RECIPES
on Parade
QUICK & EASY
DISHES

TABLE OF CONTENTS

Acknowledgments

We wish to thank the many military wives who submitted their favorite recipes for inclusion in this book. We regret that lack of space made it impossible to include all of them.

We also wish to express our appreciation for the use of photographs supplied us by the following: Cover—Standard Brands Products: Royal Puddings and Gelatins, Planter's Nuts, Blue Bonnet Margarine (recipes on pages 268, 284 and 303).

Title and order blank page photographs were supplied us by the following: South African Rock Lobster Service Corp.; Angostura—Wuppermann Corp.; Keith Thomas Company; National Association of Frozen Food Packers; U. S. Dept. of Interior, Bureau of Commercial Fisheries; The Campbell Soup Company; International Tuna Fish Association; Artichoke Advisory Board; National Dairy Council; McIlhenny Company (Tabasco); National Cherry Growers and Industries Foundation; and Florida Citrus Commission.

Favorite Recipes Press   © 1969
Post Office Box 3177
Montgomery, Alabama 36109
Library of Congress Card Catalog No. 75-83189

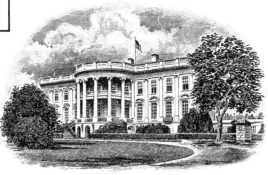

CONTINENTAL SALAD

1 pkg. lemon or orange flavored gelatin
1½ cups canned grapefruit juice
1 can or jar (16 oz.) diced beets
½ cup sliced celery
    salad greens

Dissolve gelatin in hot grapefruit juice and add ½ cup liquid drained from beets: chill until partially thickened—fold in drained beets and celery. Pour into large salad mold—chill until firm. Unmold on salad greens and top with Sesame Seed Dressing.

SESAME SEED DRESSING

Gradually blend 1 tbsp. canned grapefruit juice into 1 pkg. (3 oz.) cream cheese, beating until fluffy.

Fold in ¼ cup mayonnaise and 1 tbsp. toasted sesame seed.

INTRODUCTION

Military officers' wives thoroughly enjoy entertaining. Sometimes our parties and dinners are last-minute, hurry-up affairs when we want to prepare something delicious and yet quick and easy. The life of a military officer's wife is a busy one; she is constantly on the go.

Moreover, we must keep our husbands in trim. Certainly we want to look our best as well.

The outgrowth of these needs is this Quick and Easy Cookbook, with a section on low-calorie recipes.

Although these recipes are simple to make and can be prepared in a minimum of time, many of them are elegant. They are so delicious that your family and friends will think you spent hours in the kitchen.

Each recipe has been home-prepared time and again by the homemaker whose name appears with it. Her family and friends have asked for it many times and have called it a favorite. Soon you will find these recipes are your favorites as well.

Mary Anne Richards, Editor

Anne Weiss—Executive Editor

Mary Jane Blount—Associate Editor
Melba Colvin—Assistant Editor

Janell Webster—Assistant Editor
Joyce Miller—Assistant Editor

BOARD OF ADVISORY EDITORS

Mrs. Von Dean Clark
Headquarters 12th Air Force, Texas

Mrs. Virginia Rutledge
Ramstein AFB, Germany

Mrs. Lorraine Cummins
Arlington, Virginia

Mrs. Rhoda Serrin
Ft. Benjamin Harrison, Indiana

Mrs. Kay Gueymard
East Point, Georgia

Mrs. Bonnie Sexton
Tuscaloosa, Alabama

Mrs. Mary Prager
Fullerton, California

Mrs. William D. Shattuck
U. S. Naval Air Station, Florida

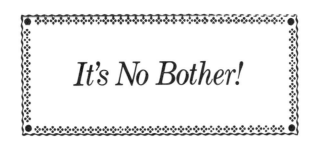

It's No Bother!

Every one of us, at some time, has been forced to "make do" in the meal department with what's on hand. Whatever the occasion—a visit from your husband's old school chum, Aunt Clara's drop-in visit to see how you're getting along, or the guest who came over to watch television and got caught in a storm which forced an overnight stay—life is much easier if you can smile serenely and say, "Oh it's no bother. There's plenty." Especially if it's true! To earn (and deserve) the gracious hostess award, plan an emergency shelf for your pantry.

Here is a basic list for your emergency shelf. These foods are mix-or-matchers. They are planned to fit several different menus equally well. As time goes on, you will want to add others and delete those little-used items.

Soups, canned
   Cream of chicken
   Cream of celery
   Cream of mushroom
   Tomato
   Consomme

Meats, canned
   Ham
   Chicken and dumplings
   Potted meats
   Pressed meat

Fish, canned
   Salmon
   Tuna
   Crab or lobster
   Sardines
   Oysters

Vegetables, canned
   Tomatoes—whole pack,
      puree, sauce, paste
   Onions, whole
   Carrots, cubed
   Corn—cream style, kernels
   Asparagus
   Beets
   Beans—limas, baked beans,
      string beans, kidney
   Green peas

Starches
   Potatoes, instant mashed
   Rice—brown and white, quick-cooking
   Spaghetti
   Macaroni
   Noodles

Breads
   Biscuit mix
   Pancake mix
   Corn bread mix
   Muffin mix
   Crackers—soda, fancy round, flavored,
      snack crackers, oysterettes
   Holland rusk or English muffins
   Brown bread
   Melba toast

Desserts
   Puddings—instant, canned
   Cake mix
   Pie crust mix
   Prepared pie crust
   Frosting mix
   Cookie mix

Fruits
   Fruit cocktail, canned
   Peach halves, canned
   Pear halves, canned
   Cherries, canned
   Applesauce, canned

Miscellaneous
   Pimentos
   Olives
   Milk—evaporated, condensed,
      powdered
   Cream substitute
   Mayonnaise
   Nuts
   Spaghetti sauce mix
   Parmesan cheese, grated
   Bread crumbs
   Lemon juice
   Pickles

```
┌─────────────────────────────────────┐
│                                       │
│      Quickie Lunches                  │
│         Or Suppers                    │
│                                       │
└─────────────────────────────────────┘
```

Whether you call it lunch or supper, one quick, small meal a day is a necessity for diet and peace of mind.

Following are suggested menus for jiffy meals:

Lamb kabobs

>Curried or yellow rice
>Grilled tomatoes
>Lemon pie

Rice with veal or

>Beef tips on rice or noodles
>Braised celery
>French beans
>Hot rolls
>Raspberry ice

Chicken a la king

>Served on corn bread
>Buttered broccoli
>Sliced tomato salad

Soup
>Bacon, tomato and cheese
> toasted sandwich
>Ice cream and cake

Hash

>Tossed green salad
>Banana sundae

Vegetable—beef soup

>Toasted rolls
>Fruit cobbler

Vegetable soup
>Cheese crackers
>Celery
>Pickles
>Fresh fruit cup

Bean and bacon soup

>French bread
>Lettuce salad—favorite dressing
>Fruit cup

Spanish chicken

>Tossed salad
>Upside-down cake

Beef Stroganoff

>Asparagus
>Hot rolls
>Chocolate sundae

Stuffed cabbage leaves

>Carrot and raisin salad
>Biscuits and butter
>Rice pudding

Chicken pilau

>Orange salad
>Canned pears

Potato soup

>Deviled ham sandwich
>Peach—cottage cheese salad

Fried link sausage

>Apple sauce
>Buttered green beans
>Orange ice

Cream of tomato soup

>Peanut butter sandwich
>Baked apple

Quick Cooking Vegetables

10 minutes—nearly all frozen vegetables may be cooked in 10 minutes.

10-15 minutes—allow water to reach steaming point, then add the following fresh

vegetables:

Asparagus
Brussels sprouts
Cabbage (shredded)
Carrots (sliced)
Celery
Eggplant (cubed)
Lima beans
Peas
Spinach
Summer squash
Tomatoes

20-25 minutes
Beets
Broccoli
Cabbage (cut)
Snap beans
Carrots (halved lengthwise)
Cauliflower
Kale
Onions
Potatoes (cut)
Turnips (sliced)

RICE

Rice is a versatile and quick-cooking food. To vary rice to combine with other dishes, try cooking it in different liquids.

Chicken or beef stock: Use chicken or beef broth or add a bouillon cube to the water.

Orange juice: Instead of water, use canned orange juice (good with poultry, in curry dishes).

Tomato juice: Use equal parts water and tomato juice.

Clear onion or vegetable soup: Make packaged soup mix according to directions, add rice.

Yellow rice: Add 1/8 teaspoon saffron powder to 8 ounces rice.

Herb rice: Cook regular way, but add 1 tablespoon each chopped fresh parsley, chives or spring onions.

Curry: Fry 1 tablespoon finely chopped onion until soft in 1 tablespoon butter. Stir in 1 teaspoon curry powder. Add water and rice and cook by regular method. Add 1 tablespoon butter before serving.

To reheat cooked rice, place in a covered saucepan with a few tablespoons water. Place on low heat. Shake pan a couple of times while heating. Heat for 5 to 10 minutes.

Sauces In A Jiffy

Sauces can spice a casserole, top open sandwiches deliciously, give vegetable leftovers zing and change ground beef into something elegant! Some quick and easy sauces can be made from a mixture of canned soup and a little imagination.

Sour cream sauce: To a can of cream of celery, chicken or mushroom soup add ½ cup sour cream. Heat, stirring occasionally. Thin with milk, if needed. Makes 1½ cups.

Mock hollandaise: Add ¼ cup mayonnaise to 1 can cream of celery, chicken or mushroom soup. Add 3 tablespoons water, 3 teaspoons lemon juice, slowly. Stir; heat. Makes 1½ cups.

Sauce with cheese: Take 1 can of cream of mushroom, chicken or celery soup. Add 3 tablespoons milk and ½ cup grated Cheddar cheese. Heat until cheese melts and blends in. Stir constantly.

JIFFY CEREAL DISHES

These quick and easy dishes have one thing in common—each uses packaged ready-to-eat cereal. There the similarity ends. Cereal, anyone?

Quick croutons: Instead of croutons, try bite-size cereals (Chex) in soups or salads. Place tablespoon of butter in skillet. Dust with garlic salt. Add cereal. Stir until browned.

Dessert crumbles: Top ice cream, pudding or custard with ¼ cup Grape-Nuts. Add dash of nutmeg.

Green bean crunch: Cut 1 cup leftover ham into strips. Add 2 packages green beans (cooked). Place in casserole. Add 1 cup bite-size shredded wheat. Season to taste with basil, salt and pepper. Add 2 cups cheese sauce. Heat through.

Stuff cabbage leaves with ground beef, rolled oats (uncooked) and sour cream. Cook cabbage in boiling water. Stuff with meat mixture, roll up, and place in pan. Cover with spicy tomato sauce. Cook, covered, over low heat for 25 to 30 minutes.

Add extra punch to hot cereal by topping with ready-to-serve cold cereal crumbles.

Throw a handful of crispy cereal into the mixture when scrambling eggs.

Make pastry cups from popped rice cereal and butter. Brown in oven. Fill with hot chow mein or chicken a la king.

Top loaf cake with ready-made frosting. Sprinkle on toasted wheat cereal crumbles.

Tomatoes nitty-gritty: Mix crushed cereal crumbs with butter and season to taste. Sprinkle tomato halves or thick slices with crumbs. Broil 6 inches from heat for 4 to 5 minutes.

Quick And Easy Soup Dishes

Split pea: Start with 1 can split pea soup. Add bacon fat and pinch of ginger.

Tomato spice: Start with 1 can tomato soup. Add can of rich milk. Add onion slice. Stir in bay leaf, pinch of cinnamon, pinch of dried cloves. Heat just to simmer.

Chicken delight: Start with 1 can each cream of chicken and chicken with rice soup. Add ½ cup milk. Stir in 1 teaspoon tarragon.

Mock turtle stew: Start with 1 can turtle soup and 1 can green pea soup. Add sherry flavoring to taste. Garnish with whipped cream.

Mock shimp chowder: Start with 1 can frozen condensed cream soup. Brown ½ cup chopped onion in 1 tablespoon butter. Blend into soup. Add 1 cup sour cream, ½ teaspoon curry powder and 1 cup shrimp. Heat. Serve over rice.

Quickie borsch: Start with 1 can bouillon. Dilute according to directions on can. Add 2 finely shredded raw beets and 2 tablespoons chopped onion. Bring to boil. Garnish with tablespoon of dairy sour cream dusted with parsley.

Mock she-crab soup: Start with 1 can cream of mushroom soup. Add 1 can condensed asparagus soup. Add 1 soup can each milk and water. Stir in 1 cup heavy cream. Add ½ cup shredded crabmeat. Use sherry flavoring, if desired.

Tomato soup creole: Start with 1 can cream of tomato soup and 1 can chicken gumbo. Add 2 soup cans water. Bring just to boil.

Celery soup: Start with 1 can condensed cream of celery soup. Add 1 can cream of chicken soup. Thin with ½ can each water and milk.

Clam bisque: Mix together 1 can condensed clam chowder, 1 can condensed chicken gumbo and 1 soup can light cream.

Tomato-pea: Start with 1 can cream of tomato soup and 1 can condensed pea soup. Add 2 cups milk. Bring to full boil. Just before serving, add sherry flavoring to taste, float grated Parmesan cheese on top.

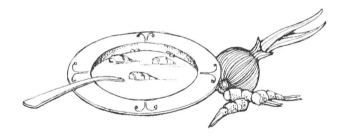

9

CANAPES

Take a head of red cabbage. Hollow it out as a bowl to hold cocktail dip.
Dips:

a. California dip—mix a package of onion soup mix with a pint of sour cream or yogurt.

b. Mash a ripe avocado. Add package of onion soup mix and 1 tablespoon lemon juice. Mix well.

c. Add mayonnaise to pint of sour cream. Mix until smooth. Add can of smoked oysters, chopped, and ½ cup minced ripe olives. Add garlic salt and lemon juice to taste.

SOUPS

Your pressure cooker can be a marvelous help in making soup stock. Although bouillon cubes and prepared gravy mixes may be used as stock, they cannot compare to the flavor added by homemade soup stock. Homemade stocks can be made in half an hour or less in your pressure cooker. Bones and scraps of meat placed in the cooker with very little water (fill cooker less than half full) at 15 pounds pressure will yield a concentrated broth. This may be poured into ice cube trays and frozen. Then when a recipe calls for stock, pop out one or two cubes, add a cup of water and simmer for a few minutes.

To remove fat from soup stock, place a lettuce leaf in hot stock. Remove leaf when it has absorbed fat.

SALADS

When washing greens, always lift them from the pan. Never drain off water. Grit and sand will settle to bottom of pan. If water is drained off, dirt can get back on greens.

For a quick salad dressing, add juice of half a lemon to a cup of yogurt or sour cream. Blend well. Add salt and pepper to taste.

Add crumbled blue cheese to French dressing. Mix well. Delicious on salads.

Easy dressings for fruit salad:

a. Honey-lime: Thin honey with bottled lime juice to taste.

b. Orange-aise: Mix mayonnaise with orange juice (fresh or frozen).

If you have leftover bits of roast beef, chicken or ham, plan a Caesar salad for dinner. It's even worth a trip to the delicatessen for the other ingredients if roast beef is your only leftover.

Serve persimmon slices with grapefruit sections and avocado slices. Add blue cheese dressing for a stand-out salad.

Fill pitted cooked prunes with seasoned cottage cheese. Add chopped nuts. Top with mayonnaise.

To keep bubbles in carbonated beverage used in geletin salad, pour liquid down side of bowl. Stir with an up-and-down motion.

BREADS

Make a loaf of bread glamorous by taking a loaf of French bread, buttering top and sprinkling generously with toasted sesame or benne seeds. Heat in oven.

Take a package of refrigerator biscuits, split them, and to each half add half an anchovy fillet or a whole smoked oyster. Fold biscuit over fish and seal edges. Brush tops with oil from fish can. Bake at 450 degrees for 8 minutes.

Take refrigerated biscuits and cut each into four wedges. Roll in melted butter and grated cheese. Bake at 400 degrees for 12 minutes.

Make pastry mix according to package directions. Roll out thin. Cover with grated Parmesan. Fold over once and roll out. Top with cheese. Repeat five or six times. Cut in strips. Sprinkle with paprika, and bake at 400 degrees for about 10 minutes.

A package of brown-and-serve rolls can be turned into an exciting coffee bread with the use of a little imagination. Butter rolls, sprinkle with a mixture of ¼ cup sugar to 1 teaspoon cinnamon. Or spread tops with a thin confectioners' sugar icing. Sprinkle on silver dragees, confetti candy dots or fine-cut citron or candied cherries, if you like.

VEGETABLES

Open a can of asparagus spears from the bottom. Vegetable can be removed without knocking off tips of spears.

Fresh asparagus can be cooked easily by standing tips up in coffee maker with works removed. Little water is used, and spears do not move around to bruise easily.

To peel onions without tears, peel under water. Hold onion directly under running water. Or you can pour boiling water over them, then cold. Skins will slip off. Start peeling from root end. Keeping onions in refrigerator will also make them less "teary" to peel.

To add sparkle to green peas: Add tablespoon chopped fresh mint to peas. Do not cook fresh green peas in pressure pan, they will cook to pieces.

Butter seasoned with any herbs you like will rescue any number of vegetables from the humdrum.

A small amount of sugar, in addition to other seasonings, will bring out the flavor of vegetables.

Combine a can of drained small onions with two cups of cream sauce. Add a dash of Worcestershire. Sprinkle generously with grated Parmesan. Bake in flat pan at 325 degrees for 25 minutes.

Mash instant potatoes with hot milk. Pile in greased casserole. Top with grated sharp cheese. Bake, uncovered, at 350 degrees until slightly browned, about 15 minutes.

Drain a can of small Irish potatoes. Rinse and slice. Place in skillet with 1 tablespoon melted butter, half a teaspoon of onion juice and pepper to taste. Brown over medium heat. Dust with paparika or parsley.

Thin celery soup with milk. Add ½ teaspoon dry mustard and dash of Worcestershire. Pour over canned new potatoes in casserole. Top with cheese slices. Bake at 350 degrees until cheese is melted, 20 to 25 minutes.

As a garnish for ham or pork roast, try broiled peach halves. Fill canned peach halves with orange marmalade. Broil until lightly browned.

To peel tomatoes easily, dip them in boiling water, then cold water. Or you can rub skin with back of table knife. Peel with sharp knife.

Add a little dried tarragon to water in which white potatoes are boiling. Most unusual.

Take frozen vegetables from package in block. Place on square of foil. Place 2 pats of butter on top. Season with salt and pepper. Fold foil over in drugstore wrap. Leave a little room for steam expansion. Place in oven at 425 degrees for 30 to 40 minutes.

Cut cored, tart apples into ½-inch slices. Place in skillet in hot sausage drippings after sausage is removed. Sprinkle apples with granulated or brown sugar. Turn once with wide spatula. Serve with sausage.

Spread deviled ham on toast slices. Top each slice with 4 or 5 asparagus spears. Cover with cheese sauce. Serve hot.

Roll 4 stalks of asparagus in thin slice of boiled ham. Fasten with toothpick. Place on broiler 3 inches from heat for 5 minutes each side. Serve covered with cheese sauce.

FRUITS

Do not remove hulls from fresh strawberries before washing them. Hulls protect sweetness of fruit. Do not wash until ready to serve.

For a pretty luncheon or breakfast dish, serve half a grapefruit on clear glass plate. Surround it with garnish of watercress or mint leaves. Top with crushed strawberries.

Serve small bunch of grapes in glass of cold water. Allow grape stem to protrude at top.

Place a ring of orange sections around a center of cooked prunes for breakfast dish.

Scald pears rather than peeling them for canning. Skins will slip off.

Two tablespoons of vinegar added to strawberries when canning will preserve their color.

MAIN DISHES

To fry pork chops, sprinkle salt over bottom of ungreased skillet. Add chops and fry slowly, 10 to 15 minutes to a side. They make their own grease and will brown nicely without sticking.

To grind liver, parboil it, remove outside membrane. Grind in food chopper.

To add extra flavor to broiled chicken, rub cavity with herbs, marinate for 2 or 3 hours in French dressing, or baste with lemon juice or barbecue sauce while broiling.

For easy chuck steak grilling, select a ½-inch thick piece of meat. Marinate in ¾ cup bottled Italian salad dressing overnight or for 10 hours. Turn meat to coat both sides. Cover with foil and grill close to coals as possible for 5 to 7 minutes a side.

Quick ham bake: Brown ½-inch thick ham slice; cut in half. Place each half on square of foil. Top each piece with pineapple slice, candied cherry and 1 tablespoon brown sugar. Fold package tightly. Place on baking sheet. Bake at 425 degrees for 30 minutes.

To broil a ham slice quickly, slash fat on edges. Place on broiler rack 3 inches below heat. Cook for 5 to 10 minutes on each side. Garnish with broiled peach or apricot halves.

Chill a can of corned beef hash. Remove both ends of can and push meat out. Cut into four rounds. Place on broiler 3 inches from heat for 7 minutes. Turn. Spread each round with mild horseradish. Top with tomato slice. Sprinkle with grated cheese. Broil 5 minutes more.

Noodles cooked in water to which 1 teaspoon instant bouillon has been added will have a different flavor. Drain, add butter and paprika or poppy seeds.

DESSERTS

Cake layers will come out of their pans without sticking if you will set the pans on a damp cloth when they come out of the oven.

A quick chocolate frosting can be made by placing chocolate-covered peppermints on surface of warm cake, covering to within ½ inch of edges. Cake will melt candies, then you spread frosting evenly over cake with table knife.

To whip gelatin, mixture must be partially set. Chill bowl, beaters of electric mixer. Whip until fluffy.

To tint coconut, place a few drops of food coloring in a jar. Add a few drops of water and shredded coconut. Shake until evenly tinted.

MISCELLANEOUS

Never leave cooked chicken at room temperature. Always refrigerate immediately following the meal. In refrigerating roast chicken that has been stuffed, remove stuffing and store separately.

Add extra calcium and protein to cream soups or casseroles by stirring in 1 or 2 tablespoons of powdered milk in addition to the liquid milk.

Yogurt is an excellent low-calorie substitute for sour cream.

Salt fish may be "freshened" by shredding or cutting in chunks. Pour boiling water over it. You may have to change water several times before fish is fresh enough to suit your taste.

For a real morning eye-opener, shave maple sugar over cereal in bowl, sprinkle with chopped nuts.

To save dishwashing, mix pancake or waffle batter in wide-mouthed pitcher. Pour batter directly onto griddle. Leftover batter can be stored, covered, in refrigerator. Thin with milk to use again. Freeze leftover waffles and toast them unthawed.

As additional treat with pancakes or waffles, serve warm syrup. Place container, uncovered, in pan of water. Heat on low.

Blend softened butter with honey. Use on waffles.

Reconstitute dry milk and frozen juice concentrates in electric blender. Place water in container, add juice or milk solids. Process until blended.

KITCHEN TRICKS

To ripen fruit more quickly, "bury it" in your meal bin. This will usually work overnight with avocados and apples.

In recipes that call for scalded milk in sauces, custards, etc., a timesaver is using cold milk. Cold milk blends in just as well with less danger of curdling and a smoother product results. Cold milk will increase cooking time a little, but this is more than compensated for in the saving of one pan and the time needed to scald milk.

To save washing an extra cup, measure dry ingredients first, place them on a sheet of waxed paper, then use same cup for measuring liquids.

When measuring thick liquids (cooking oils, syrup, molasses, honey) scrape out the measuring cup with a rubber spatula to get full measure.

Butter, margarine or lard are easy to measure if you buy them in ¼-pound sticks. One stick (¼ pound) equals ½ cup or 8 tablespoons.

To test eggs for freshness, place in deep bowl of cold water. Fresh egg will sink to bottom of bowl.

Do not wash eggs before you store them. Eggs have a protective film on shell which helps keep them fresh. Exceptionally dirty eggs may be "dry cleaned" by rubbing with paper towel or nylon net pan washer.

Thaw frozen foods quickly by placing package in front of electric fan.

To make milk sour quickly, mix a half cup of evaporated milk with a half cup of water and a tablespoon of strained lemon juice. Add sour milk slowly to other ingredients so it will not curdle mixture.

Another method of souring sweet milk is to stir lemon juice or vinegar (1 tablespoon to 1 cup) into milk. Let stand a few minutes.

To keep brown sugar from hardening, keep in jar in refrigerator. Lumpy brown sugar may be saved by placing in oven until it softens enough to crumble. Your electric blender will break up lumps in brown sugar, too.

Cheddar or process cheese which has become hard and dry after long storage in the refrigerator may be cut into small pieces and grated in your blender. Store in plastic bag to use for casserole toppings, in sauces.

If gravy or cream sauce becomes lumpy, put about ½ cup into electric blender. Cover and start on low speed. With motor running, gradually add remaining sauce. Continue to mix until smooth.

You can make buttered bread crumbs in a jiffy in your electric blender. Place bread which has been buttered and torn into small pieces into container. Run blender on low for medium crumb; high, for very fine crumbs.

Reheat leftover noodles, macaroni, spaghetti or rice. Rinse first with cold water. This removes excess starch. Place in boiling water for 5 minutes. Drain.

Quickest and best way to cook wieners is to bring pot of water to rolling boil. Turn off heat. Place wieners in pan. Wait 5 minutes. Serve. Wieners will not split or darken when cooked this way.

To save time in making iced tea, fill quart container with cold water. Suspend three or four tea bags in water. Place in refrigerator for several hours or until tea is desired strength. Tea will be clear and flavor sparkling.

Place hard or sugary jam or jelly in warm oven until sugar softens.

```
┌─────────────────────────────────────────┐
│                                           │
│         Desirable Weights                 │
│                                           │
└─────────────────────────────────────────┘
```

Weight in Pounds According to Frame (in indoor Clothing)

HEIGHT (with shoes on) 1-inch heels Feet Inches		SMALL FRAME	MEDIUM FRAME	LARGE FRAME
5	2	112-120	118-129	126-141
5	3	115-123	121-133	129-144
5	4	118-126	124-136	132-148
5	5	121-129	127-139	135-152
5	6	124-133	130-143	138-156
5	7	128-137	134-147	142-161
5	8	132-141	138-152	147-166
5	9	136-145	142-156	151-170
5	10	140-150	146-160	155-174
5	11	144-154	150-165	159-179
6	0	148-158	154-170	164-184
6	1	152-162	158-175	168-189
6	2	156-167	162-180	173-194
6	3	160-171	167-185	178-199
6	4	164-175	172-190	182-204

Men of Ages 25 and Over (left bracket for the table above)

HEIGHT (with shoes on) 2-inch heels Feet Inches		SMALL FRAME	MEDIUM FRAME	LARGE FRAME
4	10	92-98	96-107	104-119
4	11	94-101	98-110	106-122
5	0	96-104	101-113	109-125
5	1	99-107	104-116	112-128
5	2	102-110	107-119	115-131
5	3	105-113	110-122	118-134
5	4	108-116	113-126	121-138
5	5	111-119	116-130	125-142
5	6	114-123	120-135	129-146
5	7	118-127	124-139	133-150
5	8	122-131	128-143	137-154
5	9	126-135	132-147	141-158
5	10	130-140	136-151	145-163
5	11	134-144	140-155	149-168
6	0	138-148	144-159	153-173

Women of Ages 25 and Over (left bracket for the table above)

For girls between 18 and 25, subtract 1 pound for each year under 25.

Courtesy of the Metropolitan Life Insurance Company

ABBREVIATIONS

Cup . . . . c.
Tablespoon . . . . .tbsp.
Teaspoon . . . . .tsp.
Pound . . . . .lb.
Ounce . . . . oz.
Gallon . . . . .gal.

Large . . . . .lge.
Package . . . . pkg.
Small . . . . sm.
Dozen . . . . doz.
Pint . . . . pt.
Quart . . . . qt.

CAN CONTENTS

AVERAGE CONTENTS   CAN SIZE

1 c. . . . . .8 oz.
1¾ c. . . . . No. 300
2 c. . . . . No. 1 tall
2 c. . . . . No. 303
2½ c. . . . . No. 2
3½ c. . . . . .No. 2½
4 c. . . . . No. 3

OVEN TEMPERATURE

Temperature   Term
(degrees F.)
250-300 . . . . .Slow
325 . . . . .Moderately slow
350 . . . . Moderate
375 . . . . .Moderately quick
400 . . . . .Moderately hot
425-450 . . . . .Hot
475-500 . . . . Extremely hot

Accompaniments

RECIPES FOR GINGER-PEACH CONSERVE, MINTED GRAPEFRUIT SECTIONS, SPICED MELON BALLS, STRAWBERRY-RHUBARB MEDLEY AND SPICED PEACH SLICES ON PAGES 26 AND 32

BACON-CHEESE ROLL-UPS

8 slices white bread, trimmed
2 3-oz. pkg. cream cheese, softened
8 slices bacon

Spread bread generously with cream cheese. Roll up each slice gently as for jelly roll; wrap with bacon strip, securing with toothpick if necessary. Toast under broiler until bacon is cooked. Yield: 4 servings.

Mrs. Thomas G. Murnane, Treas.
Army Surgeon-Gen. Office Women's Club
Washington, D. C.

BAKED COCKTAIL FRANKS

2 tbsp. soft butter or margarine
2 tsp. prepared mustard
1 8-oz. pkg. refrigerator crescent
    dinner rolls
1/2 lb. Smokie wieners, quartered
1 egg yolk
1 tbsp. water
1 tbsp. caraway seeds

Preheat oven to 375 degrees. Combine butter with mustard in small bowl, mixing well. Unroll dough; separate into 4 rectangular pieces. Pinch each together at perforations to make dough solid. Spread with mustard-butter; cut each crosswise into 6 strips. Place Smokie on end of each strip; roll up, pinch dough to seal. Place seam-side down on greased cookie sheet. Beat egg yolk with water; brush over top of rolls. Sprinkle with caraway seeds. Bake for 10 to 12 minutes. Serve hot. Yield: 24 servings.

Mrs. Ralph Centioli, Asst. Treas. OWC
Duluth AFB, Minnesota

BITE-SIZED CREAM PUFFS WITH SHRIMP

2/3 c. boiling water
1/2 pkg. pie crust mix
2 eggs
5 oz. shrimp
1 tbsp. finely chopped chives
1/4 tsp. salt
2 tsp. lemon juice
1/2 c. mayonnaise
2 dashes of Tabasco sauce

Preheat oven to 400 degrees. Measure water into a saucepan. Heat water to boiling; stir in pie crust mix. Heat, stirring, until mixture leaves sides of pan; stir for 30 seconds longer. Remove from heat; beat in eggs 1 at a time. Drop by tablespoonfuls onto greased cookie sheet, 1 inch apart. Bake until brown. Combine remaining ingredients; mix with fork. Slice cooled puffs half-way across; insert about 1 teaspoon filling. Puffs may be warmed in hot oven for 3 minutes just before serving. Yield: 35-40 servings.

Mrs. Cary A. Kennedy, Hon. Pres. OWC
Sunny Point, Military Ocean Terminal
Southport, North Carolina

CHEESE BALL

10 oz. extra sharp cheddar cheese, grated
2 lge. pkg. cream cheese
1/4 c. sliced green olives
2 tbsp. minced green onion
2 tbsp. minced green pepper
1 tsp. garlic powder
2 tsp. Worcestershire sauce
1 tsp. lemon juice
Chopped walnuts or pecans

Blend first 8 ingredients together; form into large ball. Roll in walnuts. Serve with crackers or rye bread.

Mrs. Boyce W. Wiltrout, Bridge Chm. OWC
Mather AFB, California

CHEESE COCKTAIL COOKIES

1/2 c. flour
1/4 c. butter
1 jar bacon-cheese spread

Mix all ingredients; shape into neat roll. Wrap in waxed paper; refrigerate. Slice as for cookies when firm; place on ungreased cookie sheet. Bake at 400 degrees for 10 minutes. Yield: 40 servings.

Mrs. Joseph Schreiber, Hon. Pres. OWC
Mountain Home AFB, Idaho

CHEESE CRUNCHIES

2 c. grated cheese
2 sticks oleo
2 c. flour
Salt to taste
Red pepper to taste (opt.)
2 c. Rice Krispies

Have ingredients at room temperature; mix all together, adding Rice Krispies last. Roll into small balls; flatten each slightly. Place in ungreased pan. Bake at 350 degrees for 10 to 12 minutes.

Mrs. Jerald W. McCoy, Rec. Sec.
Redstone Arsenal OWC
Huntsville, Alabama

CHEESE PUFFS

1 jar Old English cheese spread
1/4 c. margarine
3/4 c. flour, sifted
Green olives
Pitted ripe olives

Mix first 3 ingredients together. Flatten 1 teaspoonful cheese mixture in palm; mold around each olive, rolling into ball. Place on cookie sheet in freezer until firm. Remove from sheet; place in plastic bag in freezer. Remove as many cheese

(Continued on next page)

balls as desired to serve; place on cookie sheet. Bake at 450 degrees for 8 to 10 minutes. Yield: 34 cheese puffs.

Mrs. Thomas B. Craddock, OWC
South Weymouth NAS, Massachusetts

COCKTAIL MEATBALLS

3 lb. round steak, ground
1 med. minced onion
2 c. grape jelly
2 lge. bottles catsup
1/2 tsp. garlic powder
1/2 c. dried parsley

Shape ground round with onion into small meatballs; brown slowly. Drain on paper towel; arrange in large freezing dish. Place jelly and catsup in saucepan; heat till melted. Add garlic powder and parsley. Mix well; simmer for 5 minutes. Pour over meatballs; cover with foil and freeze. Place in 350-degree oven 30 minutes before use; keep foil cover on till heated. Place in chafing dish to serve. Yield: 35-40 meatballs.

Mrs. Roger Mehle, Hon. Pres. NSC OWC
Naval Air Station
Norfolk, Virginia

CRAB AND CHEESE HORS D'OEUVRES

1/4 c. margarine
8 oz. Velveeta cheese
1 7-oz. can crab, drained
Rounds of toasted bread or croutons

Melt butter in double boiler. Add cheese; melt. Add crab; cook for 3 minutes. Place in chafing dish or any other dish not requiring direct heat. Serve with small rounds toast or croutons. May be used as main dish. Place crab and cheese mixture on large rounds of bread; broil for 30 seconds. Yield: 4 servings.

Mrs. Karl L. Keay, Sec.
P. H. Naval Shipyard OWC
Pearl Harbor, Hawaii

FRESH PINEAPPLE LUAU

3 1/2 to 4 lb. ripe pineapple
Confectioners' sugar

Cut 1 1/2-inch slices bottom and top of pineapple, including frond. Remove pineapple from trimmed shell in 1 piece, leaving shell intact, using long sharp knife. Cut pineapple slices lengthwise into 8 spears; remove core from tip. Roll each spear in confectioners' sugar. Place spears in shell; replace bottom and top of pineapple. Stand upright in shallow dish; refrigerate for at least 2 hours until chilled. Serve right from shell. Wrap securely in foil and carry in insulated carryall to take on picnic. Yield: 8 servings.

Coreen C. Haydon, 1st VP
Sandia Women's Club
Albuquerque, New Mexico

LIPTAR PASTE

2 6-oz. pkg. cream cheese
4 walnut-sized balls butter
1/2 tsp. anchovy paste
1/4 sweet onion, grated
1 tsp. capers
1/2 tsp. mustard
1 tsp. paprika
Garlic

Mix cream cheese and butter well; add remaining ingredients except garlic. Serve in bowl rubbed with garlic. Serve on crackers or as dip with chips.

Mrs. Alfred L. Ufer, Chm. OWC
Glynco NAS, Georgia

MARINATED MUSHROOMS

1 envelope salad dressing
2 tbsp. sherry
1/4 c. vinegar
2/3 c. salad oil
1 can button mushrooms, drained

Mix first 4 ingredients together; pour over mushrooms. Marinate for at least 2 hours in refrigerator. Serve with toothpicks.

Mrs. James J. Monaghan, OWC
Whiting NAS, Florida

MUSHROOMS IN OYSTER SAUCE

1 lb. fresh whole mushrooms
5 tbsp. butter, melted
2 tbsp. oyster sauce
2 tbsp. rice wine or sherry
1 tsp. sugar
2 tsp. soy sauce
1 tsp. Accent

Wash whole mushrooms; dry in towel. Saute mushrooms slowly in butter until golden. Add remaining ingredients; cook until sauce becomes thick, stirring constantly. Serve hot. Yield: 4 servings.

Patricia Stewart, Artcrafters' Chm. OWC
Langley AFB, Virginia

OLIVE-FILLED CHEESE BALLS

1/4 lb. shredded sharp cheddar cheese
2 tbsp. butter
1/2 c. flour
Dash of cayenne
25 med. olives, well drained

(Continued on next page)

Cream cheese and butter together; blend in flour and cayenne. Wrap 1 teaspoon dough around each olive, covering completely; place in shallow pan. Bake in 400-degree oven for 15 minutes. Yield: 25 balls.

Mary LaQuay Symons, Flower Chm. OWC
Miramar NAS, California

PARTY PUFFS

1 8-oz. pkg. refrigerator biscuits
1/4 lb. butter or margarine
1 envelope onion soup mix
Parmesan cheese (opt.)

Preheat oven to 425 degrees. Cut each biscuit into 4 sections. Melt butter in saucepan. Stir in onion soup mix and biscuits over very low heat, tossing gently until just light golden. Place biscuits on cookie sheet lined with brown paper. Bake for 5 minutes. Serve hot. Roll baked puffs in Parmesan cheese before serving if desired. Yield: 40 puffs.

Mrs. Richard J. Powers, Hosp. Chm.
Adair OWC
Corvallis, Oregon

SESAME-CHEESE HORS D'OEUVRES

1 2-oz. pkg. sesame seeds
1/2 tsp. soy sauce
1 8-oz. pkg. cream cheese, at room
    temperature

Brown sesame seeds lightly in ungreased skillet; mix in soy sauce. Pour sesame seeds over block of cream cheese. Serve with crackers. Yield: 4 servings.

Mrs. Edward H. Murray, Pres.
Fort Wadsworth OWC
Staten Island, New York

SHRIMP AND BACON HORS D'OEUVRES

1/2 c. white wine
1/3 bottle chili sauce
Garlic salt
Pepper
Parsley and tarragon to taste
11 bacon slices, cut into thirds
1 bag frozen shrimp

Combine wine, chili sauce, garlic salt, pepper, parsley and tarragon; pour in frozen shrimp. Marinate for 1 day, turning and separating occasionally. Wrap 1/3 of each bacon slice around each shrimp, securing with toothpick. Broil or charcoal grill until bacon is crisp. Serve hot. Yield: 8 servings.

Mrs. James D. West, VP OWC
Wakkanai Air Station, Japan

SHRIMP MOLD

1 1/2 lb. boiled shrimp
1 1/2 envelope unflavored gelatin
1/2 c. chicken stock
Dash of Worcestershire sauce
1 c. chopped celery
2 hard-boiled eggs
2 c. mayonnaise
1/2 tsp. onion juice
Paprika to taste

Reserve half the smaller shrimp for garnish; cut remaining shrimp into very small pieces. Soften gelatin in stock. Combine with cut shrimp and remaining ingredients, mixing well. Pour into mold. Garnish with caviar, if desired, on top of mold. Place shrimp and crackers on or around mold. Serve with crackers and small knife for spreading. Yield: 25 servings.

Mrs. Robert N. Ladson, Hosp. Mem. OWC
Fort McClellan, Alabama

SHRIMP AND MUSHROOMS HORS D'OEUVRES

1 12-oz. can beer
Salt to taste
1 bay leaf
1 to 1 1/2 lb. shrimp, peeled and deveined
1 4-oz. can mushrooms, drained
Juice of 1 lemon
1/2 c. mayonnaise
1/4 c. sour cream
2 tbsp. green onion, chopped

Bring beer, salt and bay leaf to boil. Add shrimp; bring to boil again. Remove from heat; let stand for 5 minutes. Drain and rinse. Sprinkle shrimp and mushrooms with lemon juice; let stand for 30 minutes. Mix with mayonnaise, sour cream and green onion; chill. Garnish with paprika and parsley. Yield: 8-12 servings.

Mrs. E. G. Copen OWC
Fort McClellan, Alabama

SHRIMPY DEVILED EGGS

1 doz. hard-boiled eggs
Salad dressing
Seasonings
Minced pickle
Minced onion
2 doz. med. to lge. sized shrimp, boiled

Make deviled eggs with first 5 ingredients, using as little salad dressing as possible. Place whole shrimp atop each egg half; sprinkle with paprika.

Ginger Edenfield, Pres. OWC
Carswell AFB, Texas

TOASTED CHEESE ROUNDS

1/3 c. grated Parmesan cheese
3/4 c. mayonnaise
1/2 c. chopped onion
Dash of Worcestershire sauce
Salt and pepper to taste
Rye bread squares

Combine first 5 ingredients; spread on rye bread squares. Toast under broiler for 1 or 2 minutes. Mixture may be kept in refrigerator up to 1 week.

Mrs. Linda Matulis, Corr. Sec. OWC
Griffiss AFB, New York

CHEESE-CHILI DIP

1 sm. jar Cheez-Whiz pasteurized cheese
spread
1 4-oz. can green chilies, roasted and
peeled
1 pkg. corn chips

Mix cheese spread and 3 or 4 chilies together until creamy and smooth. Serve with corn chips. Yield: 3-4 servings.

Peggy Harnisch, Corr. Sec. OWC
Fort Leonard Wood, Missouri

COMPANY CRAB DIP

1 8-oz. pkg. cream cheese, room temperature
1 bottle chilled chili sauce
1 8-oz. pkg. frozen crab, drained

Form cream cheese into patty. Combine ice cold chili sauce with crab; mix thoroughly. Pour over cheese patty. Yield: 4-6 servings.

Autumn M. Reed, Pres. OWC
Tempelhot AFB
Berlin, Germany

HOT CRAB DIP

1 8-oz. pkg. cream cheese, softened
2 tbsp. milk
1 can white crab meat or 1 1/2 c. fresh
crab, cooked, drained and flaked

Combine cream cheese and milk, little at a time, beating well until light and fluffy. Add crab meat. Place mixture in small casserole; cover. Bake at 350 degrees for 25 minutes. Yield: 6 servings.

Evelyn Siebert, OWC, NAS
Willow Grove, Pennsylvania

DIPPERS DIP

1 15 1/2-oz. can chili without beans
8 oz. Cheeze Whiz

Heat chili in chafing dish to boiling point. Stir in Cheez Whiz. Serve in chafing dish to keep warm. Yield: 6-8 servings.

Mrs. Phillip A. Serrin
Fort Benjamin Harrison OWC
Indianapolis, Indiana

MUSTARD DIP

1 c. hot dry mustard
1 c. wine vinegar
3 eggs
1 c. sugar

Mix mustard and vinegar; let stand overnight. Mix eggs and sugar; add to mustard mixture. Cook in double boiler until thick and smooth, stirring constantly. Keeps indefinitely. Yield: 1 2/3 pints.

Lois Abbott, Adv. OWC
Castle AFB
Atwater, California

OLD ENGLISH CLAM DIP

2 jars Old English sharp cheese
1 sm. can minced clams, drained
3 tsp. mayonnaise
1/4 tsp. dried minced garlic or more to taste

Mix all ingredients together thoroughly. Place in 7 or 8-inch pie plate. Bake at 425 degrees until bubbly throughout. Yield: 8 servings.

Mrs. Arthur Van Horn, 1st VP
Eielson AFB OWC
Fairbanks, Alaska

SOMBRERO DIP

1/2 lb. ground beef
1/2 c. chopped onion
1/4 c. hot catsup or taco sauce
1 1/2 tsp. chili powder
1/2 tsp. salt
1 8-oz. can refried beans
1/2 c. sharp American cheese, shredded
1/4 c. chopped green olives

Brown meat and 1/4 cup onion in skillet. Stir in catsup, chili powder and salt. Mash in beans; heat through. Serve in chafing dish; garnish top with cheese, olives and remaining onion. Use with corn chips or Mexican taco-flavored tostados. Yield: 20 servings.

Mrs. Pat Dawson, 2nd VP OWC
Cherry Point AFB, North Carolina

GINGER-PEACH CONSERVE

1 12-oz. pkg. frozen sliced peaches, defrosted
1/4 c. sugar
1/2 tsp. ground cinnamon
1/2 c. coarsely chopped walnuts
2 tbsp. finely chopped crystallized ginger
1/4 c. maraschino cherries

Drain juice from peaches into small bowl containing sugar and cinnamon. Stir until sugar is dissolved. Pour mixture over peaches. Add walnuts, ginger and cherries; mix well. Chill until ready to serve. Yield: 2 1/2 cups.

Photograph for this recipe on page 17.

GOURMET WINE JELLY

2 c. wine
3 c. sugar
1/2 bottle liquid fruit pectin

Mix wine and sugar in top of double boiler. Place over rapidly boiling water; stir about 2 minutes until sugar dissolves. Remove from heat; stir in liquid fruit pectin. Pour immediately into 5 medium or 6 small glasses; cover with 1/8-inch melted paraffin. Serve with meats. Any wine may be used as desired.

Mrs. W. C. Hushing, Hon. Pres. OWC
Portsmouth Naval Shipyard, New Hampshire

MRS. JOHNSON'S SPICED TEA

2 c. boiling water
6 tsp. tea
1 sm. can frozen lemon juice
1 sm. can frozen orange juice
1 1/2 c. sugar
2 qt. water
1 stick cinnamon

Pour water over tea in saucepan. Let cool; strain. Add remaining ingredients. Simmer mixture for 20 minutes. Add water if too strong. Add extra sugar to taste. Yield: 16 to 20 cups.
PERSONAL NOTE: This was a great favorite of White House guests.

Mrs. Lyndon B. Johnson
Wife of Former President of United States
Johnson City, Texas

MINTED GRAPEFRUIT SECTIONS

2 13 1/2-oz. cans frozen grapefruit sections,
    thawed
1/8 tsp. mint extract or 2 tsp. crumbled
    dried mint or 2 tbsp. chopped fresh
    mint
Green vegetable coloring

(Continued on next page)

Add mint to grapefruit sections. Add coloring to tint a delicate mint green. Chill until ready to serve. Two 13 1/2-ounce cans frozen pineapple chunks or 1 can of each grapefruit sections and pineapple chunks may be substituted for grapefruit sections. Yield: 3 1/2 cups.

Photograph for this recipe on page 17.

PICKLED BLACK-EYED PEAS

2 No. 2 cans black-eyed peas, garbanzos or
   kidney beans
1 c. salad oil
1/4 c. wine vinegar
2 cloves of garlic
1/4 c. thinly sliced onions
1 tsp. salt
1 tsp. pepper

Drain peas; place in refrigerator container. Add remaining ingredients; mix well. Store in refrigerator for 1 day. Remove garlic. Mixture may be stored 2 weeks. Yield: 8-10 servings.

Mrs. John L. Bradley
Walter Reed Army Med. Ctr. Chapel Guild
Washington, D. C.

QUICK CORN RELISH

1 12-oz. can corn, drained
1/4 c. sweet pickle relish
1 tbsp. diced pimento
4 tbsp. vinegar
1 tsp. salt

Combine all ingredients; mix well. Serve immediately or refrigerate, if desired.

Mrs. James Sandvik, Parlm. OWC
Loring AFB, Maine

QUICK BORDELAISE SAUCE

2 tbsp. minced shallots or green onions
2 tbsp. butter
3/4 c. red wine
1 10 3/4-oz. can beef gravy
2 tbsp. each, lemon juice and minced parsley
Salt and cayenne to taste

Cook shallots in butter till transparent; add wine. Simmer until half the liquid is reduced. Add beef gravy, lemon juice, parsley, salt and cayenne. Serve with roast beef or steak. Yield: 6 servings.

Frances W. Kosmicki, W and M Chm. OWC
Moron AFB, Spain

SO GOOD HORSERADISH SAUCE

1 c. sour cream
1/4 c. grated horseradish
Salt
Dry mustard and beer to make paste
Dash of lemon juice

Stir all ingredients together vigorously; set in refrigerator for chilling and thickening. Good with corned beef prime rib and boiled beef or spread for French bread.

Marie Cima, Hon. Adv. OWC
Custer AF Station
Battle Creek, Michigan

COLD SOUP (SPAIN)
GAZPACHO SEVILLANO

1 clove of garlic, peeled
1/4 green pepper, diced
1/2 sm. onion, diced
2 lge. tomatoes, chopped
1/2 cucumber, diced
6 tbsp. olive oil
2 tbsp. wine vinegar
Salt to taste
2 c. ice water

Mix all ingredients except water in blender. Blend on low speed, for few seconds. Add water; stir. Extra diced cucumbers, green peppers, boiled egg, chopped tomatoes and cubed toast may be served with soup, if desired. Yield: 4 servings. PERSONAL NOTE: Soup is pleasant noonday meal served during the terribly hot summer in Southern Spain.

Mrs. J. N. Pica, NOWC
Navy Supply Corp. Sch.
Athens, Georgia

CORN-PEA BISQUE

1 pkg. frozen peas
1 pkg. frozen corn in butter
3/4 c. milk
3/4 c. light cream
Onion salt to taste
1/4 c. dry sherry

Place all ingredients except sherry in blender. Blend; heat in saucepan. Add sherry; serve. Yield: 4-6 servings.

Mrs. John J. Lane, Wife of Commanding General
Military Traffic Mgt. and Terminal Service
Arlington, Virginia

CRAB BISQUE

1 can consomme
1 can tomato soup
1 can split pea soup, without ham
1 c. coffee cream
1/2 c. sherry
1 12-oz. can or frozen crab meat

Combine all ingredients; heat over low heat, stirring constantly, until thoroughly mixed and hot. Yield: 4 servings.

Mrs. G. W. Gaiennie, Cinclant OWC
Norfolk, Virginia

CREAM OF CRAB MEAT SOUP

1 can cream of mushroom soup
1 can cream of asparagus soup
1 1/2 cans milk
1 c. cream
2 cans crab meat, shredded
2 oz. sherry
Butter

Combine soups in saucepan; add milk and cream. Stir well; heat but do not boil. Add crab meat. Add sherry just before serving. Place piece of butter in bottom of soup tureen or place pat of butter in bottom of individual bowls. Pour hot soup over; serve immediately. Yield: 4 servings.

Mrs. Robert S. Holmes, Treas. OWC
Minot AFB, North Dakota

EGG DROP SOUP

2 14-oz. cans chicken broth
1 can water
2 chicken bouillon cubes
2 tsp. cornstarch
1 tbsp. soy sauce
2 well-beaten eggs

(Continued on next page)

Boil broth, water, bouillon, cornstarch and soy sauce in 2-quart pot. Spoon eggs into boiling mixture. Heat to serve. Serve with Chinese noodles, if desired. Yield: 6 servings.

Mrs. Neil Small, ARC Chm.
MCAS All Wives Club
Iwakuni, Japan

CUCUMBER SOUP

2 chicken bouillon cubes
2 c. boiling water
4 lge. cucumbers, pared and diced
4 stalks green onion, diced
1 tsp. salt
White pepper to taste
1 box sour cream
Milk to desired consistency

Dissolve bouillon in water; add vegetables. Cook till mushy. Cool. Blend at high speed in blender till pureed. Add seasoning and sour cream; blend at low speed. Add milk; chill. Yield: 4-6 servings.

Mrs. George E. Lee, Rec. Sec. OWC
Naha AFB, Okinawa

FRENCH CHEESE SOUP

1 sm. onion, chopped
2 celery stalks, chopped
1 green pepper, chopped
2 carrots, chopped
4 1/2 tbsp. butter, melted
4 tbsp. flour
4 c. chicken stock or consomme
3 c. cheddar cheese, grated
2 c. milk
2 tbsp. sherry
Salt and pepper to taste

Cook vegetables in butter over low heat about 10 minutes. Blend in flour; add stock. Cook, stirring constantly, until soup boils and thickens slightly. Add cheese, cooking and stirring until melted. Add milk and sherry gradually. Season with salt and pepper. Serve with a sprinkling of chopped parsley, if desired. Yield: 6 servings.

Mrs. Harvey Herrigstad, Sec. OWC
New Orleans NAS, Louisiana

HEARTY ONION SOUP

1 lb. onions, sliced
4 tbsp. butter
1 qt. water
Salt
Crustless white bread
Swiss cheese, sliced

(Continued on next page)

Fry half the onions in butter until golden. Add all onions to water; bring to a boil. Simmer for 5 minutes; add salt to taste. Simmer 15 minutes longer. Turn into 2-quart casserole; cover with bread. Add 2 layers cheese. Bake at 450 degrees for 15 minutes or until cheese is raised and golden brown. Cheese will fall after removing from oven. May be prepared ahead and baked later. Yield: 6 servings.

Mrs. E. J. Harrison, Jr., Rec. Sec. OSWC
USN Postgraduate Sch.
Monterey, California

QUICK BORSCH

1/2 c. finely sliced cabbage
1/2 onion, thinly sliced
1/4 carrot, thinly sliced
1 tbsp. butter or margarine
1 10 1/2-oz. can consomme
1 c. canned beet juice
1/2 c. julienne beets
1 tbsp. white vinegar
Salt and white pepper to taste

Saute cabbage, onion and carrot in butter in saucepan until limp. Add consomme and beet juice; cover. Simmer for 15 minutes. Add beets, vinegar, salt and pepper. Yield: 3 servings.

Mrs. Z. C. Trzyna, NOWC
Patuxent River USNAS, Maryland

QUICK CLAM CHOWDER

1 can potato soup
1 8-oz. can minced clams
1 lge. can evaporated milk
2 strips bacon

Combine potato soup, clams and milk. Heat without boiling. Fry bacon until crisp. Crumble bacon into soup; serve. Yield: 4 cups.

Mrs. George R. Shepard, 2nd VP OWC
Great Lakes NTC, Illinois

QUICK CRAB BISQUE

1 can condensed green pea soup
1 can condensed tomato soup
1 1/2 soup cans milk
1/4 tsp. curry powder
1/2 tsp. paprika
1 6 to 7 1/2-oz. can crab meat, flaked
1/4 c. sherry

Combine soups, milk and seasonings in saucepan. Heat, but do not boil. Stir in crab meat and sherry. Reheat. Serve. Yield: 4 servings.

Mrs. Leighton I. Davis, Hon. Mem.
AF OWC of Los Angeles
North Hollywood, California

VERY GOOD VICHYSSOISE

1 can frozen cream of potato soup
2/3 c. milk
3 tbsp. chopped chives

Break soup in hunks; do not thaw. Place in blender; add milk. Blend on high speed until thoroughly mixed. Stir in 2 tablespoons chives gently. Cover; place in refrigerator for 1 hour. Pour into chilled soup bowls; top with remaining chives. Yield: 4 servings.

Judy W. Graham, Publ. Chm. NOWC
Puget Sound Naval Shipyard
Bremerton, Washington

SPICED MELON BALLS

2 12-oz. pkg. frozen melon balls, defrosted
1/4 c. firmly packed light brown sugar
1/4 c. cider vinegar
5 to 6 whole cloves
1 cinnamon stick

Drain juice from melon balls. Combine melon juice, brown sugar, vinegar, cloves and cinnamon in saucepan. Simmer for 5 minutes. Pour hot syrup over melon balls. Let stand until cool; chill until ready to serve. Yield: 3 cups.

Photograph for this recipe on page 17.

SPICED PEACH SLICES

2 12-oz. pkg. frozen sliced peaches, defrosted
2 cinnamon sticks
1 tbsp. whole cloves
1/4 c. cider vinegar
1/3 c. seedless raisins

Drain and reserve juice from peaches. Combine peace juice and remaining ingredients in saucepan; simmer for 5 minutes. Pour hot syrup over sliced peaches; let stand until cool. Chill until ready to serve. Yield: 3 cups.

Photograph for this recipe on page 17.

STRAWBERRY-RHUBARB MEDLEY

1 1-lb. pkg. frozen whole strawberries,
    defrosted
1 1-lb. pkg. frozen rhubarb, defrosted
Cornstarch
1/2 c. slivered blanched almonds
1 tsp. grated lemon rind

Drain and reserve juice from strawberries and rhubarb. Measure juice; for every cup of juice, use 1 1/2 tablespoons cornstarch. Stir juice into cornstarch gradually. Cook over low heat, stirring constantly, until smooth and thick. Stir in almonds and lemon rind. Cool slightly. Fold in strawberries and rhubarb. Chill until ready to serve. Yield: 3 cups.

Photograph for this recipe on page 17.

Meat Dishes

RECIPE FOR BAKED HALIBUT SURPRISE ON PAGE 86

COFFEE POT ROAST

1 pkg. instant meat marinade
2/3 c. cold coffee
1 med. garlic clove, minced
1/4 tsp. sweet basil
1 3 to 4-lb. pot roast
1 can cream of mushroom soup
1 lge. onion, sliced

Blend meat marinade and coffee in Dutch oven; add garlic, basil and meat. Pierce all sides of meat. Marinate for 15 minutes, turning several times. Add soup and onion; cover. Cook over low heat for 2 hours to 2 hours and 30 minutes, turning meat once. Yield: 6-8 servings.

Mrs. James C. Lonz, Sec. OWC
Yuma Proving Ground, Arizona

CHILI CASSEROLE

1 12-oz. can corned beef, finely diced
1 pkg. chili mix
1/2 c. water
1 1-lb. can whole tomatoes
1 1-lb. can kidney beans
1 pkg. refrigerated biscuits
1 tbsp. melted butter or margarine
1/2 c. chopped peanuts

Heat oven to 450 degrees. Mix corned beef, chili mix, water, tomatoes and kidney beans together; pour into shallow 2-quart casserole. Bake for 15 minutes. Remove from oven; top with biscuits. Brush biscuits with butter. Sprinkle with peanuts. Return to oven; bake for 8 to 10 minutes. Yield: 6-8 servings.

Mrs. William C. Wheaton, Corr. Sec. NOWC
Charleston USNB, South Carolina

CORNED BEEF BURGERS

2 c. corned beef
1 c. shredded sharp cheddar cheese
1/2 c. stuffed olives, chopped
1 tbsp. finely chopped onion
1 tbsp. Worcestershire sauce
3/4 c. chili sauce

Mix all together. Place on 12 hamburger buns; wrap in foil. Heat in 400-degree oven for 15 minutes. Yield: 12 servings.

Mrs. Charles A. Symroski, OWC
Fort Monroe, Virginia

CORNED BEEF AND CABBAGE SKILLET

2 lb. cabbage
1 beef bouillon cube
1 1/2 c. boiling water
1 12-oz. can corned beef, cut in 8 slices

(Continued on next page)

MUSTARD SAUCE:

2 tbsp. butter or oleo
2 tbsp. flour
1/2 tsp. salt
1/8 tsp. pepper
1 tsp. sugar
1 1/2 c. milk
2 tsp. vinegar
1 tbsp. prepared mustard

Cut cabbage in 8 wedges; arrange in large skillet in circle. Add bouillon and water; cover. Simmer for 10 minutes or until tender. Arrange corned beef between cabbage wedges; cover. Simmer for 10 minutes. Melt butter; blend in flour. Stir in salt, pepper and sugar. Add 1 1/2 cups milk gradually; cook, stirring, until thickened. Add vinegar and mustard. Pour sauce over beef and cabbage. Yield: 4 servings.

Mrs. Jack F. Lane, 1st VP OWC
Fort Riley, Kansas

CORNED BEEF MULLIGAN

1 12-oz. can corned beef
1 lge. onion, chopped
1 1-lb. can tomatoes
1 sm. can peas or leftovers
2 med. potatoes, cubed
1 tbsp. Lea and Perrins sauce or more
    to taste
1 tsp. garlic salt
2 tbsp. chili sauce or catsup or rinsing
    of almost empty bottles
Any additional leftover vegetables

Place all ingredients in stew pot; cook over medium flame. Season to taste with salt and pepper after 20 minutes. Yield: 3-4 servings.

Mrs. J. L. Gregorcyk, Prog. Chm. OWC
NCAS Cherry Point, North Carolina

CORNED BEEF AND RICE

1 12-oz. can corned beef
3/4 c. regular rice
1 No. 303 can tomatoes
1 med. onion, sliced thin
1 med. green pepper
1 tsp. salt
1/8 tsp. black pepper
1 c. water

Mix all ingredients in large pot; cover. Cook over medium heat until rice is tender, about 30 minutes from time water boils. Yield: 6 servings.

Mrs. Lyall A. Bishop, OWC
Bayreuth, Germany

BROILED FLANK STEAK

1 flank steak
4 tbsp. salad oil
2 tbsp. catsup
2 tsp. soy sauce
2 tbsp. water
1 sm. onion, chopped fine
1 clove of garlic, minced

Place flank steak in flat glass baking pan. Place remaining ingredients in jar; shake well. Pour over flank steak; marinate overnight, turning occasionally. Broil as you would for any other steak; do not cut until ready to serve. Cut slantwise across grain to serve. Yield: 4 servings.

Mrs. Samuel Lee Gabby, Adv. OWC
Ramey AFB, Puerto Rico

FLANK STEAK BURGUNDY

1 1/2 lb. flank steak
Tenderizer
1/2 c. flour
Pepper to taste
1/4 c. oil
1 med. onion, sliced
1 4-oz. can mushrooms
1 can beef consomme soup
2/3 c. Burgundy

Score flank steak diagonally on both sides; sprinkle liberally with tenderizer. Coat with flour; season with pepper but no salt. Brown in hot oil. Add onions and mushrooms; saute briefly. Add soup and wine. Place in heavy skillet or baking pan; cover. Bake for 1 hour at 350 degrees. Remove cover. Bake for 15 minutes more until liquid is thick like gravy. Yield: 4-5 servings.

Mrs. Luther C. Bush, Corr. Sec. OWC
Wheeler AFB, Hawaii

LONDON BROIL

1 2-lb. flank steak, at room temperature
Meat tenderizer
1 tbsp. salad oil
1 tsp. lemon juice, fresh if possible
1 tsp. salt
1/8 tsp. pepper, freshly ground if possible
1 clove of garlic, pressed
2 tsp. chopped parsley

Score steak at 45 degree angle; treat with tenderizer. Combine remaining ingredients in small bowl. Place on greased broiler pan; baste scored side with half the oil mixture. Broil 4 inches from heat for 5 minutes. Turn; brush with remaining mixture. Broil for 3 to 5 minutes longer. Serve immediately. Dice garlic; crush between 2 spoons if you do not have a garlic press. Yield: 4-6 servings.

Mrs. Axel A. S. Johnson
Mrs. Axel A. S. Johnson, Comfairwingslant OWC
Norfolk NAS, Virginia

FLANK STEAK ORIENTALE

2 flank steaks, trimmed
3 cloves of garlic, finely chopped
1 tsp. freshly ground black pepper
2/3 c. soy sauce
1/2 tsp. Tabasco sauce
1/3 c. dry white wine or vermouth
Salt

Rub steaks well with garlic and pepper; place in a shallow dish. Add soy sauce, Tabasco sauce and wine. Let stand for 1 to 2 hours at room temperature or overnight in refrigerator, turning steaks several times. Arrange steaks on broiling pan; broil at high heat close to broiler for 3 minutes on each side for rare meat. Salt to taste; slice into thin slices. Hold knife parallel to steak to produce wide diagonal slices. Yield: 6 servings.

Mrs. Paul M. Gowan, OWC
Fort McClellan, Alabama

PEPPER STEAK

1 1/2 lb. flank steak
3/4 c. cornstarch
1/2 c. peanut oil
1 to 2 green peppers, cut into thin strips
3/4 c. soy sauce

Slice flank steak into long thin slices; cut each slice into 2 or 3 pieces to make bite-sized, Chinese style. Cover bottom of skillet, preferably iron, with oil. Dredge steak in cornstarch just before dropping into hot oil. Shake off excess cornstarch. Do not let steak bleed into cornstarch. Put all meat in at once; cook over high heat, stirring with large spoon constantly to brown on all sides. Do not let burner cool; moisture will accumulate. Parboil green peppers for 5 minutes; drain. Add soy sauce to meat, stirring constantly; remove from heat. Takes 10 minutes to prepare. Yield: 4 servings.

Mrs. Edwin T. Donley, Hon. Pres. OWC
Wife of Commanding General
Zweibruecken, Germany

STUFFED FLANK STEAK

2 flank steaks, 1/2-inch thick
1 stick margarine, melted
2 tbsp. Worcestershire
1 to 1 1/2 c. herb stuffing mix
1 sm. can mushroom pieces, drained
1/4 c. chopped celery
1/4 c. chopped onion
Italian salad dressing

Score steak on 1 side. Pour margarine mixed with Worcestershire sauce over stuffing; add mushrooms, celery and onion, combining well. Fill steak; roll up, securing with toothpicks. Place in baking pan or casserole. Bake in 350-degree oven until tender. Baste often with salad dressing. Surround with parsley and pineapple slices centered with cherries; slice at table. May also grill outside. Yield: 4-6 servings.

Mrs. Robert C. Merritt, Publ. Chm. OWC
Bergstrom AFB, Texas

STUFFED FLANK STEAK

1/2 c. seasoned croutons
1/4 c. cut-up green onions
1/4 c. butter, melted
1 med. flank steak
1/4 c. seasoned flour
Butter
1 pkg. gravy mix, prepared

Mix croutons, onions and butter; lay on steak. Roll up; fasten with toothpicks. Roll in seasoned flour; brown in small amount of butter. Place in medium casserole dish; cover with gravy mix. Bake in 300-degree oven for 1 hour. Yield: 4-6 servings.

Mrs. Norman M. Walsh, OWC
Carswell AFB, Texas

BARBECUE SAUCE FOR ZIPPY GRILLED STEAK

1/2 lb. butter or margarine
Juice of 6 lemons
1 bottle Worcestershire sauce
1/4 c. vinegar
1/2 c. Karo syrup
1 bottle catsup
2 tbsp. grated onion
1/4 tsp. Accent
Steak, ribs or chicken

Combine first 8 ingredients; simmer for 15 minutes. Unused sauce may be stored in covered jar in refrigerator for several weeks. Brown steak on grill, brushing sauce over each piece generously. Precook ribs or chicken in covered baking dish in oven for 45 minutes to insure tenderness. Yield: 10 servings.

Mrs. W. W. Senn, OWC
South Ruislip, England

EASY SWISS STEAK

3 lb. round steak
1 envelope onion soup mix
1 med. can mushrooms, with juice

Place round steak in large oblong baking pan; sprinkle over soup mix. Pour mushrooms and juice over all; cover tightly with foil. Bake at 350 degrees for 1 hour and 30 minutes to 2 hours. Yield: 3-4 servings.

Mrs. Chester Barrett, Sec.
USCG Base Wives Club
Sault Ste. Marie, Michigan

GRANNY'S PARTY STEAK

2 lb. round steak
2 c. packaged stuffing, prepared
2 tbsp. butter
1 can cream mushroom soup
1/2 c. water
1/2 c. sour cream

(Continued on next page)

Pound steak with edge of heavy saucer; cut into long pieces. Place 1/3 cup stuffing in center; roll up, fastening with toothpicks. Brown in butter; add soup and water. Cook over low heat for 1 hour, covered. Stir in sour cream; heat for 5 minutes. Yield: 6 servings.

Mrs. Albert G. Larson, Hosp. Nursery Chm. OWC
Puget Sound Naval Shipyard, Washington
Mrs. Roger D. Wyckoff OWC
Cinclant Flt. Norfolk, Virginia

MUSHROOM STEAK

Salt and pepper to taste
2 lb. round steak
Shortening
1 sm. onion
2 rings green pepper
2 6-inch pieces celery
1 10 1/2-oz. can golden mushroom soup or
    mushroom gravy
1 soup can water

Salt and pepper steak; brown in skillet with enough shortening to prevent sticking. Place in oblong pan. Add onion, green pepper, celery, soup and water; cover. Bake at 375 degrees for 1 hour or until tender. Add water during baking according to amount of sauce desired. Remove onion, green pepper and celery to serve. Yield: 6 servings.

Mrs. Jean D. Burns, Treas. O and CWC
Fort Huachuca, Arizona

ROUND STEAK DELIGHT

2 to 2 1/2 lb. round steak
Flour
1/4 c. shortening
4 to 6 green pepper rings
5 to 6 slices onion
1 can tomato sauce
1/2 to 1 c. water
1 4-oz. can mushrooms

Cover steak with flour; brown on both sides in melted shortening. Pour off excess fat. Place in casserole. Place green pepper rings over onion slices on browned meat; cover with tomato sauce. Add water around steak; cover. Bake in 350-degree oven for 1 hour and 30 minutes. Add mushrooms the last 30 minutes. Yield: 6 servings.

Mrs. Robert L. Knoth, Treas. OWC
Great Lakes, Illinois

SKILLET MAIN DISH

Several strips bacon
1 1/2 lb. round steak, in serving-sized
    pieces
4 med. potatoes, pared and sliced
2 lge. onions, peeled and sliced
Salt and pepper

(Continued on next page)

39

Lay bacon strips in electric skillet; place steak over bacon. Place potatoes over steak and onion over potatoes; salt and pepper generously. Turn heat to high for 1 to 2 minutes; simmer, covered, for 1 hour and 30 minutes. Yield: 4-6 servings.

Mrs. Charles M. Saeger, Pres. OWC
Eielson AFB, Alaska

BEEF TERIYAKI

2/3 c. soy sauce
1/3 c. white wine
1 minced garlic clove
2 tbsp. sugar
1 tbsp. honey
1/2 tsp. powdered ginger
4 sirloin, T-bone or tenderloin steaks,
    1-inch thick

Combine first 6 ingredients; marinate steaks for at least 30 minutes. Broil or barbecue until done as desired, basting frequently with sauce. May also be used for chicken teriyaki. Yield: 4 servings.

Mrs. Thomas M. Power, Student Wives Rep. OWC
Laredo AFB, Texas

BREADED STEAKS

1/2 c. Romano cheese, grated
1/2 c. Parmesan cheese, grated
1 c. bread crumbs
4 tsp. finely chopped garlic
3 tbsp. finely chopped parsley
Salt and pepper to taste
Sirloin or T-bone for 4, fat trimmed
1/2 c. olive oil
1 bottle Vin Rose

Mix cheeses and bread crumbs; add garlic, parsley, salt and pepper. Dip steaks into olive oil, roll in cheese mixture. Place steaks on waxed paper; let set for 3 to 5 hours, depending on heat. Place between pieces of mesh; barbecue for 3 minutes per side. Serve with Vin Rose. Yield: 4 servings.

Mrs. Randolph M. Ridgel, Publ. Chm. OWC
Pearl Harbor Naval Shipyard, Hawaii

PO-KUM-BA

2 onions, sliced
Margarine
3 eggs
3 tbsp. evaporated milk
4 to 8 oz. leftover steak, any kind,
    finely chopped
1 c. instant rice, cooked according to
    directions
Salt to taste

(Continued on next page)

Sautc onions in margarine; remove from frying pan. Whip eggs with milk; scramble in same pan. Add onions and steak to scrambled eggs; add rice and salt. Keep warm until ready to serve. Fresh steak may be used; fry in usual manner before adding to eggs. Yield: 4 servings.

PERSONAL NOTE: My husband ate and enjoyed this dish during 2 Korean tours. He taught me to cook it when he returned after the second.

Mrs. Theodore R. Tuerke, VP OWC
Fort Kobbe, Canal Zone

STEAKS LORRAINE

1 clove of garlic, peeled and sliced
1/4 c. salad oil
4 8-oz. thin boneless sirloin steaks
1/4 c. butter or margarine
1 tsp. dry mustard
1/2 tsp. salt
1/4 c. chopped parsley
2 tsp. lemon juice
1 tsp. Worcestershire sauce
1/4 tsp. freshly ground pepper

Combine garlic and oil; let stand for 5 minutes. Brush steak on both sides. Stir butter, mustard and salt together on heated grill or in heavy skillet. Stir in parsley; heat until butter bubbles. Place steaks on grill; turn over to coat both sides with seasoned butter. Cook slowly for 5 minutes; do not brown. Turn steaks; cook for 5 minutes more. Remove steaks to hot platter or plates. Add lemon juice, Worcestershire sauce and pepper to sauce on the grill, stirring to blend. Heat; pour over steaks. Serve at once. Yield: 4 servings:

Mrs. Nathan T. Butcher, Treas. OWC
Whiting NAS, Florida

BEEF BIRDS ITALIANO

2 lb. round steak, sliced wafer thin
1/2 c. fine bread crumbs
1/2 c. grated Parmesan cheese
1 tbsp. dried parsley flakes

Cut steak into 2 x 4-inch pieces. Mix remaining ingredients; spread over steak. roll up; thread on skewers. Broil for 5 minutes on each side. Yield: 6 servings.

Mrs. Joseph Marciano, Asst. Treas. OWC
Ent AFB, Colorado

BARBECUED BEEF

4 c. cooked beef, cut in sm. pieces
1/4 c. vinegar
1 1/2 c. water
4 tsp. mustard
1/4 tsp. pepper
2 med. onions, chopped
1/2 c. butter or oleo
2 slices lemon
1 c. catsup
3 tbsp. Worcestershire sauce
Salt

Combine all ingredients in saucepan; simmer until thickened for about 45 minutes. Yield: 6 servings.

Mrs. Paul J. Donahoe, Pres. OWC
Dayton DESC, Ohio

BEEF INTERNATIONALE

2 lb. round steak, cut into strips
Oleo
2 med. onions, thinly sliced
2 green peppers, thinly sliced
1/2 c. water
1 10 1/2-oz. can cream of celery soup
1/2 c. salad dressing
1 3-oz. can mushrooms
Salt and pepper

Cook meat in oleo until lightly browned; add onions, peppers and water. Simmer for 30 minutes, adding more water if necessary. Add combined soup, salad dressing and mushrooms; season to taste. Serve on rice. Yield: 8 servings.

Mrs. William A. Scott, Decorating Chm. OWC
Cinclant Flt.
Norfolk, Virginia

BEEF STEW A LA KING

3 lb. stew meat
4 onions, sliced
1 green pepper, sliced
1 lge. garlic clove, chopped fine
1 tsp. dry parsley
1/4 tsp. basil
Salt and pepper to taste
2 15-oz. cans tomato sauce
1 can tomato paste

Mix all ingredients together in large pan; let stand for 30 minutes. Cook slowly for about 1 hour and 30 minutes. Serve on cooked rice with side dish of tossed salad. Yield: 4-6 servings.

Mrs. Pasco F. Siravo, Treas. OWC
Howard AFB
Albrook, Canal Zone

BEEF STROGANOFF

1 lb. round steak, cut into thin strips
1/2 c. chopped onion
Garlic to taste
2 tbsp. butter or margarine
1 10 1/2-oz. can condensed cream of
    mushroom soup
1/4 c. water
1/2 c. sour cream
1/2 tsp. paprika
Salt and pepper to taste
2 c. cooked noodles

Brown steak, onion and garlic in butter; remove garlic. Stir in soup, water, sour cream, paprika, salt and pepper; cover. Cook over low heat for 45 minutes or until meat is tender, stirring often. Serve over noodles. Yield: 4 servings.

Mrs. John K. Welch, Hospitality Chm. OWC
Wakkanai Air Station, Japan

BEEF TOMATO (CHINA)
NGO YUK FAN KAY

2 tsp. cornstarch
3 tbsp. soy sauce
1 tsp. sugar
Pinch of salt
Pepper
1/2 tsp. monosodium glutamate
Oil
1 lb. sirloin tip, sliced 1/8-inch thick
1 round onion, sliced
2 green peppers, sliced
2 stalks celery, sliced
2 tbsp. cornstarch
1/4 c. cold water
1 tsp. sugar
Salt and pepper to taste
3 to 4 tomatoes, cut into wedges

Make sauce from first 5 ingredients; marinate sirloin tip in sauce for 10 to 15 minutes. Fry tip very lightly in hot oil until it loses color; push to outer edge of pan. Add a little more oil; cook onion, green pepper and celery for 5 minutes. Make paste with cornstarch and water; stir in sugar, remaining monosodium glutamate, salt and pepper. Add to tip and vegetables, stirring until sauce clears. Add tomatoes last. Serve over rice. Yield: 4-6 servings.
PERSONAL NOTE: I obtained this recipe in Oriental cooking class.

Mrs. Edward G. Spongberg, 1st VP OWC
Wheeler AFB, Hawaii

CARBONADO FLAMANDES

2 med. onions, sliced
2 tbsp. butter
1 1/2 lb. stew meat
1 bottle beer or equivalent amount of water
Salt and pepper to taste
Pinch of thyme

(Continued on next page)

43

Bay leaves
Slice bread spread with mustard
1 tsp. vinegar
Flour
1 tbsp. brown sugar

Brown onions in butter; add meat to brown. Place beer, salt, pepper, thyme and bay leaves over meat. Place bread over all; simmer till meat is tender. Mix vinegar, enough flour to make smooth sauce and brown sugar in cup; mix with meat. Bring to boil; serve over rice or egg noodles. Yield: 4 servings.

Mrs. R. H. Jenkins, Oahu OWC
Oahu, Hawaii

FLANK STEAK (CHINA)

1 flank steak, about 1 1/2 lb.
4 tbsp. soy sauce
2 tsp. Worcestershire sauce
Dash of liquid red-pepper seasoning
3 tbsp. vegetable oil
1 med. onion, peeled and sliced
1 green pepper, seeded and cut into strips
1 sm. clove of garlic, minced
1 3 or 4-oz. can sliced mushrooms with
   liquid
2 tbsp. cornstarch
1 1/2 c. beef broth or consomme

Slice steak thin diagonally; place in bowl. Sprinkle with soy sauce, Worcestershire sauce and red-pepper seasoning; toss to mix well. Heat oil in large frying pan; add seasoned meat. Cook quickly until meat loses pink color, stirring constantly. Remove from frying pan with slotted spoon. Stir onion, green pepper and garlic into drippings in pan; saute until soft. Stir in mushrooms and liquid. Blend cornstarch into beef broth until smooth; stir into vegetables. Cook until sauce thickens and boils for 3 minutes, stirring constantly. Return meat to pan; heat slowly just until hot. Yield: 4 servings.

Mrs. Billy Hollopeter, Parlm. OWC
Mt. Home AFB, Idaho

ORIENTAL BEEF QUICKIE

1 lb. beef steak, flank, round or sirloin
   cut into thin strips
2 tbsp. cornstarch
2 tbsp. salad oil
2 green peppers, diced
1 c. sliced celery
1 clove of garlic, minced
1 1/2 c. water
2 tbsp. soy sauce
Pepper (opt.)

Coat meat with cornstarch; brown quickly in oil in frying pan. Add remaining ingredients; bring to boil. Reduce heat, simmer for 10 minutes, stirring often. Serve on rice. Two cups fresh mushrooms may be added with vegetables if available. Yield: 4-5 servings.

Mrs. Richard S. Willett, OWC
China Lake Naval Weapons Center, California

HAWAIIAN CHOPPED BEEF WITH VEGETABLES

1 1/2 lb. beef sirloin tip or top round steak,
   3/4 to 1-inch thick
Cooking oil
2 c. sliced celery
2 c. sliced white onions
1 c. sliced green pepper
1 c. fresh or canned bean sprouts
Soya sauce to taste
Salt and pepper to taste
Monosodium glutamate

Slice beef into 1/8-inch strips, 2 to 3 inches long. Heat 1/2 of the cooking oil in large frying pan; add beef strips. Push beef around in pan for a few minutes to cook evenly until no longer pink. Add remaining ingredients. Cook, stirring and turning constantly to cook evenly. Do not allow meat mixture to steam. Fry until beef is done and vegetables are tender but still very crisp. Add soya sauce, salt, pepper and monosodium glutamate; mix well. Serve with rice. Yield: 6 servings.

Mrs. Charles E. Vandeveer, Entertainment Chm.
Pearl Harbor Naval Shipyard, Hawaii

MINCED BEEF AND CORN

1/2 lb. sirloin or top round beef, cut into
   3/8-inch cubes
2 tbsp. salad oil
1 1/2 c. whole kernel corn
1 med. onion, chopped
1 green pepper, diced
1/4 c. soy sauce
1 tbsp. sherry
5 tbsp. water
2 tsp. cornstarch
1 tomato, diced
Salt

Saute beef in hot oil in skillet until just browned; remove beef from skillet. Add corn, onion and green pepper to skillet; saute for a few minutes. Combine soy sauce, sherry, water and cornstarch; add to vegetables. Cook over low heat until mixture comes to a boil and thickens, stirring constantly. Return beef to skillet; add tomato and salt. Cook for a few minutes, stirring. Yield: 4 servings.

Mrs. William W. Kingery, Hon. Pres. OWC
RAF Mildenhall, England

MOCK SUKIYAKI

1 lb. thinly sliced round steak
2 tbsp. salad oil
1 1/2 c. sliced celery
1 med. green pepper, sliced
1 lge. onion, thinly sliced
1 1/2 c. sliced fresh mushrooms or
   1 6-oz. can, drained
1/2 c. sliced green onion, 1-inch pieces
1 10 1/2-oz. can beef broth
1 tbsp. soy sauce

(Continued on next page)

1/4 c. water
2 tbsp. cornstarch
4 c. hot cooked rice

Brown steak in salad oil; add vegetables, beef broth and soy sauce. Cover; cook over low heat for 10 minutes or until vegetables are just tender, stirring often. Combine water and cornstarch; add to meat mixture, stirring until thickened. Serve over hot rice.

Mrs. Julian C. Walker, Prog. Chm.
Woodbridge OWC
RAF Bentwaters, England

SKILLET BEEF SUPREME

1/2 lb. lean beef, cut into strips
2 tbsp. oil
1 med. onion, sliced
1 green pepper, sliced
1 c. celery, sliced
1 c. green beans, sliced
4 tsp. cornstarch
1 tbsp. soy sauce
3/4 c. water
1 4-oz. can mushrooms, sliced
Salt
Cooked rice

Brown beef in oil; add onion and green pepper. Add celery and green beans; cook for 3 to 5 minutes. Combine cornstarch with soy sauce and water; add to skillet. Stir in mushrooms; cook for 5 minutes, stirring until liquid is clear and shiny and beans are tender. Salt to taste; garnish with pimento, if desired. Serve over rice. Yield: 4 servings.

Mrs. James C. Fitzwilliam, Treas. OWC
Ft. Ritchie, Maryland

STEAK TERIYAKI

1 1 1/4 to 1 1/2 lb. flank steak
1 tbsp. oil
1 tbsp. brown sugar
1 tbsp. chives
1 tbsp. green pepper
1/4 c. soy sauce

Cut flank steak diagonally into bite-sized pieces with sharp knife. Mix remaining ingredients in bowl; marinate steak in bowl for at least 30 minutes. Broil for 2 minutes; flip. Broil for 2 minutes more. Serve over steamed rice, with juices. Yield: 4 servings.

Mrs. Peter C. Einselen, 1st VP OWC
Fort Richardson, Alaska

SUKIYAKI

1 1/2 lb. top sirloin, sliced paper-thin
Suet
1 cake bean curd
2 bunches green onions

(Continued on next page)

1 lb. dry onions
3 carrots
1 lb. frozen or fresh spinach
6 stalks celery
1 can bamboo shoots, diced
1 can water chestnuts, sliced
1 can bean sprouts
1 lb. mushrooms, sliced
1/2 pt. soy sauce
1 can consomme
2 1/2 tsp. brown sugar
4-oz. saki or slightly sour sauterne

Brown sirloin in suet in large skillet; push to 1 side. Slice all vegetables on slant into skillet; keeping in separate little piles. Combine soy sauce, consomme, brown sugar and saki to make sauce. Add half the sauce to vegetables and sirloin. Cook for 15 minutes or until vegetables are slightly cooked. Serve with hot rice and remaining sauce, saki and rice cakes for dessert.

Mrs. John N. Borini, Chm. Gourmet Gp. OWC
Andrews AFB, Maryland

ALL-AT-ONCE SPAGHETTI

1 tbsp. cooking oil
1 lge. onion, chopped
1/2 lb. ground beef
1 1/2 tsp. salt
Pepper to taste
2 cans tomato sauce
1 1/2 c. water
1 bay leaf (opt.)
1/4 lb. spaghetti
Grated cheese

Heat oil in saucepan or skillet. Add onion; cook until soft. Add beef; crumble with fork. Fry until meat loses red color; sprinkle with salt and pepper. Pour in tomato sauce and water; bring to a boil. Add bay leaf. Break spaghetti in half; sprinkle in small amount at a time, stirring it into sauce and keeping it separated. Cover tightly. Simmer for 20 to 30 minutes. Stir once toward end of cooking time. Serve with cheese. Yield: 4 servings.

Mrs. Kenneth R. Lumry, 2nd VP OWC
Eielson AFB, Alaska

BEEF CURRY

1 lb. ground beef
2 tbsp. chopped onion
1/2 tsp. garlic salt
1 1/2 to 1 tsp. curry powder
1 10 1/2-oz. cream of mushroom soup
2/3 c. milk
Cooked rice

Brown ground beef. Add onion, garlic salt and curry powder; cook for 2 minutes. Add soup and milk; mix thoroughly. Simmer for 30 minutes. Serve over rice. Yield: 4-6 servings.

Mrs. Stephen Krzykoski, OWC
Adair AFS Corvallis, Oregon

BLUE MONDAY QUICK DINNER

1 to 1 1/2 lb. ground beef
1 10-oz. or 12-oz. pkg. macaroni
1 No. 303 can stewed tomatoes
1/2 can water
6 to 8 slices cheese
Salt and pepper to taste

Brown beef in large skillet. Cook macaroni according to package directions. Add macaroni, tomatoes and water to beef. Cook over low heat for 15 to 20 minutes. Add cheese; cover. Cook additional 10 minutes to melt cheese. Sprinkle salt and pepper to taste.

Mrs. James F. DuBose, OWC
Keyport NTS, Washington

CHILI MACARONI

1 lb. ground beef
1/2 green pepper, chopped
1/2 sm. onion, chopped
1 tbsp. fat or drippings
1 can cooked tomatoes
1 can kidney beans
1 tbsp. sugar
1 1/2 tsp. salt
1 tsp. chili powder
1/8 tsp. pepper
1/2 c. water
2 tbsp. vinegar
4 oz. elbow macaroni

Brown beef, green pepper and onion in fat in heavy skillet. Add tomatoes and beans. Combine sugar, salt, chili powder, pepper, water and vinegar; mix until smooth. Stir into meat mixture; cover. Simmer gently for 20 minutes. Add macaroni; mix well. Cover; simmer 20 minutes longer. Serve hot. Yield: 4 servings.

Mrs. John H. Kirby, Reservation Chm. OWC
White Sands Missile Range, New Mexico

HAMBURGER GOULASH

1 lb. ground chuck
1 med. chopped onion
1 tsp. garlic salt
1 16-oz. can tomatoes, chopped
1 8-oz. can tomato sauce
1 1 1/2-lb. can pork and beans
1 8 to 10-oz. pkg. shell-roni or other
    small noodles
Salt and pepper to taste

Brown ground chuck in electric skillet with onion and garlic salt. Add tomatoes, tomato sauce and pork and beans; simmer. Cook noodles according to package directions; drain. Add to meat mixture; salt and pepper to taste. Simmer for 10 to 15 minutes. Serve. Yield: 6 servings.

Mrs. Dale E. Conrardy, Rec. Sec. OWC
Laredo AFB, Texas

CHEESEBURGER PIE

1 lb. ground beef
2 6-oz. cans tomato paste or sauce
1 tbsp. minced onion
1 tsp. salt
3/4 tsp. crushed Italian seasonings
1/4 tsp. pepper
1 can crescent rolls
4 slices mozzarella cheese
3/4 c. water
1/4 c. butter

Brown beef; drain. Add 1 can tomato paste, onion, salt, 1/2 teaspoon Italian seasonings and pepper; blend well. Separate crescent roll dough into 8 triangles. Place in ungreased 9-inch pie pan, pressing pieces together to form crust. Spread meat mixture over crust; top with cheese. Bake at 375 degrees for 25 to 30 minutes. Combine remaining tomato paste, water, butter and 1/4 teaspoon Italian seasonings. Heat until boiling. Serve sauce with meat pie. Yield: 6 servings.

Mrs. R. K. Hawley, Ways and Means Chm. OWC
Ft. Leonard Wood, Missouri

DOC'S STEW

1 lb. hamburger
1/4 c. chopped onion
1 sm. clove of garlic
4 carrots, sliced thin
2 potatoes, diced
1/2 c. water
Salt and pepper to taste

Brown hamburger, onion and garlic in large skillet. Add carrots and potatoes to meat. Pour in water; cover. Simmer for 1 hour or until vegetables are tender. Yield: 4 servings.

Mrs. L. L. Fry, Sec. FICPAC OWC
Ford Island, Hawaii

HAMBURGER SOUPLE JOE

1 lb. hamburger
1 10 3/4-oz. can condensed
    vegetable soup
4 to 6 split hamburger rolls

(Continued on next page)

Brown hamburger in skillet, breaking into crumbles. Add soup; heat until bubbly. Serve over hamburger rolls or as sloppy Joes. Yield: 4-6 servings.

Mrs. John D. Yamnicky
NAS Cecil Field, Florida

HAMBURGER STROGANOFF

1 1/2 lb. hamburger
1 tsp. salt
1/2 tsp. pepper
1/8 tsp. garlic salt
1/2 tsp. instant minced onion
2 tbsp. flour
1 can cream of chicken soup
1 can sliced cooked carrots
1 2-oz. can mushroom stems and pieces
1 c. sour cream
1/2 10-oz. pkg. noodles, cooked

Combine hamburger, salt, pepper, garlic salt, onion and flour in large skillet. Cook until meat is not red in color. Add soup; stir until hot. Stir in carrots, mushrooms and sour cream just before serving to warm through. Serve with noodles. Yield: 4-6 servings.

Mrs. Ray A. Walker, Pres. OWC
Moran AFB, Spain

HARVEST STEW

1 lb. ground beef
1/4 c. chopped onion
1 8-oz. can tomato sauce
1 1/2 c. water
1 tsp. chili powder
1 tsp. salt
1/2 No. 303 can cream-style corn
1/2 No. 303 can chili beans
4-oz. quick-cooking noodles
1/2 c. sliced ripe olives
1/4 lb. grated American cheese

Brown meat in 10-inch electric frypan. Add onion; cook till tender. Add tomato sauce, water, seasonings, corn and beans. Bring to a boil. Add dry noodles; stir. Cook about 15 minutes at 320 degrees. Add olives and cheese; continue cooking until cheese is melted. Yield: 6-8 servings.

Mrs. Richard G. Kidd, Treas. OWC
Ft. Campbell, Kentucky

LABADIE'S CHILI

1 lb. hamburger
Water
1 tsp. cumin
1 garlic pod
2 tbsp. chili powder

(Continued on next page)

Salt and pepper to taste
1 can tomatoes, mashed
2 chopped onions
1 can or fresh-cooked pinto beans
3 tbsp. flour

Place meat in enough water to make thick soup; add cumin, garlic, chili powder, salt, pepper, tomatoes, onions and pinto beans. Cook over medium heat about 30 minutes. Mix flour with water to make thin paste. Add to chili; let thicken. may be served with crackers or over noodles, if desired. Yield: 4 servings.

Mrs. Edwin J. Labadie, 2nd VP OWC
Laredo AFB, Texas

APPLESAUCE MEAT LOAF

1 1/2 lb. ground beef
1 1/2 c. bread crumbs
1 1/2 c. applesauce
2 tbsp. catsup
2 tbsp. Worcestershire sauce
1 tsp. salt
1 tbsp. dried bell pepper
1 tbsp. minced onion
Catsup to taste

Combine all ingredients except catsup; shape into balls. Place in muffin tins. Make hole in center of each; fill with catsup. Bake at 350 degrees for 30 minutes. Yield: 4 servings.

Mrs. Stanley A. Ault, Pres. OWC
US Naval Station Adak, Alaska

BEER MEAT LOAF

1 c. beer
1 egg, slightly beaten
1 c. soft bread crumbs
3/4 tsp. salt
1/4 tsp. pepper
1 tbsp. instant onion
1/2 tsp. thyme
1 lb. ground chuck
2 tbsp. margarine, melted
1/3 c. chili sauce

Add 1/3 cup beer to egg; stir in crumbs, salt, pepper, onion and thyme. Add meat; mix thoroughly. Shape into 1 large patty. Brown meat patty on both sides in margarine in skillet. Add remaining beer; cover. Simmer for 20 minutes. Spread chili sauce on meat. Yield: 4 servings.

Mrs. Ralph J. Swanson, Corr. Sec. OWC
Ellsworth AFB, South Dakota

FRENCH HAMBURGER LOAF

1 loaf French bread
1 6-oz. can tomato paste
1/4 c. Parmesan cheese
2 to 3 tbsp. sliced olives
1 tsp. salt
1/2 tsp. monosodium glutamate
Dash of pepper
1 1/2 lb. hamburger
Tomato slices
Cheese slices

Cut French bread in half lengthwise separating top from bottom. Combine remaining ingredients except tomato and cheese slices; mix well. Spread meat mixture over both halves of bread. Broil about 4 inches from flame 8 to 10 minutes until meat is done. Top with alternating slices of tomatoes and cheese. Return to broiler; broil until cheese melts. Cut into portions; serve immediately. Yield: 4 servings.

Mrs. John M. Gilreath, 1st VP OWC
Malmstrom AFB, Montana

KIDNEY BEAN MEAT LOAF

1 tbsp. minced onion
1/2 c. milk
1 1/2 lb. ground beef
1 beaten egg
Salt and pepper to taste
1/2 to 1 c. bread crumbs (opt.)
Green pepper chopped (opt.)
Dash Worcestershire
Dash Tobasco sauce (opt.)
1 8-oz. can spagetti sauce
1 8-oz. can kidney beans

Combine first 9 ingredients together; mix well. Form meat loaf into star shape; place in frying pan or baking dish. Pour spagetti sauce and kidney beans over top. Cover; simmer slowly on top of stove or bake, if desired. Bake in 350-degree oven for about 25 minutes. Yield: 4-6 servings.

Mrs. A. M. Patterson, Jr., OWC
Marine Barracks, NAS, Bermuda

MIX-IN-THE-BOWL MEAT LOAF

1 1/2 lb. ground beef
2/3 c. soft crumbs
1 c. milk
2 slightly beaten eggs
1 tsp. salt
1/8 tsp. pepper
1 tbsp. dehydrated chopped onions
1/2 tsp. dried sage
3 tbsp. brown sugar
1/4 c. catsup
1 tsp. mustard
1/4 tsp. nutmeg

(Continued on next page)

Place first 8 ingredients in 2-quart oven-proof bowl. Stir until well mixed. Combine remaining ingredients; pour sauce over meat loaf. Bake for 1 hour at 400 degrees. Serve in same bowl. Yield: 6 servings.

Mrs. Samuel B. Walker, NOWC
Norfolk NAS, Virginia

SKILLET MEAT LOAF

1 1/2 lb. ground meat
1 c. soft bread crumbs
1 c. chopped celery
1 sm. onion
1 1/2 tsp. salt
1/4 tsp. pepper
1 egg
1 can tomato sauce
2 tbsp. salad oil
Chopped parsley to taste

Combine first 7 ingredients and 1/4 cup tomato sauce. Heat salad oil. Press meat mixture into skillet; cover tightly. Cook over low heat from 30 to 40 minutes. Drain juice; add remaining tomato sauce. Sprinkle parsley over top for garnish. Yield: 6 servings.

Mrs. Donald A. Guetig, Cookbook Chm. OWC
Birkenfeld USAFB, Germany

TOMATO MEAT LOAF

1 med.-sized onion, sliced
1 1/2 lb. ground beef, crumbled
1/2 tsp. salt
1/2 tsp. basil
1/4 tsp. oregano
1 can condensed tomato soup

Place half the onion slices in bottom of 8 x 8 x 2-inch baking pan; cover with ground beef. Sprinkle with salt, basil and oregano; top with remaining onion slices. Pour tomato soup over top. Bake in 375-degree oven for 45 minutes or until brown. Yield: 4-6 servings.

Mrs. Jesse C. Gatlin, Jr., Pres. USAF Academy OWC
USAF Academy, Colorado

VIP LOAF

3 lb. ground chuck
1 c. quick-cooking oatmeal
1 c. pickle relish
1 tbsp. onion juice
1 c. tomato juice
1 tbsp. seasoned salt
1 c. cheddar cheese, shredded
1 1/2 tsp. salt
1/2 c. apricot preserves
Chopped nuts

(Continued on next page)

Mix first 8 ingredients in order given with hands. Pat into mounded loaf in 8 x 10-inch pan. Bake for 45 minutes at 350 degrees. Drain off fat and juices as loaf bakes. Spread with preserves; sprinkle with nuts. Bake for 15 minutes longer. Yield: 8 servings.

Mrs. R. D. Morgan, 1st VP NOWC
Sangley Point, Philippine Islands

BAVARIAN MEATBALLS

12 oz. catsup
12 oz. beer or gingerale
2 lb. ground chuck in 1-inch meatballs,
    unseasoned
Saffron to taste

Pour beer and catsup into pot or electric frypan at 350 degrees. Add meatballs; add saffron. Cover; cook for 30 minutes on high heat. Do not stir. Serve with rice or with toothpicks as hot hors d'oeuvres, if desired. Yield: 6 servings.

Mrs. John J. Stewart, Reservation Chm. OWC
USS Mazama-Homeport, Davisville CBC, Rhode Island

MEATBALLS

1 lb. hamburger
1/2 c. rolled oats
1 tbsp. chopped onion
1/2 c. milk
1 tsp. salt
1/2 tsp. pepper
Flour
1 tbsp. fat
1 can tomatoes or 2 c. juice
2 tbsp. Worcestershire sauce
3 tbsp. vinegar
2 tbsp. sugar
1 tsp. chili powder

Mix meat, oats, onion, milk, salt and pepper together; form into balls. Roll in flour; brown in fat on all sides. Mix remaining ingredients together; pour over meatballs. Cover; cook slowly for 20 minutes on stove. Serve with spaghetti, or as a main meat with sauce served over the meatballs. Yield: 6 servings.

Mrs. William R. McEuen, 2nd VP OWC
New Cumberland Army Depot, Pennsylvania

PORCUPINES

1 lb. ground beef
1/2 c. rice
1/4 c. minced onion
1 tsp. salt
1/2 tsp. monosodium glutamate
1/8 tsp. pepper
1 10 1/2 to 11-oz. can condensed tomato
    soup
1 tsp. Worcestershire sauce

(Continued on next page)

Lightly grease 1-quart casserole having tight-fitting cover. Mix beef, rice, onion, salt, monosodium glutamate and pepper together lightly. Form into 8 balls; place in casserole. Combine soup, water and Worcestershire sauce in saucepan; heat to boiling. Pour over meatballs. Cover. Bake at 350 degrees about 1 hour and 15 minutes or until visible rice is tender. Serve with tomato sauce. yield: 6 servings.

Mrs. T. A. Burzenski, Publ. OWC
Incirlik, Turkey

PRONTO MEATBALLS

1 lb. ground beef
1 tbsp. minced onion
1/2 tsp. salt
1/4 tsp. basil
Dash of pepper
Margarine
1 pkg. brown gravy mix
1 c. water

Combine beef, onion, salt, basil and pepper; shape into balls. Brown in margarine. Add gravy mix; stir in water. Cook until thickened. Cover, simmer for 15 to 20 minutes. Yield: 4 servings.

Mrs. Lowell L. Davis, Special Activities Chm. OWC
McKea Barracks
Crailsheim, Germany

MEXI-BURGER

1/4 c. chopped onion
2 tbsp. butter
1 lb. ground beef
1 15 1/2-oz. can chili con carne
1 c. canned yellow corn with sweet
    peppers
1/2 tsp. salt
1 7-oz. pkg. corn bread rounds,
    toasted
3 slices cheddar cheese

Saute onion in butter until transparent. Crumble beef; saute until meat loses pink color. Add chili, corn and salt; mix well. Heat for 10 minutes. Mound the beef-chili mixture on corn bread. Top with crossed strips cheese. Broil 2 minutes or until cheese begins to melt. Yield: 6 servings.

Mrs. Herman Martina, VP OWC
USA Ord. Corps
Pirmasens, Germany

BACON-BEEF AND POTATO PATTIES

1 lb. beef hamburger
1/3 c. fine cracker crumbs
1/2 c. chili sauce
1 tbsp. onions
1 egg, beaten

(Continued on next page)

1 tsp. salt
1/2 tsp. pepper
4 bacon slices
Instant potatoes for 4, prepared
Grated cheese
Paprika to taste

Combine hamburger, crumbs, chili sauce, onion, egg, salt and pepper in large bowl. Mix well; shape into 4 patties. Wrap bacon around each patty; fasten with toothpick. Press deep hollow in patty center; fill with potatoes. Sprinkle cheese and paprika over top. Place patties on rack in broiler pan. Bake at 425 degrees for 25 minutes. Yield: 4 servings.

Mrs. Robert D. Wilson, OWC
Athello AFS, Washington

CRISP MEAT CAKES

5 slices rye bread
1 c. milk
1 lb. round steak, ground
1 grated onion
1 beaten egg
1 tsp. salt
1/2 tsp. pepper
Dried bread crumbs
1 can mushroom soup

Soak bread in milk. Squeeze out part of milk, leaving bread moist. Mix with steak, onion, egg, salt and pepper. Shape in patties; roll in crumbs. Brown quickly in fat in heavy skillet. Lower heat; cook 10 minutes. Remove meat; keep warm. Add soup to pan; heat. Serve meat cakes with gravy separately to retain crispness. Yield: 4 servings.

Mrs. James Dempsey, Hon. Pres. OWC
Fifth Naval Dist.
Norfolk, Virginia

HAMBURGER DINNER IN FOIL

1 lb. ground chuck, divided into 4 patties
1 med.-sized onion, diced
2 med.-sized potatoes, diced
2 carrots, diced
2 sm. strips green pepper, diced
1 sm. stalk celery, diced
Salt and pepper to taste

Lightly grease two 12 x 16-inch pieces of aluminum foil with vegetable oil. Place 1 hamburger patty in center of each piece of foil. Combine onion, potato, carrot, green pepper and celery. Place half the vegetable mixture on each patty. Place remaining hamburger patties on top; wrap foil around each. Place in pan. Bake at 350 degrees for 1 hour and 15 minutes. May be prepared ahead; refrigerate till ready to bake. Yield: 2 dinners.

Mrs. Richard Treptow, Ways and Means Chm. OWC
Kingsley Field AFB, Oregon

PINEAPPLE BURGERS

1 lb. ground chuck
1 tbsp. parsley flakes
1 tbsp. instant onion flakes
1 tsp. monosodium glutamate
Salt and pepper to taste
2 tbsp. water
2 slices pineapple, drained
2 slices cheese
2 toasted buns

Mix all but last 3 ingredients together; shape into 4 large thin patties. Place pineapple slices on 2 patties; cover with remaining patties, sealing edges well. Grill over hot coals or broil in oven about 15 minutes per side. Top each burger with cheese just before removing from heat. Serve on buns. Yield: 2 servings.

Mrs. Walter B. Jones, Jr., VP OWC
Wasserkuppe AFS, Germany

POOR-MAN'S SAUERBRATEN

1 1/2 lb. ground beef
1 1/2 c. grated carrots
3 tsp. minced onion
1 1/2 tsp. salt
1/4 tsp. pepper
10 ginger snaps, finely crushed
   in blender
1 10 1/2-oz. can condensed beef bouillon
   soup
3/4 c. water
1/4 c. lemon juice
Hot buttered noodles

Mix ground beef, carrots, onion, salt and pepper together; shape into 6 patties. Brown well on both sides in heavy 12-inch skillet or electric fry pan; drain grease. Add ginger snaps, soup, water and lemon juice. Stir until smooth. Cover; simmer, stirring occasionally, about 10 minutes until sauce is slightly thickened. Serve on noodles. Yield: 6 servings.

Mrs. Timothy L. Thomas, Treas. OWC
Wright-Patterson AFB, Ohio

SUPER BACON BURGERS

3 lb. lean ground beef
1/2 c. minced chives
1/2 c. minced parsley
1 tbsp. rosemary
2 eggs
6 strips bacon
Seasoned meat tenderizer

Blend first 5 ingredients together. Shape into 6 thick patties. Wrap bacon around each; fasten with toothpick. Sprinkle both sides each patty with tenderizer; do not salt. Grill over charcoal or broil until desired doneness. Yield: 6 servings.

Mrs. John E. Mitchell, Pres. OWC
Fort Detrich, Maryland

QUICK SPAGHETTI SAUCE

1 med.-sized onion, diced
1/2 med. sized green pepper, diced
2 tbsp. butter
1 1/2 lb. ground beef
2 8-oz. cans tomato sauce
1 6-oz. can tomato puree
1 6-oz. can water
1 tbsp. sugar
Salt and pepper to taste
1 tbsp. hot chili powder
4 bay leaves
Cooked spaghetti
Grated Parmesan cheese

Brown onions and green pepper in butter in large skillet. Add hamburger; brown. Add tomato sauce, puree and water; mix well with hamburger. Add sugar, salt, pepper, chili powder and bay leaves; mix well. Cover; simmer for 15 to 20 minutes. Serve over spaghetti; sprinkle Parmesan cheese as garnish. Yield: 4 large servings.

Mrs. Thomas H. Kerr, Pres. O and CWC
Granite City Army Depot, Illinois

SLOPPY JOANNAS

1 lb. hamburger
Salt and pepper to taste
2 med.-sized onions, chopped
3 sticks celery, finely cut
1 c. water
1 can cream corn
1 can tomato soup
Leftover peas and corn (opt.)

Place hamburger in large skillet; season. Start to brown. Add onion and celery to meat; cook till tender. Add water, corn and soup; stir in well. Simmer gently for 30 minutes. Add leftover peas and corn, if desired. Yield: 6-8 servings.

Mrs. John R. Morris, Memshp. Chm. OWC
Sembach AFB, Germany

SOUPER LASAGNA

1/2 lb. ground beef
1 c. chopped onion
2 lge. cloves of garlic, minced
2 tsp. oregano, crushed
2 10 3/4-oz. cans condensed tomato
    soup
1/2 c. water
2 tsp. vinegar
1/2 lb. plain lasagna noodles, cooked
    and drained
1 pt. cream-style cottage cheese
1/2 lb. mozzarella cheese
Grated Parmesan cheese

Brown beef; add onion, garlic and oregano. Cook until onion is tender. Add soup, water and vinegar. Simmer for 30 minutes; stir now and then. Place 3 alternate layers of noodles, cottage cheese, meat sauce and mozzarella in shallow 12 x 8 x 2-inch baking dish. Sprinkle with Parmesan. Bake at 350 degrees for 30 minutes. Let stand 15 minutes before serving. Yield: 6 servings.

Mrs. Terrence M. Weber, OWC
McAlester Nav. Depot, Oklahoma

LAGUNA CURRY

1 c. chopped onion
1 minced garlic clove
2 tbsp. butter
2 heaping tbsp. curry powder
2 tbsp. flour
1 tsp. ginger
1 c. chicken broth
Leftover leg of lamb, cut into 1-inch
    chunks and trimmed
2 lge. green peppers, cut into chunks
2 or 3 lge. celery stalks, cut into 1/2-inch
    slices
Rice

Saute onions and garlic in butter in skillet. Blend in dry ingredients. Stir over low heat for 2 minutes; gradually add broth. Bring to boiling point; reduce heat. Cook for 10 minutes. Add meat and vegetables. Cook slowly until vegetables are crisp-tender. Serve over rice; accompany with chutney, if desired.
PERSONAL NOTE: Had the original on our honeymoon in Laguna. Came home and copied it. Although the recipe looks long, this can be made and placed on the table very quickly!

Mrs. William A. Petry, Hosp. Chm.
Naval Safety Center OWC
Breezy Point NAS, Virginia

SPAGHETTI SAUCE

1 lb. ground round
1/2 tsp. salt
1/8 tsp. pepper
1 sm. onion, chopped

(Continued on next page)

Ground Beef Dishes

1 tbsp. Worcestershire sauce
1/2 green pepper, chopped
1/8 tsp. garlic powder
1/4 tsp. oregano
1 lge. can tomato sauce

Brown meat in skillet; add remaining ingredients. Simmer for 20 minutes. Yield: 4 servings.

Mrs. Spiro T. Agnew
Wife of Vice President of US
Washington, D. C.

STUFFED HAMBURGER CUPS

1 lb. ground beef
Salt and pepper to taste
1/4 c. catsup
1 egg
1/4 c. cracker crumbs
3 tbsp. fat, margarine or butter
1/4 c. chopped celery
1/4 c. chopped onion
3 c. soft bread cubes
1/4 c. milk
4 slices cheese

Combine beef, salt, pepper; brown in skillet. Add catsup, egg and crumbs; mix thoroughly. Saute celery and onion in shortening in small skillet. Add bread, milk and salt. Divide meat into 4 portions. Shape into patty shell with indentations in each one. Place 1/2 cup stuffing into each. Bake in 350-degree oven for 25 to 30 minutes. Place cheese slice on top; return to oven for about 2 minutes. Yield: 6 servings.

Mrs. Johnny B. McDaniel, NOWC
NAS Barbers Pt., Hawaii

TASTY BARBECUE

1 lb. ground beef
1 tbsp. fat
1/2 c. chopped onion
1/4 c. chopped celery
1/4 c. chopped green pepper
1 tbsp. sugar
1 tsp. salt
Dash pepper
1 8-oz. can seasoned tomato sauce
1/4 c. catsup
1 tbsp. vinegar
1 1/2 tsp. Worcestershire sauce
6 buns

Brown meat slowly in hot fat. Add onion, celery and green pepper; cook till tender but not brown. Stir in remaining ingredients except buns. Simmer 5 to 10 minutes or till mixture is thick. Serve on buns. May be made in advance and reheated, if desired. Yield: 6 servings.

Mrs. Henry F. Helder, Gift Chm. OWC
Naval Air Station, Norfolk, Virginia

WANG DOODLE

3/4 c. chopped celery
1 med. onion, chopped
1 lb. ground beef
1 tsp. dry mustard
1 tsp. sugar
3/4 c. catsup
1 tbsp. vinegar
1 tsp. Worcestershire sauce

Sear celery, onion and beef in skillet over medium heat. Add dry mustard, sugar, catsup, vinegar and Worcestershire sauce. Cover. Simmer about 20 minutes. Serve on hamburger buns, if desired. Yield: 4 servings.

Mrs. T. R. Brownfield, Nursery Chm. OWC
Hohenfels Training Area, Germany

BARBECUE SUPREME

3 1/2 lb. ground beef
2 12-oz. cans corned beef, finely chopped
3 c. dry onions
2 tbsp. brown sugar
2 tbsp. garlic salt
2 tsp. seasoned salt
1 qt. barbecue sauce

Brown ground beef in large electric skillet at 200 degrees. Add corned beef; blend thoroughly. Add onions, brown sugar and seasonings. Blend thoroughly. Mix in barbecue sauce. Simmer for 10 minutes. Yield: 40 servings.

Mrs. Sanders E. Clark, Sr., Cookbook Chm. OWC
Savanna Army Depot, Illinois

FOIL-WRAPPED CHICKEN DINNER

4 frying chicken breasts
1 can peas
5 med. potatoes, peeled and thinly sliced
1 pkg. link sausage
Salt
Pepper
Poultry seasoning

Tear off four 1 1/2-foot lengths of 18-inch wide foil. Place 1 piece of chicken on each piece of foil. Top chicken with peas, potatoes and sausage. Salt and pepper to taste. Sprinkle with pinch of poultry seasoning. Fold foil over; seal securely to hold in juices. Place on baking sheet. Bake at 400 degrees for 1 hour and 30 minutes or till potatoes are tender. May be cooked on barbecue grill, using double thickness of foil and cooking over slow coals. Yield: 4 servings.

Mrs. Richard P. Pendorf, Ways and Means Chm. OWC
Hof AFS, Germany

FRIED CHICKEN SURPRISES

    4 chicken breasts, boned
    Salt
    Thyme
    4 thin slices boiled ham
    4 thin slices American cheese at room
        temperature
    1/2 pt. buttermilk
    1 c. self-rising flour
    Oil

Sprinkle skinless side of chicken breasts with salt and thyme. Place 1 slice each ham and cheese on skinless side of each breast. Slices may have to be trimmed so as not to overlap chicken. Roll up chicken with ham and cheese inside; pin with toothpicks. Salt to taste. Dip in buttermilk; roll in flour. Fry in enough oil to completely cover rolls at 350 degrees until golden brown and crusty. Yield: 4 servings.

                              Mrs. Ronald G. Horne, OWC
                              Cecil Field, Florida

WASHBOILER CLAMBAKE

    Washed seaweed
    1 qt. water
    8 whole unpeeled onions
    4 Idaho potatoes, wrapped in foil
    2 chickens, cut up, each wrapped in cheese
        cloth
    2 1/2-lb. lobsters
    4 husked ears corn, wrapped in foil
    24 steamer clams
    Butter

Fill bottom of washboiler or large enamel pot with seaweed; add water. Bring to boiling over high heat. Add onions, wrapped potatoes and more seaweed; cover. Cook for 15 minutes. Add wrapped chickens and layer of seaweed; cover. Cook for 15 minutes. Add lobster and more seaweed, cover. Cook for 8 minutes; add corn. Cook for 10 minutes. Add clams; cover. Steam till clams open. Serve with butter and kettle liquid as dip. Yield: 8 servings.

                              Mrs. Edward Pillings, OWC
                              West Point, New York

COLORFUL SWEET AND SOUR PORK

    4 to 6 lean pork chops
    Salt and black pepper to taste
    Dash Accent
    1 tbsp. cooking oil
    1/2 iceberg lettuce, sliced finely
    1/2 to 3/4 bottle sweet and sour sauce
    Cooked rice

Bone chops; cut meat into thin slices about 1/4-inch wide. Heat oil in heavy skillet. Brown meat quickly on all sides on medium heat or 275-degree setting of electric skillet. Season meat after turning once. Cooking time will be about 12

(Continued on next page)

minutes. Turn out onto bed of cut lettuce; drizzle sweet and sour sauce over all meat generously. Serve with cooked rice.

Mrs. John D. Stephens, Gourmet Exchange Chm. OWC
Fort McPherson, Georgia

MANDARIN GLAZED PORK CHOPS

6 thick pork chops
1 11-oz. can mandarin oranges
3 tbsp. brown sugar
1/2 tsp. cinnamon
3 whole cloves
1 tsp. salt
1 tsp. prepared mustard
1/4 c. catsup
1 tbsp. vinegar

Brown pork chops on both sides in hot fat. Drain mandarin oranges, saving juice. Combine 1/2 cup juice and oranges with remaining ingredients; pour over pork chops. cover; simmer gently for 45 minutes or until chops are tender. Yield: 6 servings.

Mrs. Reed A. Booth, Pres. OWC
Fort Eustis, Virginia

NEAPOLITAN PORK CHOPS

2 cloves garlic, sliced
3 tbsp. olive oil
6 lean pork chops
Salt and pepper to taste
1/2 c. tomato paste
1/2 c. dry white wine
1 green pepper, diced
1/2 lb. mushrooms, sliced

Brown garlic in hot oil in heavy skillet; discard garlic. Brown pork chops; sprinkle with salt and pepper. Add remaining ingredients; cover. Simmer over low heat for 30 to 35 minutes. Yield: 6 servings.

Mrs. Philip G. Dye, OWC
Bangkok, Thailand

OVEN-BARBECUED PORK CHOPS

1/4 tsp. pepper
1/2 tsp. salt
1 sm. grated onion
1 tsp. prepared mustard
1 tsp. sugar
1 can tomato paste
1/2 c. vinegar
1/2 to 3/4 c. water
1/2 tbsp. Worcestershire sauce
1/8 c. cooking oil
6 pork chops

Place all ingredients, except pork chops in plastic container with lid. Shake well. Arrange chops in shallow baking dish or pan; pour sauce over chops. Bake, uncovered at 325 degrees, turning occasionally. Cook for 2 to 3 hours depending on thickness of chops. Yield: 6 servings.

Mrs. Charles E. Masalin, VP OWC
Pearl Harbor Sub. Base, Hawaii

PAM'S CREOLE PORK CHOPS

4 med. pork chops
3 c. boiling water
6 beef bouillon cubes
1 c. regular rice
1 lge. onion
1/4 tsp. marjoram
2 tsp. salt, or less
1/4 tsp. pepper
1 lge. firm tomato
1 green pepper

Set control on electric skillet at 360 degrees. Brown chops in small amount salad oil. Remove chops; set aside. Add water and bouillon cubes to pan; stir until cubes have dissolved. Reduce heat to 220 degrees; add rice, 1/4 cup diced onion, marjoram, salt, pepper. Stir well. Place chops on top of rice; top each chop with slice of tomato, green pepper and remaining onion. Cover. Cook for 45 minutes or until rice is done. Yield: 2-4 servings.

Mrs. William A. Chansler, OWC
Chicksands RAF Station, England

PORK CHOPS AND APPLES

4 to 6 pork chops
3 to 4 unpeeled apples, cored and sliced
1/4 cup brown sugar, packed
1/2 tsp. cinnamon
2 tbsp. butter

Heat oven to 400 degrees. Brown chops on all sides in hot fat. Place apple slices in greased baking dish. Sprinkle with sugar and cinnamon; dot with butter. Top with chops; cover. Bake for 1 hour and 30 minutes. Yield: 4-6 servings.

Mrs. John E. Martin, Treas. OWC
Edgewood Arsenal, Maryland

PORK CHOPS BOULANGERE

4 loin pork chops
Shortening
2 potatoes, thinly sliced
3 carrots, sliced
1/4 green pepper, diced
1 10-oz. pkg. frozen green peas
Salt, pepper, oregano and garlic
    to taste

Fry chops in shortening; cover. Cook for 20 minutes. Add vegetables and seasonings; cover. Cook for 20 minutes. One tablespoon water may be added, if necessary. Yield: 4 servings.

Mrs. Harvey W. Burden, Hospitality Chm. CNAL OWC
Naval Air Station
Norfolk, Virginia

PORK CHOPS WITH MILK GRAVY

8 pork chops
4 tbsp. butter
1 lge. onion, chopped
2 tbsp. flour
2 vegetable bouillon cubes
1 c. water
2 c. milk
1 tsp. Gravymaster
Salt to taste
Pepper to taste

Brown chops in butter; add onion. Brown; remove chops and onions. Add flour and bouillon; mix. Add water, milk and Gravymaster, stirring constantly till mixture boils. Add chops and onions; simmer for 30 to 45 minutes. Salt and pepper to taste.

Mrs. J. R. Jacobsen, OWC
Oslo, Norway

PORK CHOPS WITH ORANGE SAUCE

8 loin pork chops
Salt, pepper and paprika
1/4 c. water
5 tbsp. sugar
1 1/2 tsp. cornstarch
1/4 tsp. salt
1/4 tsp. cinnamon
10 whole cloves
2 tsp. grated orange rind
1/2 c. orange juice

Sprinkle chops with salt, pepper and paprika; brown on both sides in skillet. Add water; cover tightly. Simmer for 1 hour. Combine sugar, cornstarch, salt, cinnamon, cloves, rind and juice in saucepan; cook, stirring constantly until thickened and clear. Spoon over chops. Yield: 4 servings.

Mrs. Elwood C. Hintzman, Charity Chm. OWC
Kamiseya USNSGA, Japan

PORK CHOPS AND RICE

4 thick pork chops
Salt
Pepper
Accent
1 c. uncooked rice, not quick-cooking type
1 med. onion
1 green pepper
1 lge. can tomatoes

Brown chops quickly in frying pan. Place chops in 3-quart casserole; season. Sprinkle rice over chops. Slice onion and green pepper over rice; season. Pour tomatoes over all; cover. Bake in 350-degree oven for 1 hour or until rice is done. Yield: 4 servings.

Mrs. Robert W. Paulson, Hon. VP OWC
Wife of Commanding General
Air Force Communications Service
Scott AFB, Illinois

PORK CHOPS AND RICE

5 pork chops
1 1/2 tsp. salt
1 tsp. monosodium glutamate
Dash of coarsely ground pepper
1 c. uncooked rice
1/2 c. chopped onion
1/4 c. chopped green pepper
2 1/2 c. water

Trim excess fat from chops; heat fat in heavy skillet or electric skillet to obtain 2 tablespoons fat. Remove trimmings. Brown chops slowly in hot fat; drain off excess. Combine seasonings; sprinkle over meat. Add rice, onion and green pepper. Add water; cover with tight-fitting lid. Cook over low heat for 30 to 35 minutes. Yield: 5 servings.

Mrs. Herman Jacobs, CG OWC
US Coast Guard Base
St. Louis, Missouri

SPANISH PORK CHOPS

6 pork chops
1 med. green pepper, coarsely cut
1 14 1/2-oz. can stewed tomatoes
1 med. onion, chopped
1 c. frozen corn
1 15-oz. can tomato sauce
1 1/2 c. water
1 tsp. onion salt
1 tsp. seasoned pepper
2 tbsp. red hot sauce
1 c. Minute rice

Preheat oven to 350 degrees. Brown chops in frying pan. Combine remaining ingredients except rice; mix in casserole. Add chops to mixture. Bake for 20 to 25 minutes. Add rice; stir gently. Bake for 3 to 5 minutes. Yield: 4-6 servings.

Mrs. William F. Wallace, Radar Sqdn. OWC
Houma AFS, Louisiana

GLAZED HAM BALLS

2 lb. ground ham
1 lb. ground pork
2 eggs, beaten
1 c. milk
1 1/2 c. bread crumbs
1 tbsp. minced onion
1 1/2 c. brown sugar
3/4 c. vinegar
3/4 c. water
1 1/2 tsp. dry mustard

Combine first 6 ingredients. Shape into balls; place in 9 x 13-inch baking pan. Heat remaining ingredients to boiling. Pour over ham balls. Bake for 1 hour at 325 degrees, basting frequently. Yield: 8-10 servings.

Mrs. Roger W. McLain, Treas. OWC
Upper Heyford RAFB, England

HAM LOAF

1 1/2 lb. ground pork
1 lb. ground ham
2 eggs
1 1/2 c. bread crumbs
1/2 c. milk
1 c. tomato juice

Mix pork, ham, eggs, bread crumbs, milk and tomato juice. Pat into 8 1/2 x 4 1/2 x 2 1/2-inch bread pan. Top with remaining tomato juice. Bake at 325 degrees for 1 hour. Yield: 8 servings.

Mrs. Steven J. Savonen, Corr. Sec. OWC
McConnell AFB, Kansas

COMPANY HAM IN SOUR CREAM

1 c. cooked ham in julienne strips
1/4 c. chopped onion
2 tbsp. butter or margarine
2 tsp. enriched flour
1 c. sour cream
1 6-oz. can broiled, sliced mushrooms, drained
Hot cooked rice

Cook ham and onion in butter until onion is tender but not brown. Sprinkle with flour; stir in sour cream gradually. Add mushrooms. Cook over low heat, stirring constantly, just until mixture thickens for 2 or 3 minutes. Garnish with parsley. Serve with fluffy rice. Yield: 3-4 servings.

Mrs. Emory M. Shelton, Bridge Chm. OWC
Dobbins AFB, Georgia

HAM IN CORNBREAD CRUST

1 c. yellow cornmeal
1 2/3 c. water
1 tsp. salt
Evaporated milk
1/4 c. butter
1 c. chopped celery
1/4 c. chopped green pepper
1/4 c. chopped onion
1/4 c. flour
1 chicken bouillon cube dissolved
   in 1 cut hot water
1 tsp. Worcestershire sauce
2 c. chopped baked or boiled ham
1 1/2 c. shredded sharp cheddar cheese

Combine cornmeal, water and salt in saucepan; cook, stirring until mixture boils. Add 1 2/3 cup milk; cook, stirring constantly until thick. Line buttered baking dish with mush. Bake at 375 degrees for 20 to 25 minutes. Remove from oven. Melt butter. Saute celery, green pepper and onion; add flour, mixing well. Blend in bouillon, 1 cup milk and Worcestershire sauce. Cook over medium heat, stirring until sauce thickens. Add ham and 1 cup cheese; stir until cheese melts. Pour into crust; top with remaining cheese. Broil until browned.

Mrs. John H. Archer, Jr., Adv. OWC
Columbus AFB, Mississippi

JAMBALAYA

3 onions, sliced
1 green pepper, diced
1 garlic clove, minced
1/4 c. butter
2 c. diced leftover ham
1/2 c. dry white wine
3 1/2 c. canned tomatoes
1/2 tsp. thyme
1/4 tsp. basil
1/2 tsp. paprika
1/4 tsp. Tabasco
1 sm. can minced clams with juice
1 c. rice

Saute onions, green pepper and garlic in butter for 10 minutes in heavy iron pot. Add ham, wine, tomatoes, seasonings, clams and juice; mix. Bring to a boil. add rice gradually, stirring constantly. Reduce heat; cover. Simmer for about 25 minutes or until rice is done.

Mrs. D. L. Felt, OWC
Lemoore NAS, California

POLYNESIAN HAM

3 c. cooked ham, cut in cubes
2 tbsp. butter
1 13-oz. can pineapple chunks
2 med. green peppers, cut in strips
1/2 c. brown sugar
2 tbsp. cornstarch

(Continued on next page)

1/2 c. vinegar
1/2 c. chicken bouillon
2 tsp. soy sauce
3 c. cooked rice

Brown ham pieces lightly in butter. Add pineapple chunks with syrup and green pepper strips; cover. Simmer for 15 minutes. Mix brown sugar and cornstarch; add vinegar, bouillon and soy sauce. Add to ham mixture; stir until thickened. Serve over hot rice. Yield: 6 servings.

Mrs. John E. Bondioli, Pres. OWC
Hohenfels AT Center, Germany

SCALLOPED HAM WITH NOODLES

3 tbsp. butter
3 tbsp. flour
3 c. milk
Salt to taste
2 c. cooked noodles
3 c. cooked ham
1 c. fine bread crumbs

Make thin white sauce of butter, flour and milk; add salt to taste. Alternate layers of noodles and meat in shallow baking dish. Cover with white sauce; sprinkle bread crumbs over top. Bake for about 20 minutes in 375-degree oven. Yield: 6 servings.

Mrs. William F. Cochran, Rec. Sec. OWC
US Fleet Weather Facility
Sangley Point, Republic of Philippines

STEAMED HAM AND CABBAGE DINNER

1/4 c. water
1 2-lb. ham slice
4 med. potatoes, peeled and cut in
    quarters
1 med. head cabbage, quartered
Salt and pepper to taste
1 med. can sauerkraut

Pour water into Dutch oven; add ham slice, potatoes and cabbage. Sprinkle with salt and pepper; cover. Cook at medium heat for 30 minutes or until potatoes are tender. Heat sauerkraut in another pot; serve with ham. Yield: 4 servings.

Mrs. Donald L. Woodford, Sec. OWC
FAAWTC
Virginia Beach, Virginia

ORIENTAL HASH

2 tbsp. cooking oil
Dash of garlic powder
1 1/2 c. cubed cooked pork
2 c. cooked rice
3 tbsp. soy sauce
2 well-beaten eggs
2 c. shredded lettuce

Heat oil in skillet; add garlic powder and pork. Cook till meat is lightly browned. Add cooked rice and soy sauce. Cook for 10 minutes, stirring occasionally. Mix in eggs; cook for 1 minute, stirring frequently. Remove from heat; add shredded lettuce. Toss together. Yield: 4 servings.

Mrs. Eugene Robert Klein, Gourmet Chm. AOWC
Allied Forces, Southern Europe
Naples, Italy

SAUSAGE ROLLS

2 c. Bisquick
1 lb. hot sausage

Prepare Bisquick according to directions; roll out. Place sausage between 2 waxed paper sheets; roll out to same size as Bisquick. Turn sausage onto Bisquick. Roll up jelly roll fashion; slice 1/4 to 1/3-inch thick. Place on greased cookie sheet; bake for 15 minuts at 400 degrees. Yield: 22 rolls.

Mrs. Kenneth W. Langford, Rec. Sec. OWC
MCAS, Beaufort, South Carolina

SICILIAN PORK

1 tbsp. fat
1 clove garlic, minced
1 med. onion, chopped
2 c. tomatoes
1/2 c. catsup
2 tbsp. vinegar
1/4 tsp. salt
1/4 tsp. pepper
Pinch of thyme
1 pkg. frozen cut green beans,
    cooked and drained
2 c. cooked diced pork

Heat fat in large frying pan; add garlic and onion. Saute for 5 minutes. Add tomatoes, catsup, vinegar, salt, pepper and thyme; cover pan. Simmer for 15 minutes. Add beans and pork; simmer, uncovered for 15 minutes. Yield: 6 servings.

Mrs. John J. White, II, Rec. Sec. OWC
Edgewood Arsenal, Maryland

BARBECUED CHICKEN

3 1 1/2 to 2-lb. frying chickens, halved
Seasoned flour

(Continued on next page)

1/4 c. fat or drippings
1 med. onion, minced
1 7-oz. bottle Seven-Up
1 c. catsup
1 tbsp. Worcestershire sauce
1 tbsp. vinegar

Roll chickens in seasoned flour. Brown in hot fat in large skillet until lightly browned; remove to shallow baking dish. Brown onion lightly in same skillet; stir in remaining ingredients. Bring to a boil; pour over chicken. Bake in 325-degree oven for 30 to 45 minutes or until tender, basting twice during cooking. Yield: 6 servings.
PERSONAL NOTE: This recipe was found in a food section of a newspaper about 15 years ago. Copies of the recipe have been requested often by guests.

Mrs. Walter J. Davies, Hon. VP OWC
Edgewood Arsenal, Maryland

SOUTH ALABAMA BARBECUED CHICKEN

1/4 c. vinegar
1/2 c. water
2 tbsp. brown sugar
1 tbsp. prepared mustard
1 1/2 tsp. salt
1/2 tsp. black pepper
1/4 tsp. cayenne pepper
Juice of 1 lemon
1 lge. onion, chopped
1/4 c. butter or oleo
1/2 c. catsup
2 tbsp. Worcestershire sauce
1 1/2 tsp. Liquid Smoke
3 cut-up chickens, cooked till tender

Mix first 10 ingredients in saucepan. Bring to a boil. Cook for 20 minutes over low heat; add catsup, Worcestershire and Liquid Smoke. Mix well. Place chicken in large casserole dish; pour over barbecue sauce. Bake in 300-degree oven for 1 hour. Yield: 10 servings.
PERSONAL NOTE: Recipe is from a Southern family in Montgomery, Alabama.

Betty Chappell, Service Chm.
Supply Corps OWC
Norfolk Navy Base, Virginia

CHICKEN ADOBO

1 chicken, boned and diced
10 whole peppercorns
1 garlic clove, diced
1/2 tsp. pickling spices
1 tsp. Accent
Salt to taste

Place chicken pieces in electric skillet at medium-high temperature. Add all other ingredients; cover. Reduce heat to simmer when juice of chicken bubbles. Simmer for 30 to 40 minutes. Chicken will cook in its own juices; add water, if needed. Serve with rice, if desired. Yield: 4 servings.

Mrs. Paul E. Maciaz, OWC
Almaden AFS, California

BRANDIED CHICKEN BREASTS

6 chicken breasts
2 tbsp. butter
2 cans cream of mushroom soup
1 can mushrooms
1 bay leaf
1 1/2 jiggers brandy or Scotch
1/2 tsp. salt
1/4 tsp. pepper
Dash of Tabasco
1/4 tsp. cayenne

Saute chicken in butter in skillet until lightly browned. Add mushroom soup, mushrooms, bay leaf, brandy, salt, pepper, Tabasco and cayenne; cover. cook slowly until tender. Serve over rice or mashed potatoes, if desired. Yield: 6 servings.
PERSONAL NOTE: Over a cup of coffee in Turkey, a friend proffered a version of the recipe and I worked on it until my family and friends demand it often.

Mrs. Paul E. Johnson, OWC
Tinker AFB, Oklahoma

BREAST OF CHICKEN IN RUM CRUMBS

2 boneless chicken breasts, with skin
   removed
1/2 c. bread crumbs
1/4 c. plus 1 tbsp. rum
1/4 lb. butter
3 marron glaces
1 tbsp. chutney with liquid

Halve chicken breasts. Flatten each half slightly with mallet. Place bread crumbs on plate; pour 1/4 cup rum into small bowl. Dip chicken in rum, then in bread crumbs. Saute chicken pieces in butter in skillet over medium heat for 1 minute on each side. Mash marrons and chutney with 1 tablespoon rum; warm in saucepan. Add few bread crumbs to make mixture spreadable. Spread this on 1 side of 2 chicken slices. Top with another chicken slice; serve hot. Yield: 2 servings.

Mrs. William B. Owens, OWC Chm. Thrift Shop
Fort McClellan, Alabama

CHICKEN BAKE

1 chicken or 1 pkg. chicken parts
1 c. seasoned flour
1/4 c. shortening or butter
1 10 1/2-oz. can mushroom soup
1 10 1/2-oz. can cream of chicken soup
1/2 soup can milk

Dip chicken in seasoned flour. Brown for 20 minutes in shortening in skillet. Place in 13 x 9 1/2-inch baking pan. Spread both cans of soup over chicken; add milk. Bake at 350 degrees for 1 hour. Yield: 4 servings.

Mrs. Jerry Marks, Rec. Sec. OWC
FE Warren AFB, Wyoming

CHICKEN A LA BOURBON

2 lge. whole chicken breasts, split
   and preferably boned
Salt
Pepper
3 tbsp. butter
1 6-oz. can frozen orange juice
   concentrate, thawed
1/4 c. salted roasted almonds, chopped
2 tbsp. bourbon
Watercress

Season chicken generously with salt and pepper. Brown chicken in frying pan in butter on both sides over medium heat; reduce heat to low. Add orange juice, 1/2 teaspoon salt and 1/4 teaspoon pepper; cover. Cook 20 minutes more, or until chicken is tender and done. Stir sauce; spoon over chicken once or twice. Remove chicken to serving plate; sprinkle with almonds. Keep warm. Reduce liquid in pan to consistency of heavy cream. Cook over high heat, stirring till slightly brown. Add bourbon; stir to blend. Pour over chicken; garnish with watercress. Yield: 2 servings.

Mrs. Charles H. Reidenbaugh, VP OWC
Fort Benning, Georgia

CHICKEN BREAST GOURMET

4 fillet chicken breasts
1/4 c. butter
1/2 chopped white onion
1/2 c. white cooking wine
1 c. sour cream

Brown breasts in butter in skillet; add onion and wine. Cook over low heat for 15 minutes; remove breasts. Pour sour cream into pan; stir till blended. Pour sour cream mixture over breasts. Yield: 4 servings.

Mrs. Ole Dahle Melsaether, Pres. OWC
Finland, AFS, Minnesota

CHICKEN WITH CHEESE AND SHERRY SAUCE

Salt and pepper to taste
Boned chicken breasts
Oregano
Melted oleo
Grated sharp cheddar cheese
1/2 c. sherry

Salt and pepper chicken breasts to taste. Sprinkle with oregano, salt and pepper. Dip in melted oleo; arrange pieces in 1 layer in flat baking dish. Bake for 45 minutes in 350-degree oven; chicken should be golden brown. Remove from oven. Sprinkle with grated cheese. Pour sherry over this; return to oven. Cook for 15 minutes.

Mrs. James J. Kennedy, Asst. Treas. OWC
Mountain Home AFB, Idaho

CHICKEN CACCIATORE

1/4 c. vegetable oil
1 3 1/2-lb. cut-up broiler fryer
   chicken, washed and patted dry
1/3 c. coarsely-chopped onion
1 pkg. spaghetti sauce mix with mushrooms
1 1-lb. can tomatoes
1 sm. can tomato paste
1 tomato paste can water

Heat oil in large skillet over moderately high heat; add chicken. Brown on all sides; remove chicken. Discard all but 1 tablespoon oil from skillet; add onion. Cook until tender. Add sauce mix, tomatoes, tomato paste and water. Blend thoroughly. Return chicken pieces to skillet; cover tightly. Cook over moderate heat for 45 minutes, or until chicken is tender. Serve with cooked spaghetti, if desired. Yield: 6 servings.

Mrs. Axel J. Hagstrom, NOWC
Seattle, Washington

CHICKEN CACCIATORE AND NOODLES

4 chicken thigh and leg quarters
1/3 c. olive oil
3 sm. onions, sliced and separated into
   rings
1/2 green pepper, chopped
1/4 tsp. garlic powder
1/2 to 1 teaspoon basil
1/2 tsp. salt
Freshly ground black pepper
1 c. canned tomatoes
1/2 c. red wine
6 oz. noodles, boiled and drained

Saute chicken in olive oil in skillet for 10 minutes or until golden brown. Add onion, green pepper, garlic, basil, salt and pepper. Simmer for 5 minutes; add tomatoes. Bring to a boil. Reduce heat. Cover. Simmer for 20 minutes; add wine. Simmer for 10 minutes. Place noodles into warmed casserole or serving dish. Serve chicken and sauce over noodles. Yield: 4 servings.

Mrs. Robert B. Somers, OWC
Homestead AFB, Florida

CHICKEN DANDIES

1/4 lb. American cheddar cheese,
   cubed
1 c. diced chicken
1 tbsp. minced green pepper
2 tbsp. minced onion
3 tbsp. chopped stuffed olives
2 tbsp. pickle relish
1/2 c. mayonnaise
8 buttered, split buns

(Continued on next page)

Combine first 7 ingredients; spoon between buns. Wrap each in foil. Bake in wrappers for 15 minutes at 300 degrees. Yield: 4 servings.

Mrs. Louis Knafla, OWC
Finland AFS, Minnesota

CHICKEN ELIZABETH A LA EPICURE

4 chicken breasts
Salt and pepper to taste
Butter
1/2 pt. sour cream
1/4 lb. Roquefort cheese, crumbled
1 garlic clove, forced through press

Season chicken with salt and pepper. Brown in butter in skillet. Arrange in 9 x 13-inch baking dish. Pour over mixture of sour cream, cheese and garlic; cover. Bake at 350 degrees for 45 minutes or until tender. Yield: 4 servings.

Mrs. Fergus T. Gomersal, Asst. Treas. OWC
FE Warren AFB, Wyoming

CHICKEN PARISIAN

1 1/2 lb. boned chicken breasts or
    thighs, with skin removed
1 can condensed cream of mushroom
    soup
1/2 c. sour cream
1 tbsp. parsley flakes
Nutmeg

Halve chicken breasts. Place chicken in shallow, greased baking dish. Combine soup with sour cream; stir in parsley. Pour over chicken; sprinkle with nutmeg. Bake at 350 degrees for 45 minutes or until lightly browned and tender. Yield: 4 servings.

Mrs. Robert D. Bradshaw, Welfare Chm. OWC
Langley AFB, Virginia

CHICKEN A LA ORANGE

12 pieces chicken
Flour
Salt and pepper to taste
Cooking oil
1 c. fresh or frozen orange juice
1/2 c. chili sauce
1/4 c. green pepper
1 tsp. prepared mustard
1/2 to 1 tsp. garlic salt
2 tbsp. soy sauce
1 tbsp. corn syrup
1 can mandarin orange sections
Parsley

(Continued on next page)

Dredge chicken with flour; season with salt and pepper. Fry in cooking oil in skillet until golden brown all over. Remove chicken to 3-quart casserole. Drain skillet; add remaining ingredients, except orange sections and parsley. Simmer for 3 minutes; pour over chicken. Bake in preheated oven for 45 minutes or until chicken is tender. Garnish with orange sections and parsley. May be made day before, reheated and garnished just before serving. Yield: 4-6 servings.
PERSONAL NOTE: Recipe was given to me by a civilian neighbor in El Paso, Texas and originally came from her grandmother in New Orleans.

Mrs. Charles H. Spragg, Ways and Means Chm.
Kaisers Lautern O. and C. Wives Club
Vogelweh, Germany

CHICKEN JUBILEE

2 fryers, cut up or 6 chicken breasts,
   split
1 tsp. salt
1/4 tsp. pepper
1/4 c. butter, melted
1 bottle Sweet n' Sour sauce
1 1-lb. can sliced peaches, drained
1 1-lb. can dark, sweet cherries, drained
1 med. onion, sliced
1/2 c. chili sauce

Place chicken, skin side up, in baking pan. Sprinkle with salt and pepper; drizzle with butter. Broil until brown. Combine sauce, peaches, cherries, onion and chili sauce; spoon over chicken. Bake at 325 degrees for 1 hour, or until chicken is tender. Thicken sauce, if desired. Yield: 6 servings.

Mrs. Thomas P. Cagney, Ways and Means Chm.
Phiblant OWC Little Creek Amphibious Base, Virginia

COUNTRY CAPTAIN

8 chicken breasts, with skin removed
1 1/2 tbsp. shortening
1 onion, chopped
2 cloves of garlic, finely chopped
1 green pepper, chopped
2 1-lb. cans tomatoes
1/2 c. raisins or currants
1 tsp. each salt, pepper, curry
   powder, chopped parsley and
   powdered thyme

Brown chicken in shortening in skillet. Arrange in baking dish. Brown onion, garlic and green pepper in shortening in skillet; add tomatoes. Cook for 10 minutes; add remaining ingredients. Simmer for 10 minutes. Pour sauce over chicken; cover. Bake for 45 minutes or until tender in 350-degree oven. Yield: 8 servings.
PERSONAL NOTE: This recipe has been in the family for years and it comes from Charleston, South Carolina.

Mrs. Andrew J. Evans, Jr., OWC
Eglin AFB, Florida

CHICKEN PIQUANT

3/4 c. rose or dry white wine
1/2 c. soy sauce
1/4 c. salad oil
2 tbsp. water
2 cloves of garlic, crushed
1 tsp. ginger
3 tbsp. brown sugar
6 chicken breasts

Place all ingredients except chicken in 12 x 15-inch pan; mix well. Place chicken in sauce; cover. Bake in 375-degree oven for 45 minutes. Sauce may be thickened and used as gravy. Turn chicken once during baking time. Serve with rice, if desired. Yield: 6 servings.

Mrs. W. C. Kidd, Tour Chm. OWC
Upper Heyfard RAFB, England

CHICKEN ROSEMARY

4 chicken breasts
Oil
1 can cream of mushroom soup
2 tsp. rosemary

Brown chicken breasts in oil in skillet. Place each on piece of aluminum foil. Spread 1/4 can or more mushroom soup on each breast. Sprinkle 1/2 teaspoon or more rosemary over soup. Fold foil around each breast. Bake in oven at 350 degrees for 1 hour or until tender. Extra breasts may be frozen in the foil wrapper and baked at any time later. Yield: 4 servings.

Mrs. B. C. Chapla, Ways and Means Chm. OWC
Carlisle Barracks, Pennsylvania

FOXY CHICKEN

4 whole chicken legs
2 chicken breasts, split
Prepared French dressing, 1890-style
1 can cream of mushroom soup

Saute dry pieces of chicken in 1/4-inch dressing in skillet until nicely browned. Lay in Dutch oven on undiluted soup; cover tightly. Simmer until tender. Stir gravy from time to time. Serve over rice, if desired. Yield: 4 servings.
PERSONAL NOTE: This came from a cookbook put out by the Episcopal Church women of the Church of the Redeemer, Springfield, Pennsylvania.

Mrs. Donald L. Baxter, NMWC
Nav. Hospital, San Diego, California

NIWA TORI

1/2 tsp. MSG
4 chicken breasts
2/3 c. Kikkoman soy sauce
1/4 c. brandy
1 clove of garlic, minced
1 tbsp. sesame oil
2 tbsp. sugar
Dash of cracked red pepper
2 tsp. gingerroot, chopped fine
    or 1/2 tsp. ground ginger

Sprinkle MSG on chicken. Place in shallow pan or large skillet. Mix remaining ingredients together; pour over chicken. Marinate for 30 minutes at room temperature or for several hours in refrigerator. Bake for 1 hour at 325 degrees. Baste 2 or 3 times during cooking. Raise temperature to 475 degrees for last 5 minutes of cooking if necessary to crispen skin. Yield: 3-4 servings.
PERSONAL NOTE: This is an original recipe in which I have combined ingredients from Chinese and Japanese ones, and baked the dish American-style for ease.

Mrs. Guy R. Chaney, Pres. NOWC
Yokosuka Navy Base, Japan

OVEN-BAKED CHICKEN IN WINE

1 fryer chicken, cut into serving pieces
    and cleaned
Salt, pepper and paprika to taste
6 tsp. white wine or rose wine
2 tbsp. water

Place chicken in baking pan; sprinkle with salt, pepper and paprika. Add wine and water; cover. Bake at 325 degrees for 1 hour and 30 minutes. Cover may be removed last 20 minutes to brown chicken. Yield: 4 servings.

Mrs. Harry I. Shalauta, Corr. Sec. OWC
White Sands Missile Range, New Mexico

QUICK-THAW CHICKEN

1 pkg. frozen chicken thighs
    or 4 breasts
2 bunches green onions
Salt and pepper to taste

Lay chicken in large, heavy skillet on bed of onions, including green part. Season to taste; cover. Simmer until done. Raise heat to brown chicken a bit in own fat. Add remaining green onions. Cook just until wilted. Yield: 3-4 servings.
PERSONAL NOTE: I made it up myself during a long and depressing diet siege and simple as it is, it is an entree I make frequently.

Mrs. Richard McCarty, Publ. OWC
Great Lakes Naval Training Ctr., Illinois

OVEN-FRIED LEMON CHICKEN

1/2 c. lemon juice
1 tbsp. soy sauce
1/2 tsp. salt
1/2 tsp. pepper
1/4 c. salad oil
2 tbsp. grated lemon peel
1 clove of garlic, crushed
2 1/2 to 3 lb. frying chicken, cut up
1/2 c. flour
1 tsp. salt
1/4 tsp. paprika
1/2 c. butter or margarine

Mix lemon juice, soy sauce, salt, pepper, oil, lemon peel and garlic together; let stand for several hours. Shake chicken pieces in bag with flour, salt and paprika. Melt margarine in pan; add chicken pieces. Pour over lemon sauce. Bake in 350-degree oven for 1 hour or until tender. Yield: 4-5 servings.

Mrs. H. D. Warden, Hon. Pres. NDWC
Naval Hosp., San Diego, California

POULET SUPREME

4 chicken breasts
1 tbsp. butter or oleo
1 tbsp. cooking oil
1 med. onion, minced
1/2 c. white wine
1 c. sour cream
Salt and pepper to taste
1 tsp. lemon juice
Slivered almonds

Broil chicken for 20 to 30 minutes watching carefully to prevent burning. Heat butter and cooking oil in small frying pan. Brown onions until yellow, not brown. Add wine; stir well. Let liquid reduce to almost nothing. Pour in sour cream; stir constantly until mixture is well blended. Simmer slowly for 5 minutes; season with salt and pepper to taste. Add lemon juice just before serving, if desired. Arrange chicken breasts on small platter; pour wine sauce over. Sprinkle with almonds. Yield: 4 servings.

Mrs. Robert O. Frazier, VP OWC
Shaw AFB, South Carolina

CHICKEN HAWAIIAN

1 lge. green pepper, cut into strips
1 clove of garlic, minced
2 tbsp. salad oil
2 10-oz. cans cream of chicken soup
1 13-oz. can pineapple tidbits with juice
2 c. cubed, cooked chicken
2 tbsp. soy sauce
3 c. cooked rice

Cook green pepper and garlic in oil in saucepan until tender. Blend in soup and

(Continued on next page)

pineapple juice. Add chicken, pineapple and soy sauce. Heat, stirring now and then. Serve over rice or toasted bread, if desired. Yield: 6 servings.

Mrs. Jan Dazey, W and M Chm. OWC
Eleventh Coast Guard Dist., Long Beach, California

CHICKEN PILAF

2 tbsp. margarine
1 c. rice
1/2 c. chopped celery
1/2 c. chopped onion
2 c. water
1 4-oz. can sliced mushrooms, undrained
1 tsp. salt
1/4 tsp. black pepper
6 pieces or more frying chicken
Paprika

Melt margarine in casserole; swish rice and vegetables around in it. Add water, mushrooms, seasonings and chicken. Sprinkle with paprika for color; cover. Bake at 350 degrees for 1 hour. Chicken will rise to top of rice as it cooks. Recipe may be enlarged easily. Yield: 4-6 servings.

Mrs. E. G. Zellmann, VP Wives Club
Navy Med. Serv. Corps, San Diego, California

CURRIED CHICKEN BREASTS

8 half chicken breasts, seasoned and floured
1/4 lb. butter
1 can cream of mushroom soup
1 can cream of chicken soup
1 1/2 c. milk
1 tsp. celery flakes
1 tsp. parsley flakes
2 tsp. curry powder
Salt and pepper to taste

Brown chicken in frying pan in butter. Arrange in foil-lined 13 x 9 x 2-inch baking pan. Make sauce in frying pan with soups, milk, seasonings and remaining butter. Bring to a boil; pour over chicken breasts. Cover with foil. Bake at 325 degrees for 1 hour and 30 minutes. Yield: 8 servings.

Mrs. Robert Q. Old, Pres. OWC
Clark AFB, Philippines

ORANGE MARMALADE-CURRY CHICKEN

4 floured breasts, thighs or drumsticks
Butter
1/2 c. orange marmalade
1/2 c. warm water
1/2 tsp. (or more) curry powder
Salt and pepper to taste

(Continued on next page)

Brown chicken well in butter in frying pan. Mix together marmalade, water and curry powder. Baste chicken well with this mixture. Pour remaining mixture into frying pan; cover. Cook for 30 minutes or until chicken is tender. Remove cover last 5 minutes of cooking. Yield: 4 servings.

PERSONAL NOTE: I wrote this recipe after reading a description of a dinner in a novel. So far it has been received well by family and friends.

Mrs. Ronald A. Stephens, Thrift Shop Chm. OWC
Iwakuni MCAS, Japan

CURRY SOMETHING

2 tbsp. butter
1/2 c. flour
1 c. milk
2 c. chicken bouillon
1 tsp. lemon juice
1 tsp. salt
2 tbsp. chopped onions
2 tsp. curry powder
2 c. cubed chicken, ham, turkey or fresh
    shrimp
Hot, fluffy rice

Melt butter in saucepan; blend in flour and milk for smooth paste. Add bouillon. Cook, stirring, till mixture thickens over low heat. Add lemon juice, salt, onions and curry powder. Simmer for 5 minutes; stir occasionally. Add chicken. Heat thoroughly, stirring. Serve over rice using condiments of grated coconut, chutney, crisp bacon bits, plumped raisins and nuts, if desired. Substitute beef bouillon for chicken when using ham. Yield: 8 servings.

PERSONAL NOTE: Actually this all came about due to the large amounts of Thanksgiving turkey left over and the limited ways the family would accept it.

Mrs. Richard Hawley, Pres. OWC
New River MCAS, North Carolina

SOUR CREAM OVEN CHICKEN

1 pt. sour cream
4 tbsp. lemon juice
4 tsp. Worcestershire sauce
2 tsp. paprika
2 tsp. celery salt
1 tsp. salt
1 tsp. garlic salt
Dash of pepper
3 lb. chicken breasts, legs and thighs
1 pkg. herb-seasoned stuffing, crushed
Melted butter

Mix first 8 ingredients together. Dip chicken pieces in sour cream mixture; roll in stuffing. Arrange chicken in shallow, greased baking dish. Brush with melted butter. Bake, uncovered, in 350-degree oven for 1 hour or until chicken is tender and crusty brown. Yield: 6 servings.

Mrs. Shelton E. Lollis, Hon. Pres. OWC
Wife of Commanding Gen. TACOM
Warren, Michigan

QUICK CHICKEN CURRY

3 tbsp. butter or oleo
3 tbsp. flour
1 tbsp. or more curry powder
2 c. milk
1 hard boiled egg, chopped
1/2 c. chopped celery
3 tbsp. applesauce
1 5-oz. can boned chicken
1 tbsp. sugar
Dash of Tabasco sauce
Dash of Worcestershire sauce
2 c. cooked Uncle Ben's rice, prepared
    according to pkg. directions

CONDIMENTS:

1/2 c. chopped nuts
1/2 c. chutney
1/2 c. pickle relish

Blend butter and flour in saucepan over medium heat to make smooth paste. Add curry powder; mix well. Add milk gradually, stirring constantly. Cook, stirring till thickened. Add next 7 ingredients. Blend well. Serve over rice with Condiments of remaining ingredients. Yield: 4 servings.

Mrs. Mac A. Graham, Hon. Pres. MOWC
South Weymouth NAS, Massachusetts

MAMALLETT'S CHICKEN DISH

1 c. raw rice
Butter
1 envelope dried onion soup mix
6 raw, skinned chicken breasts
1 can condensed cream of celery soup
1 can condensed cream of mushroom soup
1 can clear chicken broth

Place rice in buttered teflon or pyrex loaf pan. Add onion soup and chicken. Combine cream soups; pour over chicken. Bake in 300-degree oven for 2 hours. Pour chicken broth over during cooking, pouring half-can at a time. Yield: 4-6 servings.
PERSONAL NOTE: As is the case with so many of my recipes, they had their maiden voyage in the kitchen of my mother-in-law, Mrs. Pierre Mallett.

Mrs. Charles S. T. Mallett, Hon. Pres. OWC
Fort Kobbe, Canal Zone

STUFFED CHICKEN THIGHS

6 chicken thighs
1 tbsp. chopped onion (opt.)
2 tbsp. butter
1 c. croutettes stuffing, prepared according to
    pkg. directions
1/2 c. red wine
1 can condensed cream of chicken soup

(Continued on next page)

Cut small pocket in chicken thighs, going under bone but not through to other side. Saute onion in 1 tablespoon butter in skillet; mix with stuffing. Prepare stuffing mix as package directs. Stuff thighs with mix. Secure with toothpicks. Brown thighs in remaining butter on both sides in skillet. Simmer in wine for 40 minutes over medium heat. Pour off all but 1/2 cup liquid in pan; add soup. Simmer for 10 minutes.

PERSONAL NOTE: I loved stuffed pork chops and got weary of stuffing the same meat; so I came up with stuffed chicken thighs.

Mrs. Leonard Russ, Sec. O and CWC
Darmstadt, Germany

TANGY CHICKEN

1 2 1/2-oz. pkg. Italian Shake 'n' Bake
1/2 c. finely ground bread crumbs
1/4 to 1/2 c. Parmesan grated cheese
2 to 3 lb. chicken, thawed and cut up
Milk

Combine Shake 'n' Bake, bread crumbs and cheese in plastic bag. Rinse chicken in cold water; drain. Dip each piece into milk. Place 3 or 4 pieces in plastic bag; shake well. Place on large baking pan or dish lined with heavy foil. Repeat until all chicken has been coated. Do not overlap chicken. Bake at 350 degrees for 1 hour to 1 hour and 30 minutes or until golden brown. Yield: 6-8 servings.

Mrs. K. L. Nellermoe, Hosp. Chm. OWC
Mt. Home AFB, Idaho

CHICKEN A LA KING

1 can College Inn chicken a la king
1 can cream of mushroom soup
1 sm. can Le Sueur small early peas
Cooked chicken pieces (opt.)

Heat all ingredients together in skillet or saucepan. Serve over toast or rice, if desired. Yield: 4 servings.

Mrs. Judith A. Alderman, Sec. ESSA OWC
Washington Science Center, Maryland

COMPANY CHICKEN 'N' POTATOES

2 chicken bouillon cubes
1 c. hot water
1 2 1/2 to 3-lb. cut-up chicken
1/4 c. butter or margarine
2 tbsp. flour
1 med. onion, sliced
1 clove of garlic, minced
1 1-lb. can tiny potatoes, drained
3 tbsp. cooking sherry
Dash of pepper

Dissolve bouillon cubes in water; cool. Slowly brown chicken in butter in skillet for 10 to 15 minutes. Push chicken to 1 side. Blend in flour; slowly stir in bouillon. Cook, stirring, till mixture thickens. Add onion and garlic; cover. Cook for 30 minutes or till tender. Add potatoes; heat. Stir in sherry and pepper. Yield: 3-4 servings.

Mrs. S. E. Moore, Joint OWC
Naval Air Facility, El Centro, California

EASY CHICKEN PIE

1 can cream of chicken soup
1/4 c. milk
1 c. diced, cooked chicken
1 1/2 c. cooked or canned mixed vegetables
Dash of pepper

TOPPING:

1 c. Bisquick
1/3 c. milk
Dash of salt

Combine soup, milk, chicken, vegetables and pepper in 1 1/2-quart casserole. Combine Topping ingredients. Top with Topping that has either been rolled out thin or dropped by spoonfuls. Bake in 450-degree oven for 25 minutes. Yield: 4 servings.

Mrs. F. R. Wallace, Jr., Pres. OWC
Fort Lee, Virginia

QUICK GAME HEN

1 clove of garlic
4 tbsp. butter
4 Cornish game hens
1 can cream-style golden mushroom soup
1 can cream of celery soup
1 soup can dry white wine
1 sm. can mushroom pieces, drained

Preheat oven to 350 degrees. Rub inside of 3-quart direct heat-proof casserole with cover with cut clove of garlic. Melt butter in casserole till bubbly. Brown game hens in butter, turning often to insure uniform color. Remove casserole from heat; stir in remaining ingredients. Return to heat until sauce bubbles; cover. Bake for 45 minutes or until hens are tender. Decorate with chopped parsley if desired. Yield: 4 servings.

Mrs. Donald E. Gately, OWC
Naval Amphibious Base, Virginia

DUCK WITH TANGERINES

1 3 1/2-lb. duck, quartered
2 c. chicken broth
Juice of 3 lge. tangerines
Water or orange juice
1 tbsp. cornstarch
1 tbsp. lemon juice
12 drops artificial sweetener
Grated peel of 1 tangerine

Place duck in roasting pan; add chicken broth. Bake at 325 degrees for 2 hours or until duck is very tender. Remove duck; pour off all but 3 tablespoons pan drippings. Measure tangerine juice; add enough water to make 1 cup liquid. Add to pan. Blend cornstarch and lemon juice; stir into liquid in pan. Cook until thickened and clear, stirring. Remove from heat; stir in artificial sweetener and tangerine peel. Pour over duck. Yield: 4 servings.

Mrs. William W. Momyer, Hon. Pres. OWC
Wife of Commanding General
Tactical Air Command, Langley AFB, Virginia

TURKEY PILAF

1/4 c. butter
1 c. uncooked rice
1 c. chopped celery
2 1/2 c. water
1 envelope onion soup mix
1 tsp. salt
1/4 tsp. marjoram
1/4 tsp. thyme
1/8 tsp. pepper
2 c. diced turkey
1/4 tsp. chopped parsley

Melt butter in large saucepan; saute rice and celery until rice is golden brown. Add water; stir in soup mix and seasonings. Bring to boil, stirring occasionally. Cover, reduce heat to simmer for 15 minutes. Stir in turkey; cover. Simmer for 10 minutes or until liquid is absorbed. Remove from heat; let stand for 10 minutes. Garnish with parsley. Yield: 4-6 servings.

Mrs. Warren W. Daboll, Memshp. Chm. OWC
Robinson Bks., Stuttgart, Germany

ROAST VENISON

3 2 to 3-lb. roasts of young venison
Thick sliced bacon
1 fifth Rhine wine

Place roasts on rack in shallow oblong 13-inch metal pan. Cover tops of roasts completely with bacon slices. Generously pour 1/3 bottle wine over all. Bake at 325 degrees for 20 to 25 minutes per pound. Baste with remaining wine at 15 to 20 minute intervals. Total baking time is 40 minutes to 1 hour. Yield: 10-12 servings.
PERSONAL NOTE: My husband is an avid hunter and likes me to entertain friends by serving his game. I have tried numerous recipes and have found this to be the easiest and the best with rave notices from all.

Mrs. Allen R. Weeks, 1st VP OWC
McClellan AFB, California

APPLE FISH (TURKEY)
ELMALI BALIK

    1/2 lb. butter
    5 med.-sized onions, sliced
    4 tart apples, sliced
    2 1/2 lb. fresh flounder, perch or cod
    Salt and pepper to taste
    1 tsp. garlic powder
    3 bay leaves
    Paprika

Preheat oven to 350 degrees. Cut 1/4 pound butter into large baking dish; place half the onions in baking dish. Add half the apples. Place fish over onion and apple mixture. Add salt, pepper and garlic powder; cover with remaining onions, apples and butter. Set in bay leaves; sprinkle with paprika. Bake for 30 minutes. Yield: 4-6 servings.
PERSONAL NOTE: Received this recipe from Turkish artist named Fahir Aksoy.

Alice Brister, Cookbook Chm. OWC
Tuslog, Ankara, Turkey

BAKED HALIBUT SURPRISE

    2 lb. halibut steaks or other fish
        steaks, fresh or frozen
    1/2 c. French dressing
    2 tbsp. lemon juice
    1/4 tsp. salt
    1 3 1/2-oz. can French-fried onions
    1/4 c. grated Parmesan cheese

Thaw frozen steaks; cut into serving-size portions. Place in shallow baking dish. Combine dressing, lemon juice and salt. Pour sauce over fish; let stand for 30 minutes, turning once. Remove fish from sauce; place in well-greased 12 x 8 x 2-inch baking dish. Crush onions. Add cheese; mix thoroughly. Sprinkle onion mixture over fish. Bake in 350-degree oven for 25 to 30 minutes or until fish flakes easily when tested with fork. Yield: 6 servings.

Photograph for this recipe on page 33.

BLUE NOODLE BAKED FISH

    1 1/2 to 2 lb. white fish
    1 pt. sour cream
    1 can frozen cream of shrimp soup, thawed
    Salt and pepper to taste
    Dash of Tabasco sauce
    4 tbsp. (or more) sherry

Place fish into baking dish; add sour cream and soup. Season with salt, pepper and Tabasco sauce. Add sherry. Bake at 350 degrees for 30 minutes to 1 hour or until bubbly. Yield: 6 servings.
PERSONAL NOTE: This recipe is served at Blue Noodle Restaurant on Long Beach Island, New Jersey.

Mrs. Alan F. Wentworth, VP OWC
USN Hosp., Philadelphia, Pennsylvania

BAKED SARDINES

3 eggs, separated
1 can sardines, finely chopped
1/2 c. bread crumbs
3 tbsp. melted butter
1 tbsp. lemon juice
Salt
Pepper
3 stalks celery, chopped
2 med.-sized onions, minced
1 green pepper, minced
1/2 tsp. minced parsley

Beat egg yolks until light; add sardines, bread crumbs, butter, lemon juice, salt, pepper, celery, onions, green pepper and parsley. Beat egg whites; add. Place in oiled baking dish. Bake at 350 degrees for 30 minutes. Yield: 4 servings.

Mrs. Allan R. Smelley, VP OWC
Monterey NAS, California

FISH 'N' CHIPS

1 c. crushed potato chips
1/4 c. Parmesan cheese
1/4 tsp. thyme
2 lb. fish fillets
1/4 c. milk
1/4 c. butter or margarine

Combine chips, cheese and thyme. Dip fish in milk, then in potato chip mixture. Place in buttered baking dish; sprinkle with any remaining crumbs. Drizzle butter over top. Bake in 500-degree oven for 12 to 15 minutes. Yield: 6 servings.

Mrs. R. F. Fornia, Pres. OWC
Fairchild AFB, Washington

FLOUNDER ROLLS

1 egg, beaten
Salt and pepper
1 pkg. instant mashed potatoes, prepared
2 or 3 tsp. chopped chives or scallions
1 lb. flounder fillets
1/8 lb. margarine, melted
Cornflake crumbs

Add egg, salt and pepper to potatoes; blend. Add chives. Dip flounder in margarine; place portion of potatoes in center of flounder. Roll like jelly roll; secure with toothpick. Dip in cornflake crumbs. Place on cookie sheet. Bake in 350-degree oven for 20 minutes. Yield: 4-6 servings.

Gloria E. Suthowski, Asst. Welfare Chm. OWC
US Navsecgruact, Bremerhaven, Germany

EASY SALMON LOAF

1 c. broken, cooked spaghetti
1 c. dry bread crumbs
1 1-lb. can salmon
1 1/2 c. milk
1/4 c. oil
1 c. grated American cheese
1/4 c. chopped green peppers
1 tsp. salt
3 slightly beaten eggs

Mix all ingredients together well; place in greased 5 x 11-inch baking dish. Bake at 325 degrees for 1 hour. Yield: 6 servings.

Mrs. James A. Wagner, 1st VP OWC
Plattsburgh AFB, New York

SALMON CAKES

1 lb. fresh or canned salmon
1 c. Bisquick
2 tbsp. Worcestershire sauce
1/3 c. chopped onion
1 to 2 tbsp. parsley flakes
1 egg, beaten
Shortening

Combine all ingredients except shortening; mix well. Drop by heaping table-spoonfuls into hot shortening; flatten. Fry until deep brown. Serve with cocktail sauce.

Sonya Lee Spittler, OWC
Makah Air Force Station, Washington

SALMONETTES HELOISE

1 15-oz. can pink salmon
1 egg
1/2 c. sifted flour
1 tsp. (heaping) baking powder
Hot oil

Drain juice from salmon into measuring cup; reserve. Add egg to salmon; mix well. Add flour; stir with fork. Mixture will be thick. Add baking powder to 1/4 cup reserved salmon juice; beat with fork. Pour into salmon mixture; mix again with fork. Dip a half spoonful of batter with ice tea spoon; scoop out with other spoon into deep fryer, half full with hot oil. Salmonettes will float on top of oil and turn themselves. Yield: 4-6 servings.

Mrs. W. T. Silva, Pres. OWC
Otis AFB, Massachusetts

SALMON PIE

1 1-lb. can salmon
4 med. potatoes, cubed and cooked

(Continued on next page)

1 1/2 tsp. salt
1 tsp. pepper
2 unbaked 9-inch pie crusts

Drain salmon; reserve juice from 1/2 can. Pick out bones. Drain potatoes; mix with salmon. Add salt and pepper; place in pie crust lined pie pan. Cover with top crust. Bake 35 to 40 minutes at 350 degrees. Serve with white sauce or catsup on top, if desired. Yield: 6 servings.

Mrs. Robert Horrobin, Pres. OWC
National Naval Med. Ctr., Maryland

SOLE SURVIVOR

1 can frozen shrimp soup, thawed
4 sole fillets

Heat soup; place fish in shallow greased baking dish. Bake at 400 degrees for 20 minutes. Reduce temperature to 300 degrees; pour soup over fish. Bake for 15 minutes more. Yield: 4 servings.

Kathy Bode, Treas. OWC
Ramey AFB, Puerto Rico

SWORDFISH STEAK

1 lb. swordfish fillet
1 c. dry white wine
1 tsp. salt
1/2 c. mayonnaise
1/2 c. sour cream
1/4 c. chopped onion
1 c. dry bread crumbs
1/2 tsp. paprika

Soak fillet in wine and salt for 1 hour or more; remove. Dry well on both sides with paper towel. Mix remaining ingredients together; coat fillet with mixture. Place in uncovered baking dish. Bake in 400-degree oven for 30 to 40 minutes or until done. Yield: 4 servings.

Mrs. Thomas L. Trace, Adv. OWC
Roanoke Rapids, North Carolina

FAST TUNA DINNER

1/4 c. instant minced onions
2 tbsp. margarine
1 can frozen cream of shrimp soup
1/2 c. milk
1 1/2 c. frozen or fresh peas
1 lge. can tuna
Dash of pepper

Cook onion in margarine in skillet till tender; add soup, milk and peas. Cover; heat just to boiling, stirring occasionally. Add tuna and pepper; heat. Serve over hot noodles or rice. Yield: 4 servings.

Mrs. W. E. Carman, Pres. NOWC
Naval Air Station, Virginia

GOLDEN CREAMY TUNA

1 10 1/2-oz. can golden cream of mushroom
soup
1/2 soup can milk
1/4 tsp. Worcestershire sauce
2 tbsp. catsup
Dash of celery salt
Pepper to taste
1 tsp. dry parsley flakes
1 7-oz. can tuna, drained
1 4-oz. can sliced button mushrooms, drained
1 8-oz. can peas, drained
Instant mashed potatoes

Mix soup and milk; heat slowly. Add Worcestershire sauce, catsup, celery salt, pepper and parsley; mix well. Add tuna, mushrooms and peas; mix well. Heat to bubbling point. Serve over mashed potatoes. Yield: 4 servings.

Mrs. Roger D. Williams, W and M Chm. OWC
USCG New York Base, New York

TUNA-RICE DELIGHT

1 1/2 tbsp. butter or margarine
1 7-oz. can tuna, drained
1 tbsp. parsley flakes
1 10 1/2-oz. can cream of celery soup
1 1/2 c. water
1 1/3 c. rice
1 8-oz. can cooked carrots
1/2 tsp. salt
Freshly ground pepper
1/4 tsp. Worcestershire sauce
2 tsp. lemon juice
2 drops Tabasco sauce

Melt butter in electric skillet; add tuna and parsley. Heat through. Stir in remaining ingredients; cover. Cook on low temperature for 30 minutes. Add additional water if needed. Yield: 4 servings.

Mrs. Wilford F. Johnson, OWC
USN Ammunition Depot, McAlester, Oklahoma

SWEET AND SOUR TUNA

1 can chunk pineapple
2 tbsp. butter
2/3 c. pineapple juice
2 green peppers, cut in 1-inch pieces
3 tbsp. cornstarch
2 tsp. soy sauce
2 tbsp. vinegar
1/3 c. sugar
1 c. chicken bouillon or 2 cubes in 1 c. water
2 7-oz. cans tuna
1/2 tsp. salt
1/8 tsp. pepper
Chinese noodles or rice

Saute pineapple in butter for 5 minutes; add 1/3 cup juice and green pepper. Cover; simmer 10 minutes. Mix cornstarch with remaining juice; add to pineapple with soy sauce, vinegar, sugar and bouillon. Cook, stirring constantly, until thick. Add tuna and seasoning. Heat; serve on noodles. Yield: 6 servings.

Mrs. Ralph H. S. Scott, Pres. NOWC
Camp Pendleton Marine Corps Base, California

TUNABURGERS

2 6 1/2-oz. cans tuna
1/4 c. mayonnaise
3 tbsp. chopped sweet pickles
1/4 c. Velveeta cheese, cubed
8 hamburger buns, sliced

Mix tuna with mayonnaise; add pickles and cheese. Place on buns. Wrap in aluminum foil. Bake at 400 degrees for 15 minutes. Yield: 8 servings.

Mrs. J. L. Burns, Hosp. Chm. OWC
Kamiseya Navy Base, Washington

BAKED SCALLOPS

1 lb. scallops
1 sm. can mushrooms
1 green pepper, diced
Oregano, garlic salt and paprika to taste
1/2 c. tomato juice

Combine scallops, mushrooms and green pepper in baking dish; cover with seasoned tomato juice. Bake 30 minutes at 350 degrees. Yield: 3-4 servings.

Mrs. Kenneth H. White, Treas. OWC
Fort Carson, Colorado

CLAMS AND RICE

2 cloves of garlic, minced
2 tbsp. olive oil or other oil

(Continued on next page)

1 can clams
Pinch of parsley
1 c. rice
2 c. water
Salt to taste
Dash of pepper

Brown garlic in oil; add clams, parsley and rice. Brown slightly. Add water, salt and pepper; cook till rice is done. May need to add additional water. Yield: 4 servings.

Mrs. Larry A. Kocher, W and M Chm. OWC
Chicksands AFB, England

STUFFED CLAMS WITH BACON

2 c. or 2 7-oz. cans minced clams
1/3 c. minced green pepper
1/2 c. minced celery
1 1/2 c. dry bread crumbs
1 c. heavy cream or evaporated milk
2 eggs, beaten
2 tbsp. butter or other fat, melted
2 tsp. prepared mustard
1 1/2 tsp. salt
1 tsp. pepper
Grated Parmesan cheese
Bacon

Mix all ingredients except cheese and bacon together; spoon into clam or scallop shells. Bake in 350-degree oven for 20 minutes. Remove; sprinkle top with cheese and place half a strip of bacon across top of each shell. Return to oven until bacon is crisp. Yield: 6 servings.

Mrs. K. E. Van Buskirk, OWC
Walter Reed Army Med. Ctr. Chapel Guild
Washington, D. C.

CLAM-CRAB SANDWICH

2 tbsp. butter
6 oz. cream cheese
1/4 c. salad dressing
1 tsp. minced onion
Dash of garlic salt
1 can minced clams, drained
1 can shredded crab meat
Dash of Tabasco sauce
1 tsp. Worcestershire sauce
8 English muffins

Blend butter, cream cheese, salad dressing, onion and salt; add clams, crab meat, Tabasco and Worcestershire sauce. Spread mixture on split muffins. Place under broiler until slightly browned and bubbling. Yield: 8 servings.

Mrs. Robert P. Daly, Pres. OWC
Wright-Patterson AFB, Ohio

CIOPPINO

3 onions, chopped
2 cloves of garlic, chopped
3 tbsp. olive oil
1 No. 2 can solid-pack tomatoes
2 8-oz. cans tomato sauce
2 6-oz. cans tomato paste
2 c. water
1 tsp. sweet basil
1 tsp. oregano
Salt and pepper to taste
4 pieces firm fish
Cracked crab
Prawns in shell
Clams in shell

Saute onions and garlic in olive oil until lightly browned; add tomatoes, sauce, paste, water and seasonings. Simmer for 1 hour. Add fish and shellfish; simmer additional 20 minutes. Serve in large bowl for each person with nutcracker for shells and oyster fork to pick meat from shell. Yield: 6 servings.

Mrs. William A. McKean, Hon. Chm. OWC
Fort McClellan, Alabama

SEAFOOD TRIO

1/2 c. butter
3/4 c. chopped onion
3/4 c. chopped green pepper
1 6-oz. can sliced mushrooms, drained
2/3 c. all-purpose flour
2 tsp. salt
1/4 tsp. pepper
4 c. milk
1 1/2 c. shredded sharp American cheese
1 tbsp. lemon juice
1 tsp. powdered dry mustard
1/2 tsp. Worcestershire sauce
1 12-oz. pkg. frozen cooked lobster meat
1 12-oz. pkg. frozen crab meat
1 8-oz. pkg. fresh or frozen shrimp, cooked

Melt butter in a saucepan over moderate heat; stir in onion, green pepper and mushrooms. Cook until onions are soft, about 5 minutes, stirring occasionally. Remove from heat. Blend in flour, salt and pepper. Stir in milk gradually. Continue cooking, stirring constantly until thickened. Stir in cheese, lemon juice, mustard and Worcestershire sauce; cook until cheese melts. Break lobster and crab meat into large pieces; add with shrimp. Heat to boiling. Garnish with parsley and seafood pieces. Serve over rice or macaroni shells. Yield: 8-10 servings.

Mrs. Albert F. Arant, Corr. Sec. OWC
Hickam AFB, Hawaii

SHELLFISH SORRENTO

1 8-oz. pkg. elbow macaroni
2 10-oz. cans cream of mushroom soup
1 c. milk
1 6 1/2-oz. can crab meat
1 5-oz. can shrimp
1/4 c. diced pimento
1 3-oz. can sliced mushrooms
1 tsp. garlic salt
1/8 tsp. cayenne pepper
1 c. grated Parmesan cheese
2 tbsp. butter

Cook and drain macaroni. Heat soup and milk until bubbly; add macaroni, crab, shrimp, pimento, mushrooms, seasonings and 1/2 cup cheese. Spoon into 6 individual baking dishes; sprinkle with remaining cheese. Dot with butter. Brown under broiler. Yield: 6 servings.

Mrs. Fredrick A. Linville, OWC
Itazuke Air Base, Japan

CRAB BUNS

1 7 1/2-oz. can crab meat
2 stalks finely diced celery
1/4 c. finely chopped onion
1 tsp. caraway seed
Mayonnaise
3 buns, split and toasted
6 bacon slices, cooked
6 cheese slices

Combine crab meat, celery, onion and caraway seed; add mayonnaise to moisten. Spoon mixture onto bun halves. Cover with slice of bacon, then slice of cheese. Broil until cheese begins to melt. Yield: 6 servings.

Mrs. Joseph Kmiecik, Pres. OWC
Valley Forge General Hosp., Pennsylvania

CRAB MEAT BAKED IN AVOCADO HALVES

1 10 1/2-oz. can mushroom soup
1 10 1/2-oz. can cream of celery
  soup
1 1/2 lb. King crab meat
2 tbsp. chopped green onion
1/4 tsp. Tabasco sauce
1/2 tsp. salt
2 tsp. Worcestershire sauce
2 oz. sherry wine
3 lge. avocados
1/2 c. grated cheese

Mix soups, crab, green onion, Tabasco sauce, salt and Worcestershire sauce together; add sherry. Cut avocados in half; fill with crab meat mixture. Sprinkle with cheese. Bake 20 minutes at 350 degrees. Yield: 6 servings.

Mrs. Richard J. Fry, Asst. W and M Chm. OWC
Kelly AFB, Texas

CRAB FOO YUNG

4 eggs, well beaten
1 7 1/2-oz. pkg. fresh bean sprouts
1/3 c. sliced green onions
1 c. crab meat
1/2 tsp. salt
1/8 tsp. pepper
1/8 tsp. garlic powder
2 tbsp. salad oil

Combine eggs, sprouts, onions, crab meat, salt, pepper and garlic powder; mix lightly. Heat oil. Use 1/4 cup of mixture for each crab cake, turning as pancakes. Cook until set and lightly browned.

FOO YUNG SAUCE:

1 tsp. cornstarch
1 tsp. sugar
2 tsp. soy sauce
1 tsp. vinegar
1/2 c. chicken stock or 1 bouillon
   cube, dissolved in 1/2 c. water

Combine first 4 ingredients; stir in chicken stock. Cook over low heat till thickened. Serve with crab cakes. Yield: 5 servings.

Mrs. R. K. Langenbach, NOWC
Comoptevfor, Norfolk, Virginia

CRAB MORNAY

1/3 c. butter
5 tbsp. flour
1 1/3 c. chicken broth
1/2 c. light cream
1 1/2 lb. crab meat
4 tbsp. grated cheese

Combine butter, flour and chicken broth; cook until smooth. Add cream. Fold in crab meat. Pour into well-buttered dish; sprinkle with cheese. Place under broiler to brown. Serve on toast or shells. Yield: 6-8 servings.

Mrs. Raymond D. Fortmeyer, W and M Chm. MOWC
Cherry Point MCAS, North Carolina

CRAB PUFF SOUFFLE

1/4 c. butter
1/4 c. flour
1 tsp. salt
1 c. milk
3 eggs, separated
1/2 c. mayonnaise
Dash of pepper
1 tsp. each paprika and chopped fresh
   parsley
1/2 lb. or 1 6 1/2-oz. can crab meat

(Continued on next page)

Melt butter over low heat in saucepan; stir in flour and 1/2 teaspoon salt to make smooth paste. Add milk slowly, stirring constantly, until thickened. Remove sauce from heat; cool. Beat egg whites until stiff but not dry; set aside. Beat egg yolks into white sauce; fold in mayonnaise. Stir in remaining salt, pepper, paprika, parsley and crab meat. Gently fold in egg whites; pour into 1 1/2-quart souffle dish. Bake in 400-degree oven for 25 minutes or until brown and puffed. Serve immediately. Yield: 4 servings.

Mrs. Paul F. Cottrell, Decorations Chm. OWC
Castle AFB, California

CRAB RAREBIT

2 tbsp. chopped green pepper
2 tbsp. butter
2 tbsp. flour
1/2 tsp. dry mustard
1/4 tsp. salt
1 c. chopped stewed tomatoes
8 oz. Velveeta cheese, cubed
1 egg, slightly beaten
1/2 c. milk
1 c. crab

Cook green pepper in butter for 5 minutes; blend in flour. Add seasonings, tomatoes and cheese. Cook until cheese melts; add egg and milk. Cook until egg thickens mixture; add crab. Heat. Serve in patty shells. Yield: 4 servings.

Mrs. Charles E. Whiteside, NOWC
Puget Sound Navy Shipyard, Washington

CRAB TOTO

1 4 to 6-oz. box mushrooms, sliced
1 sm. onion, chopped
1 tsp. each chopped parsley and chives
5 tbsp. butter
1/3 c. white wine or vermouth
1 lb. crab meat, rinsed and drained
2 tbsp. flour
1 c. heavy cream
1/4 tsp. each ground mustard and seasoned pepper
1 tsp. seasoned salt
2 dashes each cayenne and paprika
Parmesan cheese seasoned bread crumbs

Saute first 3 ingredients in 3 tablespoons butter till limp; add wine and crab. Cook over medium high heat till moisture evaporates. Make cream sauce with 2 tablespoons butter and remaining ingredients except bread crumbs; add to crab. Sprinkle top with bread crumbs; dot with additional butter. Bake at 350 degrees for 15 minutes. Crumbs may be omitted and mixture poured into 8 baked vol au vent shells or into 8 or 9-inch pie shell. Bake for 15 minutes at 350 degrees. Yield: 6 servings.

Mrs. Edward H. Mortimer, NOWC
Puget Sound Naval Shipyard, Washington

DEVILED CRAB

1 1/2 c. milk
1 1/2 c. soft bread crumbs
2 c. flaked crab meat or shrimp
5 hard-cooked eggs, separated
1 1/2 tsp. salt
1/3 tsp. dry mustard
1/8 tsp. cayenne pepper
1/2 c. butter, melted
Buttered bread crumbs

Combine milk and bread crumbs; gently stir in crab and thinly sliced egg whites. Mash egg yolks; blend with crab meat, seasonings and butter. Pour into 10 x 6-inch pan; sprinkle with buttered bread crumbs. Bake at 450 degrees for 15 minutes. Yield: 6 servings.

Mrs. Earl N. Bridgman, Jr., Cookbook Chm. OWC
Defense Depot, Memphis, Tennessee

DEVILED CRAB IN SHELLS

1 10 1/2-oz. can cream of mushroom soup
1 7 3/4-oz. can flaked crab meat
1/2 c. bread bits
2 hard-boiled eggs, diced
Salt and pepper to taste

Combine all ingredients in double boiler; heat about 10 minutes. Place in buttered shells. Yield: 3-4 servings.

Mrs. Peter C. Weaver, Treas. OWC
Charleston AFS, Maine

ENGLISH MUFFIN WITH CRAB MEAT

1 5-oz. jar pimento cheese
2 tbsp. butter
Garlic powder to taste
4 English muffins, split
1 lb. crab meat, fresh, frozen or canned

Mix cheese, butter and garlic powder; spread on muffins. Sprinkle with crab meat. Place under broiler until cheese melts, about 5 to 8 minutes. Yield: 4 servings.

Mrs. W. K. Morgan, Games Day Chm. OWC
Aviano AFB, Italy

NEVER-FAIL CRAB MEAT SOUFFLE

2 tbsp. butter or oleo
2 tbsp. flour
1/2 tsp. paprika
Dash of cayenne pepper
1 tsp. salt
2 c. milk

(Continued on next page)

2 tsp. lemon juice
2 7 1/2-oz. cans King crab or white crab
    meat, flaked
4 eggs, separated

Melt butter; blend in flour and seasonings. Gradually add milk, stirring until thick and smooth. Add lemon juice, crab meat and beaten egg yolks. Fold in stiffly beaten egg whites; turn into greased baking dish. Bake in 400-degree oven about 30 minutes. Yield: 6 servings.

Mrs. Paul F. Opitz, Pres. OWC
Yorktown Naval Weapons Station, Virginia

QUICK CRAB CURRY

1 6 1/2-oz. can crab
1 tsp. lemon juice
1 10 1/2-oz. can cream of mushroom soup
1/2 c. milk or light cream
1 to 2 tsp. curry powder
1/8 tsp. allspice
1/8 tsp. mace
1/8 tsp. nutmeg
Dash of cayenne pepper
1 4-oz. can sliced mushrooms and liquid

Remove cartilage from crab meat gently, keeping chunks whole. Sprinkle with lemon juice; set aside. Combine soup with milk, spices and mushrooms; cook over low heat or in top of double boiler until heated through and smooth. Stir in crab. Heat; serve over rice with curry accompaniments. Yield: 4 servings.

Mrs. Mearl Gallup, Welfare Chm. OWC
Fort Wadsworth, New York

QUICK CRAB NEWBURG

2 cans frozen cream of shrimp soup, thawed
1 sm. can sliced mushrooms
2 tbsp. grated Parmesan cheese
12 oz. frozen cooked King crab
1/4 c. dry sherry

Heat soup in heavy saucepan or double boiler; add remaining ingredients in order listed. Serve hot over rice or chow mein noodles, if desired. Yield: 6-8 servings.

Mrs. Frank M. Kyes, Hon. Pres. NDOWC
Eleventh Naval Dist. Hq., San Diego, California

SUMPTUOUS SANDWICHES

English muffins
1 6 1/2-oz. can crab meat
1/4 c. mayonnaise
1/4 c. sour cream
1/8 tsp. instant minced onion

(Continued on next page)

Spread toasted English muffins with crab meat; cover with mixture of mayonnaise, sour cream and onion. Broil until browned. Yield: 3-4 servings.

Mrs. Carl Stapleton, OWC
Kelly AFB, Texas

SEAFOOD SCRAMBLE

1 6-oz. can crab meat or lobster
1 tbsp. butter
1 tsp. grated onion
1 tsp. curry powder
4 eggs
3 tbsp. cream
Toast
Catsup

Pick over crab for bones. Melt butter in skillet; blend in onion and curry powder. Add crab; saute for 5 minutes. Beat eggs with cream; pour into skillet. Scramble together. Serve on buttered toast that has been covered with thick layer of catsup. Yield: 4 servings.

Mrs. Richard E. Tiede, Hon. Pres. OWC
Rhein-Main Air Base, Germany

ESCARGOTS

1/2 lb. butter
1 bouillon cube
1 tbsp. chopped onion
2 tbsp. dry parsley
1 tbsp. chives
2 tbsp. Worcestershire sauce
1/2 tsp. salt
Dash of pepper
1 tsp. white wine or dry vermouth
2 doz. escargots with shells

Melt butter with bouillon cube; add onion, parsley, chives, Worcestershire sauce, salt, pepper and wine. Place small amount in shells; add escargots and more of sauce. Bake at 400 degrees for 15 minutes. Yield: 4 servings.

Mrs. B. V. Duclos, Parlm. OWC
Wheeler AFB, Hawaii

LOBSTER NEWBURG

2 c. diced, boiled lobster, crab or shrimp
2 tbsp. sherry
1/4 c. melted butter
1 tbsp. flour
1 c. thin cream
2 egg yolks, beaten
1/4 tsp. salt
1 tsp. lemon juice
Paprika

Heat lobster thoroughly with sherry and 3 tablespoons butter. Blend remaining butter in saucepan with flour; add cream. Stir constantly until sauce boils. Remove from heat; stir into egg yolks. Return to saucepan; cook over low heat, stirring constantly for about 2 minutes or until thickened. Add lobster and seasonings; mix well. Do not heat again or sauce may curdle. Serve immediately

(Continued on next page)

on crisp toast, toasted crackers or in patty shells. Garnish with watercress or parsley. Yield: 5 servings.

Mrs. William D. Baker, NWC
Naval Ammunition Depot, Nevada

LOBSTER MIDWAY

1/2 c. butter
1 c. chopped scallions
1 8-oz. can sliced mushrooms, drained
3 tbsp. flour
2 c. milk
1/2 tsp. salt
1/4 tsp. pepper
2 c. lobster, chunked
1 8-oz. can chunk pineapple
1 egg yolk, beaten
Paprika

Melt butter in 9-inch skillet; saute scallions and mushrooms until tender. Blend in flour; cook over low heat 3 to 5 minutes, stirring constantly. Stir in milk until smooth; add salt and pepper. Cook about 5 minutes longer. Add lobster and pineapple; heat thoroughly. Remove from heat; quickly beat in egg yolk. Spoon into individual casseroles or 1 large one. Sprinkle with paprika. Heat under broiler; serve piping hot. Yield: 4 servings.

Mrs. Michael Alan Rij, Jr., Corr. and Rec. Sec. OWC
Whiting Field NAS, Florida

LOBSTER NEWBURG

4 tbsp. butter
2 c. boiled diced lobster
1/4 c. dry sherry or Madeira
1/2 tsp. paprika
3 egg yolks
1 c. cream

Melt butter in double boiler; add lobster. Stir and cook for 3 minutes. Add sherry; cook gently for 2 minutes more. Add paprika, egg yolks and cream; cook and stir until thickened. Do not let boil. Serve at once on hot buttered toast. Yield: 3-4 servings.

Mrs. Clifford C. Collins, Sec. OWC
Charleston AFS, Maine

SHRIMP-LOBSTER ELEGANTE

2 cans frozen cream of shrimp soup
1 lge. can frozen lobster
2 tbsp. sherry
1 5-oz. can water chestnuts, drained and
   sliced
1/4 green pepper, cut in small strips

Place soup, lobster and sherry in top of double boiler. Add water chestnuts and green pepper; heat over boiling water. Serve over hot rice or toast points. Yield: 6 servings.

Mrs. Billy L. Van Horn, OWC
Charleston AFS, Maine

ARTICHOKES-CHEESE SAUCE AND SHRIMP

4 lge. artichokes, cooked
Salted water
2 4 1/2-oz. cans shrimp
1 sm. garlic clove, cut fine
Butter
3 tbsp. flour
1 1/2 c. milk
1 c. grated mild cheddar cheese
1/2 tsp. salt
1/4 tsp. cayenne

Trim stems and tough outer leaves from artichokes; boil 25 to 30 minutes in salted water. Turn upside down to drain. Probe deep into center to remove hairy chokes. Drain and rinse shrimp. Saute garlic in small amount of butter; blend in flour. Add milk, cheese and seasoning. Cook and stir until thick and smooth. Fill artichokes with shrimp; cover with sauce. Yield: 4 servings.

Mrs. George A. Demers, VP OWC
Windsor Locks, Connecticut

FRESH FRIED SHRIMP (JAPAN)
EBIFUIAI

24 lge. fresh shrimp, washed and cleaned
1/2 c. flour
2 egg whites
2 c. cornflake crumbs
Cooking oil
Salt

Dip each shrimp in flour until completely coated; dip in egg white until coated. Roll in cornflake crumbs. Deep fat fry in oil until golden brown; sprinkle with salt. Serve hot with hot buttered rice. Yield: 4 servings.
PERSONAL NOTE: My Japanese cooking class teacher was wife of Wakkanai City's mayor.

Mrs. John P. Kelly, Publ. Chm. OWC
Wakkanai Air Station, Japan

BARBECUED SHRIMP

1/3 c. chopped onion
1/3 c. chopped celery
1/2 clove of garlic, minced

(Continued on next page)

2 tbsp. fat
1 can tomato soup
2 tbsp. Worcestershire sauce
1 tbsp. brown sugar
2 tsp. prepared mustard
2 tsp. vinegar
Few drops Tabasco sauce
1 lb. boiled shrimp

Cook onion, celery and garlic in fat until golden. Add remaining ingredients except shrimp; simmer until flavors are blended. Add shrimp; cook 20 minutes longer. Serve over rice. Canned shrimp may be substituted for freshly cooked. Yield: 4 servings.

Mrs. Daniel E. Farr, II, W and M Chm. OWC
Clark AFS, Philippines

KRIS' SHRIMP

1 med. chopped onion
2 cloves of garlic, minced
1/4 c. butter or oleo
1 4-oz. can mushrooms, sliced and drained
1 1/2 lb. frozen shelled shrimp, cooked
    and drained
1 pt. sour cream
3 tsp. soy sauce

Saute onion and garlic in butter until clear but not browned; add mushrooms and shrimp. Cook 5 minutes more, stirring. Remove from heat; add sour cream and soy sauce. Return to heat until hot, but do not boil. Serve over hot rice. Yield: 4 servings.

Mrs. Rowland F. Schlegel, Pres. NOWC
Great Lakes USN Training Ctr., Illinois

QUICK SHRIMP CURRY

1/2 c. chopped onion
1 tbsp. butter or margarine
1 can frozen cream of shrimp soup
1 c. sour cream
1 tsp. curry powder
1 c. cleaned, cooked or canned shrimp
Paprika
3 c. cooked rice

Cook onion in butter until tender but not brown. Add soup; heat and stir until smooth. Stir in sour cream and curry powder. Add shrimp; heat. Sprinkle with paprika; garnish with sprig of parsley. Serve with hot rice and curry condiments. Yield: 4 servings.

Mrs. Donald G. Iselin, Adv. OWC
Davisville NCBC, Rhode Island

QUICK SHRIMP NEWBURG

2 tbsp. butter
1 3/4 tbsp. flour
1 c. half and half cream

(Continued on next page)

3 tbsp. catsup
3/4 tbsp. Worcestershire sauce
1 lb. cleaned, cooked shrimp
2 tbsp. sherry

Melt butter; stir in flour. Add cream slowly; cook over low heat, stirring until thick and smooth. Stir in catsup and Worcestershire sauce. Add shrimp; stir until heated through. Add sherry just before serving. Serve over rice. Yield: 4 servings.

Mrs. Arthur McDonald, Jr., NOWC
Lakehurst NAS, New Jersey

SAMPAN SHRIMP

1 8 1/2-oz. can pineapple chunks
1/4 c. vegetable oil
1 lb. frozen shrimp, shelled and
    deveined
2 sm. onions, cut in rings
1 green pepper, cut in thin strips
2 tbsp. cornstarch
1/4 c. brown sugar
1/2 tsp. salt
1 tsp. powdered ginger
2 tbsp. soy sauce
1/4 c. vinegar
1 lge. tomato, cut in wedges

Drain pineapple; reserve syrup. Heat oil in large skillet; saute shrimp until pink. Set aside. Add onion and pepper to skillet; saute until softened but not browned. Mix cornstarch with sugar, salt and ginger; gradually stir in soy sauce, vinegar and reserved syrup. Pour into skillet; cook gently until liquid thickens. Add pineapple, tomato and shrimp; bring to a boil, stirring constantly. Serve over rice. Yield: 4 servings.

Mrs. A. M. Henderson, Golf Chm. OWC
Inglewood AFS, California

PEPPERED SHRIMP AND EGGS

3 strips bacon
2 tbsp. butter or margarine
1 green pepper, sliced thin
1 sm. onion, sliced
1 c. peeled shrimp, canned or precooked
Salt to taste
1/4 tsp. cayenne pepper
4 eggs, slightly beaten
1 tbsp. coffee cream
1/2 tsp. Worcestershire sauce
Minced bacon

Fry bacon crisp; break into small pieces. Drain nearly all bacon fat from pan; add butter. Cook green pepper and onion until nearly tender, but not brown. Add shrimp; cook gently 1 to 2 minutes or until nearly moisture free. Season with salt and cayenne. Combine eggs, cream and Worcestershire sauce; stir in slowly. Add minced bacon; cook slowly for about 5 minutes. May use frozen or fresh shrimp; add 1 teaspoon salt and cook 5 to 6 minutes. Yield: 3 servings.

Mrs. Alton D. Slay, Hon. Pres. OWC
Edwards AFB, California

SHRIMP (ECUADOR)
CEBICHE

25 shrimp
Salted water
2 red onions
2 cloves of garlic
Juice of 2 lemons or limes
Salt and pepper to taste

Cook shrimp in salted water with 1 onion and garlic; cool and clean. Cut remaining onion in thin slices; add lemon juice, salt and pepper. Cook until onion becomes pink in color. Add shrimp; serve. Yield: 2-3 servings.

Mrs. L. E. Coira, OWC
Kelly AFB, Texas

SHRIMP AMANDINE

1/4 c. slivered almonds
1 tbsp. butter or margarine
2 lb. shelled, deveined shrimp
1 tsp. salt
Dash of pepper
2 tbsp. snipped chives

Saute almonds in butter until golden in medium skillet; remove. Saute shrimp, sprinkled with salt and pepper, until pink and tender. Sprinkle with chives and almonds. Serve from skillet. Yield: 3 servings.

Mrs. James H. Cross, Treas. NOWC
USN Advisory Gp. Detachment, Chinhae, South Korea

SHRIMP CREOLE

3 tbsp. salad oil
1 med. onion, chopped
1 med. green pepper, chopped
6 to 8 mushrooms
1 No. 2 can tomatoes
2 tsp. salt
4 peppercorns
Pinch of sugar
Worcestershire sauce to taste
1 lb. shrimp

Heat salad oil in heavy skillet; add onion and green pepper. Cook until shiny and slightly limp. Stir in remaining ingredients except shrimp; cook slowly until most of liquid evaporates or about 10 minutes. Add shrimp; heat through. Yield: 4 servings.

Mrs. Benson W. Peak, Parlm. OWC
McKee Barracks, Crailsheim, Germany

SHRIMP CREOLE

3 tsp. flour
3 tsp. bacon drippings
2 1/2 c. cooked tomatoes
1/3 c. tomato paste
6 tsp. onion, chopped

(Continued on next page)

6 tsp. green pepper, chopped
1 clove of garlic, chopped
1 1/2 tsp. parsley, chopped
2 tsp. salt
1/4 tsp. pepper
1 1/2 lb. shrimp

Brown flour in bacon drippings as for gravy; add remaining ingredients except shirmp. Bring to rolling boil. Reduce heat to simmer; cook for 20 minutes. Add shrimp; continue cooking for another 10 to 15 minutes. Simmer 5 to 10 minutes longer if fresh or frozen shrimp are used. Yield: 6 servings.

Mrs. Walter S. Bloomfield, Rec. Sec. OWC
Fort Leonard Wood, Missouri

SHRIMP E'TOUFFEE

3 lb. fresh or canned shrimp
Salt and pepper to taste
Cayenne pepper to taste
1/2 c. cooking oil
1 c. chopped onions
1/2 c. chopped celery
1/4 tsp. tomato paste
1/4 tsp. cornstarch
1/2 c. cold water

Season shrimp with salt and peppers; set aside. Combine oil, onions, celery and tomato paste; cook slowly in uncovered heavy pot until onions are wilted. Dissolve cornstarch in water; add to mixture. Add shrimp; cook over medium heat for 20 minutes. Serve with rice. Yield: 6 servings.

Mrs. Forrest E. Asher, Pres. OWC
Red River Army Depot, Texas

SHRIMP NORFOLK

1/2 c. chopped green onion
1 lge. garlic bud, crushed
1/4 lb. butter or oleo
1 lb. clean, cooked shrimp
2 c. seedless green grapes

Saute green onion and garlic in butter in skillet; add shrimp. Toss lightly until shrimp is thoroughly heated and coated with butter. Add grapes; toss. Serve immediately. Yield: 4 servings.

Mrs. M. E. Carl, Hon. Pres. MOWC
Cherry Point, North Carolina

SHRIMP SUPREME

1 c. sour cream
1 tbsp. sugar
1/4 c. soft butter
2 tbsp. lemon juice
1/4 tsp. basil
2 c. shrimp

(Continued on next page)

Combine all ingredients except shrimp for sauce. Place shrimp in shells; pour sauce over shrimp. Bake at 350 degrees for 30 minutes. Yield: 4 servings.

Mrs. Theodore M. Smyer, Welfare Chm. NOWC
Alameda NAS, California

SHRIMP FOO YUNG

1 c. cooked shrimp
1 can bean sprouts, drained
1/2 c. shredded onion
1/2 c. sliced celery
3 tbsp. oil
1/2 c. minced water chestnuts
6 eggs
3 tbsp. soy sauce
1 c. chicken stock
1 tbsp. cornstarch

Combine shrimp and bean sprouts in bowl. Saute onion and celery in oil, about 5 minutes or till clear. Add onion, celery and water chestnuts to shrimp. Beat eggs; add 1 tablespoon soy sauce. Pour over shrimp; mix well. Place 1 tablespoon at a time on well greased skillet; brown on both sides. Mix chicken stock, remaining soy sauce and cornstarch in saucepan; cook, stirring, till thickened. Pour over shrimp.

Mrs. John J. Morrow, OWC
Letterkenny Army Depot, Pennsylvania

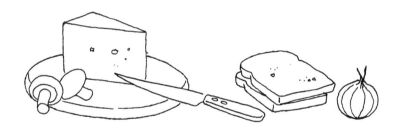

SHRIMP ORLEANS

1 tbsp. butter
1 med. onion, sliced
1 clove of garlic, crushed
1 can cream of mushroom soup
1 c. sour cream
1/4 c. catsup
1 3-oz. can broiled sliced mushrooms,
    drained
2 c. canned shrimp or 1 1/2 lb. cooked fresh
    shrimp
1/4 c. sherry

Melt butter in chafing dish or skillet; add onion and garlic. Cook till tender but not brown. Combine soup, sour cream and catsup; stir in onions. Add mushrooms, shrimp and sherry; cook over low heat just till mixture is heated through. Serve over fluffy hot rice.

Mrs. Glenn S. Chapman, Sr., CGOWC
Naval Air Facility, Naples, Italy

SHRIMP TOAST

2 4 1/2-oz. cans shrimp, drained and coarsely chopped
1/3 c. finely chopped water chestnuts or celery
1 tbsp. cornstarch
2 eggs
1/2 tsp. sugar
1/2 tsp. soy sauce
6 slices 2-day old bread, crust removed
Cooking oil

Combine all ingredients except bread and oil; mix well. Spread over bread to edges; cut each slice into triangles. Fill heavy skillet with cooking oil to 1-inch deep; heat to 375 degrees. Lower filled bread, shrimp side down, into hot oil; fry for 15 seconds. Turn; fry other side for few seconds or till golden brown. Drain on absorbent paper; serve hot. Yield: 12 servings.

Mrs. Allen S. Kaplan, Paper Ed. OWC
Lindsey Air Station, Germany

SWEET AND PUNGENT SHRIMP

1/4 c. brown sugar
2 tbsp. cornstarch
1/2 tsp. salt
1/4 c. white vinegar
2 tbsp. soy sauce
1 No. 2 can pineapple chunks, drained
    and juice reserved
1 green pepper, sliced in rings
2 sm. onions, sliced in rings
1 lb. (about) shrimp, cooked

Mix brown sugar, cornstarch, salt, vinegar, soy sauce and reserved juice in sauce-pan; cook until slightly thick. Add green pepper, onions and pineapple; cook 2 or 3 minutes. Remove from heat; add shrimp. Let stand 10 minutes. Heat before serving over hot rice. Yield: 4 servings.

Mrs. John P. Santry, OWC
Sunny Point Military Ocean Terminal, North Carolina

BAKED HASH

3 sm. cubed potatoes, cooked for 10 minutes.
1 sm. diced onion, cooked for 10 minutes
1 15 1/2-oz. can corned beef hash
1 8-oz. can biscuits

Place potatoes and onion in greased 9 x 9 x 2-inch pan; add hash. Stir all to-gether. Place biscuits over mixture. Bake in oven at 350 degrees for 10 minutes or until biscuits are browned. Yield: 4-6 servings.

Mrs. Richard Riedel, Reservation Chm.
Sangley Point OWC
San Francisco, California

FLYING SAUCERS

1 can Spam or Prem
1 lb. American process cheese
1 lge. onion, chopped
1 lge. package hamburger buns, halved

(Continued on next page)

Grate with large grater Spam and cheese into bowl; add onion. Mix together. Spread on hamburger buns; place buns, meat side up on your broiler pan. Broil until meat mixture turns color of toast. Serve immediately. Mixture may also be spread on hot dog buns and called submarines. Leftover meat mixture may be mixed in with scrambled eggs. Mixture will keep for several days in refrigerator or may be frozen.

Mrs. James M. Hesson, 2nd VP OWC
The Pentagon, Washington, D. C.

CALF'S LIVER PARIS

12 tbsp. butter
8 whole shallots, peeled and chopped
1 1/2 c. dry white wine
2 pinches of nutmeg
2 tbsp. lemon juice
8 thin slices calf's liver
2 egg yolks, beaten
4 lge. pinches of salt
8 sprigs parsley, chopped

Melt butter in skillet; add shallots. Cook for 1 minute over high heat. Add wine and nutmeg. Continue to cook over high heat for 2 minutes. Add lemon juice; turn heat very low. Quickly sear liver on both sides over high heat in large skillet. Remove from pan; keep warm. Add egg yolks to sauce with salt. Stir until slightly thickened. Place liver slices on serving dish; cover with sauce. Sprinkle with chopped parsley; serve immediately. Yield: 4 servings.

Mrs. Richard Barbera, 2nd VP OWC
Moron AFB, Spain

CHICKEN LIVERS

1/2 lb. chicken livers, floured
Butter
Salt
Pepper
Garlic powder
1 pt. sour cream
1 c. chopped green onions

Saute chicken livers in butter in skillet until brown. Add salt, pepper and garlic powder to taste. Stir in sour cream. Heat slowly. Garnish with chopped onions. Yield: 4 servings.

Mrs. Robert E. Waller, Pres. OWC
Keesler AFB, Mississippi

CHICKEN LIVERS ALOHA

1 lb. chicken livers, cut in thirds
1/2 tsp. celery salt
1/2 tsp. onion salt
1/2 tsp. paprika
1 tsp. curry powder
1 diced apple
1 8-oz. can low-calorie pineapple tidbits
    or 1/4 diced fresh pineapple
1/4 c. soy sauce
2 tbsp. water
Rice

(Continued on next page)

Sprinkle livers with celery salt, onion salt, paprika and curry. Turn and toss lightly, combining with apple and pineapple. Mix soy sauce with water; pour liver and fruit. Let stand for 30 minutes. Transfer to skillet. Cook over low heat for 30 minutes. Serve over rice. Yield: 4 servings.
PERSONAL NOTE: Recipe was clipped from an article in a newspaper last year. This has proven to be a delightfully tasty dish to be low calorie.

Mrs. Ben H. Ward, VP Women's Club
Armed Forces Staff College
Norfolk, Virginia

FRIED CHICKEN LIVERS AND RICE

1/4 c. flour
1/2 tsp. salt
1/8 tsp. pepper
2 tbsp. cornmeal
2/3 to 1 lb. chicken livers
2 tbsp. butter or margarine

CHICKEN-OLIVE SAUCE:

1 can condensed cream of chicken soup
1/3 c. sliced pimento-stuffed olives
Rice or noodles

Combine flour, salt, pepper and cornmeal in small paper bag. Add chicken livers; shake well. Heat butter in skillet; add livers. Cook for 10 to 12 minutes or until delicately brown. Add soup to pan in which livers were fried. Heat to bubbling, stirring frequently. Add olives. Serve livers on top of rice; cover with Chicken Olive Sauce. Yield: 4 servings.

Mrs. Robert E. Strange, Memshp. Chm. NDWC
Philadelphia, Pennsylvania

JAPANESE RUMAKI

3/4 lb. bacon slices, halved
1 can water chestnuts, sliced
8 oz. chicken livers, cut in pieces the size
    of small walnuts
Soy sauce
1/2 tsp. crushed hot peppers

Wrap bacon around slice of chestnuts and piece of liver. Secure with toothpick. Marinate in soy sauce and peppers for several hours. Place in shallow pan. Bake in 350-degree oven for 40 minutes or until bacon is crisp, turning once. Bacon grease should be drained after 20 minutes. May be frozen, thawed and reheated as needed. Yield: 35 servings.
PERSONAL NOTE: This recipe was simplified to this point after making many many Rumaki for Officers' Wives Club Foreign Foods luncheon and the International cooking group.

Mrs. F. T. Watts, Rec. Sec. OWC
Carlisle Barracks, Pennsylvania

RICE AND MUSHROOM RING

2 med.-sized onions, diced
1/2 lb. butter
2 4-oz. cans mushrooms

(Continued on next page)

1 lb. chicken livers
2 c. rice, cooked and drained
Salt and pepper to taste
Green vegetable

Brown onions in butter in skillet; add mushrooms. Brown slightly. Cook chicken livers in butter until tender. Combine all with rice; season to taste. Bake in greased mold in 350-degree oven with pan of water underneath for 30 minutes. Unmold; fill center with green vegetable. Wild rice may be substituted for regular rice. Yield: 6 servings.

Mrs. Robert Burke, Parlm. OWC
Hickam AFB, Oahu, Hawaii

VENETIAN CALF'S LIVER

1/2 c. butter or margarine
2 lge. onions, thinly sliced
2 lb. calf's liver, cut into matchstick
    pieces
Salt and pepper to taste
Juice of 1 lemon
2 tbsp. dry white wine
Minced parsley

Melt 4 tablespoons butter in skillet; add onions. Cook until onions are golden. Remove onions; set aside. Add remaining butter to pan; add liver. Cook over medium heat, stirring constantly, until pink is gone and liver is tender. Do not overcook. Add salt, pepper, lemon juice and wine, stirring up brown bits in bottom of pan. Serve immediately with rice or polenta, if desired; garnish with parsley. Yield: 6 servings.

Mrs. Robert G. Rubright, Treas. OWC
Suffolk Co. AFB, New York

PRONTO PUPS

1 c. pancake mix
2 tbsp. cornmeal
1 tbsp. of sugar
2 1/2 c. water
10 hot dogs

Heat deep fat to 375 degrees. Mix pancake mix with cornmeal; add sugar. Mix in water until batter is smooth. Dip hot dogs into batter; letting excess run off. Drop into fat. Fry until golden brown. You may insert small, round stick into hot dog to serve. Yield: 10 Pronto Pups.

Mrs. V. H. Wiegand, OWC
Willow Grove NAS, Pennsylvania

STUFFED DOGS

1/2 c. crushed potato chips or corn chips
1 c. grated American cheese
1/2 med. onion, chopped
1 tsp. Worcestershire sauce
4 tbsp. tomato sauce or catsup
10 hot dogs, split lengthwise

Mix together chips, cheese, onion, Worcestershire sauce and tomato sauce. Fill

(Continued on next page)

split hot dogs with mixture. Place on baking sheet. Bake at 350 degrees for 20 minutes. Serve hot. Yield: 5 servings.

Mrs. William Greene, Coast Guard OWC
Port Angeles, Washington

BARBECUED HOT DOGS AND POTATOES

1 med. onion, chopped
3 tbsp. salad oil
1 tbsp. sugar
1 tsp. dry mustard
Salt and pepper to taste
1 tsp. paprika
1/2 c. catsup
1/2 c. water
1/4 c. vinegar
1 tbsp. Worcestershire sauce
5 med.-sized cubed potatoes, cooked and drained
1 pkg. hot dogs, halved

Cook onion in salad oil in skillet till golden. Combine and add remaining ingredients, except potatoes and hot dogs. Simmer for 15 minutes. Place hot dogs, cut side down, in shallow baking dish. Spread potatoes over hot dogs; pour barbecue sauce over potatoes. Bake in 350-degree oven for 20 to 25 minutes. Yield: 4-5 servings.

Mrs. S. R. Miller, W and M Chm. OWC
Bitburg AFB, Germany

FORDS' FAVORITE FRANKS

4 tbsp. margarine, melted
10 slices white bread
4 tbsp. chopped onion
4 tbsp. prepared mustard
1/2 c. grated Parmesan cheese
10 frankfurters

Brush margarine on 1 side of bread. Combine onion, mustard and cheese. Spread on other side of bread. Place 1 frankfurter, diagonally, across mustard mixture on each slice of bread. Fasten 2 opposite corners of bread with wooden toothpicks. Place on cooky sheet. Bake in 400-degree oven for 12 minutes. Yield: 5 servings.

Mrs. John T. Ford, Adv. OWC
Tinker AFB, Oklahoma

FRANK-SAUERKRAUT GOULASH

2 tbsp. butter
2 tbsp. minced onion
1 lb. frankfurters, each cut in 5 diagonal slices
2 c. (packed) canned sauerkraut, rinsed in cold
    water and drained
1/2 c. sour cream
Paprika
1 tbsp. parsley (opt.)

Melt butter in large skillet; add onion and frankfurter slices. Cook over medium heat for 5 minutes or until onion is tender and frankfurters are slightly browned.

(Continued on next page)

Veal Dishes

Add sauerkraut to frankfurters. Simmer, covered, for 10 minutes, stirring occasionally. Stir in sour cream and paprika; stir for 1 minute. Spoon onto heated platter; garnish with parsley. Yield: 4 servings.

Mrs. Billy G. Smith, Pres. OWC
Barbers Point NAS, Oahu, Hawaii

AFRICAN CHOW MEIN

1 1/2 lb. veal cutlets, chopped
1 c. rice, uncooked
2 c. onion, chopped
2 c. celery, chopped
1 can mushrooms, drained
2 cans cream of mushroom soup
2 cans cream of chicken soup
2 c. water
1/4 lb. cashew nuts

Brown veal and onion separately. Mix all ingredients except nuts. Bake for 1 hour at 350 degrees. Remove from oven; add nuts. Bake for 30 minutes. Yield: 12 servings.

Mrs. Elmo L. Moss, AOWC
Lakehurst NAS, New Jersey

VEAL CUTLET CORDON BLEU

12 thin veal slices
Salt
Freshly-ground black pepper
6 thin Swiss cheese slices
6 thin ham slices
Flour
3 eggs, beaten
3/4 c. bread crumbs
3/4 c. butter
24 cooked asparagus tips

Flatten veal slices with cleaver; sprinkle with salt and pepper. Place 1 cheese slice and 1 ham slice on each of 6 veal slices; cover with remaining veal slices. Pound edges together; dip in flour. Dip in eggs, then in crumbs. Fry in butter for about 8 minutes. Serve with hot asparagus tips. Yield: 6 servings.

Mrs. Lloyd F. Salisbury, Pres. OWC
Fort Monmouth, New Jersey

VEAL SUPREME

1 lb. thinly-sliced veal cutlets
Flour
3 tbsp. butter
1 thinly-sliced green pepper
1 thinly-sliced onion
1 can condensed cream of chicken soup
1/4 c. white wine or sauterne
Salt and pepper

Dip veal cutlets into flour. Brown well in hot butter, for about 10 minutes; add green pepper and onion last few minutes. Stir in soup and wine; cover. Cook for 15 minutes or until veal is tender. Season to taste. Yield: 4 servings.

Mrs. John M. Collins, Treas. OWC
Concord Naval Weapons Station, California

Casseroles

RECIPE FOR CHINESE PORK SUPPER ON PAGE 122

CORNED BEEF CASSEROLE

1 1/2 c. broken noodles
Water
1 can cream of mushroom soup
1/2 c. canned milk
1 12-oz. canned corned beef
1 c. grated American cheese
1/4 c. chopped onion
1/2 c. crumbled potato chips

Cook noodles in boiling unsalted water; drain. Combine all ingredients except potato chips in greased casserole; top with potato chips. Bake for 20 minutes at 425 degrees. Yield: 6 servings.

Mrs. Charles B. Beach, OWC
Saw Vito Dei Normanni, Italy

CORNED BEEF CASSEROLE

1 can corned beef, chopped up
1 1 1/2-lb. can corned beef hash
1 8-oz. can corn, drained
1/2 c. chopped onions
2 tbsp. prepared mustard
1/2 lb. Velveeta cheese, cubes
1 can refrigerator biscuits or 1 c. biscuit
    mix

Combine corned beef, corned beef hash, corn, onions, mustard and cheese; mix well. Place in shallow casserole. Bake at 425 degrees for 30 minutes. Add refrigerator biscuits after first 20 minutes of baking. Biscuit made from mix may be added for entire baking. Mix biscuit mix, 1/3 cup milk, 1/4 cup green pepper, if desired, and egg together; spoon around edge of casserole. Corn may also be added to biscuit mix, if desired. Yield: 6 servings.

Mrs. Daniel Sevin, OWC
McClellan AFB, California

DRIED BEEF CASSEROLE

1/4 c. chopped onion
1/4 c. chopped celery
1/4 lb. dried beef, shredded
1/4 c. fat
4 tbsp. enriched flour
2 c. milk
2 c. cooked macaroni
1/2 tsp. salt
1/4 tsp. pepper
1 tbsp. minced parsley
1/3 c. grated American cheese

Cook onion, celery and dried beef in hot fat till onion is golden. Stir in flour; add milk gradually, stirring till slightly thickened. Add macaroni, seasonings and parsley. Pour into greased 1 1/2-quart casserole; sprinkle with cheese. Bake in 350-degree oven for 15 minutes. Yield: 6 servings.

Mrs. William F. Dulin, Ways and Means Chm. OWC
Malmstrom AFB, Montana

LAZY JANE'S WEEKEND BEEF CASSEROLE

1 lb. beef chuck or stewing beef, cut into 2-inch
    chunks
1/2 c. burgundy, claret or other red
    dinner wine
1 10 1/2-oz. can undiluted, condensed
    consomme
3/4 tsp. salt
1/8 tsp. pepper
1 med. onion, sliced
1/4 c. sifted all-purpose flour
1/4 c. fine dry bread crumbs

Combine beef, wine, consomme, salt, pepper and onion in casserole. Mix flour with crumbs; stir into casserole mixture. Cover. Bake in 300-degree oven for 3 hours or until beef is tender. Yield: 4 servings.

Mrs. Alex W. Talmant, Hon. Pres. OWC
Castle AFB, California

STEAK AND SPAGHETTI DINNER

1 1/2 to 2 lb. round steak
Salt and pepper
4 c. cooked spaghetti
2 No. 303 cans stewed tomatoes
2 c. grated cheddar cheese

Brown steak quickly on both sides; cut into serving-sized pieces. Season to taste. Place meat in large baking dish; cover with spaghetti. Cover spaghetti with tomatoes; sprinkle cheese over top. Bake in 325 to 350-degree oven for 30 minutes or until cheese has melted. Stewed tomatoes may be thickened and seasoned as spaghetti sauce before pouring over spaghetti. Yield: 4-6 servings.

Mrs. John C. Kempf, Jr., Corr. Sec. OWC
Los Alamitos NAS, California

STROGANOFF CASSEROLE

1 lb. round steak, trimmed and cut into
    thin strips
Shortening
2 tbsp. flour
1 17-oz. can peas, undrained
1/2 c. sour cream
3/4 tsp. salt
1 8-oz. pkg. thin noodles, cooked and
    drained
1 No. 2 1/2 jar sliced mushrooms, drained

Brown steak in small amount shortening in frying pan. Stir in flour and liquid from peas; cook until thick. Stir in peas and remaining ingredients. Place in a 1 3/4-quart casserole; cover. Bake at 325 degrees for 40 minutes. Yield: 4-6 servings.

Mrs. Laughlan C. Laurie, OWS
Kings' Point USNS, Bermuda

BEEF 'N' BEAN CASSEROLE

1 lb. ground beef
1/4 c. diced green pepper
1/2 c. minced onion
1/2 c. diced celery
Fat
1 8-oz. can tomato sauce
1/2 c. water
1 clove of garlic, minced
2 tbsp. wine vinegar
1 tsp. dry mustard
1/2 tsp. thyme
1 tbsp. brown sugar
Salt and pepper
1 No. 2 can pork and beans

Cook ground beef and vegetables in small amount hot fat until vegetables are soft; add tomato sauce, water, garlic, vinegar, mustard, thyme, brown sugar and seasonings. Blend well. Simmer 5 minutes. Pour beans into 1 1/2-quart casserole; pour meat mixture over beans. Bake at 375 degrees for 45 minutes. Yield: 5-6 servings.

Mrs. William N. Webb, Chm. OWC
Glynco NAS, Georgia

CHILIES RELLENOS CASSEROLE

2 lb. ground beef
1 c. chopped onion
1 clove of garlic
1 tsp. salt
1/2 tsp. pepper
3 4-oz. cans whole chilies
3 c. shredded sharp cheese
5 eggs
1 1/2 c. milk
1/2 tsp. hot pepper sauce (opt.)
1/4 c. flour
1/2 tsp. salt

Brown beef and onion in skillet; drain off fat. Sprinkle with salt and pepper. Place 1/2 of the chilies in 10 x 10 x 2-inch casserole; sprinkle with half the cheese. Top with meat mixture. Arrange remaining chilies on top; sprinkle with remaining cheese. Mix eggs, milk and hot sauce together; gradually add flour and salt. Beat until smooth. Pour over meat and chili mixture. Bake in preheated 350-degree oven for 45 to 50 minutes or until knife inserted in center comes out clean. Let cool 5 to 10 minutes. Yield: 6-8 servings.

Mrs. Franklin L. Tims, Treas. NOWC
Yuma, Arizona

FIESTA SPAGHETTI

2 lge. onions, diced
3 stalks celery, diced
2 garlic cloves
1/2 c. cooking oil
1 lb. ground beef

(Continued on next page)

1 4-oz. can mushrooms, drain and reserve
   liquid
3 cans tomato paste
2 to 3 tsp. chili powder
1 c. tomato juice or water
Salt
1 lb. spaghetti, cooked
1/2 lb. American cheese, grated
3/4 c. evaporated milk

Saute onions, celery and garlic in oil until limp. Add ground beef; cook until grey and crumbly. Add mushrooms and tomato paste; stir in chili powder, reserved mushroom liquid and tomato juice. Salt to taste. Layer spaghetti and meat mixture in large casserole with grated cheese. Reserve small amount of cheese for topping. Pour milk over top. Top with reserved cheese. Bake at 350 degrees for 30 minutes. Yield: 8 servings.

Mrs. James C. Morgan, Comm. Service Chm. OWC
Yongsan, Seoul, Korea

GOLF GIRL GOULASH

1 c. onion, chopped
1/2 lb. ground round
1/2 lb. bacon, broiled and crumbled
1/2 c. catsup
3/4 c. brown sugar
1 tsp. salt
1/4 tsp. pepper
2 tsp. vinegar
1 tsp. prepared mustard
1 can pork and beans
1 can garbonzos, drained
1 can red kidney beans, drained
1 can green lima beans, drained

Brown onion; add ground meat and brown. Add remaining ingredients; blend well. May be refrigerated for later use, if desired. Bake in 350-degree oven for 30 minutes to blend flavors. Yield: 10-12 servings.

Mrs. Walter D. Druen, Jr., OWC
George AFB, California

HAMBURGER-CORN BREAD CASSEROLE

1 lb. hamburger
1/2 c. chopped onion
2 tsp. chili powder
1 tsp. Worcestershire sauce
3/4 tsp. salt
1 c. canned tomatoes
1 can drained kidney beans
1/2 recipe corn bread or 1/2 packaged
   corn bread mix

Brown hamburger and onion; add chili powder, Worcestershire sauce, salt and tomatoes. Simmer a few minutes; add kidney beans. Simmer a few minutes; pour mixture into 3-quart greased casserole. Top with corn bread. Bake in 425-degree oven for about 20 minutes or until corn bread is done. Yield: 4-5 servings.

Mrs. Jan E. Verfurth, Corr. Sec. OWC
Albrook Howard AFB, Canal Zone

BEEF CASSEROLE

1 1/2 lb. ground beef
1/2 c. chopped onion
Dash of garlic salt
Salt and pepper to taste
1 tsp. basil leaves
1 tbsp. Worcestershire sauce
1 16-oz. can tomatoes
1 8-oz. can tomato sauce
1 c. sour cream
1 8-oz. package macaroni
Parmesan cheese
2 bay leaves

Brown ground beef and onion; add garlic salt, salt, pepper, basil leaves, Worcestershire sauce, tomatoes and tomato sauce. Simmer for 10 minutes. Add sour cream; simmer for 10 minutes. Layer beef mixture with macaroni in 2 1/2-quart casserole; top with Parmesan cheese. Add bay leaves. Bake at 350 degrees for 30 minutes. Yield: 8 servings.

Mrs. William J. Cance, 1st VP OWC
Ft. Fisher AFS, North Carolina

GROUND BEEF CASSEROLE

1 to 1 1/2 lb. hamburger
2 med. onions, chopped
Oil
1 tsp. salt
1/2 tsp. pepper
1/2 tsp. each oregano, chili powder and
    garlic powder
2 8-oz. cans tomato sauce
1 can undrained kidney beans
1 c. cooked macaroni
Dash of Accent
1/2 c. cheddar cheese, grated

Brown hamburger and onions in small amount of oil; add remaining ingredients except cheese. Mix well. Place in 2-quart casserole; sprinkle cheese on top. Bake at 350 degrees for 20 minutes or until cheese is bubbly. Yield: 4-6 servings.

Mrs. Charles R. Snavely, Rec. Sec. OWC
Fort Detrick Medical Research Lab., Maryland

HAMBURGER-CORN CASSEROLE

1 1/2 lb. ground beef
1 c. chopped onion
1 12-oz. can whole kernel corn, drained
1 can condensed cream of mushroom soup
1 can condensed cream of chicken soup
1 c. sour cream
1/4 c. chopped pimento
3/4 tsp. salt
1/2 tsp. monosodium glutamate
1/4 tsp. pepper
3 c. cooked noodles, drained
1 c. soft bread crumbs
3 tbsp. melted butter

(Continued on next page)

Lightly brown ground beef. Add onion; cook till tender, but not brown. Add corn, mushroom soup, chicken soup, sour cream, pimento, salt, monosodium glutamate and pepper; mix well. Stir in noodles; pour into 2-quart casserole. Mix bread crumbs and butter; sprinkle over top. Bake at 350 degrees for 30 minutes or till hot. Yield: 8-10 servings.

Mrs. Robert M. Paul, OWC
Wasserkuppe Air Station, New York

LASAGNA CASSEROLE

1 lb. ground beef
2 garlic cloves, crushed
1/4 c. minced onion
2 tbsp. salad oil
1 8-oz. can tomato sauce
2 1/2 c. canned tomatoes
1 1/2 tsp. salt
1/4 tsp. pepper
1 tsp. oregano
6 oz. wide egg noodles, cooked and
    drained
1/2 lb. thinly-sliced mozzarella cheese

Brown ground beef, garlic and onion in salad oil; stir in tomato sauce, tomatoes, salt, pepper and oregano. Cover; simmer for 15 to 20 minutes. Fill casserole by alternating noodles, cheese and meat mixture. Bake at 350 degrees for 20 to 25 minutes. Serve with Parmesan cheese, if desired. Yield: 4-6 servings.

Mrs. Richard H. Houlder, Ed. Right Angle, Hospitality Chm. OWC
ESSA Rockville, Maryland

LASAGNA PRESTO

1/2 lb. ground beef
1 c. chopped onion
2 lge. cloves of garlic, minced
2 tsp. oregano, crushed
2 10 3/4-oz. cans tomato soup
1/2 c. water
2 tsp. vinegar
1/2 lb. lasagna noodles, cooked and
    drained
1 pt. cottage cheese or ricotto
1/2 lb. mozzarella cheese, thinly sliced
Grated Parmesan cheese

Brown ground beef and onion in saucepan; add garlic, oregano, soup, water and vinegar. Simmer for 30 minutes, stirring occasionally. Arrange 3 alternate layers of noodles, cottage cheese, meat sauce and mozzarella in 12 x 8 x 2-inch baking dish; top with Parmesan cheese. Bake at 350 degrees for 30 minutes. Let stand for 15 minutes before serving. Yield: 6 servings.

Mrs. Kenneth W. Shaffer, Memshp. Chm. OWC
Bainbridge USNTC, Maryland

WASHDAY CASSEROLE

2 c. chopped celery
1 c. chopped onion
1 c. chopped green pepper
2 cans tomato soup
1 soup can water
1 tbsp. sugar
1 tbsp. Worcestershire sauce
Onion salt and garlic salt to taste
2 lb. hamburger
1 tsp. salt
Pepper to taste
1 lge. pkg. crinkle noodles, cooked
1 lb. grated cheese

Simmer celery, onion and green pepper for 15 minutes. Bring soup, water, sugar, Worcestershire sauce, onion salt and garlic salt to boil. Remove from heat. Panfry hamburger; add salt and pepper. Place 2 layers of noodles, meat, celery mixture and cheese in casserole; pour soup mixture over all, raising noodles with fork so sauce gets all through dish. Bake at 350 degrees for 20 to 25 minutes. Yield: 8 servings.

Mrs. Lincoln C. MacKay, Parlm. OWC
Kingsley Field, Oregon

DIRTY RICE

2 tbsp. butter or margarine
5 slices bacon, chopped fine
1 c. rice
1 med. bell pepper, chopped
1/2 lb. ground beef or leftover roast
1 med. onion, chopped
1 can beef consomme
1 can water
1 egg, beaten

Melt butter in skillet; add bacon and rice. Cook, stirring constantly, until rice is golden brown. Add bell pepper, ground beef and onion; stir until onion is clear and meat browned. Pour into 2-quart casserole; add beef consomme, water and egg. Cover. Bake at 300 degrees until rice is cooked and all liquid has been absorbed. May be cooked in large electric skillet. Yield: 6 servings.

Mrs. Ronald K. Campbell, OWC
Norfolk NAS, Virginia

HAMBURGER CASSEROLE

1 lb. ground beef
2 onions
1 clove of garlic
2 tsp. salt
1/4 tsp. pepper
Pinch of marjoram or oregano
3 c. cooked rice
1 c. drained green peas
1 No. 2 can tomatoes
1/4 c. grated cheddar cheese

(Continued on next page)

Cook ground beef with onions and garlic in heavy skillet; add seasonings, rice, peas and tomatoes. Mix well; place in casserole or bean pot. Sprinkle with grated cheese. Bake at 450 degrees for 20 minutes. Yield: 6-8 servings.

Mrs. Leo W. Harrison, FOCCPAC OWC
Kunia, Hawaii

SHEPHERD'S PIE

1 can green beans
1 can tomato soup
1 lb. ground round, browned
   in margarine
1 beaten egg
Instant mashed potatoes, prepared

Place beans, soup and ground meat in layers in buttered casserole. Add egg to potatoes; spread over top. Bake at 350 degrees for 30 to 45 minutes. Yield: 5 servings.

Mrs. Ben C. Rowe, VP MOWC
Yuma, Arizona

SHEPHERD'S PIE

1 sm. onion, chopped
1 lb. ground beef
Salt and pepper to taste
1 can gravy
4 or 5 lge. cooked potatoes
Butter
Milk

Brown onion and ground beef together until well done; add salt and pepper. Place meat mixture in large baking dish; pour on gravy. Mash potatoes with small amount of butter and milk; place on top of meat. Bake in a preheated 350-degree oven until potatoes are golden brown. Yield: 4-5 servings.

Mrs. William Timm, Prog. Chm. OWC
Defense Depot, Memphis, Tennessee

TEXAS FIESTA

1 lb. hamburger
Salt, pepper and garlic salt to taste
1 head cabbage, shredded
1 onion, sliced
1 lge. can tomatoes
Crumbled corn chips

Brown hamburger; season with salt, pepper and garlic salt. Drain. Place layers of cabbage, onion, hamburger and tomatoes in casserole; repeat. Top with corn chips, if desired. Bake at 350 degrees for 1 hour to 1 hour and 30 minutes. Yield: 4 servings.

Mrs. Allen R. Payne, Prog. Chm. OWC
Beale AFB, California

TASTY TATER TOTS

1 pkg. frozen mixed vegetables
1 lb. ground chuck, browned
1 can cream of mushroom soup
1/4 c. milk
1 pkg. frozen Tater Tots

Spread frozen mixed vegetables in casserole; place browned ground chuck on top. Spread soup over meat; pour milk on top. Arrange Tater Tots on top in rows. Bake at 375 degrees for 30 minutes. Yield: 6 servings.

Mrs. G. W. Umbehocker, Memshp. Chm. CGOWC
Goast Guard Base, Sault Ste. Marie, Michigan

ITALIAN EGGPLANT CASSEROLE

1/2 lb. ground beef
1/2 lb. bulk pork sausage
1/2 c. chopped onion
1 clove of garlic, minced
2 8-oz. cans seasoned tomato sauce
1 tsp. basil
1/2 tsp. oregano
1 lge. eggplant, peeled, thinly sliced
2 beaten eggs
1/2 c. salad oil
1/2 lb. mozzarella cheese

Cook meats, onion and garlic till meat is browned; pour off excess fat. Add tomato sauce, basil and oregano; simmer for about 15 minutes. Dip eggplant slices into eggs; fry in salad oil till brown on both sides. Arrange eggplant, cheese and meat sauce in alternate layers in shallow 2-quart casserole, ending with cheese. Bake at 350 degrees for 30 minutes or till bubbly and cheese melts. Yield: 8 servings.

Mrs. Richard F. Wills, ROWC
Key West, Florida

CHINESE PORK SUPPER

1 10 1/2-oz. can cream of chicken soup
1/4 cup water
1 tsp. soy sauce
1/2 c. cooked peas
1/2 c. thinly sliced celery
2 tbsp. thinly sliced green onion
1 c. diced cooked pork
4 c. finely shredded Chinese cabbage
1/2 c. Chinese noodles

Blend soup, water and soy sauce in 1 1/2-quart casserole. Stir in remaining ingredients except noodles. Bake at 350 degrees for 20 minutes. Sprinkle noodles around edge of casserole. Bake 10 minutes more. Yield: 4 servings.

Photograph for this recipe on page 113.

FRENCH HAM SOUFFLE

4 tbsp. butter or margarine
4 tbsp. flour
1 1/2 c. hot milk
1 tsp. salt
1/4 tsp. cayenne pepper
1 c. grated cheese
1/4 c. finely chopped chives
1 c. finely ground ham
6 eggs, separated

Melt butter; stir in flour. Slowly add milk; cook until smooth and thickened, stirring constantly. Add seasonings, cheese, chives and ham. Add beaten egg yolks; mix well. Cool. Fold in stiffly beaten egg whites. Place in ungreased 2-quart casserole. Bake in 300-degree oven for 1 hour and 15 minutes. Yield: 6 servings.

Mrs. Phillip L. Shackelton, VP Adj. Gen. OWC
The Pentagon, Washington, District of Columbia

HAM CASSEROLE

1 c. cooked ham, diced
2 c. canned tomatoes
1 egg, beaten
1 c. cracker crumbs
2 tbsp. mustard
2 tsp. salt
1/8 tsp. pepper
1/8 tsp. onion seasoning
1/2 c. grated cheese
2 tbsp. butter

Mix ham with tomatoes. Blend egg with 1/2 cup cracker crumbs, mustard and seasonings; add to ham and tomatoes. Place in 1 1/2-quart casserole. Mix cheese, butter and remaining cracker crumbs. Sprinkle over top. Bake in 350-degree oven for 30 minutes or until browned. Yield: 6 servings.

Mrs. Douglas C. Knox, Pres. OWC
Yuma Proving Ground, Arizona

Ham Casseroles

HAM-ASPARAGUS CASSEROLE

3 tbsp. butter
1/4 c. flour
1/2 tsp. salt
2 c. milk
1 1/2 c. cooked ham
1 can asparagus, drained
3 hard-cooked eggs, sliced
Bread crumbs

Prepare white sauce of butter, flour, salt and milk. Alternate layers of ham, asparagus and eggs in greased 1-quart casserole. Pour white sauce over top. Top with bread crumbs. Bake in 325-degree oven for 25 minutes. Yield: 4-6 servings.

Mrs. Sidney Hack, Activities Co-Chm. OWC
Fort Lewis, Washington

HAM AND KIDNEY BEAN CASSEROLE

2 c. cubed ham
4 scallions, sliced
3/4 green pepper, diced
1 6-oz. can tomato paste
1 c. red wine
2 No. 303 cans partially drained kidney
    beans
Salt and pepper to taste
4 slices bacon

Saute ham, scallions and green pepper together; add tomato paste and wine. Simmer for 5 minutes. Add beans; mix. Season with salt and pepper. Pour into 2-quart greased casserole; place bacon strips on top. Bake in 350-degree oven about 1 hour or until bacon is crisp and casserole is bubbling. Casserole may be prepared day before and refrigerated overnight. Yield: 3 servings.

Mrs. Roland M. Gleszer, Hon. Pres. OWC
Ft. Carson, Colorado

HEARTY SOUFFLE

4 tbsp. butter or oleo
4 tbsp. flour
1 c. milk
1/2 tsp. salt
1/4 tsp. pepper
3/4 c. Kraft American pasteurized cheese,
    cut-up
4 eggs, separated
1 c. diced ham
1 c. whole kernel corn

Melt butter; blend in flour. Add milk gradually; stir until thick and smooth. Add salt and pepper. Add cheese; stir over low heat until smooth. Remove from heat; add lightly beaten egg yolks. Stir until blended. Beat egg whites until stiff; stir a tablespoon of white into yolk mixture. Fold in remaining whites. Add ham and corn; spoon mixutre into 2 1/2-quart baking dish. Set dish in pan of hot water. Bake 45 minutes at 350 degrees. Yield: 6 servings.

Mrs. Robert Bergeron, Treas. NOWC
Bainbridge Naval Training Center, Maryland

HAM AND POTATO CASSEROLE

1 1/2 lb. ham or Canadian bacon, thinly
    sliced
2 6 1/2-oz. pkg. Idahoan au gratin
    potatoes
1 med. onion, thinly sliced

Layer ham, potatoes and onion in 3-quart casserole. Add liquid according to potato package directions. Stir gently so as not to disturb layer. Bake at 370 degrees for 45 minutes. Yield: 6 servings.

Mrs. Harold C. Garner, 1st VP OWC
Tuslog AFS
Ankara, Turkey

LEFTOVER PORK CASSEROLE

1 10-oz. can gravy or 1 1/2 c. homemade
    gravy
1/4 c. water
1 1/2 c. cubed cooked pork
1 10-oz. package broad noodles, cooked
1 sm. can peas, drained
1 can boiled onions, drained

Mix gravy with water in medium bowl; add pork, noodles, peas and onions. Mix lightly. Turn into greased 2 or 2 1/2-quart casserole. Bake for 30 to 40 minutes at 350 degrees or until bubbly. Yield: 4-5 servings.

Mrs. Raymond Stoetzer, Hospitality Comm. OWC
Norfolk Naval Shipyard, Virginia

MEAL IN A CASSEROLE

4 lge. potatoes, thinly sliced
2 lge. onions, thinly sliced
1 12-oz. can yellow whole kernel corn,
    drained
1 lb. lean bulk sausage
1 8-oz. can tomato sauce

Preheat oven to 400 degrees. Grease 2 1/2-quart casserole. Place potatoes in layers in bottom of casserole; add layer of onions on top. Spread corn over top. Make balls out of the sausage. Shape in 2-inch balls. Arrange on top of corn in single layer. Pour tomato sauce over sausage balls. Bake, uncovered, for 1 hour or until onions and potatoes are tender. Yield: 4 servings.

Mrs. William S. Jones, Gourmet OWC
Fort Stewart, Georgia

POINT CRUZ CASSEROLE

1 lb. bulk sausage or link sausage,
    fried and crumbled
1/2 c. chopped onion
1/2 c. chopped celery
1 c. rice
1 can cream of chicken soup

(Continued on next page)

Combine all ingredients in casserole. Bake, covered, at 350 degrees for 1 hour. Add small amount of water, if necessary. Yield: 4 servings.

Mrs. W. E. Carver, NOWC
Naval Station, Washington, District of Columbia

CHICKEN WITH ARTICHOKES

1 tbsp. (heaping) butter
1 cut-up fried chicken or 4 boned, fried
    chicken breasts
1 pkg. frozen artichoke hearts
1 can cream of chicken soup
1 tsp. poultry seasoning
1/4 tsp. ground mace
1/2 c. dry sherry
2/3 c. light cream
1 can mushrooms

Place butter in bottom of roasting pan; arrange fried chicken over it. Arrange artichoke hearts over chicken. Mix all ingredients. Pour over top; cover. Bake for 30 minutes in 350-degree oven. Garnish with parsley, if desired. Yield: 4 servings.

Mrs. Willis D. Holland, Prog. Chm. OWC
Edgewood Arsenal, Maryland

CHICKEN CASSEROLE

2 c. chopped cooked chicken
1/2 c. chopped celery
1 tbsp. chopped onion
1/2 tsp. salt
1 can mushroom soup
1 can chicken and rice soup
1 6-oz. can evaporated milk
1 sm. can chow mein noodles
3/4 c. slivered almonds
Bread crumbs

Combine all ingredients except bread crumbs in large bowl; mix well. Pour into 2-quart greased casserole; sprinkle with bread crumbs. Bake for 1 hour at 350 degrees. Yield: 6 servings.

Mrs. Harry Canham OWC
Pope AFB, North Carolina

CHICKEN CRUNCH

1/2 c. chicken broth
3 c. cooked chicken, cubed
1/4 c. chopped onion
1/2 c. slivered almonds
2 cans mushroom soup, undiluted
1 c. diced celery
1 sm. can water chestnuts, drained and
    sliced thin
1 No. 303 can chow mein noodles

(Continued on next page)

Blend all ingredients except chow mein noodles; pour into greased casserole. Bake in 325-degree oven for 40 minutes. Remove; stir in some chow mein noodles. Sprinkle remaining noodles over top. Serve on rice, noodles or by itself. Yield: 6-8 servings.

Mrs. Larry B. Hall, Activities Chm. OWC
Fort Story, Virginia

CHICKEN CRUNCH

1 3 1/2-oz. can French-fried onions
2 c. chicken
1 c. celery, cut fine
2 10 1/2-oz. cans cream of mushroom soup
   undiluted
1 5-oz. can chow mein noodles
1 5-oz. can water chestnuts, sliced

Reserve a few onions for topping. Mix all remaining ingredients; place in casserole or baking dish. Top with reserved onions. Bake at 350 degrees for 30 minutes. Yield: 6 servings.

Mrs. Pierre N. Canese, OWC
Sunny Point Military Ocean Terminal, North Carolina

CHICKEN DIVAN

2 10-oz. pkg. frozen broccoli
Salted water
2 c. sliced cooked chicken
2 cans cream of chicken soup
1 c. mayonnaise
1 tsp. lemon juice
1/2 tsp. curry powder
1/2 c. shredded sharp cheese
1/2 c. soft bread crumbs
1 tbsp. butter, melted

Cook broccoli in salted water till tender; drain. Arrange in greased baking dish. Place chicken over broccoli. Combine soup, mayonnaise, lemon juice and curry powder; pour over chicken. Sprinkle with cheese. Combine bread crumbs and butter; sprinkle over all. Bake in 350-degree oven for 25 minutes or until heated. Four skinned and boned chicken breasts may be used instead of leftover chicken. Yield: 4-6 servings.

Mrs. Donald W. Swain, Pres. OWC
RAF Mildenhall, England

CHICKEN JERUSALEM

6 chicken breasts
2 lge. cans or jars artichoke hearts
Salt and pepper to taste
Oregano
6 slices bacon
1 c. vermouth

(Continued on next page)

Placc chicken breasts on top of artichoke hearts in baking dish. Season with salt, pepper and generous amount of oregano. Place bacon on top; add vermouth. Cook, uncovered, at 350 degrees for 1 hour. Baste every 15 minutes. Yield: 6 servings.

Mrs. Vernon J. Henderson, Hon. Pres. OWC
Misawa AFB, Japan

CREAMED CHICKEN TACOS

1 sm. onion
1 bell pepper
1 lge. can tomato juice
2 cans sm. green chilies
2 c. cream or evaporated milk
2 c. grated longhorn cheese
1 doz. tortillas, cut in half
1 pkg. chicken thighs or 3 c. leftover
    chicken

Saute onion and pepper; add tomato juice and green chilies. Cover; simmer for 5 minutes. Add cream and cheese; cook slowly until cheese melts. Dip tortillas in hot fat until light brown; drain. Cook chicken thighs until tender; debone. Arrange tortillas, chicken and cheese mixture in layers until all mixture is used. Bake at 300 degrees for about 1 hour. Yield: 12 servings.

Mrs. Joseph L. Ross, 2nd VP, O and CWC
Kaiserslautern, Germany

EASY BUT GOOD CHICKEN

2 cans condensed mushroom soup
1 pt. sour cream
1 c. sauterne wine
2 cut-up chickens with breasts and thighs,
    boned
Paprika

Mix soup, sour cream and wine together. Pour over chicken in flat baking dish. Sprinkle generously with paprika. Bake at 350 degrees for 1 hour and 30 minutes or until tender. This is best cooked ahead, cooled and reheated for serving.
PERSONAL NOTE: Origin of the recipe is The Law and The Palate-Lawyers' Wives of Greater Milwaukee.

Mrs. Melvin R. Laird
Wife of Secretary of Defense
Washington, District of Columbia

CASSEROLE OF CANS

2 cans fried noodles
2 cans boned chicken
2 cans boned turkey
2 cans cream of mushroom soup
2 c. chopped celery
1/2 c. chopped onion
1/2 c. water
1 6-oz. package cashew nuts

(Continued on next page)

Mix 1 can noodles and other ingredients together; pour into buttered 2 to 3-quart casserole. Place remaining noodles on top. Bake for 1 hour at 325 degrees. Yield: 8 servings.

Mrs. E. A. Chapman, Adv. OWC
Ent AFB, Colorado

FIVE-CAN CASSEROLE

1 can chicken noodle soup
1 can mushroom soup
1 sm. can evaporated milk
1 can chow-mein noodles
1 or 2 cans boned chicken, drained

Mix all ingredients together; place in casserole. Bake at 375 degrees for 40 minutes or until done. Yield: 3-4 servings.

Mrs. Michael Fosanaro, Pres. OWC
Rome, Italy

NOODLES ROMANOFF CASSEROLE

1 pkg. noodles Romanoff, 4-serving size
1 10 1/2-oz. can cream of mushroom soup
2 c. cut-up, cooked chicken
1 10-oz. pkg. frozen chopped broccoli,
thawed and drained
1/2 c. pitted ripe olives, cut into wedges

Heat oven to 350 degrees. Prepare noodles Romanoff as directed on package, substituting 1/2 c. milk. Stir in soup, chicken, broccoli and olives. Pour into 2-quart casserole; cover. Bake for 25 to 30 minutes until broccoli is tender. Yield: 4-6 servings.

Mrs. R. A. Brown, Treas. OWC
Cherry Point MCAS, North Carolina

TURKEY STROGANOFF

1/4 c. chopped green pepper
2 tbsp. chopped onion
2 tbsp. butter or oleo
1 can condensed cream of mushroom soup
1/2 c. sour cream
2 c. cooked noodles
1 c. diced, cooked turkey
1/2 tsp. paprika

Cook green pepper and onion in butter until tender. Blend soup and sour cream in 1-quart casserole; stir in remaining ingredients. Bake in 350-degree oven for 30 minutes. Yield: 4 servings.

Mrs. Anthony N. DeBello, Club Arrangements OWC
Wright-Patterson AFB, Ohio

Chicken with Rice

QUICK CHICK CASSEROLE

1 can cream of chicken soup
1 box frozen mixed vegetables, cooked
Meat from 3 chicken breasts, cooked
1 stick pie crust mix

Combine first 3 ingredients in glass casserole; mix together. Roll out pie crust; cover top of casserole. Bake at 350 degrees for 30 minutes or until crust is brown. Serve immediately. Substitute 1 can mixed vegetables and 1 can boned chicken, if desired. Yield: 6 servings.

Mrs. Samuel I. Sifers, Jr., Pres. OWC
Ft. Ritchie, Maryland

BAKED CHICKEN CASSEROLE

1 c. Minute rice
1 fryer, cut in serving pieces
1 10 1/2-oz. can mushroom soup
1 soup can water
1 pkg. onion soup mix

Grease casserole. Add rice and chicken pieces. Mix mushroom soup, water and onion soup; pour over chicken. Cover with aluminum wrap. Bake for 1 hour at 350 degrees. Uncover; bake for 1 hour. Yield: 4-6 servings.

Mrs. Arnold A. Berglund, Hon. Pres. OWC
Sacramento Army Depot, California

CHICKEN—ALMOND CASSEROLE

2 lb. lean pork sausage
2 med.-sized onions, chopped
1 sm. stalk celery, cut fine (include
    some of tender leaves)
1 lge. green pepper, chopped
1 tsp. salt (opt.)
2 c. raw rice
3 pkg. chicken-noodle soup mix
9 c. boiling water
6 oz. sliced almonds

Brown sausage with onions in large frying pan. Add celery, green pepper, salt and rice. Turn off heat. Cook chicken-noodle mix in boiling water for 1 1/2 minutes. Divide ingredients into 2 large casserole dishes; stir once. Sprinkle nuts evenly over tops of both dishes. Bake in oven for 1 hour. Leave oven turned off for 10 to 15 minutes if mixture seems too watery. Yield: 8-10 servings.

Mrs. Martin Hurwitz, Sec. VII Corps OWC
Kelley Barracks, Germany

CHICKEN CASSEROLE

1 packet dried onion soup
3 c. water

(Continued on next page)

1 stick butter
1 c. rice
Salt and pepper
1 chicken, cut in pieces or chicken
    breasts
Paprika
Lemon juice

Heat onion soup, water and butter till butter melts. Add rice; mixture will be watery. Place mixture in greased oblong baking dish. Place seasoned chicken pieces on top. Sprinkle with paprika and lemon juice. Bake for 1 hour at 350 degrees.

Mrs. James L. Anderson, 2nd VP OW League
Saufley Field, Florida

CHICKEN CASSEROLE

1 can cream of chicken soup
3/4 c. Miracle Whip
2 c. cooked chicken or 3 cans chicken
    with broth
1 c. celery, chopped fine
1 c. cooked rice or 1/2 c. dry rice
1 tbsp. grated onion
1 tbsp. lemon juice
1/2 c. water chestnuts, sliced
Crushed potato chips

Mix all ingredients except potato chips. Place in 2-quart casserole; top with potato chips. Bake in 350-degree oven for 40 minutes. Yield: 6 servings.

Mrs. Richard Tenney, Chinhae OWC
FPO, Seattle, Washington

CHICKEN SOMETHING

1 c. Minute rice
1 sm. chopped onion
Salt and pepper
Pinch of poultry seasoning
1 can cream of chicken soup
1 can cream of celery soup
1 can cream of mushroom soup
1 c. milk
4 chicken breasts, thighs or legs

(Continued on next page)

Place rice in large casserole; add onion and seasonings. Mix soups and milk together; pour over rice. Place chicken on top. Bake at 325 degrees for 2 hours. Yield: 4 servings.

Mrs. David C. Faul, Publ. NSD OWC
Mechanicsburg, Pennsylvania

CHICKEN CURRY

1 pkg. wild rice or 2 c. cooked white rice
1 stick butter
6 lb. chicken, boiled, cut up with scissors
3 green peppers, finely chopped
3 onions, finely chopped
2 cloves of garlic, finely chopped
1 c. raisins, white preferably
1 c. blanched slivered almonds
1 1/2 tsp. salt
1/4 tsp. pepper
3 tsp. curry powder
1 lge. can mushrooms

Saute rice in butter. Combine all ingredients in baking dish; cover. Bake for 1 hour at 350 degrees. Yield: 12 servings.

Mrs. Alexander D. Surles, Jr., OWC
Ft. Monroe, Virginia

VIVA LA CHICKEN CASSEROLE

1 pkg. corn tortillas, cut in 1-inch
   strips
6 c. bite-sized chicken pieces
1 lb. extra sharp cheese
2 cans cream of chicken soup
1 soup can milk
1 7-oz. jar chilies, chopped

Grease 3-quart casserole. Layer tortillas in dish alternating with chicken and cheese. Pour mixture of soup, milk and chilies over; mix lightly. Cover. Bake for 1 hour at 300 degrees. Uncover for last 15 minutes.
PERSONAL NOTE: This is favorite standby recipe of Mrs. Robert H. Finch, wife of Sec., HEW.

Mrs. Thomas D. Farrell, OWC
McClellan AFB, California

SEAFOOD CASSEROLE

1 6 1/2-oz. can crab meat
1 6 1/2-oz. can sm. shrimp
2 hard-boiled eggs, chopped
1 4-oz. can mushroom pieces
4 c. cooked rice, quick cooking
2 10 1/2-oz. cans cream of mushroom soup

(Continued on next page)

1 1/2 c. shredded sharp cheese
3 tbsp. mayonnaise
1/2 tsp. salt
1/2 tsp. dry mustard
1/2 tsp. curry powder
1 1/2 tbsp. lemon juice
1/2 c. shredded almonds

Combine crab meat, shrimp, eggs, mushrooms and rice in 4-quart casserole. Heat mushroom soup; add 1 cup shredded cheese, mayonnaise, salt, dry mustard, curry powder and lemon juice. Add to casserole; mix well. Sprinkle with 1/2 cup of cheese and almonds. Bake for 45 minutes at 350 degrees. Yield: 6 servings.

Mrs. Salvo Rizza, OWC
Fort MacArthur, California

SEAFOOD CRUNCH

1 10-oz. can frozen condensed cream of
  shrimp soup, thawed
1/4 c. mayonnaise
1 c. crushed potato chips
1 6 1/2-oz. can crab meat, drained and
  flaked
1 c. diced celery
1/2 c. diced onion
1/2 c. diced green pepper
1 tsp. Worcestershire sauce
2 tbsp. lemon juice
1/8 tsp. Tabasco sauce
1 c. shrimp, cooked, canned or frozen
Salt and pepper

Combine soup and mayonnaise. Add 3/4 cup potato chips and remaining ingredients; stir well. Turn into greased casserole or spoon about 1 cup into individual scallop baking shells. Top with remaining potato chips. Bake at 350 degrees for 45 minutes for casserole and 15 minutes for shells. Yield: 4-6 servings.

Mrs. E. L. Casner, 1st VP OWC
Ft. Campbell, Kentucy

SHRIMP-CRAB CASSEROLE

1 to 1 1/2 c. cooked or canned shrimp
1 c. canned crab meat
1 med. onion, chopped
1 c. celery, chopped
1/2 tsp. paprika
1/2 tsp. salt
1 sm. green pepper, chopped
1 tbsp. chopped pickle (opt.)
1 to 2 tsp. Worcestershire sauce
1 c. mayonnaise

Combine ingredients, mixing lightly. Place in greased 1 1/2 or 2-quart casserole. Top may be decorated with slices of pimento. Bake in 350-degree oven for about 30 minutes. Yield: 4-6 servings.

Mrs. John S. Camper, Treas. OWC
Ft. Leonard Wood, Missouri

SHRIMP AND CRAB CASSEROLE

1 lb. crab meat
1 lb. cooked, shelled shrimp
1/2 c. chopped green pepper
1/4 c. chopped onion
1 1/2 c. finely chopped celery
1 c. mayonnaise
1/2 tsp. salt
1 tbsp. Worcestershire sauce
1 tbsp. barbecue sauce
2 c. crushed potato chips

Combine all ingredients except potato chips in buttered 2 1/2-quart casserole; top with potato chips. Bake for 20 to 25 minutes in 400-degree oven. Yield: 6-8 servings.

Mrs. Hugh S. Erskine, Women's Club
Menwith Hill USASA Station, England

SHRIMP AND LOBSTER CASSEROLE

1/2 c. chopped onion
1 med. clove of garlic, minced
2 tbsp. butter or margarine
1 10 1/2-oz. can condensed cream of
    mushroom soup
1/2 c. water
2 tbsp. sauterne or other dry white wine
1 c. cooked diced shrimp
1/2 c. drained tomatoes
3 tbsp. chopped parsley
1/8 tsp. marjoram
2 c. cooked noodles
2 lobster tails, shelled and cut in half
    lengthwise
Melted butter

Cook onion with garlic in butter in saucepan until tender. Pour soup into 1 1/2-quart casserole; gradually stir in water. Mix in all ingredients except lobster and butter. Arrange lobster on top; brush with melted butter. Bake at 350 degrees for 30 minutes. Yield: 4 servings.

Mrs. John M. Dent, Jr., Ways and Means Chm. OWC
Edgewood Arsenal, Maryland

SHRIMP AND CRAB SPECIAL

1 sm. chopped green pepper
1 sm. chopped onion
1 chopped pimento
1 4-oz. can mushrooms
3 c. cooked rice
1 4 1/2-oz. can small shrimp
1 4 1/2-oz. can crab meat
1 pkg. raw frozen peas
1 c. mayonnaise

(Continued on next page)

Mix all ingredients. Place in baking dish. Bake for 30 minutes at 350 degrees. Yield: 6 servings.

Mrs. David Lewallen, Rec. Sec. OWC
Whiteman AFB, Missouri

CRAB CASSEROLE

1 can crab meat
1 c. mayonnaise
1 sm. onion, chopped
1 c. celery, diced
1/2 c. green pepper, diced
1 tbsp. lemon juice
2 eggs
1/2 c. bread crumbs

Mix all ingredients together except bread crumbs. Place in 1-quart dish. Top with bread crumbs. Bake for 30 minutes at 350 degrees. Yield: 4 servings.

Mrs. H. S. Samuels, Rec. Sec. NDWC
Philadelphia, Pennsylvania

CRAB CASSEROLE

3 tbsp. butter
2 tbsp. flour
2 c. cream
Salt to taste
2 egg yolks, beaten lightly
1 tbsp. lemon juice
1/2 c. mushrooms
1 tbsp. minced parsley
1/2 tsp. paprika
2 tbsp. dry white wine or sherry
1 lb. crab meat, canned or fresh, coarsely
    flaked
2 tbsp. buttered bread crumbs

Make cream sauce with butter, flour and cream; season to taste. Remove from stove; blend in egg yolks. Add lemon juice, mushrooms, parsley, paprika, wine and crab meat. Pour into greased 5-cup casserole; top with crumbs. Bake at 400 degrees for about 25 minutes or until crumbs are browned. Yield: 4 servings.

Mrs. Gerald P. Schwalb, Corr. Sec. OWC
Ramey AFB, Puerto Rico

CRAB MEAT REMICK

4 slices toast
1 lb. crab meat
8 strips bacon, each cut into 4 pieces
1 1/2 c. mayonnaise
1/2 c. chili powder
1/2 tsp. paprika
Few drops of Tabasco sauce
1/2 tsp. Worcestershire sauce

(Continued on next page)

Place toast in individual casseroles; top each with crab meat. Place 8 pieces bacon on each casserole. Bake at 450 degrees until bacon is crisp, for about 15 minutes. Combine remaining ingredients in sauce; pour over casseroles. Place about 10 inches from broiler; heat until sauce bubbles and is golden brown. Yield: 4 servings.

Mrs. Richard T. Klabo, OWC
Whiting NAS, Florida

CRAB MEAT SANDWICH CASSEROLE

12 slices white bread
Butter
2 cans crab meat
1/2 to 1 tsp. oregano
1/2 to 3/4 lb. grated sharp cheddar cheese
Mayonnaise
3 c. milk and 4 eggs, beaten together

SAUCE:

1 can mushroom soup
1/2 can milk
1 sm. can mushrooms

Remove crusts from bread; spread 6 slices with butter. Place in well-greased 13 x 9 x 2 5/8-inch casserole. Sprinkle crab meat, oregano and cheese over bread layer. Top with remaining bread; spread with mayonnaise. Cover all with milk mixture. Store in refrigerator for 24 hours. Bake at 325 degrees for 1 hour and 30 minutes. Serve with mushroom Sauce topping. Yield: 6 servings.

Mrs. John J. Beck, VP JOWC
El Centro NAS, California

CRAB QUICKIE

1 c. shredded Swiss cheese
1 c. shredded Gruyere cheese
1 unbaked 9-inch pie shell
1 7 1/2-oz. can crab meat, drained and flaked
2 green onions, sliced
3 beaten eggs
1 c. light cream
1/2 tsp. salt
1/2 tsp. grated lemon peel
1/4 tsp. dry mustard
Dash of mace
1/4 c. sliced almonds

Sprinkle cheeses into pie shell. Top with meat and green onions. Combine eggs, cream, salt, lemon peel, mustard and mace. Pour over crab meat. Top with sliced almonds. Bake at 325 degrees for 45 minutes or until set. Let stand for 10 minutes before serving. Yield: 6 servings.

Mrs. F. J. Withers, OWC
Cecil Field, Florida

HOT CRAB SALAD WITH ROSE WINE

1 lb. or 2 7-oz. cans flaked crab meat
1/4 c. rose wine
1/2 c. sour cream
1/2 tsp. each dry mustard and salt
Dash of cayenne
Pinch of crumbled dried thyme
1/4 c. thinly sliced celery
2 hard-cooked eggs, chopped
1/2 c. sliced or slivered almonds
1/4 c. grated Parmesan cheese
1/4 c. melted butter

Toss crab meat gently with wine; marinate for 30 minutes. Combine sour cream, mustard, salt, cayenne and thyme; toss gently with crab, celery and eggs. Turn into buttered 1 1/2-quart casserole. Sprinkle with almonds and cheese. Pour butter evenly over top. Bake at 325 degrees for 25 minutes or until bubbling. Yield: 4 servings.

Mrs. Johnson L. Griffin, OWC
Fort McPherson, Georgia

LUCY'S CRAB CASSEROLE

1/4 c. butter
1/4 c. flour
1 c. light cream
1 tsp. salt
1/8 tsp. pepper
1/4 c. sherry
1 lb. fresh white crab meat
3/4 c. shredded cheddar cheese

Heat oven to 425 degrees. Melt butter in saucepan; stir in flour, cream, salt, pepper and sherry. Cook, stirring, over low heat, until thickened. Remove from heat; add crab meat. Pour crab mixture into buttered 10 x 6 x 2-inch baking dish. Sprinkle with cheddar cheese. Bake until cheese melts and mixture is heated through, for about 10 minutes. Yield: 4-6 servings.

Mrs. W. M. Elder, Ways and Means Chm. OWC
Kaneohe MCAS, Hawaii

MARINER'S MASTERPIECE

3 tbsp. butter or margarine
1/2 to 3/4 tsp. curry powder
1 c. thinly sliced celery
1/2 c. chopped onion
1 tbsp. lemon juice
3 c. cooked rice
1/2 c. sour cream
1/2 c. mayonnaise
1 c. ripe olives, cut into wedges
1 7 1/2-oz. can crab meat or tuna, drained
1 4 1/2-oz. can medium, deveined shrimp
1 10-oz. package frozen peas and carrots,
    cooked
Salt
Cheddar cheese strips

(Continued on next page)

137

Melt butter in saucepan; stir in curry powder, celery and onion. Cook until celery is tender. Stir in lemon juice. Place all ingredients except salt and cheese in large mixing bowl. Toss lightly to mix thoroughly. Add salt to taste. Turn into lightly-greased 1 1/2-quart shallow baking dish. Top with strips of cheese placed about 3/4 inch apart. Bake in 375-degree oven for about 25 minutes until cheese is melted. Garnish with additional wedges of ripe olives b e t w e e n strips of cheese. Yield: 8 servings.

Mrs. Thomas G. Taylor, Asst. Treas. OWC
Westover AFB, Massachusetts

QUICK CRAB CASSEROLES

1 lb. crab meat
1/2 c. cooked peas
1 10 1/2-oz. can condensed mushroom soup
Dash of pepper
1/2 c. grated cheese
Paprika

Remove any shell or cartilage from crab meat. Combine peas, soup, pepper and crab meat. Place in 6 well-greased, individual 5-ounce custard cups. Sprinkle cheese and paprika over top of crab mixture. Bake at 350 degrees for 20 to 25 minutes or until brown. Yield: 6 servings.

Mrs. John J. Kirchenstein, Ways and Means Chm. OWC
Schofield Barracks, Hawaii

FLAKED FISH CASSEROLE

2 eggs, separated
2 c. milk
2 tbsp. quick-cooking tapioca
1 1/2 tsp. salt
Dash of pepper
1/2 c. finely chopped celery
1 1/2 tsp. grated onion
2 c. flaked cooked fish
2 tbsp. chopped parsley
1/2 c. crushed cornflakes

Mix egg yolks with small amount of milk in saucepan. Add remaining milk, tapioca, salt, pepper, celery and onion; mix well. Cook, stirring over medium heat until mixture comes to a boil. Remove from heat; add fish and parsley, mixing well. Beat egg whites until they are stiff and form peaks; fold in milk mixture gradually, blending well. Spoon into greased 1 1/2-quart casserole. Sprinkle with cornflakes. Bake at 350 degrees for 50 minutes. Yield: 4 servings.

Mrs. Harold E. Ottaway, Hon. Member OWC
Seymour Johnson AFB, North Carolina

SALMON ROMANOFF

1/2 c. chopped green onion
1 chopped garlic clove
2 tbsp. butter or margarine

(Continued on next page)

1 c. cottage cheese
2 c. sour cream
5 drops Tabasco sauce
1/2 tsp. salt
1 1 lb. can salmon
6 oz. med. noodles
1 c. shredded cheddar cheese

Saute onion and garlic in margarine. Transfer to large mixing bowl; stir in cottage cheese, sour cream, Tabasco and salt. Stir in liquid from salmon. Flake and add salmon; mix lightly. Cook noodles according to package directions; drain. Stir into salmon mixture. Turn into well-greased 8-inch square baking dish; sprinkle with cheese. Bake in 325-degree oven for 30 minutes or until cheese melts and browns lightly.

Mrs. Raymond J. Reeves, Hon. Pres. OWC
Wife of Commanding General
North American Air Defense Command
Ent AFB, Colorado

SCALLOPS EN CASSEROLE

4 tbsp. butter
1/4 tsp. garlic powder
3 tbsp. cornstarch
2 tsp. salt
1/4 tsp. pepper
2 3/4 c. milk
1/4 c. dry sherry
1/2 lb. sharp cheese, grated
2 c. shell macaroni, cooked and drained
1 lb. scallops, cut in half

Make cream sauce with first 6 ingredients; add sherry. Add 3/4 of cheese. Combine macaroni, scallops and cheese sauce in buttered 2-quart casserole. Sprinkle with remaining cheese. Bake at 350 degrees for 30 minutes. Yield: 6 servings.

Mrs. R. A. Smoak, Hon. VP OWC
Fort Eustis, Virginia

LONG BEACH SEAFOOD

2 cans frozen shrimp soup
2 tbsp. sherry
2 sm. cans button mushrooms, drained
1 pkg. slivered almonds
1/2 lb. fresh or frozen crab meat
1/2 lb. fresh shrimp
Sliced American cheese
Paprika

Melt soup in saucepan; do not add milk. Place soup in 2-quart casserole; stir in sherry, mushrooms and almonds. Fold in seafood gently; cover with cheese layer. Sprinkle paprika on top. Bake at 300 degrees for 1 hour. Yield: 6-8 servings.

Mrs. Donald D. Todd, Ways and Means Chm. OWC
Fort Stewart, Georgia

JIFFY SHRIMP CASSEROLE

2 cans frozen condensed cream of shrimp
soup
1 1/2 c. boiling water
1 1/3 c. Minute rice
16 oz. frozen, cleaned shrimp
1 c. diced celery
1 c. diced green pepper
1 tsp. salt
Dash of pepper
1 c. sliced, pitted ripe olives
1/2 c. blanched, toasted slivered almonds
Parsley

Place unopened soup cans in hot water for 10 minutes to thaw. Pour shrimp soup and water into skillet. Cover; bring to a boil. Stir in rice, shrimp, celery, green pepper, salt and pepper. Cover; bring to boil. Cook for 10 minutes or until rice and shrimp are done; stir occasionally. Place in 1 1/2-quart casserole before serving; add olives. Sprinkle with toasted almonds. Garnish with parsley. Yield: 6 servings.

Mrs. John A. Bevan, Co-Ed. Newsletter OWC
Norfolk NSY, Virginia

NEPTUNE INTERNATIONALE

1 can frozen cream of shrimp soup
1 1/2 c. milk
1/2 lb. cooked, cleaned shrimp
1 7 1/2-oz. can crab, flaked
1 4-oz. can water chestnuts, sliced
1 8-oz. can button mushrooms
1/2 c. chopped green pepper
3 tbsp. chopped onion
1 1/2 tsp. salt
1/2 tsp. pepper
1 8-oz. pkg. egg noodles, cooked,
rinsed, drained
1/4 c. slivered almonds
1/2 c. grated cheddar cheese

Combine soup with milk; heat, stirring constantly until smooth. Remove from heat; add shrimp, crab, water chestnuts, mushrooms, green pepper, onion, salt and pepper. Alternate noodles and seafood mixture in layers in greased 2 1/2-quart casserole. Top with almonds and cheese. Bake in 350-degree oven for 35 minutes. Yield: 6-8 servings.

Mrs. Arthur G. Lynn, Hon. VP OWC
High Wycombe AS, England

SHRIMP CASSEROLE

Hard-boiled egg halves
Cooked shrimp
Pepperidge Farm stuffing
2 cans frozen shrimp soup, thawed

Place layers of eggs, shrimp and stuffing in flat casserole; pour soup over all. Bake for 30 minutes at 325 degrees.

Mrs. J. F. Wilhm, Hon. Bd. Member USARSO OWC
Fort Amador, Canal Zone, Panama

SHRIMP AND CHEESE CASSEROLE

8 slices bread, edges removed, broken in pieces
1 1/2 lb. shrimp, ready to eat
1/2 lb. Old English cheese slices, broken
   into bite-sized pieces
1/4 c. melted oleo
1/2 tsp. dry mustard
1/2 tsp. salt
3 whole eggs, beaten
1 pt. milk

Arrange bread, shrimp and cheese in several layers in greased casserole. Pour melted oleo over layers. Add mustard and salt to beaten eggs; add milk. Mix together; pour over ingredients in casserole. Cover; let stand minimum of 3 hours, preferably overnight in refrigerator. Bake at 350 degrees for 1 hour, covered. Yield: 6-8 servings.

Mrs. Edward Schleif, OPS Wives
Norfolk NAS, Virginia

MACARONI-CHEESE-SHRIMP BAKE

2 cans macaroni and cheese
1 can shrimp or 1 pkg. frozen shrimp
1 carton sour cream
1 hot pepper, sliced thin (opt.)

Mix all ingredients. Pour into 2-quart casserole. Bake at 350 degrees for 1 hour. Yield: 6 servings.

Mrs. Chandler B. Estes, Hon. VP OWC
Webb AFB, Texas

SHRIMP CASSEROLE HARPIN

2 1/2 lb. raw shrimp
1 tbsp. fresh lemon juice
3 tbsp. salad oil
3/4 c. raw rice
1/4 c. minced green pepper
1/4 c. minced onion
2 tbsp. butter or margarine

(Continued on next page)

1 tsp. salt
1/8 tsp. pepper
1/8 tsp. mace
Dash of cayenne pepper
1 10 1/2-oz. can tomato soup
1 c. heavy cream
1/2 c. sherry
3/4 c. slivered almonds

Cook shrimp in boiling salted water for 5 minutes; drain. Place in 2-quart casserole; sprinkle with lemon juice and salad oil. Cook rice as label directs. Saute green pepper and onion in butter for 5 minutes. Add with rice, salt, pepper, mace, cayenne pepper, soup, cream, sherry and 1/2 cup almonds to shrimp in casserole; mix well. Bake at 350 degrees for 35 minutes. Top with 1/4 cup almonds. Bake for 20 minutes or until mixture is bubbly. Yield: 6-8 servings.

Mrs. William R. Condos, Pres. OWC
Fort Bragg, North Carolina

SHRIMP AND EGGS

6 tbsp. butter
2 tbsp. minced onion
6 tbsp. flour
1/2 tsp. salt
2 1/2 c. milk
1/2 c. shredded cheddar cheese
2 c. cooked shrimp
6 hard-cooked eggs
1/4 c. mayonnaise
1/2 tsp. Worcestershire sauce
1/4 c. toasted bread crumbs
Paprika

Melt butter in large, heavy saucepan; add onion. Cook for 2 to 3 minutes. Blend in flour and salt; cook until bubbly. Add milk; cook, stirring constantly, until sauce is smooth and thickened. Add cheese; stir until melted. Combine sauce and cooked shrimp; pour into 1 1/2 to 2-quart baking dish. Cut eggs in half lengthwise; remove yolks. Mash yolks; combine with mayonnaise and Worcestershire sauce. Stuff egg whites with yolk mixture. Place stuffed eggs in baking dish on top of shrimp mixture. Sprinkle with bread crumbs and paprika. Bake in 350-degree oven for 30 to 35 minutes. Yield: 6 servings.

Mrs. H. Glenzer, Jr., Hon. Pres. NOWC
USNS, Adak, Alaska

SHRIMP NEWBURG

2 4-oz. cans mushrooms, drained
3 tbsp. butter, melted
3 lb. shrimp
2 10-oz. cans frozen cream of shrimp soup
1 10 1/2-oz. can cream of mushroom soup
1/2 c. light cream
1/3 c. sherry
2 tsp. dry mustard
1/4 tsp. salt
Pepper to taste
4 tbsp. grated Parmesan cheese

(Continued on next page)

Saute mushrooms in butter for 5 minutes, until brown. Arrange mushrooms and shrimp in casserole. Mix remaining ingredients except cheese; pour over shrimp and mushrooms. Sprinkle with cheese. Bake for 30 minutes at 350 degrees. Yield: 6 servings.

Mrs. R. J. Dougherty, 1st VP OWC
Chanute AFB, Illinois

SHRIMP WIGGLE

1 8-oz. package frozen shrimp
1 pkg. frozen peas
1 can cream of mushroom soup or 1 cup
  white sauce
1/4 c. chopped black olives
1/4 c. toasted slivered almonds

Combine all ingredients in 1 1/2-quart casserole. Bake in 350-degree oven for 30 to 40 minutes. Yield: 4 servings.

Mrs. Joseph F. DeBold, Treas. OWC
San Diego NELC, California

SHRIMP WINSTON

1 lb. frozen, shelled, deveined shrimp
3 15-oz. cans Spanish rice
1 c. sour cream
1/3 c. sherry
1/2 c. canned, slivered blanched almonds
1/4 c. reserved almonds

Preheat oven to 350 degrees about 1 hour before dinner. Cook shrimp in boiling, salted water for 5 minutes; drain. Mix all ingredients except 1/4 cup almonds in 9 x 9 x 2-inch baking dish. Top with almonds. Bake uncovered for 45 minutes.

Mrs. Philip Masenheimer, OWC
Homestead AFB, Florida

SOUTH AFRICAN STAR CASSEROLE

3 9-oz. pkg. South African rock lobster
  tails
Boiling, salted water
1 8-oz. pkg. med. noodles, cooked
4 tbsp. butter
1 med. onion, minced
4 tbsp. flour
2 1/2 tsp. salt
1 1/2 tsp. paprika
1/2 tsp. pepper
1 tsp. Angostura aromatic bitters
4 c. milk
1 8-oz. pkg. med. noodles, cooked
Buttered bread crumbs
1/4 c. melted butter

(Continued on next page)

Drop frozen South African rock lobster tails into boiling, salted water. Cook for 2 to 3 minutes after water reboils. Drain immediately; drench with cold water. Cut away underside membrane. Remove meat from shell in 1 piece. Slice each tail in half lengthwise, cutting 1/2 into chunks leaving other half whole. Melt butter; saute onion till transparent. Stir in flour and seasonings. Add milk gradually; cook until thickened, stirring constantly. Add rock lobster chunks and noodles; place in 2-quart casserole. Top with buttered bread crumbs. Bake, uncovered, for 20 minutes, at 375 degrees. Top with reserved rock lobster halves arranged in spiral star. Brush tails generously with melted butter. Return to oven. Bake for 10 minutes longer. Yield: 6-8 servings.

Photograph for this recipe on page 381.

BROWNSVILLE CASSEROLE

1 9 1/2-oz. can tuna
1 16-oz. can whole corn, drained
1 10 1/2-oz. can mushroom soup, undiluted
1 c. cooked celery
1 c. cornflakes

Heat tuna, corn and mushroom soup; add celery. Place mixture in 1 1/2-quart casserole; sprinkle cornflakes over mixture. Bake at 350 degrees for 20 to 25 minutes. Yield: 4 servings.

Mrs. S. I. Polonsky, 2nd VP OWC
Fort Monroe, Virginia

BUSY DAY MACARONI AND TUNA

1 pkg. macaroni and cheese dinner
1 can cream of celery soup, undiluted
1/2 c. milk
1 7-oz. can tuna, drained, flaked
1 3-oz. can sliced mushrooms, drained
1 tbsp. chopped pimento
1/2 tbsp. salt

Prepare macaroni and cheese dinner as directed on package. Add remaining ingredients; mix. Place in 1 1/2-quart casserole. Bake at 350 degrees for 30 minutes.

Mrs. Glen H. Wallace, NOWC
Memphis NAS, Tennessee

DAMM'S DELIGHT

1 can flaked tuna, drained
1 can cheddar cheese soup
1 can cream of celery soup
2 c. cooked rice
1 tbsp. minced, dehydrated onion
1 tsp. Accent
1/2 c. chopped celery
1/2 c. slivered almonds
Grated Parmesan cheese

(Continued on next page)

Place all ingredients except cheese in 1 1/2-quart casserole; mix thoroughly. Top with Parmesan cheese. Bake at 325 degrees for about 30 minutes. Garnish with parsley, if desired.

Mrs. John A. Damm, Memshp. Chm. NOWC
Charleston NSA, South Carolina

FISH PUFF

1 7-oz. can tuna, flaked
2 c. potato chips, crumbled
3/4 c. thin white sauce
1/2 tsp. salt
1/4 pepper
1 tsp. onion juice

Combine all ingredients. Pile loosely into greased 1-quart casserole. Bake at 350 degrees for 20 minutes. Yield: 4 servings.

Mrs. Sheryl S. Litts, OWC
USCGAS Port Angeles, Washington

HAWAIIAN DELIGHT

1 10 1/2-oz. can cream of mushroom soup
1/2 c. milk
1/2 c. chopped celery
1/2 c. chopped onions
1/2 2-oz. jar pimento
1 7-oz. can white meat tuna
1 5-oz. can water chestnuts
1 4-oz. can mushrooms
3/4 c. walnuts
1 5-oz. can chow mein noodles

Dilute mushroom soup with milk. Mix all except soup and noodles together. Butter casserole; add layer of noodles, layer of mixture and layer of soup. Top layer should be noodles with few walnuts. Bake for 35 minutes at 350 degrees. Yield: 4 servings.

Mrs. Ernest B. Wilson, Adv. OWC
Ellsworth AFB, South Dakota

QUICK TUNA PUFF

1 3 to 4-oz. can sliced mushrooms
1 tbsp. dried onion flakes
1 tbsp. butter or margarine
2 10 1/2-oz. cans condensed cream of
    mushroom soup
1 tbsp. fresh, grated lemon rind
2 6 1/2 to 7-oz. cans tuna, drained and flaked
1/8 tsp. pepper

(Continued on next page)

1 4-oz. can water chestnuts, drained and thinly
   sliced
1 1-lb. can green beans, drained
1 4-oz. can pimento, sliced
1 8-serving pkg. instant mashed potatoes
3/4 c. shredded cheddar cheese
2 tbsp. chopped parsley

Drain mushrooms; reserve liquid. Brown mushrooms and onion flakes lightly in butter; stir in soup. Add milk to mushroom liquid to fill 1/3 cup; stir into soup mixture. Add lemon rind, tuna, pepper, water chestnuts, green beans and pimento; heat slowly. Prepare instant mashed potatoes according to package directions; stir in cheese and parsley. Turn tuna mixture into 2-quart casserole. Spoon potatoes around top. Bake at 375 degrees for 10 to 15 minutes or until lightly browned. Yield: 6-8 servings.

Mrs. Richard A. Harris, Amphib. OWC
Norfolk NAS, Virginia

TUNA BAKE

1/4 c. green pepper, chopped
1 c. celery, chopped
1 med. onion, chopped
1 1/2 tbsp. butter
1 10 1/2-oz. can cream of mushroom soup
2/3 c. milk
1 c. grated cheddar cheese
1 9 1/4-oz. can tuna, drained
1 8-oz. pkg. med. noodles, cooked and drained
8 tbsp. mayonnaise
1/4 c. chopped pimento
1/2 c. toasted almonds

Brown green pepper, celery, onion and butter for 5 minutes. Cook soup, milk and cheese over medium heat till cheese is melted. Combine with tuna, noodles, mayonnaise and pimento. Mix well; pour into greased 3-quart casserole. Sprinkle with almonds. Bake for 25 to 30 minutes at 375 degrees. Yield: 8 servings.

Mrs. Eugene R. Alley, Treas. OWC
Pope AFB, North Carolina

BAKED CHILI

1 onion
2 tbsp. butter
2 c. ground cooked meat
2 tbsp. flour
1 tsp. chili powder
1 can tomato soup
1 sm. can red kidney beans or 2 c. cooked
   dried beans
Salt to taste

Chop onion; saute in butter. Add meat; brown. Blend in flour mixed with chili

(Continued on next page)

powder. Add soup and beans. Turn into baking dish; season with salt. Bake in 350-degree oven for 30 minutes. Yield: 4 servings.

Mrs. George B. Reddin, Jr., OWC
Fort Gulick, Canal Zone

CHILI CASSEROLE

1 15 1/2-oz. can chili con carne with beans
1 15 1/2-oz. can chili con carne without beans
1 15 1/2-oz. can creamed corn
1 sm. can sliced pitted black olives
1 sm. bag Fritos, crushed
1 c. grated sharp cheese

Mix first 4 ingredients together in large bowl. Pour 1/2 bag Fritos into 4-quart casserole; pour vegetable mixture over top. Cover with remaining Fritos. Sprinkle grated cheese over top. Bake for 30 minutes at 350 degrees. Yield: 6 servings.

Mrs. W. E. James, Spec. Act. OWC
Keflauik USNF, Iceland

EASY ENCHILADAS

2 1-lb. cans chili without beans
1/4 c. water
1 pkg. 12 lge. tortillas
1/2 lb. grated cheddar cheese
1 med. onion, chopped

Preheat oven to 350 degrees. Heat chili and water in large saucepan; dip tortillas into mixture until soft. Place in 13 x 9-inch pan. Spoon 2 tablespoons chili mixture, 1 tablespoon cheese and small amount onion into each tortilla. Roll up. Sprinkle remaining cheese and onion over top. Pour over remaining sauce. Bake for 30 minutes. Yield: 4-6 servings.

Mrs. M. T. Conway, OWC
Wasserkuppe AFS, Germany

CHILI-TAMALE BAKE

1 15 1/2-oz. jar or can tamales
2 15 1/2-oz. cans chili con carne with or
    without beans
1 15-oz. can kidney beans, drained
1 c. coarsely chopped onion
2 tbsp. flour
1 c. shredded process American cheese

Drain sauce from tamales. Combine drained sauce, chili con carne and kidney beans in saucepan. Mix onion and flour together; stir into chili mixture. Heat. Unwrap and slice tamales across width to form circular pieces. Pour hot chili mixture into shallow 1 1/2-quart casserole. Sprinkle with cheese; top with rows of sliced tamales. Bake in 400-degree oven for about 10 minutes. Yield: 6 servings.

Mrs. Stuart H. Smith, Hon. Pres. OWC
Cinclantflt Hq., Norfolk, Virginia

CHICKEN LIVER CASSEROLE

1 lb. chicken livers
1/4 c. butter
1/4 tsp. pepper
1 lge. bay leaf, crumbled
1 tbsp. instant minced onion
1 4-oz. can mushrooms, drained
1 1-lb. can tomatoes
1 10-oz. pkg. frozen mixed vegetables
1 1/2 c. cracker crumbs
3 slices bacon, crumbled

Saute chicken livers in butter. Add remaining ingredients except 2 tablespoons cracker crumbs and bacon. Simmer for 5 minutes, stirring occasionally. Pour into 1 1/2-quart casserole. Top with reserved crumbs and bacon. Bake at 350 degrees for 1 hour. Yield: 6-8 servings.

Mrs. Hugh Byrd, Adv. OWC
Defense Depot, Memphis, Tennessee

CHICKEN LIVER-RICE CASSEROLE

1 1/3 c. rice
1/4 c. butter or margarine
1 med. onion, minced
1/2 lb. thawed frozen or fresh chicken
    livers
Seasoned flour
1 can cream of chicken soup
1/2 c. milk
Salt and pepper to taste
Parsley and basil to taste

Preheat oven 375 degrees. Cook rice according to package directions. Melt 1 tablespoon butter; add onion. Cook till tender. Cut livers into 1-inch pieces. Roll livers lightly in flour; saute in remaining butter until browned. Combine rice,

(Continued on next page)

livers, onion, soup, milk, salt, pepper, parsley and basil in 1 1/2-quart casserole. Bake 30 minutes until hot and bubbly. Yield: 4-6 servings.

Mrs. Deane S. Parmelee, Hon. Pres. OWC
Charleston AFS, Maine

LIVER CASSEROLE

3/4 lb. lamb liver
2 lge. onions, chopped
2 oz. mushrooms, sliced
1 16-oz. can tomatoes
1 tbsp. flour
Seasoning to taste

Fry liver about 1 minute on each side; remove from pan. Fry onions and mushrooms. Add tomatoes, flour and seasoning; stir until thick. Place liver in medium dish; pour vegetable mixture over liver. Cook in 350-degree oven about 45 minutes. Add small amount water, if desired. Yield: 4 servings.
PERSONAL NOTE: Originated in Australia where liver is cheap and used in many ways.

Mrs. G. A. W. Worsell, Thrift Shop Treas. OWC
USAF Academy, Colorado

ONION-CRESTED HASH CASSEROLE

4 c. sliced onions
3 tbsp. vegetable oil
1/2 tsp. curry powder
1 tsp. Worcestershire sauce
1/2 tsp. salt
1/8 tsp. pepper
2 15 1/2-oz. cans corned beef hash
1/3 c. milk
Onion slices
1/2 c. fresh bread crumbs
1/2 c. grated cheddar cheese

Preheat oven to 375 degrees. Saute onions in oil until golden. Remove from heat; stir in curry powder. Mix Worcestershire, salt and pepper into hash; turn into 1-quart baking dish. Pour milk over hash mixture. Top with layer of onions. Toss crumbs and cheese together; sprinkle over onion layer. Bake 30 minutes. Yield: 6 servings.

Mrs. Charles Tighe, Hon. Pres. OWC
11th USCG Dist., Long Beach, California

SPAGHETTI AND CHILI BAKE

1 1-lb. 3 1/2-oz. can spaghetti in tomato
   sauce
1 15-oz. can chili with beans
Sharp cheddar cheese, grated

(Continued on next page)

Place half the spaghetti in 1 1/2-quart casserole. Add half the chili; top with grated cheese. Repeat layers, ending with cheese. Bake at 350 degrees for 20 minutes. Yield: 4 servings.

Mrs. James J. Kelly, OWC
FCPCP, San Diego, California

FRANKFURTER CASSEROLE

3 c. potatoes, sliced
1 onion, sliced thin
Salt and pepper to taste
Celery salt to taste
4 tbsp. flour
8 frankfurters
1 tbsp. butter
2 c. milk

Place half the potatoes and onion in buttered 2-quart casserole. Sprinkle with salt, pepper, celery salt and half the flour. Cut frankfurters into 1/2-inch pieces; place on potatoes. Cover with remaining potatoes. Sprinkle with seasonings and remaining flour. Dot with butter; add milk. Cover. Bake in 350-degree oven for 45 minutes. Uncover. Bake about 30 minutes longer. Yield: 6 servings.

Mrs. James F. Butler, OWC
USCGAS, Traverse City, Michigan

FRANKFURTER-SWEET POTATO-APPLE CASSEROLE

6 med. sweet potatoes, cooked, peeled and
  sliced
1/4 tsp. salt
1 1-lb. can applesauce
1/4 tsp. nutmeg
2 tbsp. butter
1 lb. frankfurters, scored

Sprinkle sweet potatoes with salt. Place half in shallow 2-quart baking dish. Cover with applesauce; sprinkle with nutmeg. Place remaining potato slices on top; dot with butter. Arrange frankfurters over potatoes. Bake in 350-degree oven for 25 to 30 minutes. May use two 17-ounce cans dry-packed sweet potatoes, if desired. Yield: 6 servings.

Mrs. James W. Morrow, 1st VP OWC
Ramey AFB, Puerto Rico

FRANKFURTER CASSEROLE

10 frankfurters
10 frozen tortillas
2 10 1/2-oz. cans chili

(Continued on next page)

1 tbsp. minced onion
6 to 8 drops Tabasco sauce
1 8-oz. can tomato sauce
1/4 c. green chili peppers, seeded and
chopped
4 oz. shredded sharp cheddar cheese

Roll up frankfurters in tortillas. Place in 12 x 7 1/2 x 2-inch baking dish. Combine chili, minced onion, Tabasco sauce and tomato sauce; pour over tortillas. Sprinkle with green chilies. Bake in 350-degree oven for 25 to 30 minutes. Top with cheese; serve. Yield: 5 servings.

Mrs. Louis Anticoli, Treas. OWC
Eielson AFB, Fairbanks, Alaska

HOT DOG CASSEROLE

1 28-oz. can baked beans
3 tbsp. catsup
2 tbsp. maple syrup
10 hot dogs
1 sm. onion, minced
3 slices cheese
3 tbsp. mustard
1 can crescent rolls

Mix baked beans, catsup, syrup and 4 sliced hot dogs together in 10 x 10-inch casserole. Split remaining hot dogs; fill with onion, cheese and mustard. Wrap in crescent rolls. Bake in 375-degree oven about 10 minutes till rolls brown and beans bubble. Fill remaining rolls with cheese, onion and mustard; bake till brown. Yield: 4 servings.

Mrs. R. M. Ward, OWC Bd.
Bainbridge NTC, Maryland

LIMA-FRANK CASSEROLE

1 10-oz. pkg. frozen lima beans, cooked
as directed on package
1 red cooking apple, unpared and thinly
sliced
6 frankfurters, sliced
1/2 c. fine, dry bread crumbs
1 can cream of chicken soup
1 tsp. Worcestershire sauce
1/4 c. toasted, slivered almonds
1/2 c. halved black olives
2 slices toast, quartered diagonally
2 4-inch square slices process American
cheese, quartered diagonally

Combine lima beans, apple and frankfurters in greased 1 1/2-quart casserole. Sprinkle bread crumbs over mixture. Combine soup, Worcestershire sauce and almonds; pour over casserole. Top with olives. Arrange toast and cheese over top of casserole. Bake at 350 degrees for 45 minutes. Yield: 4-6 servings.

Mrs. Edward R. Fye, Pres. OWC
Istanbul Air Station, Turkey

MEXICAN HOT DOG CASSEROLE

1 12-oz. can refried beans
1 pkg. hot dogs, split lengthwise
1 c. chopped onions
1 c. shredded cheddar cheese

Spread beans in 2 x 6 x 11-inch pan or baking dish. Place hot dogs in layer on beans. Sprinkle onions all over; top with cheese. Bake at 350 degrees for 25 to 30 minutes. Yield: 4-6 servings.

Mrs. Waldo J. Moulton, Arrangements Chm. OWC
Fort Detrick, Maryland

POTATO SALAD AND WIENER CASSEROLE

6 med. potatoes, sliced
Water
3 tbsp. fine bread crumbs
1 c. sour cream
1 c. salad dressing
2 tbsp. flour
2 tbsp. green onions
Salt and pepper to taste
1 lb. wieners, cut in 1/2-inch slices
4 eggs, hard boiled and sliced
1/4 c. melted butter or oleo

Cook potatoes in small amount water until tender; drain. Sprinkle 1 tablespoon crumbs into greased 2-quart casserole. Combine sour cream, salad dressing, flour and onions; blend thoroughly. Place layer of potatoes in casserole; season with salt and pepper. Add half the wieners and half the egg slices; spread with half the cream mixture. Repeat layers. Sprinkle remaining 2 tablespoons crumbs on top. Pour butter evenly over top. Bake at 350 degrees for 25 minutes. Yield: 6-8 servings.

Mrs. R. S. Hughes, OWC
NAS Whidbey Island, Oak Harbor, Washington

SCALLOPED POTATO AND HOT DOG CASSEROLE

5 med. potatoes, sliced thin
Salt and pepper to taste
Medium sharp cheese, sliced thin
5 hot dogs, sliced 1/4-inch thick
2 tbsp. butter
1 tbsp. flour
1 c. milk

Layer potatoes, salt, pepper, cheese and hot dogs in 2 1/2-quart casserole; repeat layers at least 3 times. Melt butter in saucepan over low heat; blend in flour and milk. Cook over low heat; stir until thick. Pour over casserole. Bake at 350 degrees for 1 hour and 30 minutes. Yield: 4 servings.

Mrs. Laurice G. Altman, Jr., Asst. Treas. OWC
Edwards AFB, California

Vegetable Dishes

RECIPE FOR TUNA-STUFFED ARTICHOKES ON PAGE 154

Artichoke, Asparagus Dishes

ITALIAN ARTICHOKES

2 No. 2 cans artichoke hearts
1 can condensed pea soup
1/2 c. Parmesan or Romano cheese

Drain artichoke hearts, reserving 1/2 cup liquid. Place artichoke hearts in casserole. Blend reserved liquid and pea soup; pour over artichokes in casserole. Sprinkle with cheese; cover casserole. Bake for 25 minutes at 375 degrees. Yield: 4-6 servings.

Mrs. Robert C. Cowan, Pres. OWC
Los Alamitos NAS, California

TUNA-STUFFED ARTICHOKES

2 tbsp. butter or margarine
2 tbsp. flour
1 c. milk
2 onion bouillon cubes
1/4 tsp. salt
Dash of pepper
3 6 1/2 or 7-oz. cans tuna, drained
1 1/2 c. cooked rice
1 tbsp. chopped canned pimento
6 lge. artichokes, cooked
1 c. hot water
Lemon butter

Melt butter in saucepan; quickly stir in flour. Gradually stir in milk; add 1 bouillon cube, salt and pepper. Cook, stirring constantly, until sauce boils for 1 minute and bouillon cube has dissolved. Remove from heat. Mix in tuna, rice and pimento; spoon into artichokes. Place in lightly buttered baking dish. Dissolve remaining bouillon cube in hot water; pour in bottom of dish. Cover tightly. Bake in 375-degree oven for 20 minutes or until heated thoroughly. Garnish with additional pimento, if desired. Serve with lemon butter. Yield: 6 servings.

Photograph for this recipe on page 153.

ASPARAGUS AND EGGS

1 clove of garlic, halved
Oil
1 pkg. frozen asparagus
Dash of oregano
Salt to taste
1 c. water

Brown garlic in pan in oil; cool. Add frozen asparagus, oregano, salt and water; boil until asparagus is tender. Drop in eggs; cover. Cook until eggs are set. Yield: 2 servings.

Mrs. Frank D. Andriano, OWC
Fort Hancock, Highlands, New Jersey

ASPARAGUS ON TOAST

1 15-oz. can asparagus
2 tbsp. butter or margarine
2 or 3 saltine crackers, crumbled
2 slices bread, toasted

(Continued on next page)

Heat asparagus as directed on label. Melt butter in saucepan; add cracker crumbs. Place hot asparagus on toast; sprinkle buttered cracker crumbs over asparagus. Serve immediately. Yield: 2-3 servings.

Mrs. David K. Richardson, OWC
Moron AB, Spain

CASHEW ASPARAGUS

1 lb. fresh asparagus or 1 10-oz.
   pkg. frozen asparagus
1/4 c. butter
2 tsp. lemon juice
1/4 tsp. marjoram
1/4 c. salted cashews, halved lengthwise

Cook asparagus in salted water until tender, about 12 minutes; drain. Arrange on serving dish. Melt butter; add lemon juice, marjoram and cashews. Simmer for 2 minutes. Pour over asparagus; serve. Yield: 2-3 servings.

Mrs. John A. DesPortes, OWC
US Defense Command, Taipei, Taiwan, Republic of China

ASPARAGUS-CAULIFLOWER AU GRATIN

1 10-oz. pkg. frozen asparagus spears
   or pieces
1 10-oz. pkg. frozen cauliflower
1 10 1/2-oz. can condensed cream of celery soup
1 c. shredded process American or Swiss
   cheese
1/2 c. milk
1 tsp. prepared mustard
1 tsp. Worcestershire sauce
1/2 c. wheat germ
2 tbsp. melted butter or margarine

Cook frozen vegetables according to package directions; drain. Combine soup, cheese, milk, mustard and Worcestershire sauce in large saucepan; heat slowly, stirring constantly, until cheese is melted. Add vegetables; mix carefully. Pour into shallow 1 1/2-quart casserole. Combine wheat germ and butter well; sprinkle around edges of vegetable mixture. Bake at 375 degrees for 20 to 25 minutes or until bubbly. Yield: 6 servings.

Mrs. Russell I. Brown, W and M Chm. OWC
Barbers Point NAS, Ewa Beach, Hawaii

BAKED VEGETABLES

1 No. 303 can green beans, drained
1 No. 303 can whole kernel corn
1 No. 303 can sliced carrots, drained
2 c. Onion White Sauce
1 1/2 c. grated sharp cheddar cheese
2 c. soft bread crumbs
1/4 c. melted butter
1/4 tsp. paprika

Combine vegetables, White Sauce and cheese; place in shallow baking dish. Toss crumbs with butter and paprika; place on top. Bake for 20 minutes or until browned at 375 degrees. Yield: 6-8 servings.

(Continued on next page)

ONION WHITE SAUCE:

1/4 c. butter
1/2 c. chopped onion
1/3 c. flour
1 tsp. prepared mustard
1 tsp. Worcestershire sauce
1 tsp. seasoned salt
Dash of pepper
2 c. milk

Melt butter in saucepan; saute onion in butter lightly. Stir in flour well; add seasonings. Stir in milk gradually; cook until smooth and thickened.

Mrs. Russell J. Carey, Jr., Coffee Chm. OWC
Elmendorf AFB, Alaska

CHEESY BEANS

2 tbsp. butter
2 tbsp. flour
1 c. milk
1/2 c. (or more) grated American cheese
1 1-lb. can green beans, drained
1/3 to 1/2 c. salted cashews

Melt butter; stir in flour. Cook until blended and smooth; add milk slowly, stirring. Add cheese; stir until cheese melts. Add green beans and cashews; heat through. Yield: 4-5 servings.

Mrs. Gerald D. Dyer, OWC
Yuma PG, Arizona

COPENHAGEN LIMAS

1 10-oz. pkg. lima beans
Water
1/4 c. crumbled blue cheese
1/4 c. fine dry bread crumbs
1 tbsp. butter, melted

Cook lima beans in unsalted water according to package directions. Heat milk and cheese, stirring till cheese melts; add to beans. Combine bread crumbs and butter; sprinkle over beans. Serve. Yield: 4 servings.

Mrs. Steven W. McArthur, OWC
Almaden AFS, California

CREAMY DILLED LIMAS

1 14 1/4-oz. can lima beans, seasoned
   with butter, undrained
2 tbsp. powdered coffee creamer
1/2 tsp. dillweed

Turn lima beans into saucepan; stir in powdered creamer and dillweed. Cook until blended and heated through. Serve in individual dishes. Yield: 3-4 servings.

Mrs. Jack L. Graham, Pres. OWC
NAS, San Diego, California

GREEN BEAN CASSEROLE WITH SHERRY

3 1-lb. cans French-style green beans,
    drained
American cheese, thinly sliced
Seasoning to taste
1 can cream of mushroom soup
1/4 soup can sherry

Arrange layer of beans in 2-quart casserole; add layer of cheese. Season. Repeat until beans are used. Pour soup over top; pour sherry over soup. Run spoon through mixture several times to cover layers with soup. Bake at 300 to 325 degrees for about 45 minutes. Yield: 8 servings.

Mrs. Edward H. Hirsch, Treas. OWC
Fort Gulick, Canal Zone

GREEN BEANS ELEGANTE

2 1-lb. cans cut green beans, drained
1 10 1/2-oz. can cream of mushroom soup
1/4 c. dry white wine
1/2 tsp. oregano
1 3 1/2-oz. can French-fried onion rings

Combine beans, soup, wine and oregano; place in 2-quart baking dish. Top with onion rings. Bake at 350 degrees for 25 minutes. Yield: 6 servings.

Mrs. Edward G. Jacob, Pres. OWC
Suffolk Co. AFB, Westhampton Beach, New York

HARVARD BEANS

2 tbsp. butter
1 sm. onion, sliced
5 tsp. cornstarch
1/3 c. sugar
1/4 c. wine vinegar
1 c. water
2 1/2 c. whole green beans, drained
Bacon pieces
Salt and pepper to taste

Melt butter; saute onion in butter until tender. Mix cornstarch and sugar in saucepan; blend in vinegar. Add water; cook over direct heat, stirring constantly, until mixture boils and thickens. Add onion and beans; heat through. Stir in bacon, salt and pepper. Yield: 4-5 servings.

Mrs. Daniel C. Sydow, Parlm. OWC
Laredo AFB, Texas

STRING BEANS IN TOMATO SAUCE

1 sm. onion, chopped
2 tbsp. bacon fat
1 sm. can tomato sauce
1 pkg. frozen green beans
1/2 tsp. salt
1/4 tsp. pepper
1/4 tsp. basil
2 tbsp. grated Parmesan cheese (opt.)

(Continued on next page)

Saute onion in bacon fat; add tomato sauce. Bring to a boil; add beans, salt, pepper and basil. Reduce heat; simmer for 20 minutes or until sauce is thickened. Stir cheese into beans, reserving small amount of cheese for garnish. Yield: 4 servings.

Mrs. G. B. Tamburello, OWL
Pensacola NAS, Florida

QUICK SOUTHERN GREEN BEANS

2 tbsp. margarine
1 15 1/2-oz. can green beans, undrained
Dash of pepper and paprika

Brown margarine in shallow frying pan over high heat; add beans, pepper and paprika. Reduce heat; simmer until liquid has almost boiled away about 10 minutes. Serve. Yield: 4 servings.

Mrs. Max Sansing, Parlm. OWC
Otis AFB, Massachusetts

BEETS IN ORANGE SAUCE

2 c. diced beets
2 tbsp. sugar
1 tbsp. cornstarch
1/4 tsp. salt
1/4 c. orange juice
1/2 tsp. grated orange rind
1 tbsp. butter

Drain beets, reserving 1/4 cup liquid. Combine sugar, cornstarch and salt in 2 1/2-quart saucepan; stir in reserved beet liquid and orange juice. Cook until thick, stirring constantly. Reduce heat; add orange rind, butter and beets. Mix lightly; heat thoroughly. Serve. Yield: 6 servings.

Mrs. Max Etkin, Hon. Pres.
Lexington Blue Grass Army Depot, Kentucky

COMPANY BEETS WITH PINEAPPLE

2 tbsp. brown sugar
1 tbsp. cornstarch
1/4 tsp. salt
1 9-oz. can pineapple tidbits, undrained
1 tbsp. butter
1 tbsp. lemon juice
1 1-lb. can sliced beets, drained

Combine dry ingredients in saucepan; stir in pineapple. Cook, stirring constantly, till mixture thickens and bubbles; add butter, lemon juice and beets. Heat through; serve. Yield: 4 servings.

Mrs. H. Hunter Look, 1st VP OWC
Clinton Sherman AFB, Oklahoma

SPICED BEETS

1 1-lb. can sliced beets
Juice of 1 qt. sweet pickles
2 tbsp. vinegar
1 tbsp. sugar

Drain beets, reserving liquid. Place beet liquid in saucepan. Add pickle juice, beets, vinegar and sugar. Boil for 10 minutes over low heat. Cool in liquid. Pour beets and liquid in jar; cover jar lightly. Beets will keep for several weeks. Yield: 6 servings.

Mrs. Norman C. Pardue, OWC
Picitinny Arsenal, Dover, New Jersey

BROCCOLI-ALMOND CASSEROLE

2 pkg. frozen chopped broccoli, cooked and
    drained
1 can cream of mushroom soup
1/2 c. Hellman's mayonnaise
1 tbsp. lemon juice
Dash of Worcestershire sauce
1/2 c. grated sharp cheese
1 jar pimento, chopped
1 c. crushed cheese crackers
1/4 c. slivered almonds

Arrange broccoli in buttered 2-quart casserole. Mix soup, mayonnaise, lemon juice, Worcestershire sauce and cheese; spoon mixture over broccoli. Top with pimento, crackers and almonds. Bake at 350 degrees for 25 to 30 minutes. Yield: 6-8 servings.

Mrs. James G. Daniels, Gov. Bd. OWC
Barbers Point NAS, Oahu, Hawaii

BROCCOLI CASSEROLE

2 pkg. chopped broccoli, slightly
    cooked and drained
1 can cream of mushroom soup
1/2 c. mayonnaise
1 egg, slightly beaten
1 sm. onion, grated
1 c. grated sharp cheese
1/2 pkg. Pepperidge Farm herb stuffing
1/4 c. melted butter

Combine first 6 ingredients; place in two 1-quart casseroles. Top with stuffing tossed with melted butter. Bake at 350 degrees for about 30 minutes. Yield: 6-8 servings.

Mrs. William A. Duncan, OWC
Edgewood Arsenal, Maryland

BROCCOLI CASSEROLE

1 pkg. frozen chopped broccoli
1/2 can cream of mushroom soup

(Continued on next page)

1/2 c. grated sharp cheese
1 egg, well beaten
1/2 c. mayonnaise
1 tbsp. grated onion
Salt and pepper
1/2 c. cheese cracker crumbs

Cook broccoli for 5 minutes; drain well. Combine broccoli and next 5 ingredients; season lightly. Place in casserole; sprinkle with cheese cracker crumbs. Bake at 400 degrees for 20 minutes. Yield: 4 servings.

Mrs. Lawrence H. French, OWC
USN Reg. Fin. Ctr., San Diego, California

BROCCOLI CASSEROLE

1 sm. onion, diced
1 tbsp. butter
1 c. cooked rice
1 pkg. frozen chopped broccoli, cooked
   and drained
1 can mushroom soup
1 sm. jar Cheez Whiz

Saute onion in butter; add rice and broccoli. Heat soup in double boiler; add Cheez Whiz. Stir into broccoli mixture; pour into buttered casserole. Bake at 300 degrees until bubbly. May be made ahead of time; freeze until ready to use. Yield: 8 servings.

Mrs. Warren T. Johnson, Pres. OWC
Laughlin AFB, Del Rio, Texas

BROCCOLI AND SOUR CREAM SURPRISE

2 pkg. frozen broccoli
2 oz. butter
1 pt. sour cream
Salt and pepper to taste

Cook broccoli as package directs. Remove hard stems and leaves; cut into bite-sized pieces. Add butter; cool slightly. Add sour cream, salt and pepper; pour into 1-quart casserole. Bake, covered, for 15 to 20 minutes at 325 to 350 degrees. Casserole may be assembled in advance. Bake just before serving. Yield: 6 servings.

Mrs. Kenneth Fox, Treas. OWC
Norfolk NSY, Virginia

BROCCOLI AND WATER CHESTNUTS

2 pkg. frozen chopped broccoli
Water
1 5-oz. can water chestnuts, chopped
1 envelope Lipton's onion soup mix
1/2 pt. sour cream
3 tbsp. bread crumbs

(Continued on next page)

Cook broccoli in saucepan with water until well separated; drain. Place in 2-quart casserole; add water chestnuts, onion soup mix and sour cream. Toss lightly; sprinkle with bread crumbs. Bake, covered, for 15 minutes at 350 degrees or until bubbly. Yield: 6 servings.

Mrs. Patrick W. Drennon, VP OWC
Davisville Constr. Bn. Ctr.,
North Kingstown, Rhode Island

BROCCOLI SUPREME

1 pkg. frozen broccoli
1/2 c. mushroom soup
1/2 c. mayonnaise
1 egg, beaten
1 sm. onion, grated
Salt and pepper to taste
1/2 c. grated cheddar cheese
Cracker crumbs
Butter

Cook broccoli until tender; drain well. Chop into small pieces. Combine soup, mayonnaise, egg, onion, salt and pepper; add broccoli. Pour into casserole; cover with cheese and cracker crumbs. Dot with butter. Bake 45 minutes at 350 degrees. Yield: 6-8 servings.

Mrs. Edward L. Jenkins, Treas. OWC
Hardt Kaserne, Schwaebisch Gmuend, Germany

SCALLOPED BROCCOLI

1/4 c. diced onion
3 tbsp. oleo
1 sm. box frozen chopped broccoli
2 tbsp. salted water
1 tbsp. flour
2 eggs, well beaten
1/2 8-oz. jar Cheez Whiz
Bread crumbs

Saute onion in oleo. Cook broccoli in salted water; drain well. Add onion, flour, eggs and Cheez Whiz. Mix well; place in 1 1/2-quart casserole. Bake at 325 degrees for 30 minutes. Sprinkle bread crumbs on top before serving. Yield: 6 servings.

Mrs. Frank A. Barbieri, OWC
7240 Support Squadron, Oslo, Norway

BAKED CABBAGE

1 med. head cabbage, cut in 6 or 8 wedges
6 tbsp. butter or margarine
8 tbsp. all-purpose flour
1/2 tsp. salt
2 1/2 c. milk

Place cabbage in 2-quart casserole dish. Melt butter in saucepan over low heat; blend in flour and salt. Add milk all at once, stirring constantly till mixture

(Continued on next page)

thickens and bubbles. Pour over cabbage. Bake in 375-degree oven for 1 hour. Yield: 4 servings.
PERSONAL NOTE: My mother-in-law serves this dish on New Year's Day to bring good luck throughout the year.

Mrs. Robert Jerrold Ellis, W and M Chm. OWC
Seymour Johnson AFB, North Carolina

JAPANESE CABBAGE

2 tbsp. bacon drippings
3 c. cut cabbage
3 green onions, sliced
Salt and pepper to taste
2 eggs

Melt bacon drippings in frypan; add cabbage. Cook for 3 minutes. Add green onions; cook for 2 minutes. Season. Push cabbage mixture to side of pan; add eggs. Scramble eggs; cook till done. Stir together; serve at once. Serve with soy sauce. Yield: 6 servings.

Mrs. William R. Hill, Jr., Sec. OWC
Marine Barracks, Pearl Harbor, Hawaii

STIRRED CABBAGE

1 2-lb. Chinese cabbage
1/4 c. oil
1 tsp. salt
1/2 c. water

Halve cabbage lengthwise; remove stem. Slice cabbage crosswise into 1/2-inch strips; chop stem. Fry stem in oil for 1 minute; add salt and 1/2 cup water. Cover; cook for 3 minutes. Add sliced cabbage leaves; cover. Cook over medium heat for exactly 3 minutes. Serve cabbage with any remaining pan liquid. Yield: 4-6 servings.

Mrs. Jimmie M. Jernigan, Prog. Chm. OWC
Malmstrom AFB, Great Falls, Montana

CARROTS IN ORANGE JUICE

3 tbsp. butter or margarine
6 to 8 med. carrots, peeled and sliced in 1/8-inch
    thick rounds
1 bunch green onions, thinly sliced or 4 tbsp.
    chopped onion
1/4 tsp. salt
1 tbsp. water
4 tsp. flour
1/2 c. milk
1/2 c. orange juice
Grated orange rind
Parsley (opt.)

Heat butter in heavy pan or skillet; saute carrots and onions for about 3 minutes. Add salt and water; cover. Simmer until carrots are almost tender, about 7 minutes. Sprinkle with flour; stir until mixed. Remove from heat; stir in milk gradually. Add orange juice and grated rind; chill until ready to serve. Warm

(Continued on next page)

slowly; remove carrots with slotted spoon to serving dish. Garnish with parsley. Yield: 8-10 servings.

Mrs. H. B. Lansden, OWC
MCAS, Iwakunni, Japan

CANDIED CARROTS

1/4 c. margarine
1/4 c. jellied cranberry sauce
2 tbsp. sugar
1/2 tsp. salt
2 No. 303 cans sliced carrots, drained

Combine margarine, cranberry sauce, sugar and salt in skillet; heat till cranberry sauce melts. Add carrots; mix, glazing with sauce. Bake at 350 degrees for about 10 minutes. Yield: 6 servings.

Mrs. Don E. Finney, OWC
MAAG, Addis Ababa, Ethiopia

FABULOUS CARROTS

3 c. shredded carrots
3 tbsp. butter
1 tsp. salt
1/8 tsp. pepper

Place carrots in 1-quart casserole; cover casserole tightly. Do not add water. Bake at 325 degrees for 30 minutes. Remove from oven; add butter and seasonings. Serve immediately. Yield: 5-6 servings.

Mrs. Joseph Z. Racz, Rec. Sec. OWC
American Red Cross Eur. Area Hq., Stuttgart, Germany

PIQUANT CARROTS

1 1-lb. can small whole carrots or sliced
    carrots
2 tsp. cornstarch
2 tsp. orange instant breakfast drink powder
1/8 tsp. salt
Nutmeg to taste
1 tbsp. butter or margarine

(Continued on next page)

Cauliflower, Celery Dishes

Drain carrots, reserving 1/2 cup liquid. Blend cornstarch, drink powder, salt and nutmeg in saucepan; stir in reserved liquid. Bring to a boil, stirring constantly. Reduce heat; cook until mixture thickens. Add butter and carrots; heat through. Serve. Yield: 4 servings.

Mrs. Stephen J. Balut, OSWC
USN Postgraduate Sch., Monterey, California

CAULIFLOWER CASSEROLE

1 head cauliflower, broken in flowerets
6 carrots, scraped and cut, sliced in rounds
1 box frozen green peas
1 c. bread crumbs
2 c. rich cream sauce

Cook cauliflower, carrots and peas separately; cool. Drain; layer in casserole. Cover each layer with bread crumbs and cream sauce, ending with cream sauce and bread crumbs. Bake for 30 minutes at 400 degrees. Yield: 6 servings.

Mrs. Newton H. Hodgson, Parlm. OWC
Warren AFB, Cheyenne, Wyoming

CELERY CASSEROLE

4 c. diagonally sliced celery
Salted water
1 5-oz. can water chestnuts, drained and sliced
1/4 c. diced pimento
1 10 1/2-oz. can cream of chicken soup
1/4 c. slivered almonds
1/2 c. bread crumbs
4 tbsp. melted butter or margarine

Cook celery for 4 minutes or until barely tender in small amount of water; drain. Combine water chestnuts, pimento, soup, almonds and celery; turn into greased 1 1/2-quart casserole. Mix bread crumbs and butter; spread over celery mixture. Bake at 350 degrees for 25 minutes or until crumbs brown. Yield: 4-6 servings.

Mrs. J. E. Fitzgerald, Jr., Hon. Adv. OWC
Wheeler AFB, Honolulu, Hawaii

CELERY CASSEROLE

4 c. diagonally sliced celery
1 can cream of chicken soup
1 4-oz. can water chestnuts, sliced
1 4-oz. can pimento, diced
1 2-oz. pkg. slivered almonds
1/4 c. melted butter
1/4 c. sake or soy sauce (opt.)
1/2 c. bread crumbs

Blanch celery for 4 minutes. Mix all ingredients except bread; place in casserole. Spread bread crumbs on top. Bake, uncovered, for 25 to 30 minutes at 350 degrees. Cream of mushroom soup or cream of celery soup may be substituted for cream of chicken soup. Yield: 6-8 servings.

Mrs. Thomas C. Kendrick, Treas. OWC
USMC Bks., Honolulu, Hawaii

CHINESE-STYLE CELERY CASSEROLE

2 med. bunches celery, diced
1 can cream of chicken soup
1 sm. jar pimento, diced
1 can water chestnuts, sliced or diced
1/2 c. soft bread crumbs
3 tbsp. melted butter
4 tbsp. slivered almonds or chopped
   English walnuts

Boil celery for 8 minutes; drain. Cool; add soup, pimento and water chestnuts. Place in casserole. Mix crumbs, butter and almonds; sprinkle on celery. Bake at 375 degrees for 35 minutes. Yield: 6 servings.

Mrs. W. J. Bremser, Jr., Corr. Sec. OWC
Lakehurst NAS, New Jersey

CREAMED CELERY

2 c. thinly sliced celery
2 tbsp. minced onion
1 tbsp. margarine
1/4 c. water
1/2 tsp. seasoned salt
Dash of pepper
1 tsp. cornstarch
1/4 c. milk

Saute celery and onion in margarine in medium skillet until onion is golden. Add water, seasoned salt and pepper; cover. Simmer for 10 minutes or till celery is tender-crisp. Mix cornstarch and milk to a paste; stir into celery mixture. Heat until thickened and smooth, stirring constantly. Yield: 4 servings.

Mrs. William J. Martin, III, OWC
Dugway Pvg., Utah

CHEEZY BEANS AND ONIONS

1 9-oz. pkg. frozen cut green beans
1 9-oz. jar process cheese spread
1/3 c. flour
1/2 tsp. salt
1/8 tsp. pepper
1 1/2 c. milk
1 1-lb. can onions, drained
Sliced pimento-stuffed olives

Cook beans in boiling water for 5 minutes; drain. Combine cheese spread, flour, salt, pepper and milk in same saucepan; cook over medium heat, stirring constantly, until thickened. Add onions and beans; pour into 1 1/2-quart casserole. Top with olive slices; cover with foil. Bake at 350 degrees for 20 to 25 minutes. Yield: 6 servings.

Mrs. J. F. Hill, Arts and Crafts Chm. OWC
Lowry AFB, Denver, Colorado

COMPANY VEGETABLE CASSEROLE

1 No. 1 can green beans, drained
1 No. 1 can whole kernel corn, drained

(Continued on next page)

1 No. 1 can boiled onions, drained
1 No. 1 can potatoes, drained
1 No. 1 can carrots, drained
1/4 tsp. savory
Salt to taste
1/4 tsp. pepper
1 10 1/2-oz. can cream of mushroom soup or
    cream of celery soup

Place vegetables in 3-quart casserole. Mix savory, salt, pepper and soup; pour over vegetables. Mix gently to prevent breaking vegetables; cover. Bake for 1 hour and 15 minutes at 300 degrees or 1 hour at 325 degrees or 45 minutes at 350 to 375 degrees. Casserole will hold for 2 hours in warming oven. Yield: 10-12 servings.

Mrs. Robert A. Edwards, Pres.
Transporation Women's Club, Washington, D. C.

BAKED CORN

1 No. 2 can cream-style corn
2 tbsp. flour
1 tbsp. melted butter
1 tsp. salt
2 eggs, well beaten
1/2 c. chopped green pepper
1 2-oz. jar pimento, chopped
1 c. grated sharp cheese
1/4 c. milk

Mix ingredients in order given; pour into baking dish. Bake in 350-degree oven for about 50 minutes. Yield: 4-6 servings.

Mrs. Joseph M. Kelso, Pres. OWC
Lowry AFB, Colorado

CHEESE CORN

1 tbsp. (about) butter
1/4 c. milk
1 can niblet corn, drained or 2 c. fresh corn
1/4 tsp. pepper
1/4 tsp. salt
1/4 lb. mild cheddar cheese, thinly sliced

Melt butter in casserole; add milk, corn, pepper and salt. Stir well; cover with cheese. Bake at 325 to 375 degrees until cheese is richly browned. Yield: 4 servings.

Mrs. T. I. Martin, Hon. Pres. OWC
DDMT, Memphis, Tennessee

CORN CASSEROLE

1 No. 2 can cream-style corn
8 soda crackers, crushed
1 c. diced cooked ham
3 eggs, slightly beaten
1 c. milk

(Continued on next page)

1 tsp. salt
1 tbsp. sugar

Mix corn, cracker crumbs and ham; stir in eggs, milk and seasonings. Place in greased casserole. Bake at 350 degrees for 45 minutes to 1 hour or until brown and firm when shaken. Yield: 4-6 servings.

Mrs. William Bowers, WOC
Seneca Army Depot, Romulus, New York

CORN FRITTERS

1 egg, lightly beaten
1/4 c. milk
1 c. pancake mix
1 12-oz. can whole kernel corn, drained
Wesson oil

Blend egg and milk; stir in pancake mix, just until smooth. Fold in corn. Do not overbeat. Drop by teaspoonfuls into 1 inch hot Wesson oil. Cook slowly until golden brown, about 4 minutes. Serve as vegetable or with syrup. Yield: 6 servings.

Mrs. Charles H. Whitledge, W and M OWC
Fort Eustis, Virginia

CORN FRITTERS

1 1-lb. 1-oz. can whole kernel corn, drained
1 egg, slightly beaten
1 tsp. sugar
1/2 tsp. salt
Dash of pepper
1 tbsp. butter or margarine, melted
1/4 c. all-purpose flour
1/2 tsp. baking powder
Shortening

Mix corn, egg, sugar, salt, pepper and butter; blend well. Sift flour and baking powder together; add to corn mixture. Heat small amount shortening in frypan; drop batter by tablespoonfuls into shortening. Fry on both sides until lightly brown; drain on paper towels. Serve immediately with butter or syrup. Yield: 2 servings.

Mrs. Barry L. Martin, Prog. Chm. OWC
Guilded Missile Sch., Damneck, Virginia

CORN OYSTERS

1 c. whole kernel corn
2 eggs, well beaten
1 c. flour
1 tsp. baking powder
1/2 tsp. salt
Cooking fat

Mix first 5 ingredients. Drop from teaspoon into 1/4-inch hot fat. Brown. Yield: 12 servings.

Mrs. Henry W. Fuller, Past Pres. ROWC
Key West Naval Base, Florida

FRIED CORN

1 med. onion, chopped
1 clove of garlic, chopped
1 1-lb. can whole kernel corn, drained
1/2 tsp. salt
1/4 tsp. pepper

Saute onion and garlic in medium skillet. Over medium low heat, add corn, salt and pepper. Cook for 10 minutes, stirring occasionally. Serve hot. Yield: 4 servings.

Mrs. Charles A. Meschter, Prog. Chm. OWC
Bitburg AB, Germany

SAVORY CORN

3 slices bacon
1 No. 303 can whole kernel corn, drained
1/2 c. sour cream
Onion flakes
Salt and pepper to taste
Paprika

Fry bacon till crisp; crumble. Drain fat from skillet; add corn. Stir in bacon and sour cream; season to taste with onion flakes, salt and pepper. Heat, stirring gently. Sprinkle with paprika before serving. Yield: 3-4 servings.

Mrs. John P. Byrne, Bd. Member OWC
Fort McClellan, Alabama

SCALLOPED CORN

1 can cream-style corn
1 c. milk
1 egg, well beaten
3/4 tsp. salt
1/4 c. chopped onion
1/4 c. sliced pimento (opt.)
1 1/2 c. coarse cracker crumbs
1 tbsp. melted butter

Mix first 6 ingredients and 3/4 cup cracker crumbs; pour into buttered 1 1/2-quart casserole. Top with remaining crumbs, mixed with melted butter. Bake at 350 degrees for 30 to 45 minutes or until knife inserted into center comes out clean. Yield: 4 servings.

Mrs. Judith A. Curinga, Pres. OWC
768th Med. Det., Mannheim, Germany

CHEF'S EGGPLANT

1 eggplant, sliced 3/4-inch thick
1 egg, beaten
Flour
Oil
1 jar spaghetti sauce
Parmesan cheese
Salt to taste

(Continued on next page)

Dip eggplant in egg; roll in flour. Brown in cooking oil. Place eggplant in large flat pan; cover with spaghetti sauce. Sprinkle liberally with Parmesan cheese. Bake for 20 minutes at 300 degrees. Add salt; serve hot. Yield: 6-8 servings.

Mrs. Edmund K. Hartley, Pres. OWC
FCPCP-FAAWTC, San Diego, California

EGGPLANT CASSEROLE

2 eggplants, sliced
1 c. bread crumbs
1/4 tsp. sage
1/4 tsp. poultry seasoning
1/2 tsp. salt
1/2 tsp. pepper
1 lge. onion
1 lge. can mushrooms
1 can oysters
1 egg
Mozzarella cheese

Boil eggplants for 10 minutes; drain. Combine eggplants and next 9 ingredients; place in greased casserole. Bake for 35 minutes at 350 degrees. Cover with cheese; bake for 10 minutes longer. Yield: 6 servings.

Mrs. John G. Bugenske, Hosp. Chm. OWC
Fort Wainwright, Fairbanks, Alaska

EGGPLANT CASSEROLE

3 c. cooked eggplant or squash, mashed
2 c. grated American cheese
1 pimento, diced
1 egg
2 tbsp. chopped onion
1/2 stick oleo
3 tbsp. sugar
1 tsp. salt
1 tsp. Worcestershire sauce
1 c. Waverly cracker crumbs

Combine all ingredients except 1/3 cup crumbs. Place in casserole. Sprinkle with reserved crumbs. Bake at 400 degrees until firm, about 20 minutes. Yield: 6-8 servings.

Mrs. George T. Buck, Hon. Pres. OWC
Holloman AFB, New Mexico

EGGPLANT MEDLEY

1 eggplant, peeled and sliced 1/4-inch thick
4 med. tomatoes, sliced
2 med. green peppers, cut in pieces
2 med. onions, sliced
Salt, pepper, garlic salt, sugar and MSG to taste
3/4 lb. sharp cheddar cheese, sliced

Place layer of eggplant in large casserole; add layer each of tomatoes, green peppers and onions. Sprinkle lightly with seasonings; add layer of cheese. Repeat until casserole is filled, ending with cheese; cover casserole. Bake in 400-degree oven for 30 minutes until steaming. Reduce oven temperature to 350 degrees; uncover casserole. Bake for 30 minutes longer. Yield: 6 servings.

Mrs. William C. Scarbrough, NOWC
Keyport NTS, Washington

IRISH COLCANNON

1 10-oz. pkg. frozen broccoli
1 10-oz. pkg. frozen Brussels sprouts
4 c. hot instant mashed potatoes
1/4 c. finely chopped green onions and tops
1/4 c. melted butter
1/4 c. sour cream
Salt and pepper to taste

Cook broccoli and Brussels sprouts according to package directions; drain. Chop together finely. Place potatoes in pan over hot water; add cooked vegetables, onions, butter, sour cream, salt and pepper to taste. Whip to blend; serve hot. Yield: 6 servings.

Mrs. Berwyn L. Place, VP OWC
Defense Electronics Supply Ctr., Gentile AFS, Ohio

NUT CASSEROLE

1 c. dried whole wheat bread crumbs
1 1/2 c. chopped celery
1/4 (or more) bunch parsley
3/4 c. almonds, pecans or English walnuts
2 sm. onions
1/2 c. green pepper
2 eggs, beaten
3 tbsp. melted butter
1 1/2 c. milk
Salt and pepper to taste

Grind first 6 ingredients; add remaining ingredients. Place in greased 8 x 8-inch baking dish; place dish in pan of warm water. Bake for 1 hour at 350 degrees. Serve with Mushroom Sauce or creamed peas.

MUSHROOM SAUCE:

3 tbsp. butter
3 tbsp. flour
Few drops onion juice

(Continued on next page)

1/4 tsp. salt
Dash of pepper
1 c. heated chicken stock
    or chicken bouillon
5 canned mushroom caps, sliced

Melt butter; add flour and seasonings. Stir until blended; add stock slowly, stirring constantly. Bring to boiling point; boil for 2 minutes. Add cream and mushroom caps. Cook until heated through. Yield: 8 servings.

Mrs. S. H. Runyan, Hon. 1st VP OWC
Luke AFB, Glendale, Arizona

CREAMED ONIONS

2 No. 303 cans onions
Flour
Milk
Butter
Salt and pepper to taste
Bread crumbs

Heat onions; place in small baking dish. Sprinkle onions with flour; fill dish 3/4 full with milk. Dot with butter; add salt and pepper. Brown bread crumbs in butter; sprinkle over top. Bake at 400 degrees until brown. Yield: 4-6 servings.

Mrs. Edward F. Lewis, Treas. OWC
MSCGAS, Traverse City, Michigan

CURRIED ONIONS

1 lb. onions, peeled
Salted water
1 can condensed cream of mushroom soup
1/3 c. milk
1/4 tsp. curry powder

Cook onions in boiling salted water for 20 minutes or just until tender; drain. Stir in soup, milk and curry powder; heat slowly, stirring once or twice, until bubbly and creamy. Yield: 6 servings.

Mrs. Harry Coates, Publ. Chm. OWC
Barksdale AFB, Shreveport, Louisiana

ONION CASSEROLE

2 10 1/2-oz. cans condensed cream of mushroom soup
1/2 tsp. paprika
4 1-lb. cans whole onions, drained
1/2 c. buttered bread crumbs

Blend soup, paprika and onions in 3-quart casserole; sprinkle crumbs on top. Bake for 20 minutes in 425-degree oven. Yield: 8-10 servings.

Mrs. William H. LaJeunesse, Res. Chm. OWC
Minneapolis, St. Paul Area, Minnesota

ONIONS AU GRATIN

1 lb. onions, thinly sliced
Salted water
2 tbsp. butter
2 tbsp. flour
1/2 c. cream
Salt and pepper to taste
1/4 c. chopped parsley
1 c. buttered coarse bread crumbs
1/4 c. grated Parmesan cheese

Boil onions in lightly salted water until just tender; drain, reserving 1/2 cup liquid. Melt butter in saucepan; blend in flour. Bring cream to boil; add to flour mixture, stirring vigorously. Add reserved onion liquid, salt, pepper, parsley and onions. Turn mixture into casserole; sprinkle with bread crumbs and cheese. Bake, uncovered, in 375-degree oven until heated through and brown on top, about 20 minutes.

Mrs. Morton F. Roth, OWC
Cinclant, Norfolk, Virginia

PEAS AND CELERY

Butter
1 c. thinly sliced celery
1/4 c. thinly sliced green onions
2 10-oz. pkg. frozen green peas
1 tsp. salt
1/4 tsp. pepper
1/2 tsp. nutmeg
1 tsp. lemon juice

Melt 1/2 cup butter in saucepan; saute celery and onions until slightly tender. Add peas, salt, pepper and nutmeg; cover. Cook over low heat until peas are tender; stir in lemon juice. Serve hot, topped with pat of butter. Yield: 8-10 servings.

Mrs. Robert M. Pearce, Army Liaison OWC
Pinder Barracks, Zirndorf, Germany

PEAS AND CORN SAVORY

1/4 c. minced onion
1/2 c. minced celery
3 tbsp. butter
2 cans niblet corn, partially drained
2 cans niblet peas, partially drained
1/2 tsp. dried summer savory
1/2 tsp. salt
1/8 tsp. pepper
2 tbsp. minced parsley (opt.)
1/2 c. sour cream

Saute onion and celery in butter for 3 to 4 minutes; add corn, peas, savory, salt, pepper and parsley. Cook until celery is almost tender; stir in sour cream just before serving. Serve with traditional turkey dinner at Thanksgiving and Christmas. Yield: 10-12 servings.

Mrs. Lloyd R. Wright, 1st VP OWC
Redstone Arsenal, Alabama

PETITE POIS DELUXE

2 tbsp. butter
1 pkg. frozen peas
2 c. finely shredded lettuce
1/4 c. chopped onion
1 tsp. salt
1/4 tsp. freshly ground pepper
Pinch of sweet basil, tarragon or fresh mint

Melt butter in saucepan; add frozen peas. Cook very slowly until peas defrost. Do not add water. Add lettuce, onion, salt, pepper and basil. Mix lightly. Cover with tightly-fitting lid; steam for 5 minutes. Serve at once. Yield: 4 servings.

Mrs. Robert E. Shrider, Jr., 1st VP OWC
Duluth Intl. Airport AFB, Minnesota

BAKED POTATO BITES

4 med. potatoes
1 med. onion, chopped
Butter
Salt and pepper to taste
Dehydrated parsley flakes
Grated Romano cheese

Scrub potatoes but do not peel. Cut each potato into bite-sized chunks; place in center of aluminum foil rectangle. Add onion to each mound; top with piece of butter. Season with salt and pepper; sprinkle with parsley flakes and cheese. Wrap securely in foil; bake at 375 degrees for 1 hour to 1 hour and 30 minutes. Yield: 4 servings.

Mrs. Stelvin L. Downs, Corr. Sec. OWC
Aviano AFB, Italy

BASQUE POTATOES

2 lb. potatoes, peeled and cut into 1-inch cubes
2 tsp. butter
1/2 c. chopped onion
1 clove of garlic, minced
1/2 c. chopped celery
1/2 c. grated carrot
2 beef bouillon cubes
2 c. boiling water
1 tsp. salt
2 tbsp. chopped parsley

(Continued on next page)

Cover potatoes with water; let stand while preparing sauce. Melt butter in saucepan; add onion, garlic, celery and carrot. Saute until vegetables are limp. Add potatoes; mix thoroughly. Dissolve bouillon cubes in boiling water. Add to potatoes along with salt. Cover; simmer slowly for 20 to 25 minutes until potatoes are tender. Sprinkle with parsley. Yield: 6 servings.

Mrs. Charles Y. Ashton, Ways and Means Chm. OWC
Clinton Sherman AFB, Oklahoma

CHEESY POTATO CASSEROLE

8 to 12 servings instant potatoes
1/2 tsp. garlic salt
1 tbsp. parsley
1 c. sharp cheddar cheese
1 1/2 c. crushed cornflakes
2 tbsp. butter
1/2 tsp. dry mustard
1/2 tsp. paprika
1/4 tsp. salt

Prepare instant potatoes as directed except decrease salt to 1/2 teaspoon and add 1/2 teaspoon garlic salt. Stir parsley and cheese into potatoes; turn into 1 1/2-quart casserole. Mix remaining ingredients; sprinkle over potatoes. Bake at 325 degrees for 20 minutes. May be made ahead of time. Yield: 6 servings.

Mrs. Russel M. Squires, 1st VP OWC
Hohenfels Training Area, Germany

CHEESE POTATOES

1/2 c. flour
1 stick margarine, melted
2 c. milk
1/4 lb. Velveeta cheese
1 green onion, chopped
1/2 tsp. salt
Pepper to taste
2 cans whole new potatoes, drained

Add flour to margarine in top of double boiler, stirring until creamy. Stir in milk; add cheese, stirring often until thick and creamy. Add onion, salt and pepper; add potatoes. Serve hot. Yield: 6 servings.

Mrs. Worth M. Speed, Pres. OWC
Bolling AFB, Washington, D.C.

EASY POTATO PANCAKES

6 lge. potatoes, peeled
2 eggs, well-beaten
2 tbsp. flour
1/2 tsp. baking flour
2 tsp. salt
1 sm. onion, grated
Shortening

(Continued on next page)

Grate washed and dried potatoes, using coarse grater. Drain well in colander; place in bowl. Stir eggs into potatoes. Sift flour, baking powder and salt together; add to potato mixture with onion. Saute by spoonfuls in 1/4-inch or more hot shortening. Turn to brown on second side. May be kept warm in slow oven until serving time.

Mrs. Philip Gerasimoff, OWC
Bainbridge Officer's Wives Club
Bainbridge USNTC, Maryland

EGG AND POTATO CASSEROLE

2 lb. boiled potatoes, peeled and sliced
4 hard-boiled eggs, sliced
1/2 pt. sour cream
1 tsp. salt
1/4 c. butter
1 tbsp. bread crumbs

Arrange layer of potatoes in buttered casserole dish; cover with half the egg. Cover with 2 tablespoons sour cream; sprinkle with salt. Repeat layers; add butter between. Last layer should be remaining potatoes, salt and sour cream; top with bread crumbs. Bake in 350-degree oven for 15 to 20 minutes. Yield: 6 servings.

Mrs. Martin J. Granberg, 772nd OWC
Gibbsboro AFS, New Jersey

GRATED POTATO BAKE

1/2 c. milk
3 eggs
1/2 tsp. salt
1/8 tsp. pepper
1 c. cubed sharp process cheese
2 tbsp. butter
2 tbsp. butter
3 1/2 med. onions
3 med. potatoes, pared and cubed
Green pepper rings (opt.)

Place all ingredients in blender; blend on high speed just till potatoes are grated. Pour into 10 x 6 x 1 1/2-inch baking dish. Bake in 375-degree oven for 35 to 40 minutes. Garnish with green pepper rings, if desired. Yield: 6 servings.

Mrs. George E. Rippey, OWC
Fort Monmouth, New Jersey

GOLDEN PUFF POTATOES

1 1/4 c. water
1/2 tsp. salt
1 1/3 c. instant mashed potatoes
1 c. sour cream
1/4 c. chopped green onions
2 tbsp. Spice Islands salad seasoning
2 tbsp. butter

(Continued on next page)

Heat water and salt to boiling; stir in potatoes until moistened. Blend in sour cream and onions. Turn into lightly buttered 1 1/2-quart casserole; sprinkle salad seasoning over top. Dot with butter. Bake in 375-degree oven for 15 minutes until puffed and golden. Yield: 4 servings.

Mrs. Edward Grunwald, Pres.
Forrestal Officers Wives Club
New York, New York

POTATO-CHEESE CAKES

1 c. mashed potatoes, leftover or instant
1 c. flour
3 tsp. baking powder
1/2 c. grated Parmesan cheese
2 eggs, slightly beaten
1 tsp. parsley flakes
Salt and pepper to taste
Cooking oil

Mix all ingredients except oil. Shape into rolls about 3-inches long and 1-inch wide. Fry in 1-inch hot oil in skillet until golden brown. Serve hot. Yield: 5 servings.

Mrs. Franklin C. Haskins, Wives Club
Dugway Proving Ground, Utah

POTATOES DAUPHINE

Salt
1/2 clove of garlic
1 9-oz. pkg. frozen French-fried potatoes
1 tbsp. flour
3 tbsp. soft butter
1/2 c. grated Swiss or Gruyere cheese
1/4 tsp. pepper
1/4 tsp. onion salt
1/2 c. milk, scalded

Sprinkle a little salt over bottom of baking dish; rub dish with cut side of garlic. Arrange 1/2 of the potatoes in dish. Mix flour, butter, cheese, 1/2 teaspoon salt, pepper and onion salt together; pour in milk, stirring constantly. Pour cheese sauce over potatoes in dish. Repeat layers. Bake in 325-degree oven for 30 minutes. Yield: 4 servings.

Mrs. William C. Sullivan, OWC
USAF Iceland Defense Force, Keflavik, Iceland

POTATO AND CELERY MOLD

12 stalks celery
1 leek
6 lge. potatoes, cubed

(Continued on next page)

Salted water
4 tbsp. butter
2 egg yolks
1/2 c. grated Swiss cheese

Remove threads from celery. Boil vegetables together in salted water until soft; drain. Grind through food mill; add 2 tablespoons butter, egg yolks and 1/4 cup cheese. Beat well with wire whisk or electric blender. Butter 1-quart pudding mold with remaining butter; pour mixture into mold. Bake in 350-degree oven for 15 minutes. Unmold on ovenproof platter; sprinkle with remaining cheese. Brown lightly under broiler.

Mrs. Pierre J. Dolan, Corr. Sec.
Transportation Officers Wives Club
Washington, D. C.

HOT SAUERKRAUT

1/4 c. butter or oleo
1 med. onion, minced
1 lb. sauerkraut, rinsed and drained
1 tsp. Accent
Salt and pepper to taste

Melt butter; saute onion in butter until transparent. Add sauerkraut; cook on low heat for 30 to 40 minutes until tender, stirring occasionally. Season. Yield: 4 servings.

Mrs. Thomas W. Tisler, OWC
Wasser Kuppe AFS, Fulda, Germany

SWEET SAUERKRAUT AND TOMATOES

4 slices bacon
1 med. onion, diced
1 No. 2 1/2 can tomatoes
1 No. 2 1/2 can sauerkraut
3/4 c. sugar

Fry bacon crisp; drain. Fry onion in bacon drippings. Combine tomatoes, sauerkraut, onion and sugar in saucepan; stir to mix. Crumble bacon over top of mixture; cover. Simmer for 30 minutes, stirring occasionally. Serve with fork. Yield: 6 servings.

Mrs. Charles R. Thomas, Memshp. Chm. OWC
Washington, D. C.

CREAMY SPINACH

1 pkg. chopped frozen spinach
1/2 tsp. garlic salt
Salt and pepper to taste
1 tbsp. butter
1 sm. can mushrooms, drained
1/2 c. sour cream

Cook spinach according to package directions; drain. Season spinach. Add butter to mushrooms; mix into spinach. Stir in sour cream; serve immediately. Yield: 4 servings.

Mrs. A. G. Thompson, VP OWC
Dobbins AFB, Georgia

QUICK CREAMED SPINACH

2 pkg. frozen chopped spinach
2 10 1/2-oz. cans cream of chicken soup
1/2 tsp. salt
1/4 tsp. pepper
1/4 tsp. nutmeg
2 tsp. grated onion (opt.)

Cook spinach according to package directions; do not drain. Add soup; season with salt, pepper, nutmeg and onion. Serve hot. Yield: 4-6 servings.

Mrs. Niels M. Johnsen, OWC
Sunny Point Military Ocean Terminal, North Carolina

SHERRIED SPINACH

1 pkg. frozen chopped spinach
1 tbsp. butter
1 tbsp. sherry
2 tbsp. slivered almonds or sliced water
    chestnuts
Nutmeg, salt and pepper to taste

Cook spinach as directed on package; drain. Stir in remaining ingredients; place in buttered casserole. Bake at 350 to 375 degrees until heated through. Casserole may be assembled in advance; refrigerate until ready to serve. Yield: 2-3 servings.

Mrs. John S. Lekson, OWC
Fort Campbell, Kentucky

SCRUMPTIOUS SPINACH

2 10-oz. pkg. frozen chopped spinach, thawed
    and drained
2 c. sour cream
1/2 pkg. onion soup mix
1 4-oz. can mushroom pieces, drained
1 clove of garlic, pressed
1/2 tsp. dillweed
1/2 c. buttered bread crumbs
1/2 c. grated Parmesan cheese

(Continued on next page)

Mix spinach, sour cream, soup mix, mushrooms and seasonings; place in casserole. Top with crumbs and cheese. Bake at 350 degrees for 20 minutes or until thoroughly hot. May be made in advance; refrigerate until ready to bake. Yield: 6 servings.

Mrs. C. A. Dahlen, Hon. VP OWC
Ft. Sam Houston, Texas

SCRUMPTIOUS SPINACH

2 10-oz. pkg. frozen chopped spinach, thawed
   and drained
1 egg
1 10 1/2-oz. can cream of mushroom soup

Place spinach in electric blender; add egg and soup. Blend until smooth; pour into 2-quart buttered baking dish. Bake in 350-degree oven for 30 minutes. Garnish with ground nutmeg and hard-cooked eggs. Yield: 6 servings.

Mrs. William Boehm, Pres. OWC
Navy Elec. Lab. Center, San Diego, California

SPINACH CASSEROLE

2 pkg. frozen chopped spinach
1 8-oz. pkg. cream cheese, softened
2 tbsp. horseradish
1 c. sour cream
6 slices bacon, fried and crumbled
Salt to taste
1 c. Pepperidge Farm bread stuffing mix
1/2 stick oleo or butter, melted

Cook spinach according to package directions; drain. Blend in cream cheese; add next 4 ingredients. Mix well; place in casserole. Mix stuffing mix with melted oleo; sprinkle on top. Bake for 20 to 30 minutes in 350-degree oven. Casserole may be assembled and refrigerated overnight. Add bacon; top with stuffing mix just before baking. Yield: 6 servings.

Mrs. William H. Leonard, 1st VP MOWC
Atsugi, Japan

SPINACH-ONION CASSEROLE

3 10-oz. pkg. frozen chopped spinach
1 1 1/2-oz. pkg. dry onion soup mix
1/2 pt. sour cream
3 tbsp. dry or medium sherry
1/2 3 1/2-oz. can French-fried onion rings

Cook spinach according to package directions; drain well. Combine spinach, onion soup mix, sour cream and sherry; place in greased casserole. Let stand for

(Continued on next page)

1 to 2 hours to blend flavors. Top spinach with onion rings. Bake, uncovered, at 350 degrees for 20 minutes or until bubbly. Yield: 8 servings.

Mrs. Jerry W. Mitchell, Pres. OWC
Beaufort MCAS, South Carolina

SPINACH QUICKIE

2 pkg. frozen spinach
1 can condensed cream of mushroom soup
Dash of nutmeg

Thaw spinach in strainer; press out liquid. Mix with soup and nutmeg; place in buttered casserole. Bake in 350-degree oven until bubbly. Yield: 3-4 servings.

Mrs. John B. Schley, Women's Club Exec. Bd.
Armed Forces Staff College, Norfolk, Virginia

SPINACH AND RICE

3 tbsp. dried onions
2 c. Minute rice
2 tbsp. salad oil
2 c. water
3/4 tsp. salt
1 pkg. frozen chopped spinach
1 sm. can tomato sauce
2 tbsp. catsup

Saute onions and rice in salad oil; add water and salt. Bring to a boil; cover. Remove from heat; let stand for 5 minutes. Cook spinach according to package directions. Add spinach, tomato sauce and catsup to rice, fluffing rice with fork. Heat; serve. Yield: 4-6 servings.

Mrs. George Starr, Sec. OWC
Savanna Army Depot, Illinois

SUPER SPINACH CASSEROLE

2 boxes frozen chopped spinach
1 pkg. Lipton's dry onion soup mix
1 c. sour cream

Cook spinach as directed; drain. Add onion soup mix and sour cream; place in casserole. Bake at 350 degrees for 20 minutes. May be prepared in advance; bake just before serving. Yield: 4-6 servings.

Mrs. H. M. Berthold, W and M Chm. OWC
RAF, Wethersfield, England

SPINACH VERONESE

1 box frozen chopped spinach, drained
3 tbsp. Wesson oil

(Continued on next page)

1 clove of garlic
3 or 4 small dried chili peppers
1/4 tsp. oregano
Salt

Cook spinach according to package directions. Heat oil; brown garlic and chili peppers. Remove garlic and chili peppers from oil; add oregano immediately. Cool oil slightly; add spinach. Cook slowly for 10 minutes; salt to taste. Add chili peppers; serve hot or cold. Yield: 4 servings.

Mrs. Joseph A. Rita, Rec. Sec. OWC
Wheeler AFB, Hawaii

BAKED ZUCCHINI CASSEROLE

2 No. 303 cans zucchini in tomato sauce
3 slices garlic bread, crumbled
1/4 c. grated Parmesan cheese

Spread zucchini in baking dish; cover with garlic bread crumbs. Sprinkle with Parmesan cheese. Bake at 350 degrees for 15 to 20 minutes or until liquid is reduced to desired amount. Yield: 6 servings.

Mrs. Scott T. Chandler, Pres. OWC
F. E. Warren AFB, Wyoming

CHEESE AND ZUCCHINI

3 med. zucchini
Salt and pepper to taste
3 3 1/2 x 1/8-inch slices American cheese,
    halved

Parboil zucchini; halve lengthwise. Arrange in shallow, heavily buttered baking dish; sprinkle with salt and pepper. Place cheese on each zucchini half. Bake at 350 degrees until cheese is melted and bubbly. Yield: 6 servings.

Mrs. William Ringness, OWC
Treasure Island, San Francisco, California

CHINESE ZUCCHINI

1 sm. onion, sliced
1 clove of garlic, minced
2 tbsp. bacon grease
4 unpeeled zucchini, sliced
1/4 c. soy sauce
2 tbsp. water

Cook onion and garlic in bacon grease until golden; add zucchini, soy sauce and water. Cover; simmer until zucchini is slightly tender, 5 to 8 minutes. Yield: 4-6 servings.

Mrs. William J. Gammon, Parlm. OWC
Travis AFB, California

ITALIAN-STYLE ZUCCHINI

6 zucchini
Butter
Salt and pepper to taste
Mozzarella cheese strips

Parboil zucchini; drain. Cut ends off; halve lengthwise. Place in ovenproof dish; score. Dot with butter; sprinkle with salt and pepper. Place cheese strips on each zucchini. Bake at 350 degrees until cheese is melted. Yield: 6 servings.

Mrs. Ronald J. Tribo, Pres. OWC
Ramey AFB, Puerto Rico

SAUTEED SUMMER SQUASH WITH SOUR CREAM

4 or 5 peeled yellow summer squash, julienned
1/4 c. butter
1 tbsp. flour
1 c. sour cream
1 onion, chopped fine
Dash of paprika

Saute squash in butter for 15 minutes until almost tender. Stir flour to paste with small amount of sour cream; add to squash. Stir in remaining sour cream, onion and paprika; simmer 5 minutes until onion is tender. Yield: 4 servings.

Mrs. H. E. Palmer, Treas. OWC
McGuire AFB, New Jersey

SQUASH KISHUIM (ISRAEL)

1/8 lb. butter
1 onion, minced
1 tomato, sliced
4 yellow squash, peeled and cut in 2-inch
    slices
1/2 tsp. salt
Dash of pepper
1 tsp. lemon juice

(Continued on next page)

Melt butter; saute onion until golden. Add tomato and squash. Cover; cook over low heat for 20 minutes. Season with salt, pepper and lemon juice. Yield: 6 servings.

Mrs. H. W. McCall, Cookbook Chm. OWC
Fort Campbell, Kentucky

SQUASH CREOLE

1/2 c. chopped green onions
1 tbsp. butter or margarine
2 lb. small yellow squash or zucchini,
    sliced diagonally
1 tsp. salt
Dash of pepper
1 1-lb. can stewed tomatoes

Saute green onions in hot butter in large skillet until tender, about 3 minutes. Add squash, salt and pepper; toss lightly. Cover; cook over low heat for 15 minutes or just until squash is tender. Add tomatoes; toss to combine. Cook, covered, for 1 minute longer or until mixture is heated through. Yield: 8 servings.

Mrs. Lee McClendon, Adv. OWC
K. I. Sawyer AFB, Michigan

ZUCCHINI

4 or 5 zucchini, sliced in rounds
1 lge. onion, diced
Salt and pepper to taste
Water
2 tomatoes, chopped
1/2 c. sharp grated cheese
Tabasco sauce to taste
Parmesan cheese

Simmer zucchini and onion in seasoned water until barely tender, about 10 minutes; drain. Place half the zucchini in casserole; add half the tomatoes and half the grated cheese. Season with dash of Tabasco sauce; repeat. Cover with Parmesan cheese. Bake at 325 to 350 degrees until cheese is melted. Yield: 6 servings.

Mrs. Clyde T. Earnest, Jr., Member at Large OWC
US Military Academy, West Point, New York

CANDIED SWEET POTATOES

2 cans sweet potatoes
3 tbsp. butter
1 tbsp. lemon juice
3/4 c. corn syrup
1/4 c. brown sugar

Place potatoes in frying pan; add remaining ingredients. Cook for 15 to 20 minutes. Dip sauce over potatoes when served. Yield: 6 servings.

Mrs. Samuel W. Koster, Hon. Pres. OWC
West Point, New York

HOLIDAY SWEET POTATO BALLS

1/2 c. brown sugar
1/4 c. sugar
1/2 c. finely chopped pecans
1 1-lb. 14-oz. can sweet potatoes, drained and mashed
Large marshmallows
Finely crushed cornflakes

Add sugars and pecans to sweet potatoes; mix thoroughly. Form ball of potato mixture, using 1 marshmallow as center; roll in cornflakes. Repeat procedure until all potato mixture is used. Place on cookie sheet. Bake in 350-degree oven for 20 to 30 minutes or until entire ball is warm. Marshmallow will begin to melt inside ball. Serve hot. Yield: 10-12 balls.

Mrs. Haskell L. Johnson, Pres. OWC
Schofield Barracks, Hawaii

KENTUCKY BOURBON YAMS

2 No. 2 1/2 cans yams
1 c. brown sugar
2 tbsp. butter
2 tbsp. milk
1/4 c. bourbon
Marshmallows

Heat yams; drain. Mash until light and fluffy; add remaining ingredients. Pour into 1-quart casserole; top with marshmallows. Bake for 15 minutes at 350 degrees. Fresh yams may be used. Boil until tender; peel. Yield: 4-6 servings.

Mrs. Charles L. Neugent, OWC
NAS Glynco, Georgia

SWEET POTATO SOUFFLE

1 No. 2 1/2 can sweet potatoes
1/3 c. milk
1/2 stick margarine
1/2 c. chopped pecans
1/4 c. sugar
1 egg, beaten
1/2 tsp. cinnamon
1/8 tsp. salt
Marshmallows

(Continued on next page)

Heat sweet potatoes in saucepan; drain. Mash with electric mixer. Add remaining ingredients except marshmallows, beating with mixer to desired consistency. Add more milk if necessary. Place sweet potato mixture in 1 1/2-quart baking dish; top with marshmallows. Brown in 350-degree oven for about 10 minutes. Yield: 6 servings.

Mrs. Norman F. Conant, Jr., 3rd VP OWC
Moody AFB, Georgia

TIPSY SWEET POTATOES

1 can cooked sweet potatoes or 4 to 6 fresh
    sweet potatoes, sliced
3/4 c. brown sugar
1/2 c. bourbon
2 tbsp. butter
1/4 tsp. salt
Dash of angostura bitters

Place sweet potatoes in baking dish. Combine all ingredients except bitters; cook over low heat for 3 to 5 minutes. Remove from heat; add bitters. Pour over potatoes. Bake at 350 to 375 degrees for 30 minutes. Yield: 4 servings.

Mrs. William E. Wilson, Treas. OWC
Hahn AFB, Germany

EASY SCALLOPED TOMATOES

4 slices toasted bread
1 16-oz. can tomatoes
1 tsp. instant minced onion
1 tbsp. sugar
1/2 tsp. salt
Dash of Tabasco sauce
1 tbsp. Worcestershire sauce
1/4 c. melted butter
1/4 c. shredded cheddar cheese

Cut 3 slices toast in 1/2-inch cubes. Cut remaining toast in triangles. Combine tomatoes, onion, sugar, salt, Tabasco sauce and Worcestershire sauce. Alternate layers of toast cubes and tomato mixture in buttered 1 1/2-quart casserole. Arrange toast triangles on top; pour butter over toast. Sprinkle with cheese. Bake at 375 degrees for 35 minutes. Yield: 4 servings.

Mrs. James G. Towle, Publ. Chm. OWC
Hancock AFB, Syracuse, New York

MRS. EISENHOWER'S RECIPE FOR TOMATO PUDDING

1/4 c. boiling water
1 10-oz. can tomato puree
1/4 tsp. salt
1 c. light brown sugar
1 c. white bread, cut into 1-inch cubes
1/4 c. melted butter

(Continued on next page)

Combine boiling water, puree, salt and sugar in saucepan. Boil for 5 minutes. Place bread cubes in casserole. Pour melted butter over bread cubes; add tomato mixture. Bake, covered, for 30 minutes at 375 degrees.

Mrs. Dwight D. Eisenhower
Wife of Former Pres. of US
Gettysburg, Pennsylvania

SUGAR-TOMATO BAKE

1/4 c. finely chopped onion
6 tbsp. melted butter
2 1-lb. cans tomatoes
6 tbsp. brown sugar
1 1/2 c. packaged croutons
3/4 tsp. salt

Cook onion in 2 tablespoons butter until soft. Combine onion mixture, tomatoes and 4 tablespoons brown sugar in 10 x 6-inch baking dish. Add remaining butter, remaining brown sugar and salt to croutons; mix gently. Sprinkle over tomato mixture. Bake at 375 degrees for 20 minutes. Yield: 5-6 servings.

Mrs. Charles N. Reed, Assoc. Ed. OWC
USN Hosp., Oakland, California

VEGETABLE CASSEROLE

1 10-oz. pkg. frozen peas
1 10-oz. pkg. frozen carrots
1 No. 303 can small onions, drained
2 10 1/2-oz. cans cream of celery soup
1/2 soup can milk

Combine all ingredients in 1 1/2-quart casserole. Bake in 350-degree oven for 1 hour. Casserole will hold for 1 hour; add milk, as needed. Yield: 6-8 servings.

Mrs. John R. Edwards, Corr. Sec. OWC
Fort Carson, Colorado

VENETIAN RICE AND PEAS

4 bacon slices
3 tbsp. butter
1 sm. onion, minced
1 10-oz. pkg. frozen peas
3/4 c. raw regular rice
2 c. canned chicken broth
1 tbsp. salt
Dash of pepper
1/4 c. shredded Parmesan cheese

Saute bacon until crisp in heavy skillet; remove bacon. Pour off fat; melt butter in same skillet. Cook onion and frozen peas for 5 minutes, stirring frequently. Add rice; stir until coated with butter. Stir in chicken broth, salt and pepper; cover. Simmer, stirring occasionally, for about 20 minutes or until rice absorbs all liquid. Toss with cheese and crisp bacon. Yield: 6 servings.

Mrs. Don K. Allen, Asst. Treas. OWC
K. I. Sawyer AFB, Michigan

Cereal and Pasta Dishes

RECIPE FOR CHEESE-NOODLE CASSEROLE ON PAGE 199

GARLIC GRITS

2 c. grits
1 1/2 qt. water
1/2 c. milk
2 rolls garlic cheese
4 eggs, beaten
1/4 lb. butter
Salt and pepper to taste
Parmesan cheese
Paprika

Cook grits in water in saucepan until done. Add milk, cheese, eggs, butter and seasonings. Pour into buttered 13 x 9-inch casserole dish. Sprinkle with Parmesan cheese and paprika. Bake at 300 degrees for 30 minutes. Yield: 12 servings.

Mrs. Lenson W. Graves, Pres. OWC
Jacksonville NAS, Florida

SUSIE'S PARTY GRITS CASSEROLE

1 c. grits
1 tsp. salt
4 1/2 c. water
1 roll garlic cheese
2 eggs, beaten
1/2 c. milk
2 tbsp. butter or margarine
1 c. cornflakes, crushed

Cook grits in salted water for 5 minutes. Remove from heat. Melt 3/4 the cheese into grits. Mix eggs and milk; beat into grits. Turn into a buttered casserole. Melt butter in saucepan; add remaining cheese and cornflakes. Stir into casserole. Bake for 45 minutes at 350 degrees. Yield: 10 servings.

Toby G. Mahin, Hon. Pres. NOWC
Philadelphia NAS, Pennsylvania

HOMINY AND TOMATO CASSEROLE

1 lge. onion, minced
2 tbsp. oil
1 l-lb. 12 oz. can tomatoes, drained
Chili powder, sugar and monosodium
    glutamate to taste
1 1-lb. 13 oz. can yellow hominy, drained
1 1/4 c. grated sharp cheddar cheese

Cook onion in oil in skillet until lightly browned. Add tomatoes and seasonings. Simmer, stirring frequently, for 30 minutes or until most of liquid has evaporated. Add hominy; heat through. Remove mixture from heat; stir in cheese. May also be baked in 350-degree oven for 30 to 40 minutes. Yield: 4-6 servings.

Mrs. James G. Watt, Chm. of Antiques and Home Decorations, OWC
Carlisle Barracks, Pennsylvania

BAKED RICE

1 4-oz. can mushrooms
1 onion, chopped
2 c. rice
Butter
4 c. boiling water
2 chicken or beef bouillon cubes

Saute mushrooms, onion and rice in small amount of butter in flame-proof casserole dish. Add boiling water with bouillon cubes to mixture. Bake at 350 degrees for 30 minutes. Yield: 6 servings.

Mrs. Bernard L. Weiss, 1st VP OWC
Los Angeles AFS, California

CHINESE FRIED RICE

1/2 c. coarsely ground ham, cooked chicken or
    cooked pork
2 tbsp. oil
1 sm. can mushrooms
1 1/2 tbsp. green onion, finely chopped
1 qt. cold cooked rice
3 tbsp. soy sauce
1 well-beaten egg

Fry meat lightly in oil in skillet. Add mushrooms, onion, rice and soy sauce. Cook for 10 minutes. Stir once or twice; add egg. Cook for 5 minutes, stirring frequently. Yield: 4 servings.
PERSONAL NOTE: Recipe is from our cook in Tainan, Taiwan.

Mrs. Albert Ward, Hon. VP OWC
Hahn AFB, Germany

CONSOMME AND RICE

1/2 c. uncooked rice
1 can consomme soup
1 tbsp. butter

Place rice and soup in covered baking dish. Bake in 350-degree oven for 40 minutes or until rice has absorbed all liquid, but is not dry. Add butter. Consomme may be substituted with 1 can onion soup. Both may be used when doubling recipe. Yield: 4 servings.

Mrs. Floyd Standage, Social Chm. OWC
Torrejan AFB, Spain

DIRTY RICE A LA CAMP

1/2 stick butter or margarine
1 can onion soup
1 4-oz. can sliced or chopped mushrooms
    with liquid
1 c. rice

(Continued on next page)

Combine butter, soup and mushrooms in saucepan. Heat till butter melts. Add rice; cover. Cook over low heat until tender. One package dry onion soup mix and 2 1/4 cups water may be substituted for canned soup.

Mrs. David A. Brigman, Past Pres. OWC
Tempelhof Central Airport, Germany

EASY RICE BAKE

Butter or margarine
1 c. rice
2 c. boiling water
1/2 tsp. salt

Butter generously 2-quart casserole; add rice. Pour over boiling water; dot with butter. Salt to taste. Bake at 350 degrees for 45 minutes. Serve with butter. Yield: 6 servings
PERSONAL NOTE: Being a potato fan I've never been able to boil rice to please my husband. After many tears and a letter to mother my husband now compliments my baked rice.

Mrs. Robert I. Hughes, OWC
Birkenfeld AFS, West Germany

EASY RICE PILAF

2/3 stick plus 1 tbsp. butter
2 tsp. paprika
2 c. (heaping) long grain rice
1 med. onion, finely chopped
1 can sliced mushrooms, drained
4 c. chicken or beef broth or consomme
Cayenne pepper to taste
1 tsp. salt

Melt 2/3 stick butter in pan; stir in paprika and rice. Braise, stirring briskly until it bubbles. Remove from heat. Gently saute onion in another pan in 1 table-spoon butter until transparent. Place into 2 1/2-quart casserole dish with rice, mushrooms and broth. Season with cayenne and salt; cover. Bake at 375 degrees for 30 minutes; stir. Bake for 15 minutes. Yield: 4-6 servings.

Mrs. Terry Ginsburg, OWC
San Miguel NAV STA, Philippines

GREEN CHILI—RICE

1 c. raw rice, cooked and cooled
1 c. sour cream
1/2 lb. cubed cheddar cheese
1 4-oz. can chopped green chili peppers

Mix rice and sour cream; add cheese and peppers. Place in greased 2-quart casserole. Bake for 35 to 40 minutes at 350 degrees. Yield: 6 servings.
PERSONAL NOTE: This dish is of Mexican origin.

Mrs. Richard R. Stevens, Golf Chm. OWC
Ft. Riley, Kansas

FRIED RICE

1 egg
2 tbsp. butter
2 c. cooked Minute rice
1/2 c. onions, diced
1/2 c. shrimp, crab, bacon or ham, diced
1/2 c. frozen peas
1 1/2 tbsp. soy sauce

Scramble egg in butter in skillet; add remaining ingredients except soy sauce. Mix well. Simmer for 10 minutes. Stir gently, adding soy sauce. Simmer for 2 minutes longer. Yield: 4 servings.

Mrs. Robert A. Thompson, Ed. of Publn. OWC
Laredo AFB, Texas

GOLDEN RICE BAKE

1 pt. cooked rice
1 qt. grated carrots
3 beaten eggs
1 tsp. salt
2 tbsp. minced onions
1/2 c. milk
1 lb. grated American cheese

Combine all ingredients in well-greased baking pan, reserving half the cheese. Bake at 350 degrees for 15 to 25 minutes. Sprinkle remaining cheese over top. Bake for 10 minutes longer.

Mrs. Burnette S. Harrison, Cookbook Chm. OWC
USN Supply Center
Oakland, California

MUSHROOM RICE

Precooked rice
1 3-oz. can sliced broiled mushrooms, drained
1/4 c. butter

Prepare rice as directed on package in quantity needed. Heat mushrooms with butter in pan until butter melts; pour over rice. Toss with fork until well mixed. Season to taste.

Mrs. Robert L. Cardenas, Hon. Bd. Member, OWC
Eglin AFB, Florida

OUTDOOR INDIAN PILAF

1/3 c. butter
1 c. large grain rice, uncooked
1 clove of garlic, minced
2 1/2 to 3 c. beef bouillon
1/4 c. raisins
2 tbsp. toasted almonds

(Continued on next page)

Combine butter, rice and garlic in skillet. Saute until rice turns orange; remove from heat. Add bouillon; cover with tight lid. Simmer for 45 to 50 minutes or until liquid is absorbed and rice is tender; check pilaf after 30 minutes and add bouillon if needed. Remove from heat; sprinkle with raisins and almonds. Serve immediately. Yield: 4 servings.

PERSONAL NOTE: I received this recipe from an Air Force wife, Sally Majaros, while assigned together in Naples, Italy.

Mrs. W. A. Cauthen, Jr., Projects and Activities Chm. OWC
Schwabisch Gmund, Germany

ONION RICE

1/2 c. diced celery
2 tbsp. butter or oleo
1 c. converted rice
2 c. water
1 pkg. dry onion soup mix
1 tsp. salt

Saute celery in butter in pan. Mix with remaining ingredients in 1 1/2-quart casserole with cover. Bake, covered, in 350-degree oven for 1 hour. Yield: 4-6 servings.

Mrs. Robert E. Barker, Group II Chm. OWC
Camp Lejeune, North Carolina

ORIENTAL FRIED RICE

2 tbsp. bacon grease
1 or 2 sm. green onions, chopped
1 c. chopped shrimp, ham or chicken
2 c. cold, cooked rice
1 egg, beaten

Heat grease in large cast iron skillet over medium heat. Saute onions with meat. Add rice; toss several times till rice begins to separate. Pour egg into pan; stir quickly. Serve when egg and rice are somewhat dry. Yield: 4 servings.

Mrs. Joseph C. Mellon, II, OWC
Germany

RICE CASSEROLE

1 c. uncooked regular rice
1 soup can consomme
1 soup can bouillon
1 onion, chopped
1/3 stick butter
1/2 tsp. salt

Spread rice in 1 1/2-quart baking dish. Mix other ingredients in saucepan. Heat till hot and butter is melted; pour over rice. Stir to mix. Bake for 1 hour, covered, at 325 degrees. Yield: 4 servings.

PERSONAL NOTE: Recipe was given to me by a Public Health Service Doctor's wife. We just love it.

Mrs. Joseph J. Bookout, Rec. Sec. CG OWC
Alameda, California

PARSLEY RICE

2 c. water
2 chicken bouillon cubes
1 tsp. salt
1/2 tsp. cooking oil
1 c. raw rice
1/3 c. sliced green onion
1/2 c. diced green pepper
1/3 c. slivered, unblanched almonds
2 tbsp. margarine
1/2 c. coarsely chopped parsley

Bring water, bouillon cubes, salt and oil to a boil in saucepan. Add rice; stir. Cover; turn heat down to low. Cook for 20 minutes or until rice is fluffy and water is absorbed. Saute onion, green pepper and almonds in margarine in skillet for 2 minutes. Fold in cooked rice; add parsley. Serve with soy sauce, if desired. Yield: 6 servings.

Mrs. Joseph Demarke, VP OWC
Pearl Harbor NAS, Oahu, Hawaii

RICE CASSEROLE

1 box or bag of herb or curry rice
1 c. frozen peas
1 can sliced mushrooms
3/4 stick butter
2 c. boiling water

Place all ingredients in casserole dish. Mix slightly; cover. Bake at 350 degrees for 50 minutes. Yield: 5 servings.

Mrs. Morton Bregman, Pres. OWC
Perrin AFB, Texas

RICE CASSEROLE

1 1/2 c. regular long grain rice
1 can chicken gumbo soup
1 can consomme
1 can mushrooms, drained
1 1/2 cans water
1/2 cube butter or oleo

Combine all ingredients in baking dish. Bake, covered, at 350 degrees for 1 hour.

Mrs. R. W. Musgrove, OWC
Cecil Field, Florida

RICE CURRY

2 med. onions, chopped
2 stalks celery, chopped
3 tsp. parsley
1/2 stick butter
1 to 2 tsp. curry powder
1 10-oz. pkg. Minute rice

(Continued on next page)

Saute together onions, celery and parsley in butter in pan. Add curry powder and beef consomme. Bring consomme mixture to a boil. Add rice; cover for 5 minutes. Remove from heat. Yield: 6 servings.

Mrs. John J. Paolino, 1st CP OWC
Laredo AFB, Texas

RICE AND GREEN CHILIES

3/4 lb. Monterey Jack cheese, cut in
    domino-sized strips
2 cans green chilies
3 c. cooked rice
3 c. sour cream
Salt and pepper to taste
1/2 c. grated cheddar or Monterey Jack
    cheese

Stuff cheese strips into chilies. Place in 1 1/2-quart buttered casserole. Mix rice, sour cream, salt and pepper. Add to casserole; smooth top. Sprinkle grated cheese on top. Bake at 350 degrees for 25 minutes. Yield: 6-8 servings.
PERSONAL NOTE: My husband and I enjoy the rice and chilies, but the children like only the rice. This is easily served to all of us.

Mrs. J. E. McCardell, Treas. OWC
Miramar NAS, California

RICE AND MUSHROOM CASSEROLE

2 2/3 c. precooked rice
6 tbsp. salad oil
2 sm. cans mushrooms, drained
1/2 c. chopped green onion
2 cans beef consomme
2 tbsp. soy sauce
1/2 tsp. salt

Mix all ingredients. Bake in covered casserole at 350 degrees for 30 to 45 minutes or until all liquid is absorbed. Do not stir. Prepare in advance by placing all dry ingredients in casserole. Add liquids just before baking. Yield: 6 servings.

Mrs. Ralph Graham, Adv. OWC
US NAG DET, Korea

RICE-NOODLE DISH

1/2 c. margarine
1 c. white rice
1 c. thin egg noodles
1 can onion soup
1 can beef consomme

Melt margarine in heavy saucepan. Brown slightly rice and noodles in melted margarine. Add soup and consomme; mix well. Cover. Simmer until done. Yield: 6 servings.

Mrs. Alan R. Pendleton, Projects Chm. OWC
Pearl Harbor NAS, Oahu, Hawaii

SAVORY RICE CASSEROLE

1 c. uncooked rice
1 c. boiling water
1 No. 1 1/2 can tomatoes
1 tsp. salt
2 tbsp. butter
1/4 c. vegetable flakes
2 tbsp. onion flakes
1/4 lb. grated cheese

Mix all ingredients; pour into ungreased 2-quart casserole. Bake, covered, at 350 degrees for 45 minutes; uncover. Bake for 20 minutes more. Yield: 4 servings.

Mrs. Paul Deranian, Sec. MOWC
Miramar NAS, California

STEAMED RICE IN OVEN

1 c. long grain white rice
1 tsp. salt
2 c. boiling water
2 tbsp. melted butter

Place rice and salt in 1-quart casserole. Add boiling water and melted butter; Cover casserole. Bake in 350-degree oven for 40 to 45 minutes. Recipe may be doubled and baked in a 2-quart casserole. This recipe is especially nice for buffet parties as it may be baked in oven and forgotten for 45 minutes. Yield: 4 servings.

Mrs. Leon C. Luther, Manager Thrift Shop OWC
Picatinny Arsenal, New Jersey

SURPRISE BAKED RICE

1 c. rice
2 tbsp. margarine
1 sm. onion, chopped
2 c. hot water
1 tsp. salt
1 envelope Good Seasons salad dressing
    mix, French, Italian or blue cheese
1 2-oz. can sliced mushrooms and liquid
Tomato wedges
Sour cream with chives
Diced chicken or ham (opt.)

Brown rice in margarine in skillet. Add onion, hot water, salt, salad dressing mix, mushrooms and liquid; mix well. Pour into 1 1/2-quart casserole. Bake, covered, for 45 minutes at 350 degrees or until liquid is absorbed. Remove from oven; top with tomato wedges. Return to oven for 10 minutes, uncovered. Serve with sour cream with chives. Add chicken or ham for a main dish. Yield: 5 servings.

Mrs. David F. Loomis, Pres. USOWC
Navy Section MAAG, Taiwan

WESTERN GRAIN CASSEROLE

1/4 c. butter or margarine
1 1/2 c. barley
1 envelope onion soup mix
2 3/4 c. boiling water
1 4-oz. can mushrooms
Shredded cheddar cheese (opt.)

Melt butter in saucepan; add barley. Stir until barley is lightly browned, adding more butter if necessary. Add onion soup mix and boiling water. Bring to a boil. Turn into 6-cup heatproof casserole dish. Top with mushrooms; cover. Bake at 350 degrees for 1 hour or until liquid is absorbed. Top with cheese; bake for 5 minutes. Certain brands of barley may require 30 minutes longer baking time and one-fourth cup more water, which may be added to keep barley from drying out during baking. Dish should be moist and tender. Yield: 6 servings.
PERSONAL NOTE: This is deliciously similar to Western Grain served at famous Nut Tree restaurant near Sacramento, California.

Mrs. S. W. Honeychurch, Nursery Chm. OWC
Mannehim, Germany

CHEESE AND MACARONI IN WINE

2 c. uncooked macaroni
2 tbsp. butter
1 1/2 c. cubed cheese
1/2 tsp. salt
1/2 tsp. dry mustard
2 eggs, beaten
1 1/2 c. thin cream
1/2 c. white wine
3 tbsp. chopped green pepper

Combine all ingredients; mix well. Place in buttered 2-quart casserole; cover. Bake at 350 degrees for 60 minutes. Let stand for 10 minutes before serving. Yield: 6 servings.

Mrs. Carl R. Webb, Ways and Means Chm. OWC
Naha AFB, Okinawa

MACARONI-TOMATO CASSEROLE

Hot boiled macaroni (7 or 8-oz. uncooked)
2 c. cut-up sharp cheddar cheese
1 tsp. salt
1/4 tsp. pepper
2 1/2 c. well seasoned cooked tomatoes

Preheat oven to 350 degrees. Place cooked macaroni, cheese, salt and pepper in alternate layers in buttered oblong baking dish, ending with layer of cheese on top. Pour tomatoes over all. Bake for 35 to 45 minutes or until liquid is absorbed. Garnish if desired with parsley sprigs, pimento strips or pepper rings. Yield: 6-8 servings.

Mrs. Robert S. Denehy, Hospitality Chm. O and CWC
Hardt Kaserne, Germany

GEORGIA'S MACARONI CASSEROLE

2 med. green peppers
2 med. onions
1 tbsp. liquid cooking oil
1 8-oz. box elbow macaroni
1/2 pt. sour cream
1 14-oz. can Italian tomatoes
1/2 c. Parmesan cheese

Slice green peppers and onions; fry in oil for 5 minutes over medium heat. Cook macaroni in boiling, salted water until done; drain. Pour back into cooking pot. Add fried vegetables, sour cream, tomatoes and cheese. Mix all together; taste. Add little salt, if necessary. Pour into 4-quart casserole. Bake in 325-degree oven for 25 minutes. Yield: 4-6 servings.

Mrs. William R. Cameron, Hon. VP OWC
McCoy AFB, Florida

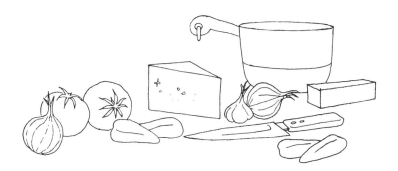

MACARONI WITH TOMATO AND CHEESE

1 12-oz. pkg. macaroni
1 15-oz. can tomato sauce
1 10 1/2-oz. can tomato puree
3/4 c. milk
1 egg
1 tsp. sugar
1 tsp. salt
1/2 tsp. pepper
1 1/2 c. sharp cheddar cheese, grated
1/2 c. crushed potato chips

Cook macaroni as directed. Mix remaining ingredients, except cheese and potato chips. Alternate layers of macaroni and cheese in large baking dish. Pour tomato mixture over macaroni; sprinkle with cheese and potato chips. Bake at 400 degrees until cheese is well browned. Yield: 6-8 servings.

Mrs. Casper R. Van Dien, VT-2 Rep. OWC
NAS, Whiting Field, Florida

MACARONI CASSEROLE

1 1-lb. box macaroni broken in pieces, cooked
    according to directions on box
8 1-oz. slices American cheese
1 green pepper, cut in strips
5 tbsp. butter or margarine
1 1-lb. can tomatoes
1 sm. onion, minced
1 clove of garlic, halved
Salt and pepper to taste

Cook macaroni in salted, boiling water; drain. Arrange macaroni, cheese and green pepper in layers in greased 1 1/2-quart casserole; dot with butter. Repeat. Heat tomatoes, onion, garlic, salt and pepper in small saucepan; pour on top of macaroni mixture. Bake for 1 hour at 350 degrees. Yield: 6 servings.

Mrs. Walter B. Forman, Hospital Chm. OWC
Lockbourne AFB, Ohio

SEABEE SURPRISE

1 pkg. sm. elbow macaroni
1/2 c. catsup
1 pkg. grated cheddar cheese
1/2 c. milk

Cook elbow macaroni according to directions on package. Layer macaroni in greased 1 1/2-quart casserole. Sprinkle 1/2 of catsup and 1/2 of cheese on top. Cover with another layer of macaroni, catsup and cheese. Pour milk over mixture; mix gently. Bake in 350-degree oven, uncovered until bubbly and brown, for 30 minutes. Yield: 6 servings.

Mrs. Stephen M. Brenner, Parlm. OWC
Port Hueneme, California

SPECIAL MACARONI AND CHEESE CASSEROLE

1/2 lb. uncooked macaroni
2 tbsp. chopped green pepper
2 tbsp. chopped onion
3 tbsp. butter
3 tbsp. flour
2 c. milk
3/4 c. sharp cheddar cheese, grated
1 tbsp. minced parsley
1/2 tsp. dry mustard
Dash of salt, pepper and garlic salt
Crumbled potato chips

Cook macaroni according to directions on package. Simmer green pepper and onion in butter until golden; set aside. Mix flour with melted butter; add milk. Cook over low heat. Stir until sauce is thick; add grated cheese. Add seasonings and vegetables; mix with macaroni. Pour into buttered 2 1/2-quart baking dish. Make deep circle with potato chips around edge of dish; sprinkle center with parsley and more grated cheese. Bake at 325 degrees for 30 to 40 minutes. Yield: 4-6 servings.

Linda V. Rodenaver, Coffee Chm. FOCCPAC OWC
Kunia, Oahu, Hawaii

FETTUCINE

4 tbsp. butter
1 c. heavy cream
3 c. hot boiled egg noodles, drained
3/4 c. shredded Parmesan cheese
Salt and pepper to taste
1/2 tsp. grated nutmeg

Melt butter until lightly browned. Add 1/2 cup cream; boil rapidly until large bubbles form. Add noodles to hot butter and cream mixture. Toss vigorously with 2 forks. Add cheese and remaining cream, a little at a time. Season with salt, pepper and nutmeg. Yield: 4 servings.

Mrs. Keith Bennett, Hospitality Chm. DDMT OWC
Memphis, Tennessee

CHEESE-NOODLE CASSEROLE

1/4 c. butter
3 tbsp. flour
3/4 tsp. salt
1/4 tsp. garlic salt
1/8 tsp. white pepper
Dash of nutmeg
2 c. milk
1/2 c. dry white cooking wine
1 8-oz. pkg. processed Swiss cheese, shredded
3 c. uncooked noodles, cooked and drained
2 tbsp. sliced green onion
2 tbsp. diced pimento
1/2 c. shredded Parmesan cheese

Melt butter; blend in flour, salt, garlic salt, pepper and nutmeg. Add milk. Cook, stirring constantly, until sauce is smooth and thickened. Add wine and Swiss cheese; stir until cheese is melted. Fold noodles, onion, pimento and 1/4 cup of the Parmesan cheese into sauce. Pour mixture into shallow 1 1/2-quart casserole. Sprinkle with remaining Parmesan cheese. Bake at 350 degrees for 25 minutes or until hot and bubbly around edges. Yield: 6 servings.

Photograph for this recipe on page 187.

PARMESAN NOODLES

1 8-oz. pkg. med. noodles
1/4 c. soft butter
1/4 c. heavy cream
Parmesan cheese

Cook noodles according to directions; drain. Cream butter with cream and cheese till smooth in small bowl. Turn noodles into hot serving dish; toss lightly with butter mixture to coat well. Yield: 6 servings.

Mrs. Sylvia Kay Schanzer, 1st VP OWC
Frankfurt, Germany

SPAGHETTI A LA DIABLE

1 8-oz. pkg. spaghetti
1 onion, cut fine
1 clove garlic, minced
2 tbsp. cooking oil
2 1/2 c. cooked tomatoes
Salt and pepper
1 tbsp. sugar
Cayenne pepper to taste
1 1/2 c. cooked and diced chicken
1 c. mushrooms, sauteed
Grated cheese

Cook spaghetti in boiling salted water till tender. Drain; place in greased casserole. Saute onion and garlic in oil until tender. Add tomatoes, salt, pepper, sugar and cayenne. Heat to boiling; add chicken and mushrooms. Pour over spaghetti; toss with a fork. Sprinkle with cheese. Bake in 350-degree oven until mixture is heated through and cheese is melted. Yield: 4 servings.

Mrs. Charles A. Bell, OWC
Maxwell AFB, Alabama

JIFFY VERMICELLI

1/2 med. onion, chopped fine
1/2 green pepper, chopped fine
1 clove of garlic, crushed
2 tbsp. oil
1 8-oz. can tomato sauce
3 c. boiling water
1/2 lb. vermicelli or thin spaghetti

Fry onion, pepper and garlic in oil until clear. Add tomato sauce and water. Break vermicelli or spaghetti in half; add to mixture. Cook for about 15 minutes in large frying pan. Yield: 4 servings.

Mrs. David E. Davenport, Pres. OWC
Plattsburgh AFB, New York

PASTA

3/4 c. olive oil
1 1/2 c. fresh basil leaves
1 to 2 cloves of garlic
1/2 c. pine nuts
1 c. fresh sprigs of parsley
3/4 c. Romano cheese, grated
1 tsp. salt
1 pkg. fine vermicelli

Combine first 6 ingredients in an electric blender; blend until smooth paste. Add salt. Cook fine vermicelli in boiling salted water until tender, for about 10 minutes; drain. Mix vermicelli and cheese mixture. Yield: 6 servings.

Mrs. Calvine F. Johnson, OWC
Treasure Island, California

Egg and Cheese Dishes

RECIPE FOR TABASCO SCRAMBLED EGGS ON PAGE 213

ALSATIAN EGGS

6 thin slices bacon
1/2 c. shredded cheddar or American cheese
6 eggs
Salt and pepper to taste
1/2 to 3/4 c. milk or light cream

Place bacon in bottom of casserole or baking dish; sprinkle cheese over top. Break eggs carefully, so as not to disturb yolk; slide over bacon and cheese. Add salt and pepper; pour milk over top. Bake in 300 to 325-degree oven for 12 to 15 minutes until eggs are set. Yield: 4 servings.

Mrs. Elpedio Basa, Ways and Means Chm. OWC
Rhein Main Air Base, Germany

BAKED EGGS WITH CHEESE

1/4 c. light cream
4 eggs
Salt and pepper to taste
1/2 c. shredded sharp process
    cheese

Butter 4 ramekins or custard cups; add 1 tablespoon cream. Break 1 egg into each; sprinkle with salt and pepper. Set cups in shallow pan; pour hot water 1-inch deep in pan. Bake in 325-degree oven for 15 minutes. Top each egg with about 2 tablespoons cheese. Bake 5 to 10 minutes longer. Serve at once. Yield: 4 servings.

Mrs. M. P. South, Hon. Pres. OWC
Fallon NAS, Nevada

BAKED EGGS IN MUSHROOM SAUCE

1 can condensed cream of mushroom soup
1/2 c. milk
1/4 tsp. celery salt
4 eggs
4 slices toast

Combine soup, milk and celery salt in bowl; blend well. Pour 2/3 sauce into 10 x 6 x 2-inch baking dish. Break eggs into sauce, placing each separately. Spoon remaining sauce over eggs. Bake in 350-degree oven for 20 minutes or until egg whites are set. Serve each egg with sauce on toast. Yield: 4 servings.

Mrs. Sigmund Alexander, OWC Publ. Chm.
Norton AFB, California

CANADIAN EGG PIE

10 slices Canadian bacon
8 sandwich-size slices Swiss cheese
6 to 8 eggs

(Continued on next page)

Salt and pepper to taste
3/4 c. light cream
2 tbsp. grated Parmesan cheese

Fit Canadian bacon around edge of 10-inch Pyrex pie plate to form scalloped rim. Place cheese slices in bottom, slightly overlapping bacon. Break each egg into small dish; carefully slide onto cheese. Season with salt and pepper; cover with cream. Sprinkle Parmesan cheese over top. Bake in 350-degree oven for 15 to 20 minutes until eggs are set and top is flecked with light brown. Yield: 6 servings.

Mrs. Paul R. Cerar, Hon. Pres. OWC
Edgewood Arsenal, Maryland

CHEDDAR EGG CUPS

2 tbsp. butter or margarine
2 tbsp. flour
1 c. milk
Liquid red-pepper seasoning to taste
1/2 c. grated sharp cheddar cheese
1 c. chopped cooked ham
4 eggs
1/4 c. soft bread crumbs

Melt butter in medium-sized saucepan. Stir in flour; cook, stirring constantly, just until bubbly. Stir in milk and red pepper seasoning; continue cooking and stirring until sauce thickens and boils 1 minute. Remove from heat. Stir in 3/4 cheese until melted. Divide ham evenly among four 6-ounce custard cups; top with cheese sauce. Break each egg in dish; slide over cheese sauce in cups. Sprinkle with bread crumbs and remaining cheese. Bake in 325-degree oven for 20 minutes or to desired doneness. Yield: 4 servings.

Mrs. John H. Murphy, 1st VP OWC
Ft. Holabird, Maryland

CHUTNEY EGGS

12 hard-cooked eggs
8 slices crisp bacon, crumbled
1/4 c. finely chopped chutney
3 tbsp. mayonnaise

Cut eggs in half lengthwise; mash yolk separately with fork. Add bacon, chutney and mayonnaise to mashed yolks. Fill egg white halves. Yield: 12 servings.

Mrs. Rush L. Canon, Pres. NDWC
San Diego, California

EASY LUNCH DISH

1 can cream of mushroom soup
1 jar pimento cheese spread
4 hard-boiled eggs, coarsely chopped
1 can chow mein noodles

(Continued on next page)

Heat soup and cheese spread in double boiler; stir well. Add eggs. Heat noodles. Serve cheese mixture over noodles. Yield: 2 servings.

Mrs. Robert E. Harrington, Pres. OWC
Langley AFB, Virginia

EASY RANCH STYLE EGGS
HUEVOS RANCHEROS FACIL

1 7-oz. can taco sauce
4 eggs
Salt

Heat taco sauce to 200 degrees in electric skillet. Poach eggs in sauce; salt to taste. Yield: 2 servings.

Mrs. Myron T. Johnston, Ways and Means Chm. OWC
Kelly Barracks, 7 Stuttgart, Mohringen, Germany

EGGS AU GRATIN

2 c. med. white sauce
1 tbsp. minced onion
1 c. grated cheddar cheese
12 eggs
1 c. bread crumbs
3 tbsp. butter
6 to 8 English muffins, cut in half
    and toasted

Prepare medium white sauce; add onion. Place half the sauce into buttered 9 x 13-inch Pyrex dish. Add half the cheese. Break eggs carefully; over sauce and cheese. Cover with remaining sauce and cheese; sprinkle bread crumbs and butter over top. Bake at 375 degrees about 15 to 25 minutes until brown. Serve over English muffins. Yield: 6-8 servings.

Mrs. Ronald W. Marshall, Newcommers Com. Chm. OWC
Fairchild AFB, Washington

EGGS WITH CHEESE

3 tbsp. butter
1/4 c. flour
1 tbsp. salt
1/4 c. grated onion
2 c. milk
3/4 c. grated cheddar cheese
6 hard-cooked eggs, sliced
1 c. buttered bread crumbs

Melt butter in saucepan. Add flour, salt, onion and milk gradually; stir until thickened. Stir in cheese; add eggs to sauce. Arrange in casserole; top with crumbs. Bake about 20 minutes at 325 degrees. Yield: 4-5 servings.

Joan Duguette, Entertainment Sec. OWC
North Bay CFB, Ontario, Canada

EGGS BENEDICT

Butter
English muffin or toast
Thin slice ham
Egg, poached

Butter round of split and toasted English muffin; cover with ham slice or spread with deviled ham. Top each with poached egg; cover with Hollandaise Sauce.

HOLLANDAISE SAUCE:

1 egg yolk, slightly beaten
1 to 1 1/2 tbsp. lemon juice
1/4 c. butter
Salt to taste

Combine egg yolk, lemon juice and butter in saucepan. Cook over low heat, stirring constantly, until butter melts and sauce is slightly thick. Season; pour sauce over egg. Serve at once. Yield: 1 serving.

Mrs. James Almond, NOWC
Camp Pendleton, California

EGG FU YONG

1 med. onion
2 tbsp. oil
4 sm. carrots, sliced
3 tbsp. sliced cabbage
2 tbsp. sliced leek or green onion
4 eggs
Salt and pepper
Dash of soy sauce
1-oz. shrimp, chopped (opt.)
1 can tomato puree
1 1/2 c. water
2 tbsp. flour
Sugar to taste
2 tbsp. cooked peas

Fry onion in oil until golden. Add carrots, cabbage and leek; simmer for 8 to 10 minutes. Beat eggs with 1/4 teaspoon salt, 1/8 teaspoon pepper and soy sauce. Add vegetables and shrimp. Bake 2-inch thick omelets in skillet. Heat tomato puree and water; add flour and thicken slightly. Season with sugar, salt and pepper; pour over omelets. Garnish with peas. Serve with rice, if desired. Yield: 4 servings.

Mrs. Henry P. Meyer, Treas. OWC
Keesler AFB, Minnesota

EGGS ON MUFFINS

1/2 c. chopped onion
1/2 c. chopped pepper
2 tbsp. butter
4 eggs
2 tbsp. milk
1/2 tsp. salt

(Continued on next page)

1/4 tsp. pepper
1 tsp. Worcestershire sauce
4 English muffin halves
4 slices American cheese

Saute onion and pepper in butter until tender. Combine eggs, milk, salt, pepper and Worcestershire sauce. Add to onion and pepper; scramble to desired consistency. Toast and butter English muffins. Place scrambled eggs on muffin halves; top each with cheese slice. Place under broiler until cheese melts. Yield: 4 servings.

Mrs. Donald Lidke, OWC
NAS New Orleans, Louisiana

EGG-MUSHROOM CASSEROLE

6 hard-boiled eggs, grated
1 10 1/2-oz. can mushroom soup
1 soup can milk
1 dozen Ritz crackers, crushed
2 tbsp. butter

Place eggs in 1 1/2-quart casserole. Mix soup and milk together; stir into eggs. Add 3/4 cracker crumbs; mix with ingredients. Dot with butter; sprinkle remaining crumbs over top. Bake for 20 minutes at 350 degrees. Yield: 6 servings.

Mrs. Richard I. Howson, OWC
Jacksonville, Florida

EGG POACHED IN CHEESE SAUCE

2 tbsp. melted butter
2 tbsp. flour
3/4 tsp. salt
1/4 tsp. paprika
1 1/2 c. milk
1/4 tsp. Worcestershire sauce
1 c. cheese, grated
6 eggs
2 tomatoes, sliced
6 pieces toast

Melt butter; add flour, salt and paprika. Mix until smooth. Add milk gradually, stirring constantly. Cook until thick and smooth. Add Worcestershire and cheese; stir until melted. Pour into shallow pan; drop eggs into sauce. Poach over low heat until eggs are set. Cut each tomato into 3 slices; season. Place under broiler for few minutes. Place tomato slice on toast; top with poached egg. Pour sauce over top. Yield: 6 servings.

Mrs. Robert W. Eager, Jr., VP OWC
FOCC PAC, Hawaii

EGGS IN SOUR CREAM

1/4 c. melted butter
1 1/2 c. sour cream
3/4 c. chili sauce
Cayenne pepper to taste
Seasoned salt
Seasoned pepper
Freshly ground black pepper
6 eggs

Melt 2 tablespoons butter in each of 6 individual baking cups. Combine sour cream, chili sauce, cayenne, salt and pepper. Spoon into cups. Break 1 egg into each cup. Bake in 400-degree oven about 10 minutes or until eggs are done. Yield: 6 servings.

Mrs. John M. Nolan, 2nd VP OWC
Ft. Campbell, Kentucky

FRENCH OMELETTE

6 eggs, separated
1/2 c. milk
Salt and pepper to taste
Parsley, 2 sprigs fresh or 1 tsp. dried
1 lge. can mushrooms
1 c. Swiss cheese, grated

Beat egg whites stiff but not dry. Place yolks, milk, salt, pepper, parsley, mushrooms and cheese in blender. Blend for 15 seconds. Fold yolk mixture into beaten whites; mix well. Pour into large buttered skillet. Bake in 300-degree oven about 40 minutes until golden brown and puffed. Yield: 4 servings.

Mrs. Henry Frohsin, Treas. OWC
Hq. Supdist, Hessen, Frankfurt, Germany

FRIED PEPPERS AND EGGS SANDWICHES

1/4 c. cooking oil
6 med. bell peppers, cut in 1/2-inch strips
3 eggs, beaten
3 hard-crust rolls or bread

Place oil in 10-inch skillet; allow to heat several minutes over medium heat. Place peppers in skillet; cook for 15 to 20 minutes until soft and fork will pierce strips. Turn occasionally to prevent burning. Add eggs; mix together until eggs are cooked. Serve with hard-crust rolls. May serve with sliced tomatoes and mayonnaise, if desired. Yield: 3-4 servings.

Mrs. Howard M. Betts, Adv. OWC
Moron AFB, Spain

GERMAN EGG BALLS

2 c. flour, sifted
1 tsp. baking powder
1 tsp. salt

(Continued on next page)

2 eggs, separated
1 1/4 c. milk
1/2 c. margarine or butter

Sift flour, baking powder and salt together. Add egg yolks and milk; stir until smooth. Melt margarine in skillet; heat till quite hot. Pour in batter. Turn with broad spatula or pancake turner when begins to thicken on bottom. Keep turning and chopping mixture until lightly browned. Looks like hash-browned potatoes. Serve instead of potatoes with any meat. Yield: 6 servings.

Mrs. Elliott Coldwater, Special Events Chm. OWC
Great Falls, Montana

GLAMORIZED SCRAMBLED EGGS

6 tbsp. butter
2 minced green onions
5 mushroom caps
4 tomatoes, peeled, seeded, drained
    and chopped
1 c. cooked shrimp halves
6 eggs, slightly whipped
Salt to taste
4 slices buttered toast
Grated cheese

Melt butter in chafing dish; add onions and mushroom caps. Simmer for 5 minutes. Add tomatoes, shrimp, eggs and salt. Cook to desired doneness. Serve over toast; sprinkle with cheese. Yield: 4 servings.

Mrs. B. McClaugherty, Hon. VP OWC
Naval Air Facility
Sigonella NAF, Sicily

HORSERADISH OMELET

2 tbsp. butter or margarine
6 tbsp. cold water
3/4 tsp. salt
1/8 tsp. pepper
6 eggs, beaten slightly
1/2 8-oz. carton horseradish dip

Preheat frying pan; add butter. Tilt frypan to grease bottom and sides. Add water, salt and pepper to eggs; beat to blend. Pour into frypan. Lift omelet edge with spatula; tilt pan so uncooked mixture spreads underneath. Repeat until omelet is creamy and set. Spread half the omelet with horseradish dip; fold over filling. Roll from handle to opposite side, using 2 turners; loosen bottom with turner. Roll out onto heated platter. Yield: 4-6 servings.

Mrs. Richard H. Searle, OWC
USMCRD, Parris Island, South Carolina

EGGS WITH LOX AND ONIONS

Butter or margarine
Lox, 1 piece per person

(Continued on next page)

Onions, 1/2 per person
Eggs, 2 per person
Milk (opt.)
Salt and pepper to taste

Melt butter in frying pan. Add cut-up lox and chopped onions; fry until onions are golden. Stir frequently. Beat eggs until foamy. Add milk, if desired; season to taste. Pour on top of lox-onion mixture. Scramble in pan. Cook until mixture sets. Serve at once.

Mrs. Saul Koss, Publ. Chm. O and CWC
Stuttgart, West Germany

EGGS STROGANOFF

4 breakfast steaks
Meat tenderizer
1/4 c. butter or margarine
1 sm. onion, finely chopped
1/3 lb. fresh mushrooms, sliced
    or 1 4-oz. can mushrooms
12 eggs
1/4 c. water
1/2 tsp. catsup
1/2 tsp. dry mustard
1 c. sour cream

Moisten both sides of steak; sprinkle with tenderizer, 1/2 teaspoon per pound. Pierce deeply with fork; cut into strips 1/8-inch wide. Do not salt. Melt half the butter in electric frying pan at 375 degrees. Add remaining butter, onion and mushrooms; saute until lightly browned. Reduce heat to 250 degrees. Beat eggs and water together; pour over onion, mushrooms and meat. Blend together; cook about 2 minutes until eggs are as desired. Mix catsup and mustard into sour cream; add to meat and egg mixture. Allow to heat thoroughly. Serve immediately with English muffins or corn bread. Yield: 6 servings.

Mrs. John W. Shong, Hon. Pres. OWC
Sangley Point USNS, Philippines

ONE-DISH BRUNCH

10 slices Canadian bacon
8 1-oz. slices Swiss cheese
8 eggs
Salt and pepper to taste
1 c. light cream
2 tbsp. Parmesan cheese
1 can sliced pineapple
1/2 c. jam, any kind
2 tbsp. melted butter

Arrange bacon around edge of deep-dish pie plate to form scalloped edge. Line bottom with cheese slices. Slide eggs carefully over cheese. Add salt, pepper, cream and Parmesan. Bake for 15 to 20 minutes at 350 degrees. Remove. Drain pineapple; brush with jam. Drizzle on melted butter. Place pineapple on cookie sheet; broil 7 to 8 minutes. May bake canned biscuits with eggs for complete brunch, if desired. Yield: 6-8 servings.

Mrs. Everett T. Nealey, Program Chm. OWC
Fort Bragg, North Carolina

RANCH EGGS

Butter
1 lge. onion, sliced
1 lge. can tomatoes
1 6-oz. can tomato paste or condensed
    tomato soup (opt.)
1 sm. green pepper, chopped
Leftover meat, cut sm. (opt.)
4 or 5 eggs
American cheese slices

Melt rounded tablespoonful butter in frypan or skillet. Heat onion; add tomatoes, tomato paste and green pepper. Simmer for 10 minutes. Add leftover meat; simmer until sauce is fairly thick. Add 2 tablespoonfuls butter. Slide in eggs; do not scramble. Add slices American cheese between partially set eggs. Serve egg, melted cheese and tomato sauce on toast. Yield: 4-5 servings.

Mrs. E. H. Tempest, Hospitality Chm. OWC
Pearl Harbor Naval Base, Honolulu, Hawaii

SCOTCH EGGS

6 hard-boiled eggs
1 1/2 lb. bulk sausage
1 egg, beaten
Bread or cracker crumbs

Cool and dry eggs well. Mold sausage around each egg. Dip in egg; roll in crumbs. Deep fry at 350 degrees until sausage is done and eggs are well browned. Cut in half lengthwise; serve either hot or cold as an appetizer. Yield: 6 servings.
PERSONAL NOTE: This is popular at coffees in England or served as a light tea with muffins.

Mrs. Alfred C. Petersen, Pres. OWC
Duluth AFB, Minnesota

OMELET ITALIANO

1 sm. can tomato sauce with or without mushrooms
1 tsp. Italian spice mix
1/2 tsp. oregano
1/2 tsp. sweet basil
6 lge. eggs
Salt and pepper to taste
1 4-oz. pkg. grated pizza or mozzarella cheese
1 tbsp. butter or margarine

Simmer sauce with spices while omelet is cooking. Beat eggs lightly with salt and pepper. Add cheese; stir. Melt butter in frypan on low heat. Pour egg mixture in pan; cook until edges brown. Fold omelet over; cook on both sides until set. Pour sauce over individual omelet servings. Yield: 4 servings.

Mrs. Harold Wilpan, W and M Chm. OWC
Altus AFB, Oklahoma

OVEN OMELET

8 slices bacon, coarsely chopped
4 green onions, thinly sliced
8 eggs
1 c. milk
1/2 tsp. seasoned salt
2 1/2 c. shredded Monterey Jack cheese
    or Swiss or cheddar

Fry bacon until browned; drain, reserving 1 tablespoon drippings. Saute onions in drippings until limp. Beat eggs with milk and seasoned salt; stir in bacon, onions and 2 cups cheese. Pour into greased, shallow 2-quart baking dish. Bake in 350-degree oven for 35 to 40 minutes until mixture is set and top lightly browned. Sprinkle with remaining cheese; return to oven until cheese melts. Serve immediately. Yield: 6 servings.

Mrs. Jack E. Russ, Parlm. OWC
Cecil Field NAS, Florida

PEPPERS AND EGGS

3 tbsp. olive oil
4 med. green peppers, thinly sliced
6 eggs, well beaten
Salt and pepper to taste

Heat olive oil in skillet; add green peppers. Cook slowly until well done and soft. Add eggs; cook until eggs are scrambled. Add salt and pepper. Serve while hot. Yield: 3-4 servings.

Mrs. Max Giovannini, Welfare Chm. OWC
Wakkanai AFS, Hokkaido, Japan

PRESIDENT'S CHEESE DISH

1 c. soda cracker crumbs
2 c. med. white sauce
1/2 lb. sharp cheddar cheese
1 4-oz. can pimentos, chopped
4 hard-cooked eggs, grated
Buttered crumbs

Place layer of crumbs in buttered square casserole; moisten well with white sauce. Add layers of cheese, pimento and eggs. Repeat in same order ending with buttered crumbs on top. Bake at 350 degrees for 25 minutes. Yield: 4 servings.

Mrs. John F. Peterson, Pres. O and CWC
Zweibruecken, Germany

QUICK EGGS BENEDICT

4 slices Canadian bacon
2 English muffins, halved and buttered
1 can cheddar cheese soup
4 eggs, poached

Place Canadian bacon and muffins on cookie sheet; broil until brown. Heat cheese soup in saucepan. Place Canadian bacon on muffin half; place egg on bacon. Pour soup over egg; serve. Yield: 4 servings.

Mrs. John D. Beeson, 2nd VP OWC
Seymour Johnson AFB, North Carolina

RANCH EGGS (MEXICO)
HUEVOS RANCHEROS

1 No. 2 can tomatoes
1 med. onion, chopped
1 clove of garlic
1 lge. green pepper, chopped
2 jalapeno peppers
1/2 tsp. salt
6 to 8 eggs
Toast

Combine tomatoes, onion, garlic, green pepper, jalapeno peppers and salt in large skillet. Stew over low heat for 30 minutes. Break eggs carefully; slide into mixture. Poach until set. Serve eggs on toast; cover with tomato sauce. Yield: 4-6 servings.

Mrs. Brooks G. Bays, 1st VP OWC
Colorado Springs, Colorado

RICH SCRAMBLED EGGS BUFFET STYLE

Butter
2 tbsp. flour
Powdered non-dairy creamer
Water
1 1/2 doz. eggs
1/2 tsp. salt
1/8 tsp. pepper

Melt 2 tablespoons butter in saucepan over low heat until frothy. Blend in flour with wire whip; cook and stir for 1 minute without coloring. Add 1/4 cup powdered creamer and 1 cup boiling water all at once; beat with wire whip to blend. Increase heat to moderately high; cook and stir sauce until comes to boil and thickens. Keep warm. Melt 3 tablespoons butter in skillet until foamy. Beat eggs, 6 tablespoons powdered creamer, salt, pepper and 3/4 cup hot water. Pour into skillet; cook slowly, stirring occasionally until eggs are partially set. Remove from heat; fold in white sauce. White sauce keeps eggs soft and moist until serving time; keep in 200-degree oven. Yield: 12 servings.

Mrs. Eugene T. Seaburn, Pres. OWC
Fort Riley, Kansas

SCRAMBLED EGGS A LA MARTIN

1 lb. hamburger
6 slices cheese, diced
1 doz. eggs
Salt and pepper to taste

Brown hamburger in frying pan. Drain excess grease. Add cheese, eggs, salt and pepper; scramble together until eggs are done and cheese is melted. Yield: 6 servings.

Mrs. Thomas D. Coss, Sec.-Treas. OWC
Bellefontaine AFS, Ohio

TABASCO SCRAMBLED EGGS

2 3-oz. pkg. cream cheese
1/2 c. milk
1 doz. eggs
1 tsp. salt
1 tsp. Tabasco
4 tbsp. butter

Place cream cheese and milk in large mixing bowl; blend until smooth. Add eggs, salt and Tabasco; beat until foamy. Melt butter in chafing dish or large skillet; pour in egg mixture. Cook over medium heat, stirring bottom and sides as eggs become firm. Continue to cook until eggs are thick and creamy. Yield: 6 servings.

Photograph for this recipe on page 201.

CHEESE DREAMS

8 slices bread
8 slices cheddar cheese
2 or 3 tomatoes, sliced
1 onion, sliced thin
16 slices bacon

Cover bread with cheese slices; arrange tomato slices over cheese. Sprinkle onion slices over tomato; top with 2 slices of bacon cut to fit bread. Place on cookie sheet. Heat under broiler till cheese melts and bacon crisps. Yield: 4 servings.

Mrs. F. P. Fardy, Adv.
F. E. Warren OWC
Cheyenne, Wyoming

CHEESE FONDUE

1 clove of garlic
1 1/2 c. dry white wine
2 lb. grated natural Swiss cheese
1/4 c. all-purpose flour
1/2 tsp. salt
1/2 tsp. dry mustard
Dash of grated nutmeg

(Continued on next page)

1/4 c. cognac, rum or kirsch
2 med. sized loaves French bread, cut into 1-inch
    cubes

Rub round 2-quart chafing dish, casserole or electric skillet with garlic; discard garlic. Add wine; heat slowly over medium heat until bubbles begin to form. Do not boil. Mix cheese lightly with flour; add cheese mixture by handfuls to wine, stirring each time till cheese is melted. Add seasonings and cognac; stir well. Adjust heat to keep fondue bubbling slowly. Dip cubes of bread into melted cheese with long-handled fondue forks. Add a small amount of hot wine if fondue becomes too thick. Yield: 8 servings.

Mrs. Curtis J. Johnson, VP OWC
Istanbul AS, Turkey

CHEESE PUDDING

1 stick butter
6 slices white bread
3 eggs
2 1/2 c. milk
1 tsp. salt
1 tbsp. mustard with horseradish
2 1/2 c. American cheese, grated

Rub butter onto bottom and sides of 3-quart baking dish. Spread remaining butter on bread; cut into cubes. Mix eggs, milk, salt and mustard. Alternate layers of bread and grated cheese in baking dish. Pour in liquid. Bake at 325 degrees for about 45 minutes or until knife comes out of center clean. May be kept for 2 or 3 days. Yield: 8 servings.

Mrs. Thomas M. Horne, Pres.
Parris Island OWC
Parris Island, South Carolina

CHEESE PUFF

2 tbsp. butter
3 tbsp. flour
1/2 c. scalded milk
1/2 tsp. salt
1/2 c. grated sharp cheese
3 eggs, separated

Melt butter. Add flour; mix well. Add scalded milk gradually. Add salt and cheese. Remove from fire; add egg yolks which have been beaten until lemon-colored. Fold in stiffly beaten egg whites. Pour into buttered 1-quart baking dish. Bake for 20 minutes in 350-degree oven. Serve at once.

Mrs. Earl Graham, Adv.
Naval Postgraduate School OSWC
Monterey, California

CHILIES RELLENOS CASSEROLE

6 oz. mozzarella cheese
6 oz. Jack cheese
6 oz. cheddar cheese

(Continued on next page)

3 sm. cans mild green chilies, seeds removed
2 eggs
1/2 c. flour
2 c. milk

Break up cheese; place in 1 3/4-quart Corning Ware buffet server in layers with chilies. Combine eggs, flour and milk; beat well. Pour over cheese. Bake at 350 degrees for 30 minutes. Yield: 6-8 servings.

Mrs. Phillip A. Rand, OWC
Kingsley Field, Oregon

CHEESE SOUFFLE

1 c. milk
3 tbsp. butter
1/4 c. flour
1/2 tsp. salt
1/4 tsp. black pepper
1/16 tsp. paprika
1/16 tsp. soda
1/4 lb. sharp cheddar cheese, cut in sm.
   pieces
4 eggs, separated

Scald milk in saucepan; melt butter in upper part of double boiler over hot water. Stir in flour until smooth. Add hot milk, salt, pepper, paprika and soda. Stir and cook until smooth and thickened. Stir cheese into sauce until melted and smooth; remove from hot water. Let stand for 30 minutes at room temperature. Beat egg yolks until lemon colored; beat egg whites until stiff. Beat yolks into cheese mixture; fold into whites. Turn into ungreased 1 1/2-quart casserole; set into shallow pan of hot water. Bake at 300 degrees for 1 hour and 15 minutes.

Mrs. Paul A. Bowles, Act. Chm. AG OWC
Washington, District of Columbia

CLASSIC CHEESE FONDUE

12 oz. or 3 c. natural Swiss cheese, cut into
   thin strips
1 tbsp. all-purpose flour
Garlic
1 1/4 c. sauterne
Dash of freshly ground pepper
Dash of nutmeg
3 tbsp. dry sherry
1 loaf French bread or 8 or 9 hard rolls, torn into
   bite-sized pieces

Toss cheese and flour together in brown sack to coat. Rub inside of fondue cooker with clove of garlic; sprinkle in 1/4 clove of minced garlic. Pour sauterne into 1 1/2-quart saucepan; warm till bubbles start to rise. Do not cover or boil. Add handfuls of cheese until all is melted and blended, stirring constantly. Stir in seasonings and sherry. Warm foil-wrapped bread in oven. Pour cheese mixture into fondue pot. If mixture becomes thick, add warmed sauterne. Dip bread cubes into fondue.

Mrs. Joseph A. Mitchell, Publ. Chm. OWC
Minot AFB, North Dakota

EASY CHEESE STRATA

12 slices bread
6 slices cheese
4 eggs
2 1/2 c. milk
Salt and pepper

Prepare 6 cheese sandwiches; place in baking dish. Beat eggs; add milk. Salt and pepper to taste. Pour over sandwiches; let stand for 45 minutes. Bake in 325-degree oven for 40 minutes or until golden. Yield: 6 servings.

Mrs. R. M. Gehrin, Hon. Pres.
Tofsham AFS, Maine

MOCK CHEESE SOUFFLE

Butter
Bread slices, crusts removed
1 lb. American cheese
6 eggs, well-beaten
1 qt. milk
Salt

Butter 9 x 11-inch baking pan. Place slices of buttered bread in pan; cover with 1/2 of the grated cheese. Repeat. Combine eggs, milk and salt to taste. Pour over bread and cheese; let mixture soak for 1 hour. Place in pan of water. Bake in 275-degree oven for 1 hour or until puffed up and brown.

Mrs. Alan Baker, Hon. Pres. OWC
Taega, Korea

NEVER-FAIL CHEESE SOUFFLE

Butter
8 slices white bread, with crusts removed
1 lb. sharp cheddar cheese, grated
6 eggs, beaten
3 c. milk
3/4 tsp. salt
3/4 tsp. dry mustard
Dash of cayenne

Butter both sides of the bread. Place alternate layers of cheese and bread in buttered 8-inch square casserole. Combine eggs, milk, salt, mustard and cayenne; pour over cheese and bread. Refrigerate overnight. Bake for 1 hour at 350 degrees. Yield: 4-6 servings.

Mrs. William Snavely, OWC
Tinker AFB, Oklahoma

QUICHE LORRAINE

1 lb. bacon, cooked and crumbled
1 1/2 c. Swiss cheese, broken up
1 unbaked 10-inch pie shell
4 lge. eggs, slightly beaten

(Continued on next page)

1 tbsp. flour
3/4 tsp. salt
Dash of pepper
Dash of nutmeg
1 c. heavy cream
1 c. half and half

Place bacon and cheese in pie shell. Mix remaining ingredients well; pour over bacon and cheese. Bake in 375-degree oven for 50 minutes or until knife comes out clean. Serve thin slices with white wine, if desired.

Mrs. Albert Brevel, VP
Karlsruhe O and CWC
Karlsruhe, Germany

QUICHE LORRAINE

1/2 lb. bacon
1 unbaked pie crust
1/4 lb. Swiss cheese
3 eggs
2 c. milk
1 tsp. salt
1/16 tsp. pepper

Fry bacon until crisp; crumble into pie crust. Shred cheese; arrange over bacon. Beat eggs slightly with rotary beater; add milk and seasonings. Blend well. Pour over bacon and cheese. Bake in 400-degree oven for 30 to 40 minutes. Remove from oven while center appears soft. Cool for 5 minutes before serving.

Mrs. David L. Freeman, Executive Bd. AFSCWC
Norfolk, Virginia

SPEEDY CHEESE FONDUE

1 10 1/2-oz. can condensed cheddar cheese soup
1/2 c. dry white wine
1/4 c. flour
6 slices crisp bacon, crumbled
1 tsp. chopped chives
French bread, cubed

Combine all ingredients. Cook over direct flame, stirring constantly, until mixture bubbles and thickens. Serve immediately. Dip cubes of French bread into fondue. Must be kept hot in chafing dish or fondue pot to serve. Yield: 6 servings.

Mrs. T. M. Quinlan, 1st VP, MCASOWC
Beaufort, South Carolina

SWISS FONDUE

1 clove of garlic
1 1/2 c. dry white wine
1 lb. Swiss cheese, grated
1 tsp. flour, combined with water to make
   paste

(Continued on next page)

1/4 tsp. nutmeg
1/4 tsp. salt
1/4 tsp. pepper
2 tbsp. kirsch

Rub top of double boiler with garlic. Add wine and cheese; bring to boil, stirring till blended. Add flour; stir. Add nutmeg, salt and pepper. Stir well. Add kirsch when ready to serve. Add additional kirsch, if necessary. Yield: 6 servings.

Mrs. Edward N. Sutton, OWC
Kaneohe Marine Corps Air Station, Hawaii

THREE-CHEESE TORTILLA CASSEROLE

12 corn tortillas
3 tbsp. cooking oil
2 lge. white onions, sliced
1 8-oz. can tomato sauce
1 tbsp. oregano
1 tsp. salt
1/2 tsp. pepper
1 10-oz. can enchilada sauce
1/2 c. Parmesan cheese
2/3 lb. Jack cheese, shredded
1 pt. sour cream
1 c. cheddar cheese, shredded
1/2 tsp. paprika

Cut each tortilla into 8 pieces. Fry in heated oil until slightly crisp; drain. Saute onions in 1 teaspoon of the oil till wilted. Add tomato sauce, oregano, salt, pepper and enchilada sauce. Simmer for 10 minutes. Place alternate layers of tortilla pieces, tomato sauce, Parmesan cheese, Jack cheese and sour cream in greased 2-quart casserole ending with sour cream. Bake in 325-degree oven for 20 minutes. Sprinkle cheddar cheese and paprika on top. Bake for 10 minutes. Serve with Italian bread and green salad with avocado, if desired.

Mrs. James W. Blunt, Jr., Pres. OWC
Ft. Sam Houston, Texas

TOMATO-CHEESE CASSEROLE

4 (about) med. tomatoes, sliced
1 c. grated cheddar cheese
1/3 c. thinly sliced onions
1/2 tsp. salt
1/8 tsp. pepper
1/2 tsp. Accent
1 c. crushed potato chips

Preheat oven to 350 degrees. Arrange half the tomato slices flat in 1 1/2-quart casserole. Arrange half the cheese and onion slices in layers over tomatoes; sprinkle with 1/2 the salt, pepper and Accent. Repeat. Top with crushed potato chips. Bake for 30 minutes or until cheese is melted and bubbly. Yield: 4 servings.

Mrs. R. E. Veruette, ROWC
Key West Naval Base, Florida

Salads

RECIPE FOR SOUTH AFRICAN SALAD ON PAGE 238

CHICKEN MOUSSE

1 envelope unflavored gelatin
1/2 c. cold water
1 c. hot chicken stock
1/4 tsp. onion salt
2/3 c. chilled evaporated milk, whipped
1 tbsp. lemon juice
1 1/2 c. diced cooked chicken

Sprinkle gelatin on cold water to soften. Dissolve softened gelatin in hot chicken stock; add onion salt. Chill to unbeaten egg white consistency; beat with rotary beater until fluffy. Fold in whipped milk and lemon juice. Blend in chicken. Turn into 5 or 6-cup mold. Chill until firm. Yield: 8 servings.
PERSONAL NOTE: Recipe from Knox Meal Planning for the Diabetic.

Mrs. Robert F. Hunt, Hon. Pres.
Norfolk, Virginia

CHICKEN SALAD

1 1/2 c. mayonnaise
1/2 tbsp. curry powder
1 tbsp. soy sauce
1 sm. can pineapple chunks
4 c. chicken, cubed
1 sm. can water chestnuts, sliced
1 lb. seedless grapes
1 c. diced celery
1 1/2 c. toasted slivered almonds

Combine mayonnaise, curry powder and soy sauce; mix with remaining ingredients; garnish with additional pineapple, if desired. Yield: 8 servings.

Mrs. Daniel Riboni, Clock Shop Chm. OWC
Tempelhof Central Airport, Germany

CHILEAN CHICKEN AND CORN SALAD

1 1/2 c. chicken chunks
1 8-oz. can whole kernel corn
2 med. tomatoes, cut in wedges
1 med. green pepper, chopped
1/2 c. mayonnaise
1/2 tsp. salt
1 tsp. chili powder
1/4 tsp. pepper
1 tsp. lemon juice
Lettuce
2 hard-cooked eggs, quartered or sliced

Place chicken, corn, tomatoes and green pepper in medium bowl. Blend mayonnaise, salt, chili powder, pepper and lemon juice. Add mayonnaise mixture to chicken mixture; toss together. Place on lettuce lined salad plate; garnish with eggs. Refrigerate until served. Yield: 4-6 servings.

Mrs. Lee E. Murphy, Gourmet Chm. OWC
Holloman AFB, New Mexico

CHICKEN SALAD EXOTIC

2 c. diced chicken or turkey
Green onion tops, chopped
2 cans bean sprouts, drained
1 can water chestnuts, drained and thinly
    sliced
1 tsp. curry powder
2 tsp. soya sauce
1 c. salad dressing
1/2 tsp. salt
2 hard-boiled eggs, cut in wedges
1/4 c. almonds

Combine first 8 ingredients. Garnish with eggs; sprinkle with almonds. Chill for several hours in refrigerator to blend flavors. Yield: 10 servings.

Mrs. Ronald E. Sweitzer, Treas. OWC
Montieth, Furth, Germany

CURRIED CHICKEN PATIO SALAD

3/4 tsp. curry powder
3/4 c. mayonnaise
1 pkg. frozen peas, cooked
1 1/2 c. precooked rice
1/2 c. chopped dill pickle
1 tsp. grated onion
Dash of pepper
1 1/2 c. diced cooked chicken
1/2 c. diced celery

Mix curry with mayonnaise. Add remaining ingredients; chill thoroughly.

Mrs. Charles W. Johnson, Treas. OWC
Dobbins AFB, Georgia

FRUIT AND CHICKEN SALAD SUPREME

2 c. cubed cooked chicken
2 tbsp. chopped green olives
3/4 c. chopped celery
1/2 c. toasted almonds
1 c. raw apple cubes
2 tbsp. chopped ripe olives
2 tbsp. chopped sweet pickle
2 hard-cooked eggs, diced
1 c. diced pineapple
1/2 c. raisins
3/4 c. mayonnaise
Lettuce
Spiced apple rings
Ripe olives
Watercress
Crushed potato chips

(Continued on next page)

Combine first 11 ingredients; toss lightly. Serve on lettuce; garnish with apple rings, olives and watercress. Top with potato chips. Yield: 6 servings.

Mrs. Charles J. Bailey, Jr., 2nd VP NOWC
San Juan NAS, Puerto Rico

HOT CHICKEN SALAD

2 c. thinly-sliced celery
1/2 c. ground toasted almonds
2 tsp. grated onion or onion juice
1/2 tsp. salt
1 c. mayonnaise
2 tbsp. lemon juice
2 c. cooked diced chicken
1/2 c. grated American cheese
1 c. crushed potato chips

Preheat oven to 450 degrees. Combine all ingredients except cheese and potato chips; spread in shallow baking dish. Sprinkle cheese over top lightly; top with potato chips. Bake for 10 to 15 minutes or until it is bubbly hot. Yield: 4 servings.

Mrs. Charles A. Harris, Publ. Chm. OWC
RAF Mildenhall, England

JELLIED CHICKEN SALAD

1 envelope unflavored gelatin
1 3/4 c. water
2 chicken bouillon cubes
1 1/2 tbsp. lemon juice
1 tsp. grated onion
1 c. diced chicken, cooked
1/2 c. diced celery
1/2 c. cooked peas, drained
Lettuce

Soften gelatin in 1/2 cup water in saucepan. Place bouillon cubes in 1 1/4 cups water; add to gelatin. Place over low heat until bouillon and gelatin are softened. Add lemon juice and onion. Chill until consistency of unbeaten egg white. Fold in chicken, celery and peas. Place in 3-cup mold; chill until firm. Serve on crisp lettuce. Yield: 4 servings.

Mrs. Marvin E. Prigmore, Treas. NOWC
Camp Pendleton, California

APRICOT-GLAZED FRUIT SALAD

1 lge. grapefruit, peeled and sectioned
1 No. 2 1/2 can pineapple chunks, well drained
1 11-oz. can mandarin oranges, well drained
3/4 c. miniature marshmallows
1 1-lb. can apricot pie filling
1 banana, diced

(Continued on next page)

Combine grapefruit, pineapple chunks, oranges and marshmallows; fold in apricot pie filling. Chill for several hours. Fold in diced banana just before serving; serve in lettuce cups. Yield: 8-10 servings.

Mrs. George G. Wees, Rec. Sec.
Signal OWC
Washington, D. C.

AVOCADO BOATS WITH HOT DRESSING

2 avocados
Lettuce
4 tbsp. butter
4 tbsp. catsup
2 tbsp. vinegar
2 tbsp. sugar
2 tsp. Worcestershire sauce
1/2 tsp. salt
Few drops of Tabasco sauce

Halve avocados; remove seed. Place on lettuce. Combine remaining ingredients in saucepan; cook over low heat only until hot, stirring thoroughly. Pour into hollowed avocados; serve immediately. Yield: 4 servings.

Mrs. Frank E. Bassett, Pres.
Guided Missile School OWC
Dam Neck, Virginia

AVOCADO QUICKIE SALAD

1/3 c. mayonnaise
1 tbsp. wine vinegar
1/2 tsp. grated onion
Salt and pepper to taste
Dash of Tabasco sauce
Dash of garlic salt (opt.)
1 med. avocado, diced
1 sm. tomato, diced

Blend mayonnaise, vinegar, onion and seasonings; mix lightly with avocado and tomato. Serve on wedges of lettuce. Yield: 4 servings.

Mrs. Richard DePrez, Hon. Pres. OWC
NAS, Norfolk, Virginia

GUACAMOLE SALAD

1/2 c. fresh or canned chopped green chilies
3 ripe avocados, mashed
3 tbsp. milk
1 sm. clove of garlic, minced
3 tbsp. French dressing
1 16-oz. pkg. cream cheese
1/4 tsp. salt

(Continued on next page)

223

Blend all ingredients to creamy consistency; serve on lettuce leaf at once. May also be used as appetizer with corn or potato chips. Yield: 4 servings.

Mrs. James L. Whiteman, OWC
Norfolk Naval Shipyard, Virginia

AVOCADO RINGS

2 avocados
1 8-oz. pkg. cream cheese
1 tbsp. heavy cream
1 tbsp. onion juice
Butter
1/2 c. toasted almond slivers

Cut avocados in half crosswise; remove pits and peel. Blend cream cheese, cream and onion juice; pack firmly into avocado halves. Seal halves together with butter; chill. Slice into 1/2-inch thick slices; serve on lettuce. Top with generous sprinkling of toasted almonds. Yield: 4 servings.

Mrs. David B. Savage, Hon. VP OWC
Fort Richardson, Alaska

SO SIMPLE SALAD

1 avocado, peeled and halved
2 lettuce leaves
2 tbsp. lemon juice
2 maraschino cherries

Remove avocado seed. Place lettuce leaf on salad plate; cut avocado half into slices; arrange on lettuce leaf pinwheel-fashion. Sprinkle 1 tablespoon lemon juice over slices. Garnish with cherry or other bright red garnish such as pimento bow. Repeat for second serving. Use more lemon juice, if desired. Yield: 2 servings.

Mrs. C. W. Robinson, Jr., Hospitality Chm. OWC
Fort Holabird, Maryland

AVOCADO SALAD

1 pkg. lime Jell-O
1 c. hot water
1/2 c. diced celery
1 tbsp. green pepper, diced
1 tbsp. onion, diced
1 tsp. (scant) salt
1 tsp. (scant) lemon juice
3 tbsp. mayonnaise
1 lge. ripe avocado, mashed

Dissolve Jell-O in hot water; add remaining ingredients. Pour into 1-quart mold; chill for 2 hours or until set. Yield: 5 servings.

Mrs. John E. McQuary, Hon. Chm. OWC
Barbers Point NAS, Hawaii

BLENDER SUNSHINE SALAD

2 envelopes unflavored gelatin
1 c. chilled orange juice
1/2 lemon, peeled and seeded
1/4 c. sugar
1/4 tsp. salt
1 1/2 c. sliced carrots
1 1/2 c. undrained crushed pineapple

Sprinkle gelatin over 1/2 cup orange juice in container of electric blender; allow to stand for a few minutes. Place remaining 1/2 cup orange juice in small sauce-pan; bring to boil over moderate heat. Add boiling orange juice to gelatin; cover. Blend at low speed until gelatin is dissolved, using rubber spatula to push gelatin granules from sides of container into mixture. Turn blender to high; add lemon, sugar and salt. Blend until mixture is smooth; stop blender. Add carrots; chop by turning to high speed for only a few seconds. Stop to add pineapple; blend for few seconds longer. Turn into 4-cup mold or individual molds. Chill for 2 to 3 hours or until firm. Yield: 8 servings.

Mrs. Gordon E. Mulvey, Newcomer Chm. OWC
Langley AFB, Virginia

CRANBERRY-SOUR CREAM SALAD

1 pkg. cherry gelatin
1 c. hot water
1/2 c. cold water
1 1-lb. can whole cranberry sauce
1/2 c. diced celery
1/4 c. walnuts or pecans, broken
1 c. sour cream

Dissolve gelatin in hot water; stir in cold water. Chill until slightly thickened. Break up cranberry sauce with fork; stir into gelatin with celery and walnuts. Fluff sour cream with fork; fold into gelatin mixture. Pour into 1-quart mold; chill until firm. Unmold onto lettuce. Yield: 4-6 servings.

Mrs. William D. VanMeter, Rec. Sec. OWC
Ft. Carson, Colorado

HOLIDAY SALAD

Water
1 can mandarin-oranges, drained and halved,
    juice reserved
1 No. 303 can pineapple tidbits, drained and
    juice reserved
2 3-oz. pkg. raspberry Jell-O
1 1-lb. can jellied cranberry sauce
Colored miniature marshmallows (opt.)
1/2 c. chopped nuts

Add enough water to combined reserved juice to make 3 cups liquid; heat. Add Jell-O to dissolve completely; cool until slightly thickened. Stir in cranberry sauce until dissolved; add remaining fruit, marshmallows and nuts. Pour into 9 x 13-inch pan; chill until set. Yield: 12-15 servings.

Mrs. Clyde A. Shay, OWC
Othello AFS, Washington

MANDARIN ORANGE SALAD MOLD

2 pkg. lemon flavored gelatin
1 c. hot water
1 12-oz. can frozen orange juice concentrate
1 c. cold water
2 tbsp. lemon juice
2 11-oz. cans mandarin oranges, drained

Grease 6 1/2-cup mold. Dissolve gelatin in hot water; add frozen orange juice concentrate, stirring until dissolved. Add cold water, lemon juice and oranges; pour into mold. Chill until partially set; stir oranges through gelatin mixture. Chill until set. Yield: 12 servings.

Mrs. Daniel W. Roderick, Hospitality Chm. OWC
Keflavik USNS, Iceland

MOLDED GUACAMOLE

1 3-oz. pkg. lemon gelatin
1 1/2 c. boiling water
1 1/2 c. mashed avocado
1/2 c. sour cream
1/2 c. salad dressing
1 tbsp. finely chopped onion
1/2 tsp. salt
Dash of Tabasco sauce

Dissolve lemon gelatin in boiling water; cool. Combine remaining ingredients; mix until well blended. Stir in gelatin; pour into oiled 1-quart mold. Chill until firm. Unmold; surround with lettuce. Yield: 6-8 servings.

Mrs. William B. Yancey, Hon. Pres. OWC
Myrtle Beach AFB, South Carolina

PINEAPPLE-CHEDDAR CHEESE MOLDED SALAD

1 sm. can crushed pineapple
Water
3/4 c. sugar
1 tbsp. plain gelatin
1 c. grated mild cheddar cheese
1 c. whipping cream, whipped

Drain pineapple; add enough water to juice to make 1/2 cup liquid. Place liquid in saucepan; add sugar. Bring to boil to dissolve sugar; remove from heat. Dissolve gelatin in 1/4 cup cold water; add to syrup, stirring until melted. Refrigerate until partially thickened; stir in cheese, pineapple and whipped cream, mixing well. Pour into slightly greased mold; refrigerate until ready to serve. Better made the day before. Yield: 8 servings.

Mrs. E. O. Swett, USCG OWC
Port Angeles, Washington

RASPBERRY-APPLESAUCE SALAD

1 c. applesauce
1 3-oz. pkg. raspberry gelatin
1 10-oz. pkg. frozen raspberries, thawed
1/2 c. mayonnaise
1/2 c. whipped cream

Heat applesauce just to boiling; add gelatin, mixing well. Stir in raspberries. Pour into 8 or 9-inch mold or individual molds; chill until set. Serve with dressing made from mayonnaise mixed with whipped cream. Yield: 6 servings.

Mrs. Herbert W. Wessell, Treas.
Tuslog OWC
Ankara, Turkey

SHERRY-CHERRY JELL-O

1 pkg. black cherry Jell-O
1 can pitted Bing cherries, drained and
    liquid reserved
1/4 c. sherry
1/2 c. chopped walnuts and pecans

Prepare Jell-O as directed, substituting cherry liquid and sherry for 1 cup cold water, adding cold water to bring liquid to full cup measure, if necessary. Add cherries and walnuts; chill until set. Excellent with turkey or chicken. Yield: 9 servings.

Mrs. Martha Sheffield, OWC
RAF Alconbury, England

SOUR CHERRY SALAD

1 can pie cherries, drained
    and juice reserved
1 pkg. lemon Jell-O
1 c. sugar
1 tbsp. unflavored gelatin
1/4 c. water
1 sm. can crushed pineapple
1 c. pecans
1 orange, juice and rind
1 lemon, juice and rind

Heat cherry juice; dissolve Jell-O in hot juice. Add sugar and gelatin dissolved in water. Add remaining ingredients; let thicken slightly. Pour into mold; chill until set. Yield: 4-6 servings.

Mrs. Robert G. Triplett, Sec.
USNAG Def. OWC
Chiwhae, Korea

STRAWBERRY SALAD

1 3-oz. pkg. strawberry Jell-O
1/2 c. boiling water

(Continued on next page)

1 pkg. frozen strawberries
1/2 sm. can crushed pineapple
2 sm. bananas, diced
1/2 pt. sour cream
1/2 c. nuts (opt.)

Dissolve Jell-O in boiling water. Add berries, breaking apart with fork as they melt; do not mash. Add pineapple and bananas. Pour 1/2 of the Jell-O mixture into long baking dish; chill until congealed. Spread sour cream over top. Spoon remaining Jell-O mixture over sour cream. Chill until firm. Yield: 4-6 servings.

Mrs. John W. Greenfield, Marine Bk. OWC
Pearl Harbor, Hawaii

SURPRISE SALAD

2 3-oz. pkg. strawberry-banana gelatin
1 1/2 c. boiling water
2 10-oz. pkg. frozen strawberries
1 sm. can crushed pineapple
2 lge. ripe bananas, mashed
2 c. sour cream

Dissolve gelatin in boiling water. Add strawberries, pineapple and bananas; stir gently. Pour 1/2 of the mixture into one 8 x 8 x 2-inch square pan or 13 x 9 x 2-inch oblong pan; congeal quickly. Spread sour cream over congealed salad. Pour remaining gelatin mixture over sour cream; refrigerate until completely jelled. Cut into squares; serve on lettuce leaf. Yield: 8 servings.

Mrs. Roger G. Steen, Social Chm. OWC
Myrtle Beach AFB, South Carolina

CRANBERRY SALAD

1 qt. cranberries, ground fine
1 1/2 c. sugar
2 c. miniature marshmallows
2 c. grapes, cut fine
1 c. cream, whipped

Mix first 4 ingredients together in large mixer bowl; chill overnight. Whip cream; fold into mixture before serving. Yield: 24 servings.

Mrs. B. G. Langhofer, Protocol Chm. OWC
Kingsley Field, Oregon

FRESH FRUIT SALAD COINTREAU

Oranges, sectioned and cut
Grapefruit, sectioned and cut
Bananas, sliced
1 avocado, cut into strips
Strawberries
Cointreau liqueur

(Continued on next page)

Combine all ingredients; place in lettuce cup. Pour cointreau over fruit; serve. Any fresh fruit in season may be used.

Mrs. Russell V. Carson, On-Base Chm. Red Cross Vol. OWC
Moody AFB, Georgia

FIVE-CUP SALAD

1 c. mandarin oranges
1 c. pineapple tidbits
1 c. coconut
1 c. miniature marshmallows
1 c. sour cream

Drain oranges and pineapple. Combine ingredients in bowl. Chill to serve. Great as dessert or a salad. Yield: 6 servings.

Mrs. N. T. Campanini, OWC
Willow Grove NAS, Pennsylvania

FROZEN CRANBERRY SALAD

1 1-lb. can cranberry sauce
1/2 pt. sour cream
1 7-oz. can crushed pineapple, drained

Combine cranberry sauce and sour cream; stir in pineapple. Pour into ice tray without sections to freeze. Serve on lettuce. Yield: 6 servings.

Mrs. Thomas C. Hunter, OWC
US Military Academy
West Point, New York

FROZEN GRAPEFRUIT SALAD

1 8-oz. pkg. cream cheese, softened
1 c. sour cream
1/4 tsp. salt
1/2 c. sugar
1 grapefruit, sectioned
1 avocado, diced
1 c. seedless grapes, halved
1/2 c. pecan pieces

Beat cream cheese until fluffy; blend in sour cream. Stir in salt and sugar until well blended; add grapefruit sections, avocado, grapes and pecans. Pour into 9 x 5-inch loaf pan; freeze until firm. Slice; serve plain or with French dressing on salad greens. Yield: 6 servings.

Mrs. Harold O. Bourne, 2nd VP OWC
Ft. Carson, Colorado

FRUIT COCKTAIL SALAD

1 lge. can fruit cocktail, drained
1 c. sm. marshmallows
1/2 c. shredded coconut
1/2 c. sour cream

Place fruit cocktail, marshmallows and coconut in bowl. Add sour cream; mix all together. Refrigerate for several hours before serving. Yield: 6-8 servings.

Mrs. K. A. Kleypas, 3rd VP Wives' Club
Sandia Base, New Mexico

FRUIT SALAD

SALAD:

4 red apples, diced
1/4 c. lemon juice
1/2 lb. seedless grapes
1 sm. can mandarin oranges
4 bananas, sliced
1/3 c. pecan halves

DRESSING:

1/3 c. orange juice
1/3 c. pineapple juice
2 tbsp. lemon juice
2 eggs, slightly beaten
1/2 c. sugar
1/4 tsp. salt
1 tbsp. cornstarch
3 tbsp. water
1 c. heavy cream, whipped

Cover apples with lemon juice; let stand while preparing remaining fruit and dressing. Drain fruit before pouring on dressing. Mix fruit juices; add to eggs with sugar and salt. Cook over medium heat until slightly thickened; add cornstarch dissolved in water. Cook until thickened; cool. Fold in whipped cream; pour over drained fruit. Makes enough for 2 salads. Yield: 6-8 servings.

Mrs. Charles H. Livingston, Pres. OWC
Arlington Hall Station, Virginia

FRUIT SALAD

1 c. mandarin orange slices, drained
1 c. pineapple chunks, drained
1 c. miniature marshmallows
1 c. Angel Flake coconut
1 c. sour cream

Combine all 5 ingredients; chill thoroughly. Salad is better the longer it keeps. Yield: 6 servings.

Mrs. Joe B. Whitt, Welfare Chm. OWC
Suffolk County AFB, New York

FRUIT SALAD

1 lge. can fruit cocktail
2 bananas, sliced
1 c. sweetened flaked coconut

Drain most of juice from fruit cocktail. Mix all ingredients; chill to serve as salad or dessert. Yield: 6 servings.

Mrs. Roy L. Gooch, Sec. OWC
Naval Weapons Station, Yorktown, Virginia

LEATH FAMILY SALAD

1 c. sugar
2 tbsp. flour
Pinch of salt
1 egg, slightly beaten
1 No. 2 1/2 can crushed pineapple, drained
   and juice reserved
1/2 to 1 lb. grated American cheese to taste

Mix sugar, flour and salt; moisten with small amount of pineapple juice. Stir in egg, mixing well. Add remaining pineapple juice; cook over low heat until thickened, stirring constantly. Cool before mixing with pineapple and cheese. Better chilled before serving. Serve with poultry; good for covered dish meals. Yield: 6-8 servings.

Mrs. Forest B. Crain, OWC
Maxwell AFB, Alabama

MANDARIN ORANGE SALAD

1 11-oz. can mandarin oranges, drained
1 13-oz. can crushed pineapple, drained
1 c. miniature marshmallows
1 c. flaked or shredded coconut
1 c. sour cream
1 c. chopped pecans (opt.)

Mix all ingredients; chill for about 2 hours or overnight. Serve in bowl or in lettuce cups. Yield: 6 servings.

Mrs. Russell W. Grunewald, 1st VP OWC
K. I. Sawyer AFB, Michigan

HOT CURRIED FRUIT SALAD

1 No. 2 1/2 can pears
1 No. 2 1/2 can peaches
1 No. 2 1/2 can pineapple
8 maraschino cherries
1/2 c. margarine
2 tbsp. curry powder
1/2 c. brown sugar

(Continued on next page)

Preheat oven to 325 degrees. Drain fruit dry on paper towels. Melt margarine slowly in saucepan; add curry powder and brown sugar, stirring until well dissolved. Fill 9 x 12-inch casserole with separate layers of pineapple, peaches and pears; dot with cherries. Fill in between pineapple sections with any remaining fruit; dribble sauce over all. Bake for about 1 hour. Serve immediately or within 24 hours. Reheat for 30 minutes before serving. Yield: 9 servings.

PERSONAL NOTE: Pakistani student friend of my husband at Command and General Staff School agreed to a dinner of exchange cooking. We estimated amounts as he cooked; this is the result.

Mrs. Thomas W. Bowen, OWC
Clark AFB, Philippines

PEACH SALAD

1 No. 2 can peach pie filling
1 11-oz. can mandarin oranges, drained
2 c. fresh seedless green grapes
2 sliced bananas, not too ripe
1 10-oz. can pineapple tidbits, drained

Combine all ingredients; chill in refrigerator. Add miniature marshmallows if desired. Salad will keep for several days. Yield: 8 servings.

Mrs. Jerry L. Yeager, 2nd VP OWC
George AFB, California

PINEAPPLE-MELON SALAD

1 16-oz. pkg. frozen melon balls
Crisp salad greens
1 1-lb. 4 1/2-oz. can pineapple slices, chilled
   and drained
Bottled clear French dressing with celery seed

Immerse melon balls package in bowl of hot water for about 45 minutes to thaw. Remove melon balls from package; drain. Arrange salad greens on 6 small plates. Place pineapple slice on each; top with melon balls. Spoon dressing over fruit. Celery French dressing may be made by adding 1 teaspoon celery seed to 1/2 cup bottled clear French dressing. Yield: 6 servings.

Mrs. John D. Schneider, OWC
USNAD, Oklahoma

PIE FILLING SALAD

1 can cherry or apple pie filling
1 lge. or 2 sm. bananas
1 sm. can diced pineapple
1 can mandarin oranges

Mix all ingredients; chill. Serve plain or with sour or whipped cream. Yield: 6-8 servings.

Mrs. Harry J. Heppner, Program Chm. AWAG Rep.
Frankfurt, Germany

QUICK FRESH FRUIT SALAD

1 can mandarin orange sections
3 med. red apples, cut up
2 bananas, cut up
1/2 to 3/4 c. raisins
1/4 c. mayonnaise or salad dressing
1 tsp. lemon juice
Sugar to taste
Maraschino cherries (opt.)

Combine first 4 ingredients. Add mayonnaise and lemon juice; sprinkle with sugar. Chill for about 15 minutes before serving on lettuce leaves, topped with cherries. Cherry juice, if desired will lend pink color; omit sugar. Tangarine sections may be substituted for orange. Cantaloupe and seedless grapes may be added when in season. Yield: 6 servings.

Mrs. J. J. Hardin, Jr., Ed. Newsletter OWC
Norfolk Naval Shipyard, Virginia

QUICK FRUIT SALAD

1 1-lb. can pears
1 1-lb. can peaches
2 bananas
1 c. bite-sized marshmallows
1 c. green grapes (opt.)
1/2 c. mayonnaise
1/4 c. milk

Cut pears, peaches and bananas into bite-sized pieces; add marshmallows and grapes. Mix mayonnaise and milk thoroughly; blend in with fruit. Chill until ready to serve. Yield: 6 servings.

Mrs. Ronald A. Boss, OSWC
USN Postgraduate School Monterey, California

GREEN SALAD CONTINENTAL

Lettuce
1 c. cubed Swiss cheese
1 fresh peach, sliced
1 9-oz. can pineapple tidbits, drained

(Continued on next page)

1/2 c. purple grapes, halved and seeded
1/4 c. walnut halves

GINGER ORANGE DRESSING:

1/4 c. vegetable oil
2 tbsp. thawed orange juice
1/4 tsp. salt
1/8 tsp. ginger

Combine salad ingredients. Mix Dressing ingredients in jar; shake well. Drizzle Dressing over salad. Yield: 6 servings.

Mrs. Richard S. Ewing, Pres. NOWC
New Orleans NAS, Louisiana

AVOCADO HALVES FILLED WITH SEAFOOD

1 6 1/2-oz. can King crab meat or lobster
1 to 2 tbsp. lemon juice
1 c. diced celery
2 tbsp. chopped green onion
1/4 c. Thousand Island dressing or mayonnaise
Salt and pepper to taste
1/4 c. unpared cucumber, diced
2 avocados

Break seafood into chunks; sprinkle with lemon juice. Add celery, onion and salad dressing; mix lightly. Season; chill. Add cucumber just before serving. Mound in 4 avocado halves brushed with lemon juice. Yield: 4 servings.

Mrs. Robert E. Webb, Hospitality Com. NOWC
Los Alamitos NAS, California

CRAB SALAD

1/2 c. low-calorie mayonnaise
2 tbsp. chopped parsley
2 tbsp. snipped chives
1 tsp. Worcestershire sauce
1/2 tsp. lemon juice
1 c. diced pared cucumber
2 7 1/2-oz. cans King crab meat, drained
Crisp lettuce cups
4 hard-boiled eggs, sliced

Combine in medium bowl mayonnaise, parsley, chives, Worcestershire sauce and lemon juice; mix well. Add cucumbers and crab meat; toss. Refrigerate, covered, for 1 hour or until well chilled. Fill lettuce cups with crab mixture; garnish with eggs. Yield: 4 232-calorie servings.

Mrs. Stanley Forster, OWC
Los Alamitos, California

CRAB SALAD

2 7 1/2-oz. cans King crab meat, drained
1/2 c. low-calorie mayonnaise

(Continued on next page)

1/2 tsp. lemon juice
1 tsp. Worcestershire sauce
2 tbsp. snipped chives
2 tbsp. chopped parsley
1 c. diced pared cucumber
Crisp lettuce cups
4 hard-cooked eggs, sliced

Remove cartilage from crab meat, if necessary. Combine in medium bowl mayonnaise, lemon juice, Worcestershire, chives and parsley; mix well. Add crab meat and cucumber; toss. Refrigerate, covered, for 1 hour or until well chilled. Fill lettuce cups with salad; garnish with egg slices. Yield: 4 servings.

Mrs. Edward Dewey, 2nd VP OWC
Little Rock AFB, Arkansas

HOT SEAFOOD SALAD

1 c. celery, minced
1 onion, chopped
1 tbsp. butter
1 lge. can peas or 1 pkg. frozen peas, cooked
1 can crab meat, diced
2 cans shrimp, diced
2 cans tuna, flaked
2 c. mayonnaise
2 tsp. Worcestershire sauce
4 hard-cooked eggs, diced
Bread crumbs or crushed potato chips

Saute celery and onion in butter in pan until tender. Mix all except last ingredient; place in buttered casserole. Cover with bread crumbs. Bake in 300-degree oven for 30 minutes. Yield: 12 servings.

Mrs. Ivey D. Drewry, Adv. OWC
Redstone Arsenal, Alabama

RICE AND TUNA SALAD

1 1/2 c. rice
1 tsp. salt
Water
1 lge. can peas, drained
1 can tuna, drained
2 med. fresh tomatoes
4 1/2 tbsp. mayonnaise
Dash of grated onion

Cook rice and salt in saucepan with enough water to cover first digit of index finger for 20 minutes or until tender. Mix peas, tuna, tomatoes, mayonnaise and onion into hot rice. Yield: 6 servings.
PERSONAL NOTE: We ate this often during the depression when I was a little girl.

Mrs. M. J. Stewart, Welfare Chm. CGOWC
St. Louis, Missouri

SALMON MOUSSE

1 envelope plus 1 tsp. unflavored gelatin
2 tbsp. lemon juice
1 tsp. dillseed
1/4 tsp. paprika
1/2 tsp. salt
1/2 c. boiling water
1/2 c. mayonnaise
1 sm. onion, sliced
1 stalk celery, cut into 1-inch pieces
1 1-lb. can salmon
2 tbsp. pimento
1 c. heavy cream
1 egg

Place first 6 ingredients in blender. Blend at high speed for 40 seconds. Turn off; add remaining ingredients. Blend on low speed for 10 seconds. Turn into a 1 1/2-quart mold. Chill overnight. Yield: 4-6 servings.
PERSONAL NOTE: I found this in magazine approximately 14 years ago when I was a new Air Force wife. It has been served with satisfaction many many times.

Mrs. James R. Singleton, Pres. OWC
Moody AFB, Georgia

ARTICHOKE HEART-SHRIMP SALAD

Romaine lettuce
Iceberg lettuce
2 sliced green onions (opt.)
1 stalk celery, diced (opt.)
1 7-oz. can deveined shrimp, rinsed
1 6-oz. jar marinated artichoke hearts
2 tbsp. (level) mayonnaise

Tear lettuce into salad bowl. Add onion, celery and shrimp. Add artichokes, reserving marinade. Add mayonnaise to marinade; shake well. Pour on salad; toss. Yield: 4-6 servings.

Mrs. Samuel J. Trabun, 1st VP OWC
Mather AFB, California

MISSOURI SALAD PLATE

Shredded crisp lettuce
2 slices pineapple
1/2 pkg. cream cheese, halved
1 lge. tomato, thinly sliced
2 slices crisp bacon
12 cooked shrimp
4 tbsp. fish cocktail sauce or French dressing

Place lettuce on large salad plates. Top with pineapple; add cheese. Place tomato on 1 side of plate; top with bacon. Arrange shrimp on opposite side. Pour over dressing. Yield: 2 servings.

Mrs. Samuel L. Hoard, 1st VP C and OWC
McKee Barracks, Germany

CREOLE SHRIMP SALAD

1 c. cold cooked rice
3/4 lb. cut-up cooked cleaned shrimp
3/4 tsp. salt
1 tbsp. fresh frozen or canned lemon juice
1/4 c. slivered green pepper
1 tbsp. minced scallions or onion
2 tbsp. Fench dressing
1 tbsp. chopped stuffed olives
1/2 c. diced raw cauliflower
1/3 c. mayonnaise
Dash of pepper

Toss together all ingredients. Serve on lettuce, if desired. Yield: 4 servings.

Mrs. W. V. Relyea, Adv. OWC
Plattsburgh AFB, New York

PINEAPPLE-SHRIMP SALAD

2 c. cooked shrimp
1/4 c. French dressing
1 c. celery, sliced diagonally
1 c. pineapple chunks, drained
Lettuce

Marinate shrimp in French dressing for 30 minutes; combine with celery and pineapple. Arrange on lettuce; serve with additional dressing, if desired. Yield: 6 servings.

Mrs. R. C. Fonda, Treas. NOWC
NAS Agana, Guam

SHRIMP SALAD

2 lb. fresh shrimp, cooked and cleaned
Dash of pepper
1 tsp. horseradish
1/4 tsp. Tabasco sauce
2 tbsp. salad dressing
1 tsp. A-1 sauce
2 tbsp. catsup
1 green pepper, chopped
1 med. onion, chopped
1/2 apple, chopped
3 med. stalks celery, chopped
1/2 c. stuffed olives, chopped
3 hard-boiled eggs, chopped
1 head lettuce, chopped
2 med.-sized firm tomatoes, cut in wedges

Let shrimp cool thoroughly. Mix pepper, horseradish, Tabasco, salad dressing, A-1 sauce and catsup together in cup. Add chopped ingredients except lettuce and tomatoes; mix. Let cool thoroughly in refrigerator. Add lettuce and tomatoes just before serving. Yield: 4 servings.
PERSONAL NOTE: This is a favorite meal in a salad recipe from my husband's uncle.

Mrs. Gilbert G. Smith, Jr., Hon. VP OWC
McGuire AFB, New Jersey

QUICK SHRIMP ASPIC

1 c. boiling water
1 pkg. lemon Jell-O
1 8-oz. can tomato sauce
1 tbsp. horseradish
1 c. canned or frozen shrimp

Add boiling water to Jell-O. Stir until dissolved. Add tomato sauce and remaining ingredients. Pour into mold. Chill until set. Yield: 4-6 servings.

Mrs. John H. Castul. Ed. Magazine OWC
Castle AFB, California

SHRIMP-TOMATO ASPIC

1 pkg. lemon Jell-O
1 c. boiling water
1 can tomato soup
1 tbsp. horseradish
2 tbsp. white vinegar
1/2 tsp. salt
1 can deveined shrimp

TOPPING:

3/4 c. sour cream
1/4 c. mayonnaise
1/4 tsp. dillweed

Dissolve Jell-O in boiling water; cool slightly. Add next 5 ingredients. Pour into mold; refrigerate until firm. Mix sour cream and mayonnaise together; sprinkle with dillweed. Yield: 4-6 servings.

Mrs. Tom Swaim, Hon. Pres. OWC
Wakkanai AFS, Japan

SOUTH AFRICAN SALAD

6 4-oz. South African rock lobster tails
Boiling water
2 lb. potatoes
1/2 c. diced onion
1 tsp. salt
1/4 tsp. white pepper
1 1/2 c. mayonnaise
1/4 c. heavy cream

Drop frozen South African rock lobster tails into boiling salted water. Lower heat when water reboils; simmer for 5 minutes. Drain immediately; drench with cold water. Cut away thin underside membrane; remove meat from shells. Chill. Boil potatoes; drain and peel. Cut into cubes while still warm. Place in large bowl. Add onion, salt and pepper immediately. Mix mayonnaise with cream until smooth. Pour over potatoes and onions; leave in thick top layer. Cool then chill. Cut chilled rock lobster tails into bite-size pieces at serving time. Add to potatoes; toss together until all ingredients are well blended. Yield: 6 servings.

Photograph for this recipe on page 219.

SOUTH-OF-THE-BORDER SALAD

2 lb. ground round
3 tbsp. salad oil
1 1/2 c. onions
1 tsp. salt
1 tsp. pepper
1 tsp. chili powder
1 sm. box Velveeta cheese
1 can hot tomatoes
1 garlic clove
1 lge. head lettuce, chopped
3 lge. tomatoes, chopped

Brown meat in oil with onions in heavy skillet; add seasonings. Cook until onions are tender and meat is cooked. Melt cheese in saucepan; add tomatoes. Rub inside of large bowl with garlic. Arrange lettuce and fresh tomatoes in bowl. Drain extra grease from meat. Pour meat on lettuce; toss. Top with cheese mixture. Yield: 6 servings.
PERSONAL NOTE: My daughter liked the inside of a taco so I now make a salad of insides for her to enjoy.

Mrs. Wendell R. Wisdom, Pres. C and OWC
McKee Barracks
Crailsheim, Germany

ASPARAGUS SALAD

1/2 head lettuce
2 green onions, sliced
1 14 1/2-oz. can asparagus pieces, drained
1/2 c. mayonnaise
Salt and pepper to taste

Break up lettuce into bite-sized pieces. Other greens may also be used. Add onions and asparagus. Add mayonnaise, salt and pepper just before serving. Yield: 4-6 servings.

Mrs. John A. Vasilopoulos, Pres. OWC
Hancockfield, New York

ASPARAGUS-TOMATO SALAD

2 med.-sized ripe tomatoes, sliced
Lettuce leaves
1 can asparagus spears
3 tbsp. salad dressing or mayonnaise

(Continued on next page)

Milk
1 tbsp. minced onion
Paprika

Place tomato slices on lettuce leaves. Lay asparagus spears on top of tomato slices. Thin salad dressing to thick pouring consistency with small amount milk in small bowl. Mix in onion; pour over salad. Garnish with paprika. Yield: 4 servings.

Mrs. Henry L. Spencer, Parlm. OWC
San Vito Dei Normanni, Italy

BEAN SALAD

1 can yellow wax beans
1/2 c. onions
1 can green beans
1/4 c. green peppers
1/2 c. water
3/4 c. vinegar
Salt
Liquid sweetener

Chop vegetables; pour water and vinegar over. Salt; add few drops of liquid sweetener to taste. Store in refrigerator.

Mrs. Arthur L. Law, Recreation Chm.
Ft. Kobbe OWC
Howard AFB, Canal Zone, Panama

CABBAGE SALAD

2 c. shredded cabbage
1 cucumber, diced
1 sm. onion, chopped
1/3 c. mayonnaise or salad dressing
Salt and pepper to taste

Combine cabbage, cucumber, onion and mayonnaise; season to taste. Yield: 6-8 servings.

Mrs. Pat H. Davis, Corr. Sec. Women's Club
Fort Detrick, Maryland

CHEESE PEPPERS

1 3-oz. pkg. cream cheese
1/2 tsp. lemon juice
2 tbsp. chopped chutney
2 green peppers, tops and seeds removed
1 head of lettuce, cut into quarters
1/2 c. mayonnaise

Mix cream cheese, lemon juice and chutney; fill peppers with mixture. Chill in refrigerator. Cut peppers into 1/4-inch slices just before serving; place in center of lettuce head. Ring pepper slices with mayonnaise. Yield: 6 servings.

Mrs. Pasquale J. Florio, Finance Chm. OWC
MCAS, Yuma, Arizona

CUCUMBER-COTTAGE SALAD

1 pkg. lime Jell-O
1 1/3 c. boiling water
3 tbsp. lemon juice
1/2 tsp. salt
1 c. sm. curd cottage cheese
1/2 c. mayonnaise
1 tbsp. minced onion
1 sm. cucumber, diced

Combine Jell-O, water, lemon juice and salt. Stir until Jell-O is dissolved; refrigerate until nearly set. Whip; add cottage cheese, mayonnaise, onion and cucumber. Allow to set for several hours before serving. Yield: 6 servings.

Mrs. Donald A. Feldman, Pres. Cape May OWC
Wildwood Electronics Center, New Jersey

EASY TOMATO ASPIC

2 sm. pkg. lemon Jell-O
2 1/2 c. boiling water
1 8-oz. can tomato sauce
2 tbsp. vinegar
1 tsp. salt
1 c. celery, diced
10 sliced olives

Dissolve Jell-O in water; add tomato sauce. Add all ingredients in order. Pour into large mold. Yield: 6-8 servings.

Mrs. Edison F. Arnold, Hon. VP OWC
Kelly AFB, Texas

CORN SALAD

2 lge. cans corn, drain 1 can
1 can drained whole tomatoes
1 lge. onion, sliced thin
1/4 c. vinegar
1 tbsp. sugar

Mix all ingredients; refrigerate for half day or overnight. Yield: 8 servings.

Mrs. Henry A. Proctor, 1st VP OWC
Reese AFB, Texas

GRANDMA'S BARBECUE SALAD

1 pkg. lemon Jell-O
1 1/4 c. boiling water
1 can tomato sauce
1 1/2 tbsp. vinegar
1/2 tsp. salt
1/2 tsp. pepper
1 c. diced celery

(Continued on next page)

2 tbsp. horseradish
Dash of Worcestershire sauce

Dissolve Jell-O in boiling water; add remaining ingredients. Pour into 1 1/2-quart mold. Refrigerate until molded; unmold on bed of greens. Serve plain or with mayonnaise. Yield: 6 servings.

Mrs. Merwyn L. Spaulding, Flying Yankee Ladies Club
Bradley Field, Windsor Locks, Connecticut

CUCUMBERS IN SAUCE

2 lge. cucumbers, peeled
Salt to taste
2/3 pt. sour cream
1/3 c. vinegar
2 tbsp. sugar
1/4 tsp. pepper
1 tbsp. mustard

Slice cucumbers very thin. Salt; wrap in paper towels for about 1 hour. Squeeze out all water. Combine ingredients for sauce; add cucumbers. Marinate in refrigerator for 1 hour or more. Yield: 6-8 servings.

Mrs. Claude Proctor, Jr., Hospitality Chm. OWC
Hof AS, West Germany

ENSALADA RUSIA (SPAIN)

6 whole potatoes, boiled in jackets
1 c. onion, chopped
2 hard-cooked eggs, cut up
3/4 c. mayonnaise
Pimento strips
8 to 10 olives
9 or 10 sm. shrimp
1 can sm. peas

Peel potatoes; cube. Place on pretty serving platter. Sprinkle onion and eggs around and through potato cubes. Cover on top with mayonnaise. Adorn with pimento strips, olives and shrimp; sprinkle peas all over salad. Yield: 8 servings.

Mrs. G. P. Pribyl, VP OWC
Topsham AFS, Maine

EASY CAESAR SALAD

4 tbsp. lemon juice
1/4 c. olive oil
1/2 tsp. ground pepper
1 tsp. Worcestershire sauce
1/2 tsp. garlic powder
1/2 tsp. salt
1 beaten egg
1/2 c. Parmesan cheese
6 chopped anchovies
1 c. croutons
2 heads romaine lettuce

(Continued on next page)

Place all ingredients except coutons and lettuce into jar; shake well. Refrigerate till just before serving. Tear up lettuce leaves when ready to serve; pour dressing over. Add croutons. Yield: 4-6 servings.

Mrs. Alan G. Schreihofer, 1st VP OWC
Torrejon AB, Spain

GERMAN POTATO SALAD

2/3 lb. bacon, fried
5 lb. cooked potatoes, diced
1 1/2 c. vinegar
2 tsp. sugar
2 tbsp. salt
1/2 tsp. pepper
1/2 c. onions, chopped
1 c. water

Crumble bacon over potatoes. Add remaining ingredients to bacon grease; simmer. Pour over potatoes when ready to serve. Yield: 25 servings.

Mrs. William Schaal, Publ. Chm. OWC
Offutt AFB, Nebraska

GREEN BEAN SALAD

1 tsp. dillweed
1 tsp. dillseed
2 1-lb. cans whole green beans, drained
1 4-oz. jar pimento
1 c. chopped celery

Mix dressing according to directions on package; add dillweed and dillseed. Combine beans, pimentos and celery in large container; add dressing. Marinate overnight or for about 8 hours in refrigerator. Yield: 8 servings.

Mrs. Wade F. Johnson, OWC
McCoy AFB, Florida

HERBED FRESH VEGETABLES

Ripe red tomatoes
Firm cucumbers
2/3 c. salad oil
1/4 c. tarragon vinegar
3 tbsp. finely-cut parsley
3 tbsp. finely-cut chives
1 tsp. salt
1/4 tsp. coarse pepper
Few leaves or 1/2 tsp. dried marjoram

Peel tomatoes, if desired; slice into 1/2-inch slices. Peel cucumbers; slice into 1/4-inch slices. Combine tomatoes and cucumbers in bowl. Mix oil, vinegar and other ingredients; pour over vegetables. Cover; chill for at least 1 hour.

Mrs. Kenneth L. Stahl, Pres. OWC
Ft. McClellan, Alabama

GREEN BEAN SALAD

1/2 head lettuce, cut or broken
1/2 c. green onion, chopped or dry moistened
1/2 c. cut green beans

DRESSING:

2 tbsp. bacon grease
2 tbsp. sugar
2 tbsp. vinegar
Salt and pepper
2 strips crisp bacon, crumbled

Prepare salad in bowl. Combine bacon grease, sugar, vinegar, salt and pepper to taste for dressing. Pour cooled, not chilled dressing over salad mixture before serving. Sprinkle crumbled bacon on top. May be tossed or not. Yield: 4 servings.

Mrs. F. J. Caron, Hon. VP OWC
Fort Fisher, North Carolina

HOT SPINACH SALAD

1 pkg. fresh spinach, washed, drained
3/4 tbsp. bacon fat
3/4 tbsp. olive oil
4 or 5 dashes of soy sauce
1 1/2 tbsp. cider vinegar
1/4 tsp. mustard
Seasoned salt
2 slices bacon, cooked and crumbled

Tear spinach into bite-sized pieces. Heat skillet. Add bacon fat, olive oil, soy sauce, vinegar and mustard; blend with spoon. Add spinach when dressing is thoroughly heated; toss. Add half the bacon; continue to toss. Add remaining bacon. Turn off heat when spinach leaves are covered with dressing; serve at once. Yield: 3 servings.

Mrs. Salvador E. Felices, OWC
McCoy AFB, Florida

ITALIAN CHEF'S SALAD

4 tbsp. salad oil
4 tbsp. wine vinegar
2 tbsp. lemon juice
1 clove of garlic, chopped
1 tbsp. chopped parsley
1/2 tsp. pepper
1/2 tsp. salt
1 c. cold cooked meat, cut in very thin strips
1 head garden lettuce, torn into pieces

(Continued on next page)

Place oil, vinegar, lemon juice and spices together in shaker or jar; mix thoroughly. Add sliced meat; marinate for 1 hour or more. Toss with lettuce just before serving. Yield: 4 servings.

Mrs. Warren K. Hilliard, Jr., Parlm. OWC
Chicksands RAF Base, England

KIDNEY BEAN SALAD

1 16-oz. can kidney beans, drained
1 med.-sized cucumber, thinly-sliced
1 lge. Bermuda onion, cut in rings
2 lge. tomatoes, cut in wedges
1 head crisp lettuce
1/3 to 1/2 c. mayonnaise
1 tsp. salt
Dash of pepper
3 hard-cooked eggs, sliced

Wash kidney beans in cold water; drain. Add cucumber, onion rings, tomato wedges and large lettuce leaves. Toss lightly with mayonnaise, salt and pepper. Place in lettuce-lined salad bowl. Garnish with egg slices. Yield: 6 servings.

Mrs. Patrick J. Kenny, Treas. OWC
Fort Monmouth, New Jersey

MABEL'S SALAD

2 eggs
Salt
Monosodium glutamate
1 tbsp. cooking oil
1 lge. unpeeled cucumber, chilled
1 1-lb. can bean sprouts, chilled and drained
2 tbsp. sesame seed oil

Beat eggs with 1/4 teaspoon salt and 1/4 teaspoon monosodium glutamate. Heat oil in large frypan to sizzling; add egg mixture. Lower heat. Slide eggs over pan until dry and like a sheet. Remove from heat; shred into pieces about 1/4 x 1-inch. Set aside. Slice cucumber into slices no more than 1/4-inch thick; cut slices into 1/4-inch wide strips. Combine with bean sprouts, 1 teaspoon salt, 1/4 teaspoon monosodium glutamate and sesame seed oil. Add about 3/4 of shredded egg; toss. Garnish with remaining egg. Yield: 4 servings.

Mrs. Royce Moser, Jr., Program Chm. OWC
Ent AFB, Colorado

MARINATED BEAN SALAD

1 No. 303 can green beans
1 No. 303 can yellow wax beans
1 No. 303 can kidney beans
1 No. 303 can garbanza beans
1/2 c. minced celery
1/2 c. minced onion
1/2 c. salad oil

(Continued on next page)

1/2 c. cider vinegar
3/4 c. sugar
1 tsp. salt
1/2 tsp. pepper

Drain each can beans into colander; rinse. Place in glass bowl; add celery and onion. Mix all other ingredients in separate bowl; pour over bean mixture, tossing to mix. Cover; refrigerate until served. Let stand for about 8 or 9 hours at least. Yield: 10 servings.

Mrs. Lawrence B. Moore, OWC
Keyport Naval Torpedo Station, Washington

MIXED VEGETABLE SALAD

1 10-oz. pkg. frozen mixed vegetables
1/4 c. vinegar
1/4 c. mayonnaise
1/4 c. sour cream
1 hard-boiled egg, chopped
1 fresh tomato, sliced

Cook frozen vegetables according to package directions; drain well. Add vinegar, mayonnaise and sour cream. Add egg and tomato, if desired. Yield: 4 servings.

Mrs. Monte G. Dickey, 1st VP OWC
Itazuke AB, Japan

MIXED VEGETABLE SALAD

1 1-lb. 8-oz. pkg. frozen mixed vegetables
1/4 c. chopped scallions, including tops
1/4 c. chopped green pepper
3/4 c. salad dressing
Salt and pepper

Cook mixed vegetables according to package directions; drain. Add scallions and green pepper; cool. Add salad dressing, salt and pepper to taste. Keep in refrigerator until ready to use. Garnish with tomato wedges, if desired. This will keep for several days in refrigerator. Yield: 6-8 servings.

Mrs. David E. Disbrown, Hail and Farewell Chm. OWC
Selfridge AFB, Michigan

PEA AND MUSHROOM SALAD

1/2 c. mayonnaise
1 med. onion, finely minced
6 tsp. evaporated milk
1 tsp. Season-All
1 tsp. sugar
Pinch of nutmeg
3 drops of Tabasco
1 No. 303 can green peas, drained
8 oz. mushroom slices, drained

(Continued on next page)

Mix mayonnaise with onion, milk and spices well. Mix in vegetables; refrigerate for 2 hours. Yield: 3-4 servings.

Mrs. Marvin R. Breaux, Pres. MAAG OWC
Addis Ababa, Ethiopia

SAUERKRAUT SALAD

1 lge. can sauerkraut
1 lge. onion
1 lge. green pepper
1 lge. sweet red pepper or 1 sm. can pimento
1 c. celery
Salt
1 c. vinegar
1 1/2 c. sugar

Chop vegetables; combine. Salt to taste. Mix vinegar and sugar; pour over vegetables. Pour into container; cover. Store in refrigerator. This keeps for long time. Use dietary sweetener instead of sugar to make low-calorie salad. Yield: 6 servings.

Mrs. James F. Meyer, Corr. Sec. OWC
Sheppard AFB, Texas

SPINACH SALAD

Fresh spinach, washed and cut up
Oil, vinegar, salt, pepper and garlic powder
Crisp bacon pieces

Toss spinach lightly with oil, vinegar, salt, pepper and garlic powder. Sprinkle bacon pieces over spinach before serving.

Mrs. Vernon L. Speicher, Corr. Sec. OWC
Edgewood Arsenal, Maryland

SUMMER SALAD

1 pt. sour cream
1 envelope onion soup mix
1/2 c. cottage cheese
1/4 c. finely-chopped cucumber
2 tbsp. finely-chopped green pepper
3 radishes, coarsely chopped

(Continued on next page)

Blend all ingredients; cover. Refrigerate until cold and firm. Serve on crisp lettuce. Yield: 4 servings.

Mrs. Jerry V. Brown, Womens' Club Corr. Sec.
Sandia Base, New Mexico

SWEET AND SOUR LETTUCE

1 med. head lettuce, torn into small pieces
1/2 c. onion, chopped
1 tsp. sugar
1 tbsp. vinegar
6 slices bacon, fried till crisp

Wash lettuce in cold water; drain. Toss lettuce with onion, sugar and vinegar. Remove bacon from pan; drain on paper towel. Pour warm bacon fat over lettuce mixture; toss lightly. Top with crumbled bacon. Yield: 6 servings.

Mrs. E. J. Krestly, Hospitality Chm. NAD OWC
Hawthorne, Nevada

WILTED LEAF LETTUCE SALAD

1 head wilted leaf or romaine lettuce
4 slices bacon, chopped into sm. pieces
1 1/2 tbsp. sugar
3 tbsp. vinegar

Break lettuce into bite-sized pieces. Fry bacon until almost crisp; add sugar and vinegar to bacon and bacon fat. Stir until well-mixed; pour over lettuce. Yield: 4-6 servings.

Mrs. R. U. Zuberbuhler, Program Chm. OWC
Hahn AFB, Germany

ZUCCHINI SALAD

6-8 zucchini squash, quartered
Salted, boiling water
2/3 c. olive oil
1/3 c. wine vinegar
2 tbsp. sweet pickle relish
Salt and pepper to taste
1 tsp. tarragon or oregano
Minced onion, green pepper if desired

Drop zucchini in boiling water. Cook for about 5 to 6 minutes until crisp but tender. Pour oil, vinegar, relish and seasonings into blender; mix. Pour over squash. Decorate with strips of pimento, capers and fresh parsley. Yield: 6 servings.

Mrs. Robert Karwoski, Publ. Chm. OWC
Griffiss AFB, New York

Breads

RECIPE FOR CHERRY HOT CROSS BUNS ON PAGE 266

CLOUD BISCUITS

2 c. flour
4 tsp. baking powder
1 tbsp. sugar
1/2 tsp. salt
1/2 c. shortening
1 egg, beaten
2/3 c. milk

Sift flour, baking powder, sugar and salt into large mixing bowl. Cut in shortening with pastry blender. Add egg to milk; pour milk mixture into dry ingredients. Stir lightly with a fork. Turn out onto floured surface; knead about 20 times. Roll dough to 3/4-inch thickness; cut with small biscuit cutter. Bake in 450-degree oven for 10 to 14 minutes. For drop biscuits increase milk to 3/4 cup. Yield: 2 dozen servings.

Mrs. Ricahrd A. Naldrett, Adv. OWC
McCoy AFB, Florida

SESAME FLAT BISCUITS

1 8-oz. pkg. or 10 refrigerator biscuits
1 tbsp. margarine or butter, melted
Sesame seeds

Place biscuits on greased cookie sheet. Pat out with fingers until 3-inches across. Leave 1-inch between biscuits. Brush with margarine; sprinkle with sesame seeds. Bake at 350 degrees for 10 minutes or until brown. May be made ahead and placed in refrigerator or frozen. Place in 200-degree oven to reheat. Yield: 5 servings.

Mrs. Marshall J. Loftus, OWC
Hickam AFB, Hawaii

TEX-EZY BISCUITS

2 c. sifted all-purpose flour
3 tsp. baking powder
1 tsp. salt
1/3 c. Wesson oil
2/3 c. milk

Sift together flour, baking powder and salt. Pour oil and milk into measuring cup; do not stir together. Pour into flour mixture. Stir with fork until mixture rounds up into a ball. Place dough on waxed paper; press out 1/4-inch thick with hands. Cut with unfloured biscuit cutter. Bake for 10 to 12 minutes on ungreased cookie sheet in 475-degree oven. Yield: 3-4 servings.

Mrs. Bill B. Lambert, Ways and Means Chm. OWC
Sembach, Germany

BACON BARS

1/2 c. shredded sharp American cheese
6 slices bacon, fried crisp and crumbled

(Continued on next page)

2 c. biscuit mix
3 tbsp. bacon drippings

Stir cheese and bacon into biscuit mix. Prepare dough according to package directions for rich biscuits, substituting drippings for shortening. Knead 10 times. Roll out to 10 x 6-inches; cut into strips 6 inches long and 1-inch wide. Cut each strip into 1/3 to make 18 bars. Place 1-inch apart on ungreased baking sheet. Bake at 450 degrees for 10 minutes. Yield: 18 rolls.

Mrs. Theodore Musachia, OWC
Chandler AFB, Minnesota

BREAD AND BUTTER STICKS

Butter or margarine
2 c. (about) packaged biscuit mix
1 tbsp. sugar
1/2 c. milk

Melt 6 tablespoons butter in 13 x 9 x 2-inch baking pan in oven. Combine biscuit mix, sugar and milk in mixing bowl; stir with fork till soft dough is formed. Beat vigorously 20 strokes. Turn out onto board lightly-dusted with biscuit mix; knead gently 10 times. Roll into 12 x 8-inch rectangle. Cut dough in half lengthwise with floured knife; cut each half crosswise into 16 strips. Dip each strip into melted butter turning to coat both sides. Arrange in 2 rows. Bake in 425-degree oven for 15 minutes or until golden. Serve warm. Yield: 32 sticks.

Mrs. Kelly E. Taggart
ESSA OWC
Rockville, Maryland

GARLIC STICKS

1 can biscuits
1/4 c. milk
1/2 c. crushed cornflakes
Garlic salt

Cut each biscuit in half. Shape into sticks 5 to 6-inches long. Dip each stick into milk; roll in cornflakes. Sprinkle with garlic salt. Place sticks on buttered baking sheet about 1-inch apart. Bake in 450-degree oven for 7 to 10 minutes. Yield: 20 servings.

Mrs. Glyn W. Ramsey, Hon. Pres. OWC
Aviano AFB, Italy

QUICK BUTTER DIPS

2 c. (about) sifted flour
1 tbsp. sugar

(Continued on next page)

1 tbsp. baking powder
Pinch of salt
1 c. milk
1 stick or 1/2 c. margarine or butter

Sift dry ingredients together into mixing bowl; add milk all at once. Stir lightly to moisten. Do not overmix. Cut stick of margarine in half; melt each half in 9-inch glass baking dish. Place dough on lightly-floured surface; sprinkle with flour. Pat into 1/4-inch thick oblong shape. Cut in half lengthwise with table knife; cut each half into 16 to 20 strips. Pick up each strip separately; place in melted margarine. Turn strips to coat. Place side by side in baking dish. Repeat for second baking dish. Bake in 425-degree oven for 10 to 15 minutes or until golden brown. Serve with jelly or honey, if desired. Yield: 6-8 servings.

Mrs. Jerry M. Plenert, Booksales Chm. OWC
Mather AFB, California

SESAME ROLLS

1 pkg. refrigerator biscuits
Milk
1 1/2 c. rice cereal, crushed coarsely
2 tsp. salt
1 tbsp. sesame seed
1 tbsp. caraway seed

Cut biscuits in half; roll each into slim stick about 4-inches long. Brush with milk. Combine cereal crumbs, salt and seeds; roll sticks in mixture. Place on greased baking sheet. Bake in 400-degree oven for about 10 minutes or until rolls are lightly browned. Yield: 20 servings.

Mrs. Douglas C. Purdy, Corr. Sec. OWC
Scott AFB, Illinois

SESAME STICKS

1/2 c. butter or margarine
2 cans refrigerator biscuits
1 box sesame seeds

Melt butter into 11 x 15-inch baking pan. Separate biscuits; pull and stretch biscuits into 7-inch sticks. Roll in melted butter; twist. Place in baking pan; sprinkle liberally with sesame seeds. Bake at 450 degrees for 8 to 10 minutes or until golden. Remove from oven; let set for 2 minutes before removing from pan. This allows sesame sticks to absorb butter in pan. Yield: 20 servings.

Mrs. Don M. Rieke, First VP OWC
Norton AFB, California

CHEDDAR CHEESE STARS

1 c. Bisquick
1 c. grated cheddar cheese
1/2 c. water
Paprika

Combine Bisquick and cheese; stir in water. Roll out 1/4-inch thick; cut into small star shapes. Sprinkle with paprika. Arrange on ungreased cookie sheet; cover with waxed paper. Refrigerate. Bake at 425 degrees for 8 to 10 minutes or until lightly brown. Yield: 2 dozen.

Mrs. Richard J. Schriver, Adv. OWC
Beaufort MCAS, South Carolina

CHEESE CORN BREAD

1 c. sifted all-purpose flour
1/4 c. sugar
4 tsp. baking powder
3/4 tsp. salt
1 c. yellow cornmeal
2 eggs
1 c. milk
1/4 c. soft shortening
1 c. grated cheddar cheese
3 tbsp. poppy seed

Preheat oven to 425 degrees. Sift flour with sugar, baking powder and salt; stir in cornmeal. Add eggs, milk and shortening. Beat with rotary or electric mixer till just smooth about 1 minute. Add cheese; mix lightly. Pour into 3 greased loaf pans; sprinkle with poppy seed. Bake in 425-degree oven for 20 to 25 minutes. Fill pans no more than 2/3 full.

Mrs. Robert C. Whitcomb
Wheeler OWC
Hickam AFB, Hawaii

CORN BREAD

3/4 c. bread flour
2 tsp. baking powder
3/4 tsp. salt
2 tbsp. sugar
3/4 c. yellow cornmeal
3 tbsp. melted butter
3/4 c. milk
1 egg, beaten

Heat oven to 425 degrees. Sift dry ingredients into mixing bowl. Melt butter in 8 x 8-inch pan. Combine dry ingredients with milk and egg. Beat well. Pour into buttered and heated pan. Bake for 25 minutes. Yield: 8 servings.

Mrs. Joe E. Ashley, Treas.
Menwith Hill WC
Harrogate, England

HAWAIIAN CORN BREAD

2 eggs
1 c. milk
2 sticks melted butter
3/4 c. sugar
2 c. Bisquick
1/2 tsp. baking soda
2 tbsp. yellow cornmeal

Beat eggs well. Add milk and melted butter. Fold in dry ingredients. Pour into greased 1-quart ring mold or loaf pan. Bake at 350 degrees for 30 to 35 minutes. Yield: 8 servings.

Mrs. J. J. Hein, Treas. NOWC
Charleston, South Carolina

JALAPENO CORN BREAD

3 c. corn bread mix
1/2 c. salad oil
1 lge. grated onion
1/2 c. pickled jalapeno peppers, chopped
    finely
1 1/2 c. grated cheese
1/2 c. pimento, chopped
2 1/2 c. milk
3 beaten eggs
1 can creamed corn
3 slices bacon, fried and chipped
Mashed garlic to taste

Mix all ingredients well. Bake at 400 degrees in greased pan until golden brown. Yield: 4-6 servings.

Mrs. Harry B. Trimble, Hon. VP OWC
George AFB, California

HOT CORN BREAD

1 1/2 c. yellow cornmeal
1/4 c. cooking oil
1 tsp. salt
2 eggs
3 tbsp. baking powder
1 c. sour cream
1 c. canned cream corn
3 jalapeno peppers, chopped fine

Preheat oven to 350 degrees. Combine all ingredients. Pour into greased deep baking dish or Dutch oven. Bake for 35 minutes. Yield: 6 servings.

Mrs. James B. Argersinger, Parlm. OWC
Misawa AFB, Japan

JALAPENO CORN STICKS

2 c. white cornmeal
1 c. flour
1 tsp. salt
6 tsp. baking powder
3 eggs
1 lge. onion, chopped fine
8 to 12 jalapeno peppers, chopped fine
1/2 c. Wesson oil
1 1-lb. can cream-style corn
1 1/2 c. grated cheddar cheese

Mix dry ingredients; add eggs, onion, jalapeno peppers, oil and corn. Mix well; fold in cheese last. Batter will be thick. Bake at 350 degrees in greased corn stick pans for about 25 minutes. These may be made and kept frozen.

Mrs. Thomas E. Moore, Adv. OWC
Elmendorf AFB, Alaska

SPOON BREAD

1 c. white cornmeal
1 c. boiling water
2 tbsp. melted butter
1 tsp. salt
2 eggs, well-beaten
1 c. milk
1 1/2 tsp. baking powder

Scald cornmeal with boiling water. Stir in remaining ingredients; mix well. Turn into buttered pan. Bake at 375 degrees for 40 minutes. Yield: 6-8 servings.

Mrs. Thomas Madison Anthony
664th Radar OWC
Bellefontaine, Ohio

HUSH PUPPIES

1 1/2 c. cornmeal
1 1/2 c. water
1/2 c. milk
1 tbsp. vegetable oil
2 tsp. grated onion
2 beaten eggs
1 c. flour
3 tsp. baking powder
2 tsp. salt
1 tsp. sugar (opt.)

Cook cornmeal and water, stirring until stiff and mixture begins to roll into ball. Remove from heat; add milk, oil and onion. Stir until smooth. Stir into eggs in 2-quart bowl. Sift flour; blend in dry ingredients. Add to cornmeal batter blending thoroughly. Heat 1-inch deep fat to 375 degrees. Drop batter by teaspoonfuls into fat; fry for 6 to 7 minutes. Drain. Increase onion and salt and add garlic for more spicy hush puppies.

Mrs. Lawrence A. Ferguson
Naval Training Center OWC
Bainbridge, Maryland

OLD VIRGINIA SPOON BREAD

1 1/2 c. plain cornmeal
2 tsp. baking powder
1 1/2 tsp. salt
3 c. cold water
1 1/2 c. milk
3 eggs
3 tbsp. butter

Sift together cornmeal, baking powder and salt; add water. Pour into pan; cook until thick, stirring constantly. Remove from stove; add milk, eggs and butter. Turn into greased 13 x 9 1/2 x 2-inch pan. Bake in 400-degree oven for 25 to 30 minutes. Yield: 6-8 servings.

Mrs. Charles H. Yeatts, Hosp. Chm.
Naval Weapons Sta. OWC
Yorktown, Virginia

QUICK CORN STICKS

    1 12-oz. pkg. corn muffin mix
    1 12-oz. can or 1 1/2 c. whole kernel corn,
        drained
    1/4 c. chopped green pepper
    1 tsp. minced onion

Prepare corn muffin mix according to package directions. Add corn, green pepper and onion; mix well. Fill greased corn stick or muffin pans 2/3 full. Bake at 350 degrees for 20 minutes or until medium brown. Yield: 24 servings.

Mrs. Raymond N. Winkel, Treas.
Norfolk, NAS, Virginia

SPOON BREAD

    1/2 c. yellow cornmeal
    1/2 tsp. salt
    2 c. milk
    2 eggs
    Butter

Cook cornmeal, salt and 1 1/2 cups of the milk over low fire until very thick, stirring constantly. Add 1 egg; beat vigorously. Spread into buttered shallow serving dish. Break remaining egg into pan to which cornmeal was cooked; beat well. Add 1/2 cup of the milk; stir to blend. Add slowly so the egg mixture cuts into cornmeal mixture without blending. Bake at 375 degrees for 30 minutes or until puffed and brown on top. Serve with butter and jam, if desired. Yield: 4 servings.

Mrs. Russell L. Taylor
Med. Serv. Corps OWC
San Diego, California

TEXAS CORN BREAD PUDDING

    1 c. cornmeal
    1/2 tsp. baking soda
    1/2 tsp. salt
    2 eggs, well beaten
    3/4 c. milk
    1/4 c. bacon drippings
    1 1-lb. 1-oz. can cream-style corn
    1 4-oz. can green chilies, chopped
    1 c. grated sharp cheese

Combine all ingredients except cheese. Place half the batter in greased baking dish; cover with half the cheese. Spoon remaining batter over this. Cover with remaining cheese. Bake in 350-degree oven about 25 minutes or till done. Yield: 8 servings.

Mrs. Urey W. Alexander, Pres. USAWC
Carlisle Barracks, Pennsylvania

SPOON CORN BREAD

2 1/2 c. milk
2/3 c. cornmeal
Butter
1/2 tsp. salt
2 eggs

Combine milk and cornmeal in saucepan. Heat to boiling; cook for 1 minute. Add 2 tablespoons butter and salt; set aside. Beat eggs until frothy; fold into cornmeal mixture. Pour into greased 1-quart casserole. Bake at 375 degrees for 35 to 40 minutes. Serve from baking dish with plenty of butter. Omit salt if using self-rising cornmeal. Yield: 5-7 servings.

Mrs. Kelly G. Moss, Pres. OWC
USPHS Hosp., Norfolk, Virginia

TEXAS TRAIL CORN BREAD

2 c. yellow cornmeal
1 tsp. salt
1 tsp. baking powder
Hot boiling water
1 egg
Salad oil

Mix cornmeal, salt and baking powder well. Add hot water till slightly moistened. Beat egg; add to mixture, stirring well. Mixture should be fairly dry. Shape heaping spoonfuls into balls; drop into hot oil. Fry until golden in color and crispy. Excellent with chili and red beans. Yield: 2-4 servings.
PERSONAL NOTE: This recipe originated with my husband's great-grandmother who was an Indian. It was used by chuckwagon cooks in the late 1800's.

Mrs. B. E. Thornton, Spec. Act. Chm. OWC
Camp Nieuw, The Netherlands

CLOUD-LIGHT DROP DUMPLINGS

1 c. flour
2 tsp. baking powder
1/2 tsp. salt
1/2 c. milk
Sprig of parsley, minced

Sift dry ingredients together into small bowl. Use scant cup of flour if not presifted, saving time to sift just once. Add milk and parsley; mix to thick batter. Drop from spoon onto boiling beef or chicken stew. Cover tightly; cook for 20 minutes. Do not raise lid while cooking. Lower heat; boil gently.

Mrs. Harry L. Gans, Ways and Means Chm.
Army Surgeon Gen. Office
Washington, D. C.

EASY DROP DUMPLINGS

1 c. sifted flour
1 1/2 tsp. baking powder
1/2 tsp. salt
1 tbsp. Crisco
1/2 c. milk or water

Sift flour with baking powder and salt. Cut in Crisco until mixture is fine as cornmeal. Add milk; mix very lightly until soft dough is formed. Drop from teaspoon onto boiling stew. Cover tightly; cook without removing cover for 12 minutes. May be used with navy beans. Beans are removed from pot; dumplings spooned onto the broth. Yield: 4-6 servings.

Mrs. William C. Westcoat, NOWC
Bremerhaven, Germany

HOMEMADE NOODLES

Flour
3 eggs
1 tsp. salt

Fill a mixing bowl about 1/3 full of flour. Make a hole in the center; break eggs into hole. Add salt; work flour into eggs with fork. Work in as much flour as possible or until dough can be handled. Work until smooth on floured board; roll out; cut into small strips 1/2 to 3/4-inch wide. Shake out each long strip; drop into boiling broth. Cook for 20 to 30 minutes, uncovered. Yield: 8-10 servings.

Mrs. Benson Frank Landrum, Special Projects Co-Chm. OWC
Stuttgart, Germany

HERB RING-ROUND

1/2 stick butter
2 tsp. Italian Good Seasons herbs
2 pkg. refrigerator butter flake rolls

Melt butter in small saucepan; stir in herbs. Separate rolls in each package into 12 pieces. Dip 1 at a time into butter mixture, coating both sides. Stand on edge in single layer in buttered 9-inch pie plate working from outside toward center. Bake in 375-degree oven for 20 minutes or until golden. Serve hot. Yield: 8 servings.

Mrs. Donald E. Sexton, Ed. Bd. Mem.
Fort Lee, Virginia

GOLDEN CHEESE FRENCH BREAD

1 loaf French bread, sliced
1 stick butter, melted
Parmesan cheese, fresh grated

(Continued on next page)

Dip each slice of bread in melted butter then Parmesan cheese. Place on baking sheet. Place slices under broiler for 1 minute; serve. Yield: 8 servings.

Mrs. James D. Johnson, Pres. OWC
MCAS Cherry Point, North Carolina

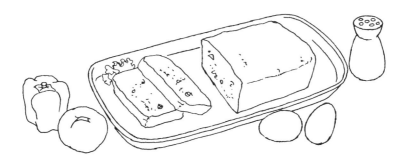

HERITAGE BROWN BREAD

2 c. graham flour
1/2 c. all-purpose flour
2 tsp. baking soda
1 tsp. salt
2 c. buttermilk
1/2 c. molasses
1 c. seedless raisins

Combine all ingredients; mix well. Spoon into 3 well-greased Number 303 or 1-pound cans. Let stand for 30 minutes. Bake at 350 degrees for 45 to 50 minutes or until cake tests done.

Mrs. Martin J. Valaske, Corr. Sec. OWC
U. S. Naval Hosp., Great Lakes, Illinois

HOT ONION BREAD

2 c. flour
4 tsp. baking powder
1/2 tsp. (about) salt
4 tbsp. shortening
1 lge. onion
3/4 c. milk

Sift dry ingredients; mix in shortening. Dice half the onion very fine; mix in. Add milk; stir well. Turn into deep 9-inch cake pan patting dough higher on sides. Slice remaining onion on top of dough. Sprinkle with salt. Bake in 470-degree oven for about 12 minutes. Cut into wedges; serve. Yield: 6-8 servings.

Mrs. Delmar G. Jacobs, Mem. Chm. OWC
Offutt AFB, Nebraska

ONION-BACON BREAD

4 strips bacon
2 c. biscuit mix
2 tbsp. instant minced onion
2/3 c. milk
3 tbsp. melted butter

Cut bacon into small pieces. Fry until crisp; drain. Combine biscuit mix with 1 tablespoon of the onion. Add milk; blend thoroughly with fork. Turn dough into greased 8-inch square pan using back of spoon to spread evenly. Combine remaining onion and butter; spoon over dough. Sprinkle with bacon. Bake in 425-degree oven for 15 to 20 minutes. Cut; serve hot. Yield: 9 servings.

Mrs. Roland H. Shamburek, Vol. Act. Chm.
Army Surgeon Gen. Office
Washington, D. C.

ONION KUCHEN

2 med.-sized onions
3 tbsp. butter
1 pkg. refrigerator biscuits
1 egg
1 8-oz. carton sour cream
1/2 tsp. salt
1 tsp. poppy seed

Slice onions; separate into rings. Saute slowly in butter until soft. Separate biscuits into layers; place single layer in ungreased 8-inch cake pan. Spoon onion mixture on top. Beat egg slightly; blend in sour cream and salt. Spoon over onion mixture; sprinkle with poppy seed. Bake in 375-degree oven for 30 minutes or until topping is set. Slice into wedges; serve warm. Yield: 6 servings.

Mrs. D. A. Panska Bd. Mem. OWC
Iwakuni M. C. A. S., Japan

QUICK FRENCH BREAD

2 cans refrigerator biscuits
1 egg white, slightly beaten
Sesame seed
Butter or margarine, melted
Garlic butter

Stand biscuits on edge on cookie sheet. Lightly press together and shape to form long loaf. Brush with egg white; sprinkle with sesame seed. Bake at 350 degree

(Continued on next page)

for 35 to 40 minutes or until brown. Remove from oven; slice almost to bottom. Spread with melted butter; return to oven. Bake for several minutes. Serve hot. Yield: 6-8 servings.

Mrs. Thomas J. Mitchell, Pres. OWC
Davisville CBS, Rhode Island

SKILLET ONION BREAD

1 c. chopped onion
4 tbsp. butter
2 pkg. refrigerator biscuits

Saute onion in butter in 10-inch skillet with ovenproof handle until soft; remove from heat. Lift out onion with slotted spoon; place in small bowl. Separate biscuits; dip to coat both sides in drippings remaining in skillet. Arrange biscuits in single layer in skillet beginning at outer edge and working toward center. Spoon onion evenly over top. Bake in 400-degree oven for 25 minutes or until lightly golden. Separate into individual biscuits before serving. Yield: 2 dozen.

Mrs. Garth E. Phillips, Ways and Means Chm. OWC
Bolling AFB Washington, D.C.

CRAIG'S MELT-IN-YOUR-MOUTH MUFFINS

Oil
2 c. flour, sifted
2 tsp. baking powder
1/2 tsp. salt
1/4 c. sugar
1 egg
1 c. milk
1/4 c. melted shortening

Heat oven to 425 degrees. Oil muffin cups well. Measure flour. Add baking powder, salt and sugar. Sift again into mixing bowl. Break egg into small mixing bowl; beat slightly. Add milk and melted shortening to egg. Pour egg mixture into flour; stir until all ingredients are blended. Fill muffin cups half full. Bake in preheated oven for 15 to 20 minutes. Yield: 10-12 servings.

Mrs. Terry P. Weyant, Treas. OWC
Whiteman AFB, Missouri

DOUBLE CORN MUFFINS

1 pkg. corn muffin mix
1 1-lb. can or 2 c. whole kernel corn, drained
1 2 1/4-oz. can deviled ham

Prepare muffin mix according to package directions; stir in corn. Spoon into greased muffin pans, filling 2/3 full. Drop 1 spoonful of deviled ham onto center of each muffin. Bake at 375 degrees for 20 minutes. Yield: 12 servings.

Mrs. Paul I. Hartman, OWC
Fort Johnston, North Carolina

GRITS MUFFINS

1 c. sifted enriched flour
1 tsp. salt
2 tbsp. baking powder
1 egg
3/4 c. milk
2 tbsp. liquid shortening
2/3 c. cooked quick grits
Butter
Jam

Preheat oven to 425 degrees. Sift together flour, salt and baking powder. Beat egg, milk and oil together. Add to dry ingredients; stir until slightly blended. Fold in grits. Spoon into well-greased muffin pans. Bake for 20 to 25 minutes or until lightly browned. Remove from oven; loosen each muffin with knife or spatula. Serve hot with butter and jam. Yield: 12 servings.

Mrs. J. B. Caughman, Past Pres. OWC
U. S. Naval Station, The Bermudas

MOM'S MUFFINS

1/4 c. shortening
1/4 c. sugar
1 egg
1 1/2 c. flour
2 1/2 tsp. baking powder
1/2 tsp. salt
1/2 c. (about) milk

Cream shortening and sugar. Add egg; blend well. Add flour, baking powder, salt and milk. Stir with spoon until just blended. Add more milk if batter is too thick; stir to blend. Fill greased muffin tins 2/3 full. Bake at 400 degrees for 12 to 15 minutes. Yield: 12-18 servings.

Mrs. John J. Noller, Pres. OWC
Kingsley Field AFB, Oregon

MYSTERY MUFFINS

1 c. self-rising flour
3 tbsp. mayonnaise
1/2 c. milk

Place flour in bowl; add mayonnaise and milk. Stir till blended. Fill greased muffin cups 2/3 full. Bake at 425 degrees for 16 to 20 minutes. Yield: 6 servings.

Mrs. F. M. Amman, OWC
Parris Island, South Carolina

APPLE PANCAKE

1 egg
3/4 c. milk
1 c. Bisquick
Butter
1/2 tsp. cinnamon sugar
1 apple, peeled and sliced thin
Maple syrup

Mix egg, milk and Bisquick together. Melt butter in large frying pan over low heat. Pour in batter; sprinkle with cinnamon sugar. Arrange sliced apples in circular pattern over mixture. Cook until nicely browned on bottom. Flip pancake over in pan with pancake turner. Cook for a few minutes; turn out on plate apple side up. Cut into 8 wedges. Serve with butter and maple syrup. Yield: 4 servings.

Mrs. Walter D. Stone, Jr., OWC
Fort Myer, Virginia

BLINTZ PANCAKES

3 eggs
1 1/4 c. milk
3/4 c. all-purpose flour
1 tbsp. sugar
1/2 tsp. salt
Cottage cheese

Beat eggs till thick and lemon-colored; stir in milk. Sift together dry ingredients; add to egg mixture. Mix until s m o o t h. Pour about 1/4 cup of the batter onto moderately hot, buttered griddle. Spread batter evenly to make thin cakes. Turn when underside is delicately brown. Spread 2 tablespoons of cottage cheese across center of each cake; roll up. Place cakes on towel-covered baking sheet in moderate oven to keep warm. Serve with syrup of your choice. Yield: 12 servings.

Mrs. Daniel R. Stefanowich, Hosp. Chm.
Yuma Proving Ground OWC
Yuma, Arizona

DELICATE PANCAKES

2 eggs
1/2 pt. sour cream, combined with
   1/2 tsp. soda
4 tbsp. flour
3 tbsp. melted butter

Beat eggs; add remaining ingredients. Mix well. Drop by tablespoonfuls onto hot griddle. Yield: 3 servings.

Mrs. Joseph McCarthy, Pres. OWC
Fort Campbell, Kentucky

FEATHERWEIGHT PANCAKES

3 eggs, separated
1/4 tsp. salt
1/4 c. flour
3/4 c. cottage cheese

Heat griddle very slowly. Beat egg whites until stiff but not dry. Beat yolks with same beater until light and lemon colored. Stir in salt, flour and cheese; fold in egg whites. Drop by small spoonfuls onto hot, lightly-greased griddle. Bake until golden brown on both sides. Serve with honey and butter, if desired. Yield: 4 servings.

Mrs. R. M. Frye, Hon. Pres.
U. S. Naval Air Facility OWC
Naples, Italy

QUICK AND EASY SOURDOUGH PANCAKES

1 c. sifted flour
1 tsp. baking powder
1/4 tsp. salt
1 tbsp. sugar
1 egg
1 c. sour milk
1/2 tsp. soda
3 tbsp. melted shortening

(Continued on next page)

Sift flour, baking powder, salt and sugar. Beat egg well. Combine sour milk and soda; add to egg. Stir in melted shortening. Add to flour mixture. Bake on hot griddle. Yield: 4 servings.

Mrs. Rudolph John Meissner, OWC
Eielson AFB, Alaska

BLUE CHEESE ROLLS

1 pkg. or 10 refrigerator biscuits
1 3 or 4-oz. pkg. blue cheese
Equal amount of butter or margarine
Paprika

Preheat oven to 425 degrees. Remove biscuits from package; separate. Cut each biscuit into 4 pieces. Place biscuits 1/2-inch apart on large cookie sheet. Cream blue cheese and butter together; spread equally onto each biscuit. Sprinkle with paprika. Bake at 425 degrees for 8 minutes. Yield: 40 servings.

Mrs. Milton A. Hintze, Jr. OWC
Ent AFB, Colorado

CHERRY HOT CROSS BUNS

1 13 3/4-oz. pkg. hot roll mix
1/4 c. chopped green glace cherries
1 1/4 c. sifted confectioners' sugar
5 tsp. milk
1 8-oz. jar red stemmed maraschino cherries

Prepare hot roll mix according to package directions, adding chopped glace cherries. Let rise; shape into 1 1/2-inch balls. Place on greased baking sheets. Let rise in warm place until doubled in size. Cut deep cross in each bun using scissors. Bake in 400-degree oven for 10 to 15 minutes or until golden brown. Cool slightly. Combine sugar and milk for frosting; mix until smooth. Pour into crosses. Top with whole maraschino cherries. Yield: 18 servings.

Photograph for this recipe on page 249.

EASY POPOVERS

1 c. milk
2 eggs
1 tbsp. oil
1 c. flour
1/4 tsp. salt

Place all ingredients in blender. Cover; blend thoroughly till smooth about 15 seconds. Pour into greased custard cups. Bake in 425-degree oven for about 30 to 40 minutes. Yield: 8 servings.

Mrs. Joseph B. Green, Jr. OWC
Davisville CBS, Rhode Island

Desserts

RECIPE FOR FLORIDA AMBROSIA ON PAGE 322

ALMOND BLOSSOM CAKE

    1 pkg. white cake mix
    3/4 c. less 3 tbsp. sour cream
    3/4 c. water
    2 egg whites
    1/2 tsp. almond extract

Blend all ingredients for cake in large mixing bowl; beat for 2 to 3 minutes at medium speed on mixer until smooth. Pour into 2 greased 8 or 9-inch layer pans. Bake for 30 to 35 minutes in 350-degree oven. Cool for 15 to 20 minutes before turning onto rack to finish cooling. Frost cake with Almond Cream Frosting.

    FROSTING:

    5 tbsp. butter or margarine
    3 c. confectioners' sugar
    3 tbsp. sour cream
    1/4 tsp. almond extract
    Toasted almonds

Cream butter; beat in sugar gradually. Add sour cream and extract; beat until light and fluffy. Spread between layers and over sides and top of cooled cake. Garnish with toasted almonds.

Mrs. John J. Eairley, OWC
Kelly AFB, Texas

CHOCOLATE ANGEL CAKE

    1 pkg. angel food cake mix
    1 c. instant chocolate mix
    1 c. heavy cream
    Semi-sweet chocolate

Beat egg white portion of cake mix as directed on package. Add instant chocolate when adding flour mixture. Bake according to package directions. Frost with whipped cream when completely cooled. Shave chocolate over top of cake; refrigerate until ready to use. Yield: 8-10 servings.

Mrs. Edward G. Haggett, Corr. Sec. OWC
Picatinny Arsenal, New Jersey

CINNAMON SWIRL PUDD'N CAKE

    1 1-lb. 3-oz. pkg. yellow cake mix
    1 pkg. instant vanilla pudding
    4 eggs
    1 c. water
    1/2 c. soft margarine
    1 tsp. vanilla extract
    1/4 c. sugar
    1 tsp. ground cinnamon
    Confectioners' sugar

Combine cake mix, pudding, eggs, water, margarine and vanilla extract in large mixing bowl; blend well. Beat at medium speed of electric mixer for 10 minutes.

(Continued on next page)

Pour into greased 10-inch tube pan or bundt pan. Combine sugar and cinnamon; sprinkle over batter. Cut through batter with spatula or knife. Bake in 350-degree oven for 45 minutes or until done. Cool in pan for 10 minutes. Remove from pan; cool on wire rack. Sprinkle with confectioners' sugar just before serving. Yield: One 10-inch tube cake.

Photograph for this recipe on cover.

COCONUT POUND CAKE

1 c. shortening
2 c. sugar
6 eggs
2 c. flour
Dash of salt
2 tsp. coconut flavoring
2 tbsp. coconut flour

Cream shortening and sugar; add eggs 1 at a time, creaming well. Add flour and salt, beating well. Beat in flavoring and coconut flour. Pour into ungreased tube pan. Bake for 1 hour at 325 to 350 degrees. Koko Whip, a coconut flour, may be obtained from a Stuckey's store.

Mrs. J. H. Kepley, Corr. Sec. OWC
RAF Mildenhall, England

COLUMBIAN CAKE

1 pkg. yellow cake mix
1 tbsp. sugar
1 tbsp. oil
2 c. light brown sugar
1 stick butter
1 No. 2 can crushed pineapple
1 c. chopped nuts
1 can coconut

Mix cake according to package instructions, adding sugar and oil. Place in greased 10 x 14-inch pan. Bake in 300-degree oven for 15 to 20 minutes until almost firm in center. Combine remaining ingredients; cook until thick. Spread on cake. Return to oven until toothpick in center comes out clean.

Mrs. Bruce K. Pierson, VP
NAS Command OWC
NAS Mainside, Florida

FLUFFY ELEGANTE ANGEL

1 pkg. angel food cake mix
Strong cold coffee
1 pkg. fluffy frosting mix
1/2 c. sour cream

(Continued on next page)

Prepare cake mix as directed on package, substituting coffee for water; pour into ungreased tube pan. Bake as directed. Prepare frosting mix as directed; fold in sour cream. Frost top and sides of cake; garnish with sliced toasted almonds. Refrigerate. Yield: 10 servings.

Mrs. John J. Maynihan
Forrestal OWC
Norfolk, Virginia

FRUIT COCKTAIL CAKE

1 No. 2 can fruit cocktail
1 c. sugar
1 egg
1 1/2 c. unsifted flour
1 tsp. baking soda
1/2 tsp. salt
1 c. brown sugar (firmly packed)
1/2 c. chopped nuts

Mix fruit cocktail, sugar and egg together; add flour, baking soda and salt. Place in greased and floured 9 x 13-inch pan. Mix brown sugar and chopped nuts; sprinkle over batter. Bake in 350-degree oven for 45 minutes. Top with whipped cream, if desired. Yield: 6-8 servings.

Mrs. Rodney O. Radke, Newsletter Ed. Women's Club
Fort Detrick, Maryland

FRUIT COCKTAIL CAKE

1 c. flour
1 c. sugar
1 tsp. soda
1 tsp. salt
1 8 3/4-oz. can fruit cocktail
1 egg
2 tbsp. brown sugar
1/2 c. nuts

Sift dry ingredients together. Mix or blend fruit cocktail and egg. Pour into 8 x 8-inch greased pan; sprinkle brown sugar and nuts on top. Bake in 350-degree oven for 30 minutes. Yield: 9 servings.

Mrs. F. R. Van Laethem, 3rd VP OWC
Washington, D. C.

GRAHAM CRACKER CAKE

30 graham crackers, crushed
1 c. chopped walnuts or pecans
1 c. shredded coconut
1 c. sugar
2 tsp. baking powder
1/8 tsp. salt
2 tbsp. melted butter
2 whole eggs
1 tsp. vanilla
1 c. milk

(Continued on next page)

Place all ingredients in large bowl in order given, stirring well with large spoon. Do not beat. Pour into greased and floured 8 x 10-inch or 9 x 9-inch pan. Bake at 350 degrees for 40 to 45 minutes. Serve warm or cold, plain or topped with whipped cream or orange butter frosting. Cake will keep for long time and may be frozen. Yield: 8-10 servings.

Mrs. John D. Libey, Hon. Pres. VT-1 OWC
Saufley Field NAS, Florida

LEMON-LIME CAKE

1 box lemon cake mix
1 pkg. lime Jell-O
3/4 c. water
3/4 c. oil
4 eggs
Juice of 2 lemons
1 c. powdered sugar

Mix cake mix and Jell-O. Add water, oil and unbeaten eggs; beat together. Pour into 2 greased 7 1/2 x 3 1/2-inch loaf pans. Bake in 350-degree oven for 40 minutes. Mix lemon juice and powdered sugar; spread on cake while warm. Yield: 12 servings.

Mrs. Warren E. McElheny, OWC
New Orleans NAS, Louisiana

PANIC CAKE

1 21-oz. can pie filling, any flavor
1 box yellow cake mix
2 sticks butter, melted
1/2 c. chopped nuts

Grease 8-inch square cake pan. Spread pie filling in pan; pour dry cake mix over filling. Pour melted butter and nuts on top. Bake for 45 minutes at 350 degrees. Yield: 9 servings.

Mrs. Curtis C. Heinrich, Special Activities Chm. OWC
Minot AFB, North Dakota

PEACH CAKE

1/2 c. sugar
Peaches, sliced
2 tbsp. butter
1 egg
Pinch of salt
1 tsp. (heaping) baking powder
1/2 c. milk
1 c. flour
1/2 tsp. vanilla

(Continued on next page)

Pineapple Cakes

Place 1/4 cup sugar in greased 7 1/2 x 7 1/2-inch pan; line pan generously with peaches. Mix remaining ingredients; pour over peaches. Bake at 375 degrees for 30 minutes. Yield: 4-6 servings.

Mrs. Barry D. Bennett, Welcoming Com. Chm. OWC
Bitburg AFB, Germany

PINEAPPLE BAR CAKE

1 1/2 c. flour
1/4 tsp. baking soda
1 tsp. baking powder
1/8 tsp. salt
1/2 c. melted margarine
2 c. sugar
4 eggs
1 9-oz. can crushed pineapple, drained
1/2 c. chopped nuts

Sift flour, baking soda, baking powder and salt together. Set aside. Beat margarine and sugar together. Beat in eggs, one at a time. Add sifted ingredients, pineapple and nuts; mix well. Pour into greased and floured 13 x 9-inch pan. Bake for 30 to 40 minutes at 350 degrees. Yield: 12 servings.

Mrs. B. H. Klein, 2nd VP OWC
Selfridge AFB, Michigan

PINEAPPLE CAKE

2 c. flour
1 1/2 tsp. soda
1 1/2 c. sugar
3 lge. eggs
1 No. 2 can crushed pineapple or fruit
    cocktail, including syrup
1/2 c. nuts, chopped

Mix all ingredients together; pour into greased, flat loaf pan. Bake for 45 minutes at 350 degrees.

ICING:

1 c. evaporated milk
1 stick margarine
1 c. sugar
1 c. flaked coconut
1/2 c. pecans

(Continued on next page)

Cook milk, margarine and sugar together until thickened. Add coconut and pecans; pour over warm cake. Cut into serving pieces. Yield: 12 servings.

Mrs. Edward D. Higgins, Ways and Means Chm. OWC
Norton AFB, California

PINEAPPLE CAKE

2 c. flour
3 c. sugar
1 tsp. soda
1 No. 2 can crushed pineapple
1 stick margarine
1 sm. can sweetened condensed milk
1 c. pecans
1 c. coconut

Mix flour, 1 1/2 cups sugar, soda and pineapple; pour into greased, but not floured, oblong pan. Bake at 300 degrees for 45 minutes or until done. Bring remaining sugar, margarine and milk to boil; cook for 4 minutes or until creamy. Mix in pecans and coconut; spread over cooled cake. Yield: 12 servings.

Mrs. Michael S. Pearcy, Past Pres. OWC
Finley AFS, North Dakota

PETITS FOURS

1 1-lb. 3-oz. pkg. white cake mix
2 egg whites
1 pkg. fluffy white frosting mix
Food coloring
Chocolate shot
Toasted coconut
Chopped nuts
Candied cherries
Currant jelly

Preheat oven to 350 degrees. Line bottom of ungreased 15 x 10-inch jelly roll pan with waxed paper. Make cake as package directs; pour into pan. Bake for 25 to 30 minutes until cake tests done. Cool cake in pan for 5 minutes; turn out onto wire rack. Remove paper; cool completely. Cut cake into five 2-inch strips lengthwise; cut strips into seven 2-inch pieces on the diagonal or square. Frost; decorate with remaining ingredients. Yield: 35 pieces.

Mrs. D. K. Layman, NAV Commsta OWC
FPO Honolulu, Hawaii

QUICK TOMATO SPICE CAKE

1 pkg. spice cake mix
1 can condensed tomato soup
Eggs (opt.)
1/4 c. water
1/2 c. seeded raisins
1/2 c. chopped nutmeats

(Continued on next page)

Mix cake as directed on package, substituting 1 cup soup and water for liquid. Add eggs, if desired. Place in 8 x 12-inch round cake pans or 13 x 9 x 2-inch pans. Bake at 350 degrees for 30 to 35 minutes or 35 to 40 minutes. Cake may be dusted with confectioners' sugar or frosted with Cream Cheese Frosting.

CREAM CHEESE FROSTING:

2 3-oz. pkg. cream cheese
1 tbsp. milk
1 1-lb. pkg. sifted confectioners' sugar
1/2 tsp. vanilla extract (opt.)

Blend cream cheese and milk. Add confectioners' sugar gradually; blend well. Mix in vanilla extract. Makes enough frosting for two 8-inch layers. Sprinkle top with maple sugar, if desired.

Mrs. Rondel L. Waldo, Publ. Chm.
US Armed Forces OWC
Bangkok, Thailand

RUM CAKE

1 18 1/2-oz. pkg. deluxe yellow cake mix
4 lge. eggs
3/4 c. salad oil
3/4 c. apricot nectar
1 stick butter
2/3 c. sugar
1/3 c. Meyers rum

Place cake mix, eggs, oil and apricot nectar in mixing bowl together; beat with mixer for 10 minutes. Lightly grease and flour 9 or 10-inch angel food pan; pour cake batter into pan. Bake at 325 degrees for 50 minutes. Place butter, sugar and Meyers rum in saucepan; bring to boil on top of stove. Prick cake with long pronged fork; pour topping over. May be served warm or at room temperature. Freezes well with sauce on it. Yield: 8 servings.

Mrs. Alan D. Breed, VP OWC
Philadelphia Coast Guard and Marine Inspection Office, Pennsylvania

SURPRISE CAKE

1 1-lb. 6-oz. can fruit pie filling
1/2 c. coconut
1/2 c. nutmeats
1/2 c. butter, melted
1 sm. pkg. white or yellow cake mix
Water
Egg

(Continued on next page)

Mix pie filling with coconut, nutmeats and butter; spread in 9-inch square cake pan. Prepare cake. Mix with water and egg as directed on box; spread over pie filling. Bake for 40 minutes at 350 degrees. Yield: 8 servings.

Mrs. Richard P. Pawson, Thrift Shop Chm. OWC
Fort Wadsworth, Staten Island, New York

STRAWBERRY-JELL-O CAKE

CAKE:

1 pkg. white cake mix
1 sm. pkg. strawberry Jell-O
1 c. salad oil
1/2 c. water
1/2 sm. pkg. frozen strawberries, thawed
4 eggs

Mix all ingredients together; pour into cake pan. Bake at 350 degrees until done.

FROSTING:

1 box powdered sugar
1/2 sm. pkg. frozen strawberries, thawed
1/4 lb. butter or oleo

Mix ingredients together with electric mixer. Spread over cake. Yield: 8 servings.

Mrs. J. R. McDonnell, OWC
Portsmouth Naval Shipyard, New Hampshire

THREE-IN-ONE CAKE

1 pkg. yellow cake mix
1 pkg. chocolate cake mix

(Continued on next page)

Prepare each cake mix separately according to instructions. Grease a 11 x 17-inch rectangular roasting pan; place cake batter at each end. Marble center where 2 cakes come together with knife. Bake at 350 degrees for 35 minutes until cake is done. Cool; frost with favorite frosting. Yield: 28 servings.

Mrs. F. O. Caron, Hist. and Publ.
Forrestal OWC
Norfolk, Virginia

VELVET FUDGE CAKE

1 1/3 c. Bisquick
3/4 c. sugar
1/3 c. cocoa
3 tbsp. soft shortening
1 egg
3/4 c. milk
1 tsp. vanilla

Preheat oven to 350 degrees. Grease and flour 8-inch square pan. Mix Bisquick, sugar and cocoa together; add shortening, egg and 1/4 cup milk. Beat vigorously for 1 minute. Stir in remaining milk and vanilla; beat for 1/2 minute more. Pour half the batter into pan; spread with half the Topping. Cover with remaining batter. Bake for 35 to 40 minutes. Spread with remaining Topping immediately. Serve warm.

TOPPING:

1/2 c. semisweet chocolate pieces, melted
1/3 c. water
2 c. finely grated coconut (opt.)

Mix ingredients together thoroughly. Yield: 6-9 servings.

Mrs. William H. Wilhelmi, Parlm. OWC
Eglin AFB, Florida

MINT SWIRLS

3 tbsp. butter or margarine
3 tbsp. milk
1 pkg. creamy white frosting mix
Oil of peppermint
Red food coloring

Melt butter with milk in top of double boiler. Add frosting mix; stirring till smooth. Cook over rapidly boiling water for 5 minutes, stirring occasionally. Add about 8 drops of oil of peppermint. Tint with few drops of food coloring. Drop by teaspoonfuls onto waxed paper, swirling tops of candies with teaspoon.

(Continued on next page)

Keep candy over hot water while dropping candies. Add few drops of hot water if mixture thickens; cool. Yield: about 5 dozen mints.

Mrs. Frank E. Smith, Treas. MCAS OWC
Beaufort, South Carolina

JINGLE BALLS

1/2 c. soft butter
2 tsp. vanilla
2 c. powdered sugar
3/4 c. peanut butter
1 c. chopped walnuts
1 12-oz. pkg. chocolate bits
2 tbsp. parawax

Cream butter, vanilla, sugar, peanut butter and nuts together; form into balls. Melt chocolate bits with parawax in top of double boiler. Dip balls into chocolate. Set on waxed paper; chill.

Mrs. John Walsh, OWC
Naval Torpedo Station, Keyport, Washington

UNBAKED FRUIT ROLL

1 7 1/4-oz. box vanilla wafers
1 can sweetened condensed milk
1 1-lb. box raisins
1 c. chopped nuts
2 c. coconut flakes

Roll vanilla wafers into crumbs. Add all ingredients in mixing bowl; mix well. Shape into 3 rolls on waxed paper. Place in refrigerator; chill for 1 to 2 hours. Yield: 15-20 servings.

Mrs. Daley D. Dougherty, Treas. Supply Corps OWC
NAS, San Diego, California

ROCKY ROAD CANDY

4 4 1/2-oz. milk chocolate bars
3 c. tiny marshmallows
3/4 c. coarsely broken California walnuts

Melt chocolate partially over hot water; remove from heat. Beat till smooth; stir in marshmallows and nuts. Spread in buttered 8 x 8 x 2-inch pan; chill. Cut into squares when firm. Yield: 36 squares.

Mrs. C. E. Hogan, Ways and Means Chm. MOWC
Camp H. M. Smith, Hawaii

EASY CHEESE CAKE

3 8-oz. pkg. cream cheese
4 eggs
1 c. sugar
1/4 tsp. almond extract

Beat all ingredients till well blended. Pour into 2 well-greased 9-inch pie pans. Bake at 350 degrees for 40 to 50 minutes.

TOPPING:

1 c. sour cream
3 tbsp. sugar
1 tsp. vanilla

Combine topping ingredients; spread on cake. Bake for 10 minutes at 350 degrees. Cool; refrigerate. Yield: 8-12 servings.

Mrs. Theodore Sudinsky, Ways and Means Chm. OWC
KI Sawyer AFB, Michigan

LEMON CHEESE PIE

1 1/4 c. graham cracker crumbs
3 tbsp. sugar
1/3 c. butter or margarine
2 dashes ground cinnamon
1 8-oz. pkg. cream cheese
2 c. milk
1 sm. pkg. instant lemon pudding

Combine crumbs and sugar. Melt butter; add to crumbs. Press mixture firmly into 9-inch pie pan. Bake at 350 degrees for 8 minutes. Remove from oven; sprinkle lightly with cinnamon. Stir cream cheese until very soft. Blend in 1/2 cup milk gradually, until creamy. Add remaining milk and instant lemon pudding. Beat slowly with egg beater for 2 minutes. Pour into cooled pie shell; refrigerate until serving time. Yield: 6 servings.

Mrs. George H. Carswell, OWC
Sigonella NAF, Sicily

STRAWBERRY-CHEESE DELIGHT

2 c. flaked coconut
2 tbsp. sugar
1 tbsp. flour
2 tbsp. margarine, melted

(Continued on next page)

1 10-oz. jar strawberry preserves
1 8-oz. pkg. cream cheese
3/4 c. confectioners' sugar
1/2 c. chopped pecans
1 tbsp. milk
1 tsp. almond extract
1 c. heavy cream

Make crust with coconut, sugar and flour. Blend in margarine; press into 9-inch spring pan or 8-inch square pan. Bake at 350 degrees for 10 minutes. Chill; spread on half of preserves. Combine cream cheese with 1/2 cup sifted confectioners' sugar, pecans, milk and almond extract. Blend well; spread over layer of preserves. Combine cream and remaining confectioners' sugar; whip until stiff. Spoon over cream cheese layer. Garnish with remaining preserves. Yield: 6-8 servings.

Mrs. John B. Ogas, 3rd VP OWC
Los Angeles AFS, California

CHERRY-BERRY CREAM

1 box black cherry Jell-O, mixed according
    to directions
1 sm. pkg. frozen strawberries, thawed
2 c. vanilla ice cream
2 lge. bananas, sliced
1/2 c. miniature marshmallows

Let Jell-O set until it starts to thicken; whip. Add strawberries and ice cream; whip again. Fold in bananas and marshmallows. May be served in parfait glasses. Yield: 6 servings.

Mrs. Darrell Max Smith, Corr. Sec. MOWC
Beaufort MCAS, South Carolina

CHERRY-PUDDING DESSERT

1 3 1/4-oz. pkg. vanilla pudding and pie-filling
    mix
2 c. milk
1 1-lb. 4-oz. can cherry pie filling

(Continued on next page)

Prepare pudding mix with milk as directed on package; chill. Place cherries in 6 parfait glasses. Top with pudding. Yield: 6 servings.

Mrs. Jack W. Kunkel, Sec. OWC
Red River Army Depot, Texas

COFFEE FLUFF

6 egg yolks
Liquid sweetener equal to 5 teaspoons sugar
Dash of salt
3/4 c. strong coffee

Combine egg yolks, liquid sweetener and salt in top of double boiler. Beat with rotary beater until mixture is very thick. Place over hot, not boiling water; gradually add coffee and continue to beat. Beat until pudding thickens and forms mounds when dropped from beater. Chill, covered, until ready to serve. Yield: 4 servings.

Mrs. Charles E. Boeing, NOWC
Alameda NAS, California

COFFEE MALLO

16 marshmallows
1/2 c. strong coffee
1 c. whipping cream, whipped

Melt marshmallows in coffee; let stand for 1 hour or until thickened. Beat in whipped cream; pour in parfait glasses; refrigerate until ready to serve. Yield: 6 servings.

Mrs. Stuart Henry Smith, Hon. Pres. Cinclant OWC
Norfolk, Virginia

ENGLISH TRIFLE

1 pkg. ladyfingers or pound cake, sliced
1/4 c. sherry wine
1 box fresh strawberries, sliced and sugared
1 sm. pkg. vanilla pudding mix, prepared as directed
1 c. whipping cream, whipped
Sliced almonds

Arrange ladyfingers around sides and on bottom of 4 dishes. Scatter sherry over cake. Set aside for 10 minutes. Spread strawberries over ladyfingers; add cooled custard. Top with whipped cream. Scatter almonds over top. Refrigerate no more than 2 to 3 hours. Yield: 4 servings.

Mrs. Alan Roach, NOWC
Norfolk, Virginia

JELL-O ANGEL FOOD

1 6-oz. pkg. red raspberry Jell-O
1 c. hot water
2 c. cold water
1 sm. can crushed pineapple
1 pt. whipping cream, whipped
1/2 lge. angel food cake, broken into pieces

Dissolve Jell-O in hot water; add cold water. Let set until almost firm. Combine pineapple and whipped cream. Fold into Jell-O. Pour mixture over cake in 9 x 13 x 2-inch glass pan. Refrigerate until firm. Cut into squares; serve. May be prepared a day ahead. Yield: 10-12 servings.

Mrs. Ralph H. Smith, Jr., Pres. OWC
Mather AFB, California

JEWEL SQUARES

1 No. 2 can crushed pineapple
1 3-oz. pkg. strawberry gelatin
1 c. boiling water
2 tbsp. lemon juice
1 c. heavy cream, whipped
2 tbsp. sugar
1/2 tsp. vanilla
1/3 c. chopped California walnuts
18 graham cracker squares
Canned pineapple tidbits, halved
Whipped cream

Drain crushed pineapple, reserving syrup. Dissolve gelatin in boiling water; add syrup and lemon juice. Chill till partially set. Whip cream with sugar and vanilla; fold in crushed pineapple and nuts. Line 8 x 8 x 2-inch baking dish with 9 graham crackers; spread with cream layer. Gently press remaining crackers over top. Arrange pineapple tidbits on each cracker. Spoon gelatin over; chill till firm. Top with whipped cream. Cut between crackers. Yield: 9 servings.

Mrs. Philip J. Walsh, Pres. OWC
Othello AFS, Washington

LEMON SNOW

1 envelope dessert topping mix, prepared as directed
2 egg whites, beaten till stiff but not dry
1 can lemon pie filling

Gently fold prepared topping and egg whites into pie filling. Pour into parfait glasses; chill. May garnish with dollop of whipped cream and grated lemon rind, if desired. Yield: 6 servings.

Mrs. Eugene D. Schultz, Treas. NOWC
NOB Norfolk, Virginia

POTS DE CREME

1 c. semisweet chocolate chips
1 1/4 c. light cream, scalded
2 egg yolks
3 tbsp. brandy

Place all ingredients into Osterizer container; cover. Blend on low speed until smooth. Pour into 6 cups or small sherbet dishes, filling 2/3 full; cover. Chill for 3 hours or until consistency of pudding. Yield: 6 servings.

Mrs. Thomas A. Gilson, NOWC
Glynco NAS, Georgia

QUICK ANGEL FOOD DESSERT

1 bakery angel food cake, sliced into 3 layers
1 can cherry pie filling
1 pkg. pistachio instant pudding
1 carton Cool Whip

Spread bottom layer of cake with cherry filling. Prepare pudding mix according to package directions, using little over 1 3/4 cups milk instead of full 2 cups. Chill pudding till firm; spoon over second layer. Place third layer on top; frost top and sides with Cool Whip. Refrigerate. Yield: 10 servings.

Mrs. Ben Bellis, 1st VP OWC
Wright-Patterson AFB, Ohio

QUICK CHERRY-CREAM PARFAITS

1 c. milk
1 c. sour cream
1/4 tsp. almond extract
1 3 5/8 or 3 3/4-oz. pkg. instant vanilla pudding
   mix
1 1-lb. 5-oz. can cherry pie filling
Toasted slivered almonds

Combine in mixer bowl milk, sour cream and almond extract. Add pudding mix; beat with rotary or electric beater till creamy and well blended. Fill parfait glasses with alternate layers of pudding, cherry filling and almonds; chill. Garnish with additional almonds. Yield: 6 servings.

Mrs. Leland W. Hutcheson, OWC
Chandler AFS, Minnesota

LEMON FLUFF CITRON FROMAGE (DANISH)

6 eggs, separated
1 c. sugar
1 tbsp. unflavored gelatin
1/4 c. water
Boiling water
Juice and grated rind of 1 lemon
Whipped dessert topping
Maraschino cherries

Combine egg yolks and sugar; beat well. Dissolve gelatin in 1/4 cup water. Add just enough boiling water to dissolve gelatin completely. Add lemon and rind to yolks and sugar. Add gelatin. Fold in stiffly beaten egg whites slowly; chill. Serve with whipped topping and a maraschino cherry for festive light dessert. Yield: 8 servings.
PERSONAL NOTE: My grandmother brought this recipe with her from Denmark in 1910.

Mrs. Philip R. Korzilius, OWC
Othello AFS, Washington

STRAWBERRY-CHEESE COUPE

1/2 c. heavy cream, whipped
1/2 c. canned crushed pineapple, well drained
1 c. cottage cheese
1/4 c. sugar
1/4 tsp. almond extract
1 pkg. frozen sliced strawberries, thawed
2 tbsp. grenadine syrup

Whip cream. Combine in bowl pineapple, cottage cheese, whipped cream, sugar and almond extract; refrigerate. Mix strawberries and grenadine syrup; refrigerate. Alternate layers of cottage cheese mixture and strawberries in sherbet glasses. Top each serving with strawberry, if desired. Yield: 6 servings.

Mrs. Ken Randall, OWC
Minot AFB, North Dakota

STRAWBERRY DESSERT

Graham cracker crumbs
2 c. powdered sugar
3/4 c. butter
2 well-beaten eggs
1/3 c. chopped walnuts
1 1/2 pkg. strawberry Jell-O
1 1/2 c. hot water
2 sm. pkg. frozen sliced strawberries
1 pt. whipping cream, whipped

Spread layer of cracker crumbs in 13 x 9-inch pan or glass baking dish. Cream powdered sugar, butter and eggs. Pour over cracker crumbs; sprinkle with nuts. Dissolve Jell-O in hot water; add frozen strawberries immediately. Refrigerate till it starts to jell. Pour over mixture in pan. Spread whipped cream over mixture; sprinkle with graham cracker crumbs. Keep refrigerated until serving. Yield: 10-12 servings.

Mrs. Gordon E. Williams, OWC
Kelley Barracks, Stuttgart, Germany

STRAWBERRIES AU NATUREL

2 pt. washed strawberries, hulled and sliced
Sour cream
Light brown sugar

Place berries in large bowl; add 2/3 cup sour cream and 1/2 cup brown sugar. Mix gently. Spoon into 6 dishes. Top each with 1 tablespoon sour cream and 1 teaspoon brown sugar. Chill for 1 hour. Yield: 6 servings.

Mrs. C. H. Kemp, 1st VP Women's Club
Army Transportation Corps, Washington, District of Columbia

SUMMER PARFAIT

1/2 c. crushed pineapple, well drained
1 c. cottage cheese
1/2 c. heavy cream, whipped
1/4 c. sugar
1/4 tsp. almond extract
1 pkg. frozen raspberries
    or strawberries
2 tbsp. grenadine syrup (opt.)
Chopped pecans

Combine pineapple, cottage cheese, whipped cream, sugar and extract; refrigerate. Mix berries and grenadine; refrigerate. Alternate layers of cottage cheese

(Continued on next page)

mixture and berries in sherbet or parfait glasses. Top each with whole berry or spoonful pecans. Keep refrigerated until served. Yield: 4 servings.

Mrs. Paul D. Arvin, Reservation Chm. OWC
Ft. Wadsworth, New York

SYLLABUB

4 oz. confectioners' sugar
Juice of 1 lemon
1/2 c. sweet white wine
2 egg whites, whipped till stiff
1/2 pt. heavy cream, lightly whipped
Peel of 1 lemon

Fold sugar, lemon juice and wine into egg whites. Combine with whipped cream. Spoon mixture into 6 to 8 serving glasses. Decorate with twisted slice of lemon peel. May be prepared day ahead and refrigerated. Mixture will separate. Yield: 6-8 servings.
PERSONAL NOTE: This recipe was published in an English Good Housekeeping Diary and Account Book.

Mrs. E. B. Wellman, 2nd VP OWC
Rhein Main, Germany

STRAWBERRY WHIP

1 pkg. strawberry Jell-O
1 c. boiling water
1 c. cold water
1 envelope Dream Whip
1/2 c. cold milk
1/2 tsp. vanilla
1 10-oz. pkg. frozen strawberries,
    thawed and drained

Dissolve Jell-O in hot water. Add cold water; let set until it has consistency of thick gravy. Whip with electric mixer until Jell-O is light and fluffy; set aside. Mix Dream Whip, milk and vanilla; whip until stiff. Stir Jell-O fluff and Dream Whip together to make marble effect. Fold strawberries into mixture. Store in refrigerator until ready to serve. Yield: 6 servings.

Mrs. Robert L. Hood, Pres. CGOWC
C. G. Rad. Sta. Pt. Higgins, Ketchikan, Alaska

ELLEN'S STRAWBERRY CREAM DESSERT

1 3-oz. pkg. strawberry Jell-O
1 c. boiling water

(Continued on next page)

1 10-oz. pkg. frozen strawberries
1 8 1/2-oz. can crushed pineapple,
   drained
1 lge. ripe banana, finely diced
1 c. sour cream

Dissolve Jell-O in boiling water; add frozen strawberries. Stir until thawed; add pineapple and banana. Pour 1/2 of the mixture into 1-quart mold; chill until firm. Spread sour cream over top. Cover with cooled remaining Jell-O mixture; chill until firm. Top with additional sour cream at serving time, if desired. Yield: 6-8 servings.

Mrs. Robert M. Price, Welfare Com. Chm. OWC
High Wycombe Air Station, Buckinghamshire, England

TIPSY SQUIRE

1 pkg. custard-flavored dessert mix
2 1/4 c. milk
1 3-oz. pkg. sliced almonds
2 sponge cake layers
1/2 c. sherry
1 tbsp. sugar
1 c. heavy cream, whipped

Empty dessert mix into saucepan; stir in milk. Cook over medium-high heat, stirring occasionally, until mixture begins to boil. Mixture will thicken as it cools; chill thoroughly. Measure 1/4 cup almonds; set aside. Place 1 cake layer in large deep dessert dish. Set almonds into surface and sides of cake. Combine sherry and sugar. Pour half the wine mixture over cake. Repeat with second layer. Beat custard until smooth; gradually fold in whipped cream. Spread mixture over entire cake. Garnish with reserved almonds and fresh Bing or maraschino cherries, if desired. Yield: 8-10 servings.

Photograph for this recipe on cover.

ARCTIC VALLEY NUGGETS

1 1-lb. 3-oz. box white cake mix
1/2 c. cocoa
2 eggs
1 tbsp. water
1/2 c. liquid oil
1 tsp. vanilla
1/2 to 3/4 c. chopped pecans
Powdered sugar

Mix all ingredients together, except sugar, to form stiff dough. Drop half teaspoonfuls into sugar; roll to form sugar coated balls. Place on ungreased cookie sheet about 1-inch apart. Bake in 375-degree oven for 10 to 14 minutes. May substitute coconut and almond extract for pecans and vanilla; drop directly on cookie sheet without rolling in sugar.

Mrs. Clyde J. Harger, Pres. OWC
Fort Richardson, Anchorage, Alaska

BROWNIES IN A HURRY

17 graham crackers, crumbled
4 squares chocolate, melted
1 can sweetened condensed milk
1/2 tsp. salt
1/2 c. nuts

Combine all ingredients; mix well. Pour into greased 7 x 11-inch pan. Bake at 350 degrees for 20 minutes. Cool; cut. Yield: 24 pieces.

Mrs. Homer B. Davis, OWC
El Centro NAF, California

CHOCOLATE-PEPPERMINT SQUARES

1 pkg. devil's food cake mix
1 tsp. peppermint extract
1 recipe confectioners' frosting or
1 can prepared frosting
3 sq. bitter chocolate
3 tbsp. butter or oleo
Paraffin (opt.)

Prepare cake mix as directed, adding peppermint. Place in 15 x 10-inch jellyroll pan. Bake according to package directions taking care not to overbake. Cool; frost with vanilla frosting. Melt chocolate with butter; few shavings of paraffin will make topping glossy. Cover white frosting. May be cut into large squares for dessert or small pieces for teas.

Mrs. Linus T. Stitham, OWC
Charleston AFS, Maine

CHOCOLATE SQUARES

1 c. chocolate chips
1 c. nuts, chopped
2 c. graham cracker crumbs
1 can sweetened condensed milk

Grease 8-inch square pan lined with waxed paper and grease paper. Combine all ingredients; place in prepared pan. Bake at 350 degrees for 35 minutes. Remove

(Continued on next page)

from oven; turn upside down and peel off waxed paper. Cut into squares while still warm. Yield: 12 servings.

Mrs. Carl Ratz, Pres. OWC
Ft. Harrison, Indiana

COMPANY BROWNIES

1 pkg. brownie mix
1/2 c. chopped nuts
Miniature marshmallows
Canned chocolate frosting

Mix brownies according to package directions; add nuts. Place in greased 9 x 9-inch pan. Bake according to package directions. Remove from oven; place marshmallows over top. Turn oven heat off; return brownies to oven to melt marshmallows. Cool; frost with chocolate frosting.

Mrs. T. R. Fitzsimmons, Treas. NOWC
Mechanicsburg NSD, Pennsylvania

HELLO DOLLY COOKIES

1 stick oleo or butter
1 c. graham cracker crumbs
1 c. chocolate chips
1 c. coconut
1 c. chopped pecans
1 can sweetened condensed milk

Melt oleo in 9 x 9-inch pan. Place in layers crumbs, chocolate chips, coconut and pecans. Pour milk over top. Bake at 350 degrees for 30 minutes. Cool; cut in squares.

Mrs. Jaime H. MacInnis, Memshp. Chm. OWC
Ellsworth AFB, South Dakota

GRAHAM CRACKER BROWNIES

20 crackers, crumbled
1 6-oz. pkg. chocolate chips
1 can sweetened condensed milk

Combine all ingredients; stir until well blended. Pour into greased 8-inch square pan. Bake for 30 minutes in 350-degree oven. Cut into squares while hot. Pecans or walnuts may be added for variation. Yield: 12 squares.

Mrs. John D. Sharp, Treas. OWC
High Wycombe AFS, England

MOCK BABY RUTH BARS

4 c. oatmeal
1 c. brown sugar
1/4 c. corn syrup
2/3 c. butter or margarine, melted
1/4 c. crunchy peanut butter
1 tsp. vanilla
1 6-oz. pkg. chocolate bits
1/2 6-oz. pkg. butterscotch bits
2/3 c. crunchy peanut butter
1 c. salted peanuts

Mix oatmeal, brown sugar and corn syrup together. Pour butter over mixture; stir. Add 1/4 cup peanut butter and vanilla. Mix; pat into a 9 x 13-inch pan. Bake at 400 degrees for 12 minutes. Melt chocolate and butterscotch bits; add 2/3 cup peanut butter and peanuts. Spread over top; cool.

Mrs. K. A. Murphy, Act. Chm. OWC
Fort Snelling, Minnesota

NEW ENGLAND SQUARES

2 c. graham cracker crumbs
1 1/3 c. ready-to-use mincemeat
1 15-oz. can sweetened condensed milk

Blend crumbs, mincemeat and condensed milk together. Turn into well-greased 9 x 13 x 2-inch pan. Bake in 350-degree oven about 30 minutes until lightly browned. Let cool in pan before cutting. One 9-ounce package condensed mincemeat may be used, if desired. Crumble mincemeat into small-sized saucepan; stir in 3/4 cup water. Cook over medium heat, stirring constantly. Bring mixture to a boil. Boil for 1 minute. Yield: 24 squares.

Mrs. Raymond L. V. Pearson, Parlm. OWC
Istanbul Air Station, Turkey

QUICK BROWNIES

1 pkg. devil's food cake mix
1 egg
1/4 c. water
Nuts (opt.)

Place cake mix in bowl; add remaining ingredients. Stir until blended. Batter will be very thick. Press batter into greased 9 x 14-inch pan. Bake at 350 degrees for 20 to 25 minutes for chewy type brownie. Bake slightly longer for cake type.

Mrs. N. Jack Hansen, Pres. OWC
McClellan AFB, California

NO-BAKE BARS

1/2 c. sugar
1/2 c. light corn syrup
1 c. crunchy peanut butter
4 c. corn flakes
1 6-oz. pkg. chocolate chips
1/2 c. chopped walnuts

Melt sugar and syrup together in saucepan. Remove from heat; add peanut butter and corn flakes. Heat oven to 350 degrees; turn off. Place cookie bar mixture in lightly buttered 6 1/2 x 10 1/2-inch pan. Sprinkle chocolate chips over mixture. Place in oven until chocolate is melted. Swirl chocolate with knife; sprinkle with walnuts. Cut into squares. Yield: 24 cookies.

Mrs. Charles R. McFadden, OWC
Monteith Barracks, Furth, Germany

SAD CAKE BROWNIES

1 lb. brown sugar
3 eggs, slightly beaten
2 c. Bisquick
1 c. chopped nuts

Add sugar to eggs; mix well. Add Bisquick; stir until moistened. Add nuts; stir well. Place in heavy pan or iron skillet. Bake at 350 degrees about 30 minutes. Cake will fall when cool and be chewy like brownies. Yield: 10 servings.

Mrs. Charles M. James, Pres. OWC
Holloman AFB, New Mexico

CHOCOLATE FUDGIES

1/2 stick butter
1 12-oz. pkg. chocolate chips
1 tsp. vanilla
1 15-oz. can condensed milk
1 c. flour
1 8-oz. pkg. pecans, broken

(Continued on next page)

Melt butter and chocolate in top of double boiler. Add vanilla; remove from heat. Stir in milk and flour; add nuts. Spoon small amounts onto cookie sheet. Bake at 350 degrees for 5 minutes only. Freeze before eating; delicious when thawed. Yield: 6-7 dozen.

Mrs. Paul McMehan, OWC
Charleston Naval Base, South Carolina

CHOCOLATE-OAT COOKIE

2 c. sugar
1 stick margarine
4 tbsp. cocoa
1 tsp. vanilla
1/2 c. milk
2 tbsp. peanut butter
3 c. quick oats

Combine sugar, margarine, cocoa and vanilla; mix well with milk. Place over heat, stirring constantly; bring to a boil. Boil about 2 minutes or until mixture forms soft ball in cold water. Remove from heat; stir in peanut butter and oats. Drop by spoonful onto waxed paper; cool. Yield: 24 cookies.

Mrs. Jack G. Albert, Corr. Sec. OWC
C. G. Training Center, Cape May, New Jersey

CHOCOLATE-OATMEAL COOKIES

2 c. sugar
1/3 c. cocoa
1 stick oleo or butter
1/2 c. milk
2 1/2 c. quick-cooking oatmeal
1/2 c. peanut butter
1 tsp. vanilla

Place first 4 ingredients in saucepan; boil 3 minutes. Add remaining ingredients. Mix well. Drop on greased cookie sheet or waxed paper with greased spoon; pat down. Yield: 28 cookies.

Mrs. Clifford W. Hargrove, Hon. Pres. OWC
Ramey AFB, Puerto Rico

FUDGE-RITZ COOKIES

1 12-oz. box quick fudge mix
1 box ritz crackers

(Continued on next page)

Prepare fudge according to package directions. Reduce heat when fudge begins to thicken. Dunk crackers in fudge. Place fudge-covered crackers on waxed paper for fudge to harden. Yield: 30 cookies.

Mrs. Anthony R. Marrical, Rec. Sec. OWC
Patuxent River NATC, Maryland

FUDGE-LIKE CHOCOLATE COOKIES

1 15-oz. can sweetened condensed milk
1 12-oz. pkg. chocolate chips
2 tbsp. butter
1 c. flour
1 tsp. vanilla
1 c. nuts

Mix milk, chocolate chips and butter together; melt over low heat. Add remaining ingredients; mix well. Spoon walnut-sized portions onto greased cookie sheet. Bake at 350 degrees for 7 minutes. May be served with vanilla ice cream for dessert.

Mrs. O. I. Meadows, OWC
Norfolk Naval Base, Virginia

MELTING MOMENTS

3/4 c. butter or margarine
2/3 c. confectioners' sugar
1 1/2 c. flour
1/2 c. cornstarch

Cream butter and sugar together. Add flour and cornstarch; mix well. Roll dough into walnut-sized balls; place on lightly greased cookie sheet. Flatten slightly with fork. Bake at 350 degrees about 15 minutes or until light brown. May be frozen, if desired. Yield: 3 dozen cookies.

Mrs. Robert E. Taylor, 2nd VP OWC
Red River Army Depot
Texarkana, Texas

GINGER-CHOCOLATE CHIP COOKIES

1/2 c. water
1 6-oz. pkg. chocolate bits
1 14-oz. pkg. gingerbread mix

(Continued on next page)

Add water and chocolate bits to gingerbread mix; mix well. Drop by spoonfuls onto greased cookie sheet. Bake at 375 degrees for 5 to 8 minutes. Yield: 3 dozen cookies.

Mrs. Robert W. Nelson, Treas. OWC
Fort Lewis, Washington

NO BAKE-COOKIES

2 c. sugar
1/2 c. milk
1/2 c. shortening
3 tbsp. cocoa
Oatmeal
1 c. coconut
1 c. nuts
1 tsp. vanilla

Mix sugar, milk, shortening and cocoa in 2-quart saucepan; bring to a boil. Boil for 1 minute, stirring all the time. Remove from heat; add oatmeal, coconut, nuts and vanilla. Drop by teaspoonfuls onto waxed paper. Let cool. Yield: 3 dozen cookies.

Mrs. Stanley E. Brereton, Prog. Chm. OWC
Ankara, Turkey

NO-BAKE DATE RICE KRISPIE COOKIES

1 1-lb. box dates
1/4 lb. butter
1/2 c. sugar
2 c. Rice Krispies
1/2 tsp. vanilla
1 c. shredded coconut

Cook dates, butter and sugar in double boiler, stirring constantly until mealy. Remove from heat; stir in Rice Krispies and vanilla. Roll into balls; roll balls in coconut. Yield: 3 dozen cookies.

Mrs. Russell N. Shablow, Bowling Pres. OWC
Cigli AFB, Turkey

PEANUT BUTTER COOKIES

1 c. peanut butter
1 c. sugar
1/2 c. water
2 c. biscuit mix
1 c. chocolate chips (opt.)

(Continued on next page)

Blend peanut butter, sugar and water. Add biscuit mix; blend well. Add chocolate chips. Drop by small teaspoon onto lightly greased cookie sheet; flatten with fork. Bake in 400-degree oven about 8 minutes. Yield: 5 dozen.

Mrs. Joseph F. Herrity, Sunshine Chm. OWC
Ft. Richardson USA Sig. C., Alaska

UNBAKED COOKIES

1 pkg. chocolate chips
1 pkg. butterscotch chips
1 can chow mein noodles
6 oz. blanched salted peanuts

Melt chocolate and butterscotch chips over low heat; add noodles and peanuts. Mix well; drop by teaspoonfuls onto waxed paper. Chill. Yield: 3 dozen.

Mrs. C. M. Isaacson, Hon. Pres. OWC
Hancock Field, New York

ROMANIAN HONEY COOKIES

2 eggs
1 c. sugar
2 c. flour
2 tbsp. honey
1/2 tsp. soda
1/2 tsp. cinnamon
Pinch of cloves

Mix ingredients together well; knead about 2 minutes. Add small amount flour, if necessary. Roll out small portions at a time to 1/8-inch thickness. Cut with cookie cutter. Place in greased pan. Bake at 350 degrees to desired doneness. Yield: Several dozen.

Mrs. Harold Otiker, Hon. Pres. OWC
Vint Hill Station, Warrenton, Virginia

UNBAKED PEANUT BUTTER DROPS

1 1/2 c. sugar
1/4 tsp. salt
1/2 c. milk
1/4 c. light corn syrup
1/2 c. peanut butter
1 tsp. vanilla
2 c. rolled oats
1 c. coconut
Salted peanuts (opt.)

Mix sugar, salt, milk and corn syrup together in saucepan. Cook, stirring occasionally, until mixture forms soft ball. Remove from heat; stir in peanut butter and vanilla. Mix well; stir in rolled oats and coconut. Drop from teaspoon onto waxed paper; press a few salted peanuts into top of each cookie, if desired. Yield: 3 dozen.

Mrs. David I. Scott, Pres. CGOWC
Traverse City Coast Guard Air Station, Michigan

BUTTERMILK SCONES

4 tbsp. shortening
2 tbsp. sugar
2 c. all-purpose flour
1/2 tsp. baking soda
1/2 tsp. salt
2/3 c. buttermilk
1 beaten egg
1/2 c. raisins

Cut shortening into dry ingredients with pastry blender till texture is mealy. Make well in center of mixture; gradually add buttermilk and egg, stirring with fork. Mix till soft dough is formed. Add raisins. Turn onto lightly floured board; divide into 2 portions. Roll each gently with rolling pin or pat with hands into circle 1/2-inch thick. Place on ungreased cookie sheet; mark into 4 quarters with knife. Bake at 450 degrees for 12 to 15 minutes.

Mrs. Felix Muller, OWC
Handorf Kaserne 570 Artillery Group, Germany

CINNAMON COFFEE CAKE

1 egg
Sugar
1/2 c. milk
1 c. pancake mix
3 tbsp. shortening, butter or lard, melted
1/2 tsp. cinnamon

Beat egg until light and fluffy; beat in 1/2 cup sugar, small amount at a time. Add milk, pancake mix and shortening, stirring in lightly. Pour batter into greased

(Continued on next page)

8-inch square pan. Sprinkle 2 tablespoons sugar and cinnamon on top. Bake in 400-degree oven for 20 minutes. Thinly sliced, peeled apple may be placed on top before adding cinnamon mixture, if desired. Yield: 4-6 servings.

Mrs. McPherson G. Legare, Memshp. Chm. OWC
Savanna Army Depot, Illinois

COFFEE CAKE

1/2 c. shortening
3/4 c. sugar
1 tsp. vanilla
3 eggs
2 c. flour
1 tsp. baking powder
1 tsp. baking soda
1/2 pt. sour cream
1/2 c. butter
1 c. brown sugar
2 tsp. cinnamon
1 c. chopped walnuts

Cream shortening, sugar and vanilla together. Add eggs 1 at a time, beating after each addition. Sift flour, baking powder and soda together. Add alternately to creamed mixture with sour cream. Combine butter, brown sugar, cinnamon and walnuts together. Grease tube cake pan. Pour half the batter in pan; add half brown sugar mixture. Repeat. Bake at 350 degrees for 50 minutes. Drip confectioners' icing on top and sides, if desired. Yield: 8 servings.

Mrs. William J. Dixon, OWC
Portsmouth Naval Shipyard, New Hampshire

COFFEE CAKE EXCEPTIONALE

3/4 c. soft butter or margarine
1 1/2 c. sugar
3 eggs
1 1/2 tsp. vanilla
3 c. flour
1 1/2 tsp. baking powder
1/4 tsp. salt
1 1/2 tsp. soda
1 1/2 c. sour cream
Cinnamon-Nut Filling

Preheat oven to 350 degrees. Grease 10 x 4-inch tube pan. Cream butter and sugar thoroughly; beat in eggs and vanilla. Sift flour, baking powder, salt and soda together; mix into creamed mixture alternately with sour cream. Spread 2 cups batter into pan. Sprinkle with 1/3 Cinnamon-Nut Filling; repeat layers twice. Bake for 50 to 60 minutes; cool slightly in pan before removing.

(Continued on next page)

CINNAMON-NUT FILLING:

1/2 c. (packed) brown sugar
1/2 c. chopped nuts
1 1/2 tsp. cinnamon

Mix filling ingredients together; layer in pan according to cake batter directions. Yield: 12-14 servings.

Mrs. Jack A. Robinson, OWC
Bitburg AFB, Germany

JOLLY BREAKFAST RING

2/3 c. milk
2 c. Bisquick
1/3 c. butter
3 tbsp. brown sugar
12 cherries
Nuts, chopped
1/2 c. sugar
1 tsp. cinnamon

Add milk to Bisquick at once; stir with fork. Beat dough vigorously. Shape dough into 12 balls. Melt butter; pour 3 tablespoons into a 9-inch ring. Sprinkle with brown sugar; place cherries and 1/4 cup nuts in pan. Roll balls in remaining butter; then in mixture of sugar, cinnamon and 3 tablespoons nuts. Place in ring mold. Bake for 30 minutes in 400-degree oven. Remove from pan while warm. Yield: 8 servings.

Mrs. Douglas Finch, 2nd VP OWC
Canadian Forces Base North Bay, Ontario, Canada

QUICK COFFEE CAKE

All-purpose flour
2 tsp. baking powder
Sugar
Butter or margarine
1 egg
1/2 c. milk
1/2 tsp. cinnamon

Mix 2 cups flour, baking powder, 1/2 cup sugar, 6 tablespoons butter, egg and milk together in large bowl; beat with mixer for 3 minutes at medium speed. Place batter into greased 8 x 8-inch square pan. Pour 2 tablespoons melted butter over top of batter. Mix 4 tablespoons sugar, 1 tablespoon flour and cinnamon together; sprinkle over butter. Bake at 400 degrees for 20 to 25 minutes. Nuts may be sprinkled on top, if desired. Serve warm. Yield: 12 servings.

Mrs. William L. Skliar, Program Chm. OWC
Edwards AFB, California

GOLDEN NUGGET COFFEE CAKE

1 12-oz. jar peach preserves
2 cans flaky refrigerator biscuits
1/2 c. chopped walnuts
Maraschino cherries

Heat peach preserves in saucepan. Separate each biscuit into 3 layers. Overlap from 1 can to form 9-inch circle on ungreased baking sheet. Brush with preserves; sprinkle with 1/4 cup walnuts. Dip remaining biscuits in preserves; overlap on top. Bake at 400 degrees for 18 minutes. Brush with remaining preserves. Sprinkle with remaining walnuts; garnish with cherries. Yield: 6 servings.

Mrs. John A. Moulson, Welfare Chm. OWC
Pearl Harbor Naval Shipyard
Honolulu, Hawaii

RAISIN-MINCEMEAT COFFEE CAKE

2 1/2 c. biscuit mix
2/3 c. milk
Melted butter
1 c. seedless raisins
1 c. prepared mincemeat

POWDERED SUGAR FROSTING:

3/4 c. sifted powdered sugar
1/4 tsp. vanilla
1 tbsp. warm water

Combine biscuit mix, milk and 2 tablespoons melted butter, stirring to make soft dough. Turn out onto floured board. Roll to 8 x 18-inch rectangle. Cut in half lengthwise. Spoon raisins mixed with mincemeat down center of dough strips. Fold edges over, pinching together to cover filling. Coil strips in buttered 9-inch layer cake pan, joining ends of 2 coils to make 1 continous strip. Snip part way through rolls at 2-inch intervals. Brush with melted butter. Bake in 400-degree oven for 25 to 30 minutes until browned. Mix powdered sugar with vanilla and water; drizzle frosting over cake. Yield: 1 cake.

Mrs. James W. Osmar, Adv. OWC
US Nav. Sec. Gru Act
Bremerhaven, Germany

DOUGHNUTS

1 pt. salad oil
1 pkg. refrigerator biscuits
1/2 c. sugar

Heat oil in skillet on top of stove. Separate biscuits; punch hole in center of each with empty soft drink bottle top. Drop biscuits and holes into hot oil; cook for 3 to 5 minutes until golden brown. Place sugar in paper sack; shake doughnuts and holes in sack until well-covered with sugar. Yield: 10 servings.

Mrs. Spurgeon H. Neel, Pres. OWC
Army Surgeon General
Washington, District of Columbia

APPLESAUCE DROP DOUGHNUTS

2 c. enriched flour
1/2 c. sugar
2 tsp. baking powder
1/2 tsp. salt
1 tsp. cinnamon
1 egg
1/2 c. applesauce
1/2 c. milk
1 1/2 tbsp. shortening, liquid or melted

Sift flour, sugar, baking powder, salt and cinnamon together. Beat egg; add applesauce and milk. Add egg mixture to dry ingredients, mixing well. Stir in shortening. Drop batter by teaspoon into 375-degree fat; fry until golden brown on all sides. Dough may be kept in refrigerator for 2 to 3 weeks and used for quick fresh doughnuts at any time.

Mrs. George M. Geer, OWC
Sembach AFB, Germany

QUICK DOUGHNUTS

Oil
1 can biscuits
Sugar and cinnamon mixture or powdered
sugar

Heat 1/2-inch oil in skillet. Separate biscuits; fry in oil till golden brown, turning once. Drain on absorbent paper; cool. Shake in bag with sugar and cinnamon mixture.

Mrs. Roy L. Laughton, Games Day Chm. OWC
Fairchild AFB, Washington

QUICK CHOCOLATE-FILLED DOUGHNUTS

1/4 c. sugar
1/2 tsp. cinnamon
2 pkg. refrigerator biscuits
Chocolate chips
Cooking oil

Mix sugar and cinnamon; set aside. Cut out centers of biscuits. Press 5 or 6 chocolate chips into half the biscuits; top with plain halves. Press together firmly. Deep fry in cooking oil; drain. Shake in paper bag with sugar-cinnamon mixture. Yield: 3-4 servings.

Mrs. Ray L. Barry, Welfare Chm. OWC
MAAG, Taipei, Taiwan, China

APPLESAUCE-NUT BREAD

2 c. flour
3/4 c. sugar
3 tsp. baking powder
1/2 tsp. cinnamon
1 tsp. salt
1/2 tsp. baking soda
1 c. chopped walnuts
1 egg
1 c. canned applesauce
2 tbsp. melted shortening

Preheat oven to 350 degrees. Grease 9 x 5 x 3-inch loaf pan. Sift flour, sugar, baking powder, cinnamon, salt and soda together; add walnuts. Beat egg in bowl; add applesauce and shortening. Add flour mixture; stir just until blended. Turn into prepared pan. Bake for 1 hour. Cool in pan for 10 minutes. Remove from pan. Cool in refrigerator before slicing. Yield: 25 slices.

Mrs. Paul J. Rice, Treas. OWC
Cooke Barracks, Goeppingen, Germany

BANANA-NUT BREAD

2 c. biscuit mix
3/4 c. sugar
1/4 tsp. baking soda
1/4 c. finely chopped black walnuts
1 c. mashed, ripe banana
2 eggs
1/2 c. sour cream

(Continued on next page)

Combine all ingredients; mix well. Pour into 1 pound loaf pan. Bake in 350-degree oven for 45 minutes. Yield: 1 loaf.

Mrs. John J. Lighter, OWC
Bentwaters RAF Station, England

JIFFY ORANGE-NUT BREAD

2 c. sifted all-purpose flour
1 tsp. baking soda
1 tsp. baking powder
1/2 tsp. salt
2 tbsp. butter or margarine
1/2 c. boiling water
2 tbsp. grated orange rind
1/3 c. orange juice
1 c. sugar
2 tsp. vanilla
1 egg, slightly beaten
1/2 c. coarsely chopped walnuts
6 walnut halves

Sift flour, baking soda, baking powder and salt together. Melt butter in boiling water in medium-sized bowl. Blend in orange rind and juice, sugar, vanilla and egg. Add dry ingredients and chopped walnuts. Stir just until all flour is dampened; batter will be lumpy. Pour batter into greased loaf pan; place walnut halves on top. Bake at 350 degrees for 1 hour or until wooden pick inserted in center comes out clean. Remove from pan; cool on wire rack. Wrap in waxed paper. Bread keeps well; slices better day after baking.

Mrs. John E. Bircher, Pres. OWC
Harrogate, Yorkshire, England

MAPLE-GLAZED CINNAMON LOAF

2 cans refrigerator cinnamon rolls with
    raisins
1/4 to 1/2 tsp. imitation maple flavoring
2 tbsp. chopped walnuts
Maraschino cherries, drained

(Continued on next page)

Preheat oven to 375 degrees. Separate dough into 16 rolls. Stand rolls up, seam side down in 9 x 5-inch loaf pan. Place together, seam side down, forming loaf until all rolls are used. Bake at 375 degrees for 35 to 40 minutes or till deep brown and centers are done. Remove from pan immediately. Combine cans of frosting in packages with maple flavoring; blend well. Sprinkle walnuts; garnish with cherries. Yield: 16 servings.

Mrs. Richard D. Ensor, VP OWC
Seymour Johnson AFB, North Carolina

MAUI MANGO BREAD

1 c. butter
2 c. sugar
4 eggs
3 c. flour
1 tsp. salt
2 tsp. baking soda
2 c. mango pulp
1 1/2 tsp. banana extract
1 c. nuts
1 c. coconut

Cream butter and sugar together. Add eggs, flour, salt and baking soda; stir until flour is moistened. Add mango pulp, extract, nuts and coconut. Mix until all ingredients are moist. Place in bread loaf pan. Bake for 50 minutes at 350 degrees. Yield: 1 loaf.

Mrs. W. B. Monson, III, Sec. OWC
Pearl Harbor, Honolulu, Hawaii

MINCEMEAT BREAD RING

1 3/4 c. all-purpose flour
3 tsp. baking powder
1/2 tsp. salt
2 eggs
1/4 c. milk
1/2 c. brown sugar
Butter
1 c. prepared mincemeat
1/4 c. orange marmalade

Sift flour, baking powder and salt together. Beat eggs well; stir in milk, brown sugar, 3 tablespoons melted butter and mincemeat. Add flour mixture; stir until just blended. Place in 8-inch greased ring mold. Bake for 1 hour at 350 degrees. Cool 10 minutes. Remove from pan. Cream orange marmalade and 1/2 cup butter together. Serve bread ring with orange butter. Yield: 12 slices.

Mrs. Edward A. Vivian, Adv. OWC
Little Rock AFB, Arkansas

PETITE DATE-BANANA LOAVES

3/4 c. boiling water
1 8-oz. pkg. pitted dates, cut up
1 3/4 c. sifted all-purpose flour
1/2 c. sugar
1 tsp. soda
1/4 tsp. salt
1 beaten egg
1 c. mashed bananas
3/4 c. crushed pineapple
1 c. broken walnuts

Pour boiling water over dates; let stand 5 minutes. Sift flour, sugar, soda and salt together. Add dates, egg, bananas, pineapple and walnuts, mixing well. Turn batter into 4 greased 4 1/2 x 2 3/4 x 2 1/4-inch loaf pans. Bake in 350-degree oven for 35 minutes or till done. May bake in greased 9 1/2 x 5 x 3-inch loaf pan for about 55 to 60 minutes or till done.

Mrs. Spiro S. Babalis, Property Chm. OWC
Selfridge AFB, Michigan

ULU MAU HAWAIIAN BREAD

1 No. 2 1/2 can crushed pineapple
1 10-oz. pkg. moist coconut
1 1/2 c. sugar
4 eggs, beaten
4 c. flour
2 tsp. salt
2 tsp. soda
1/2 c. crushed macadamia nuts

Combine pineapple and coconut in bowl. Add sugar to beaten eggs; mix well. Sift flour, salt and soda; add to mixture. Mix well until blended. Add nuts; stir to blend. Pour into greased 5 x 9-inch loaf pans. Bake at 325 degrees for 1 hour. Place on wire racks to cool. Yield: 3 loaves.
PERSONAL NOTE: Authentic recipe used at the Ulu Mau Village in Honolulu.

Mrs. James R. Smith, 3rd VP OWC
Hickam AFB, Hawaii

PUMPKIN-RAISIN-NUT BREAD

1 c. salad oil
4 eggs
2/3 c. water
2 c. canned pumpkin
3 1/3 c. flour
3 c. sugar
1 1/2 tsp. salt

(Continued on next page)

1 tsp. nutmeg
1 tsp. cinnamon
2 tsp. baking soda
1 c. raisins
1 c. chopped walnuts

Mix oil, eggs, water and pumpkin together in large bowl. Add flour, sugar, salt, nutmeg, cinnamon and soda; beat until well blended. Add raisins and walnuts. Pour into 4 greased and floured 7 3/8 x 3 5/8 x 2 1/2-inch pans. Bake at 350 degrees about 50 minutes to 1 hour. Serve with cream cheese, if desired.

Mrs. Joseph R. Rokous, OWC
West Point USMA, New York

APPLE MUFFINS

1 egg, beaten
1 c. milk
1/4 c. oil
1 c. chopped apples
2 c. flour
Sugar
4 tsp. baking powder
1/2 tsp. salt
1 tsp. cinnamon

Mix egg, milk, oil and apples together. Sift in flour, 1/2 cup sugar, baking powder, salt and 1/2 teaspoon cinnamon. Place in greased 9 x 13-inch pan. Combine 2 tablespoons sugar and remaining cinnamon; sprinkle over top. Bake at 425 degrees for 15 to 20 minutes. Yield: 8 servings.

Mrs. Gerald F. Maneri, Treas. OWC
Hancock Field, New York

APPLE MUFFINS

1 c. minced apple
1 tbsp. honey
1 tsp. cinnamon
1 2/3 c. all-purpose flour
1/4 tsp. salt
2 tsp. baking powder
1/4 c. sugar
1 egg, slightly beaten
2/3 c. skim milk
1/4 c. butter or margarine, melted

Mix apple with honey and cinnamon; set aside. Sift dry ingredients into mixing bowl. Combine egg, milk and butter; add to dry ingredients. Blend until flour is moistened. Do not overmix; batter should be lumpy. Fold in apple. Fill paper baking cups 2/3 full. Bake in 400-degree oven for 16 to 20 minutes. Yield: 12 servings.

Mrs. W. J. Klump, Gourmet Chm. OWC
Clinton Sherman AFB, Oklahoma

BANANA MUFFINS

1/2 c. flour
1 tsp. baking powder
1 tsp. soda
Dash of salt
3 ripe med. bananas
2 eggs
1/4 c. vegetable shortening
3/4 c. sugar
1 tsp. vanilla

Combine flour, baking powder, soda and salt in mixing bowl. Place bananas, eggs, shortening, sugar and vanilla in blender container. Blend for 20 seconds at high speed. Add banana mixture to dry ingredients; stir to combine. Fill paper-lined muffin tins half full. Bake at 325 degrees for 25 minutes. Yield: 15 muffins.
PERSONAL NOTE: Recipe came from old Hawaiian family on the island of Oahu. Muffins are soft.

Mrs. Robert D. Gamble, O and CWC
Pirmasens USAH Muenchweiler, Germany

CINNAMON-BANANA MUFFINS

2 c. Bisquick
2 1/4 tsp. cinnamon
Sugar
1 egg
1 c. milk
1/4 c. vegetable oil
3 bananas, mashed

Stir Bisquick, 2 teaspoons cinnamon and 1/3 cup sugar, egg, milk and oil; add to dry mixture. Add bananas; stir until all ingredients are blended. Batter will be lumpy. Fill lined or greased muffin tins 3/4 full. Combine remaining cinnamon and 1 tablespoon sugar; sprinkle over top of each muffin. Bake in 425-degree oven for 20 minutes. Yield: 18 muffins.

Mrs. Richard L. Moore, Ed. OWC
Reese AFB, Texas

NUTTY BISCUITS

1 tbsp. butter
1 tbsp. nuts
1 tbsp. light brown sugar
1 pkg. oven-ready biscuits

(Continued on next page)

Place butter, nuts and brown sugar in bottom of each muffin tin. Top with oven-ready biscuits. Bake according to package directions. Yield: 10 biscuits.

Mrs. Austin M. Wilgus, W and M Chm. OWC
Fort Richardson, Alaska

QUEEN'S SURF BANANA MUFFINS

2 c. sugar
1 c. shortening
6 ripe, mashed bananas
4 eggs, well-beaten
2 1/2 c. cake flour
1 tsp. salt
2 tsp. baking soda

Cream sugar and shortening together until blended. Add bananas and eggs. Sift dry ingredients together 3 times; blend with batter. Do not overmix. Pour into greased muffin pans. Bake at 350 degrees for 45 to 50 minutes. Yield: 2 dozen.

Mrs. N. P. Hanna, Cookbook Chm. OWC
Ft. Sam Houston, Texas

QUICK CINNAMON ROLLS

1/4 c. sugar
1 tsp. cinnamon
1 pkg. oven-ready biscuits
2 tbsp. melted butter or margarine

Mix sugar and cinnamon. Dip each biscuit in melted butter, then in cinnamon-sugar mixture. Place in pans. Bake according to package directions. Remove from oven; loosen rolls immediately. Yield: 10 biscuits.

Mrs. Robert V. Hemm, OWC
Bolling AFB, Washington, District of Columbia

ANGEL JAG

Angel food cake loaf, thinly sliced
1 can chestnut paste or maron glace
Brandy to taste
1 qt. boiled custard

(Continued on next page)

1 pkg. shaved almonds
Whipped cream

Spread cake slices with chestnut paste; place together in desired shape, loaf or circle. Pour over brandy; top with custard. Sprinkle with nuts; let stand until chilled. Top with whipped cream. Yield: 10-12 servings.
PERSONAL NOTE: This is an old family recipe from General Jean Lafitte adapted for post wedding party of Major General and Mrs. Kenneth Joe Hodson.

Mrs. Kenneth Hodson, Army Judge Advocate Wives Club
The Pentagon, Washington, D.C.

WHIPPED CREAM PUFFS

PUFFS:

1/4 c. vegetable shortening
1/2 c. boiling water
1/2 c. flour, sifted
Dash of salt
2 eggs

FILLING:

1/2 pt. whipping cream
2 tbsp. confectioners' sugar

Melt shortening in water; bring to a boil. Remove from heat; dump in flour and salt. Stir to paste until mixture separates from pan. Add eggs, 1 at a time. Fill large tablespoon 2/3 full; drop on cookie sheet, evenly spaced. Bake at 450 degrees for 10 minutes; reduce temperature to 400 degrees. Bake for 20 minutes longer. Whip cream until stiff peaks form; add confectioners' sugar. Cool cream puffs; split. Fill puffs with whipped cream; sprinkle with additional confectioners' sugar. Yield: 10-12 servings.

Mrs. Joseph McElroy, OWC
Fort Lesley J. McNair, Washington, D.C.

CONFEDERATE PUDDING SAUCE

1 pkg. lemon-flavored pie filling
1/2 c. sugar
2 1/2 c. cold water
2 egg yolks, slightly beaten
1/4 c. brandy
1/4 c. white wine
Cinnamon-pudding cake or plain cake

Combine pie filling and sugar in saucepan. Gradually stir in cold water and egg yolks, stirring to keep mixture smooth. Cook over medium high heat, stirring

(Continued on next page)

steadily until mixture starts to boil. Break flavor capsule if undissolved; stir into filling. Stir in brandy and white wine; chill. Stir sauce to soften before serving. Serve over cake. Yield: 3 cups.

Photograph for this recipe on cover.

BEAT AND EAT ICING

1 egg white
1/4 tsp. cream of tartar
3/4 c. sugar
1 tsp. vanilla
1/4 c. boiling water

Mix ingredients in small bowl. Add boiling water; beat until stiff.

Mrs. Robert A. Plummer, OWC
San Veto Dei Normanni AS, Italy

FONDUE CHOCOLATE

9 oz. Swiss chocolate
1/2 c. cream
2 tbsp. Kirsch

Break chocolate into small pieces. Combine chocolate, cream and Kirsch in saucepan or small chafing dish. Stir over low heat until chocolate is melted and smooth. Stir constantly, being careful heat is not too high to burn chocolate. Dunk angel food cake bits, ladyfingers, mandarin orange or tangerine slices, pineapple chunks, marshmallows or fresh strawberries into chocolate.

Mrs. William H. Doolittle, 2nd VP OWC
Fort Wainwright, Alaska

QUICK CAKE TOPPING

1/2 c. oleo
1 c. brown sugar
1 c. pecans
1 c. coconut
1/2 c. evaporated milk

Mix above ingredients in order listed; spread on a hot cake layer. Broil until bubbly.

Mrs. John F. Lewis, Tour Chm. OWC
R. A. F. Wethersfield, England

RICH THICK CHOCOLATE SAUCE

2/3 c. warm milk, cream, coffee or sherry
1 c. sugar
4 sq. unsweetened chocolate, cut in sm. pieces
1 tsp. vanilla
Dash of salt

Pour warm liquid, sugar, chocolate, vanilla and salt into blender. Blend until smooth. Sauce may be used for ice cream, pudding, for frosting cakes or flavoring malted milk. Yield: 1 3/4 cups.

Mrs. William J. Simpson, Pres. OWC
Afsouth Post, Bagnoli
Naples, Italy

SOPA BORACHA

1 pound cake or plain loaf cake, cut into
1-inch thick slices
1 tsp. cinnamon
1 c. rum or brandy
1/2 c. sugar
1 1/4 c. water

Place cake slices in large flat dish or individual flat serving dishes. Sprinkle with cinnamon; pour 3 to 4 tablespoons rum or brandy on each cake slice. Make syrup from sugar and water; boil about 10 minutes. Pour over cake when ready to serve.

Mrs. Charles E. Seiler, 1st VP OWC
Whiteman AFB, Missouri

STRAWBERRY SNOW

1/2 c. sugar
1 egg white
1 c. strawberries, diced
Pinch of salt

Place all ingredients in medium-sized bowl; whip with electric beater until mixture forms stiff peaks. Serve over pound cake, angel cake or shortcake; garnish with whole strawberry. Recipe can be made with bananas and apples and served with light cornstarch sauce over top instead of cake. Yield: 6 servings.

Mrs. Joseph M. Madden, OWC
USAF Academy, Colorado

SWISS TOAST WITH RUM SAUCE

12 slices white bread
3/4 c. butter
6 slices Swiss cheese
2 eggs
1 c. milk
1/2 tsp. salt

RUM SAUCE:

1/4 c. dark rum
2 tbsp. butter
1 c. sugar
1/3 c. water

Spread bread with 1/2 cup softened butter; make 6 Swiss cheese sandwiches. Beat eggs until foamy; beat in milk and salt. Dip sandwiches in egg mixture to coat them thoroughly. Saute at 400 degrees in remaining 1/4 cup butter for 10 minutes or until golden brown on both sides. Combine all ingredients for sauce; cook over low heat, stirring constantly, until sugar is dissolved and sauce is hot. Serve sandwiches with hot rum sauce. Yield: 6 servings.

Mrs. L. C. Laitsch, VP OWC
Comfair, Hawaii

COFFEE LOVERS' DELIGHT

1 qt. coffee ice cream
6 tbsp. kahlua
1/4 c. uncooked coffee grounds
Whipped cream (opt.)

(Continued on next page)

Spoon ice cream onto dessert plates or sherbet glasses, if preferred. Pour at least 1 tablespoon kahlua over each serving. Sprinkle few coffee grounds on top. If whipped cream is used, add cream after kahlua. Sprinkle coffee grounds over all. Yield: 6 servings.

Mrs. Paul Ignatius
Wife of former Sec. of the Navy
Washington, District of Columbia

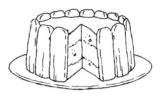

EASY STRAWBERRY DESSERT

5 marshmallows, cut up
1 box frozen strawberries
1/4 pt. whipping cream
1/4 c. chopped walnuts or pecans

Add marshmallows to strawberries; let stand for about 45 minutes. Whip cream until stiff; fold into strawberry mixture. Add nuts; pour into refrigerator tray. Remove from freezer; store in refrigerator for about 1 hour before serving. Yield: 6 servings.

Mrs. Richard W. Leighton, Pres. OWC
USNSY, Portsmouth, New Hampshire

FRESH ORANGE DESSERT

1 orange, peeled, sliced
Sugar
1 tbsp. almonds, toasted in butter
1/4 c. whipping cream
Brown sugar
Sour cream

Sugar orange slices lightly; drop several toasted almonds on each slice. Stack them to resemble orange shape. Whip cream; add brown sugar and sour cream to taste. Spoon sauce over orange. Yield: 1 serving.

Mrs. Karl H. Grosh, OWC
Williams AFB, Arizona

FROZEN FRUIT CUP

2 c. canned pears
1 No. 2 can fruit cocktail
1 sm. can pineapple tidbits and juice
1 box frozen strawberries, partially thawed
1 c. water
3/4 c. sugar

Drain juice from pears and fruit cocktail; place in serving dish. Add pineapple tidbits and strawberries. Combine water and sugar in saucepan; boil for 3 minutes. Pour hot syrup over fruit mixture; freeze. Let stand at room temperature for few minutes before serving. Yield: 4 servings.

Mrs. E. S. Hutchinson, Parlm. OWC
Cape May Receiving Center, New Jersey

FROZEN LEMON CHIFFON PIE

2 eggs, separated
Sugar
1/2 tsp. lemon rind
1/4 c. lemon juice
8 graham crackers, rolled
3/4 c. whipping cream, whipped

Cook egg yolks, 6 tablespoons sugar, lemon rind and juice. Beat egg whites stiff with 2 tablespoons sugar. Fold into cooked lemon mixture; chill. Butter inside of pie plate or tray. Sprinkle with 1/2 of crumbs. Fold cream into chilled lemon mixture; pour into tray. Cover with crumbs; freeze. Yield: 4-6 servings.

Mrs. Charles E. Abbott, 2nd VP OWC
Sheppard AFB, Texas

FROZEN STRAWBERRY CAKE

1 1/2 c. crushed strawberries
2/3 c. sugar
1 tbsp. lemon juice
3 c. graham cracker crumbs
1/2 c. cream
1 1/2 tsp. vanilla extract
Whipped cream
Chopped pecans

Combine ingredients in order listed; blend well. Line freezing tray with waxed paper; fill with mixture. Cover; freeeze until firm. Cut into squares; top with

(Continued on next page)

whipped cream and few pecan meats and strawberries. Keeps in freezer for weeks. Yield: 6-8 servings.

Mrs. W. E. Bragunier, Pres. OWC
NAV COMSTAPHIL
San Miguel, Puerto Rico

FROZEN LEMON MOUSSE

2 envelopes unflavored gelatin
1 6-oz. can frozen lemonade concentrate,
    thawed
Yellow food coloring
1 qt. vanilla ice cream

Sprinkle gelatin over undiluted lemonade concentrate to soften, in small sauce-pan. Place over low heat, stirring until gelatin is dissolved. Remove from heat; stir in few drops of food coloring. Cut ice cream into chunks; place in large bowl. Beat with electric mixer at medium speed just until softened. Pour lemonade mixture into ice cream; beat at medium speed just until blended. Turn into 4 or 5-cup mold. Refrigerate for 15 minutes or until set. Unmold onto serving plate. If desired, garnish with lemon leaves and thin slices.

Mrs. Stephen Sherwood, Hon. Pres. NSC OWC
San Diego, California

FROZEN LEMON PIE

2 eggs, separated
Sugar
Juice and grated rind of 1 lemon
2/3 c. evaporated milk, whipped
1 pastry or graham cracker crust baked and
    cooled

Mix egg yolks and 1/2 cup sugar well. Add juice and rind of lemon. Stiffly beat egg whites; add 3 tablespoons sugar. Add egg white mixture to egg yolk mixture. Add milk to other ingredients. Pour filling into crust. Freeze until 1 hour before serving; pie should be placed in refrigerator to soften slightly. Yield: 8 servings.

Mrs. Earl M. Thompson, Pres. OWC
Norton AFB, California

HOMEMADE ICE CREAM

2 1/2 c. sugar
2 eggs
1 pt. of heavy cream
1 tbsp. vanilla
Whole milk

(Continued on next page)

Blend sugar and eggs in mixer. Beat together until color is very light yellow. Stir cream into egg mixture. Add vanilla. Add enough milk to fill 1 gallon freezer to about 2 inches from top. Freeze according to freezer directions. Yield: 12-14 servings.

Mrs. Exley E. Wical, OWC
Clinton County AFB, Ohio

GRASSHOPPER DELIGHT

Vanilla ice cream
White creme de cacao
Green creme de menthe

Place 1 or 2 scoops ice cream in individual dessert dish or sherbet glass. Pour one jigger white creme de cacao and 1 jigger green creme de menthe over ice cream.

Mrs. Rallin J. Aars, Sec. OWC
Tempelhof AFB, Germany

LEMON SHERBET DELIGHT

1 c. sugar
Few grains of salt
1 c. water
1/2 c. milk
1 c. lemon juice
2 egg whites

Combine 3/4 cup sugar, salt and water; cook for 5 minutes. Cool; add milk, then juice. Freeze until firm in refrigerator. Turn into chilled bowl; beat thoroughly. Beat egg whites; gradually add remaining sugar. Continue beating until stiff and sugar is dissolved; fold into frozen mixture. Return to tray; freeze until firm. Yield: 6 servings.

Mrs. Ralph Carlson, Treas. OWC
Clinton County AFB, Ohio

LIME FROST

1 egg, separated
1/3 c. water
1/3 c. nonfat dry milk
1/3 c. sugar
1/4 tsp. grated lime peel
2 to 3 tbsp. lime juice
Dash of salt
3 tbsp. graham cracker crumbs

(Continued on next page)

Combine egg white, water and dry milk; beat until stiff peaks form. Mix beaten egg yolk, sugar, peel, juice and salt; gradually beat into egg white. Spread 2 tablespoons crumbs in refrigerator tray; spoon in lime mixture. Dust with remaining crumbs. Freeze; cut in squares or wedges to serve.

Mrs. Frederick O. Hutchinson, Corr. Sec. OWC
Williams AFB, Arizona

LIME SHERBET

1 c. sugar
2 c. water
1/2 c. lime juice
Green vegetable coloring

Heat sugar and water until sugar is dissolved. Add lime juice and drop of food coloring, if desired. Cool; freeze for 2 to 3 hours, stirring every 30 minutes for the first 2 hours. Yield: 4 servings.

Mrs. C. B. Jones, Pres. OWC
Cooke Barracks
Geoppingen, Germany

MELON-DUE

1 qt. watermelon pulp
1 1/4 c. sugar
1 tbsp. lemon juice
6 tsp. brandy or B and B

Place all ingredients in blender; blend until of blended pulp consistency. Pour into freezer container; freeze. May be prepared while melon is in season for future use. Yield: 8 servings.

Mrs. Gordon Bennett, Pres. OWC
Bentwaters Woodbridge RAF Base, England

MOCHA MOUSSE

8 oz. semisweet chocolate
3 tbsp. strong coffee
4 tbsp. creme de cacao
1 c. heavy cream, whipped with 3 tbsp.
    sugar

Combine chocolate, coffee and creme de cacao in double boiler; melt, stirring to blend. Cool. Fold chocolate mixture into whipped cream. Pour into mold or paper muffin cups; freeze. Remove from freezer 10 minutes before serving, if molded. Yield: 8-10 servings.

Mrs. Truman Clark, OWC
MCAS, Beaufort, South Carolina

OVER THE RAINBOW DESSERT

1/2 gal. rainbow sherbet or multi-flavored
    ice cream, sliced into 2-inch squares
1 pkg. coconut macaroons, crushed
1 qt. Cool Whip
Walnuts for garnish

Place 1/2 package macaroons in 13 x 9-inch casserole. Top with 1/2 of sherbet. Top with 1/2 of Cool Whip. Repeat layer. Garnish with walnuts. Freeze. Let thaw slightly before serving. Yield: 12 servings.

Mrs. G. Brian, OWC
Port Hueneme, California

PEANUT BRITTLE FREEZER DESSERT

3 c. whipping cream
Vanilla to taste
1 lb. peanut brittle, crushed

Whip cream until stiff. Add vanilla to taste. Fold peanut brittle into whipped cream. Place in 8 x 8 x 2-inch pan; freeze. Cut into appropriate serving pieces; serve frozen. Yield: 8 servings.

Mrs. Henry E. Davis, Corr. Sec. OWC
Naha AFB, Okinawa

SHERBET SPECIAL

1 qt. orange sherbet
Mandarin oranges, coconut, nuts or
    marshmallows

(Continued on next page)

Soften sherbet by letting set out of refrigerator for 30 minutes. Place in bowl; stir to soften further. Add remaining ingredients; mix lightly. Place in ice tray or shallow pan; refreeze. Serve with garnish of ingredients used, as nuts or coconut. Lime sherbet may be used instead of orange sherbet; use fruit cocktail for remaining ingredients. Yield: 6 servings.

Mrs. Donald Westrom, Pres. O and CWC
Special Service Crafts
Grofenwohr, Germany

SPEEDY SUNDAES

1 3 1/4-oz. pkg. pudding and pie filling
  mix, any flavor
2 c. milk
Ice cream

Cook pudding according to package directions; spoon while hot over ice cream. Vanilla ice cream allows for variety with topping. Try adding flavorings to chocolate and vanilla mixes, such as mint, instant coffee or banana. Top with chopped nuts, whipped cream or marshmallow creme, if desired. Yield: 6 servings.

Mrs. Lawrence M. Schilling, OWC
USCGAS
Traverse City, Michigan

SUMMER FIVE-IN-ONE DESSERT

3 bananas, quartered and sliced
Juice and pulp of 3 oranges
Juice and pulp of 3 lemons
3 c. sugar
3 c. water

Mix fruits, sugar and water; pour into ice cube tray and freeze. Garnish with mint leaf. Yield: 6 servings.

Mrs. Paul H. Running, Sec. OWC
US Naval Comm. Sta., Western Australia

AMBROSIA

1 lge. can pineapple chunks, well drained
2 or 3 bananas, sliced
1 c. maraschino cherries, well drained
2 c. tiny marshmallows or 1 c. coconut
1/2 c. chopped walnuts (opt.)
2 envelopes Dream Whip or sour cream

(Continued on next page)

Combine all ingredients gently; refrigerate for about 2 hours. Yield: 6-8 servings.

Mrs. Emery W. Young, OWC
Keyport Naval Torpedo Station, Washington

BAKED FRUIT DISH

Pears, pineapple, peaches and apricots
1/4 lb. butter
1 tbsp. brown sugar
1 tsp. curry powder
1 tsp. cinnamon
1/2 tsp. nutmeg

Wipe fruit well; refrigerate for 1 hour. Remove from refrigerator; place in casserole. Dot with butter. Mix brown sugar and spices together; sprinkle onto each piece of fruit, dividing mixture equally among them. Bake, uncovered, for 45 minutes at 325 degrees.

Mrs. Keith A. Kelling, Howard Kobbe OWC
Fort Kobbe, Canal Zone

BANANAS IN RUM

6 ripe bananas
1/2 c. olive oil
3 tbsp. rum
1/2 tsp. vanilla extract
1/4 c. powdered sugar

Cut bananas into slices. Fry in hot oil until browned. Place in serving dish. Mix rum and vanilla; sprinkle over bananas. Sieve powdered sugar over top. Yield: 6 servings.

Mrs. Edward Lange, OWC
Chandler AFS, Minnesota

BERRY FLAMBE

1 1-lb. can blueberries
1 1-lb. pkg. frozen strawberries
1 1-lb. pkg. frozen raspberries
1 jigger plus 1 tsp. Triple Sec
Ice cream or meringue shells

Defrost berries in hot water as package directs. Place berries in blazer pan of chafing dish; bring to boil gradually. Add 1 jigger Triple Sec; warm. Flame 1 teaspoon Triple Sec; ignite berries. Pour over ice cream or meringue shells. Yield: 6 servings.

Mrs. Michael B. Blaisdell, Bridge Chm. OWC
Cannon AFB, New Mexico

BANANA DELIGHT

6 bananas, split
1 c. orange juice
1 c. brown sugar
1/2 c. dry bread crumbs or cake crumbs
1/2 c. grated coconut
1/4 tsp. nutmeg
1/4 tsp. cinnamon

Place bananas in buttered baking dish. Mix orange juice and sugar; pour over bananas. Mix crumbs with coconut and spices; sprinkle over bananas. Bake for 20 minutes. Yield: 6 servings.

Mrs. M. J. Carucci, Luncheon Chm. OWC
Itazuke AFB, Japan

CHERRIES JUBILEE

1 1/8 c. currant jelly
5 1-lb. cans Bing cherries, drained and
    pitted
1 c. brandy
Hard ice cream balls

Melt jelly in large chafing dish; add cherries. Heat until bubbly; add brandy in center. Do not stir. Light brandy when warm; let flame. Stir; serve on ice cream balls. Yield: 10 servings.

Mrs. Homer R. Adrianse, Treas. Mare Island OWC
San Francisco Bay NSY, California

CANTALOUPE ALASKA

3 ripe cantaloupes, well chilled
4 egg whites

(Continued on next page)

Dash of salt
1/2 c. sugar
1 pt. firm vanilla ice cream
2 tbsp. almonds, sliced

Preheat oven to 500 degrees. Cut cantaloupes in half; remove seeds. Level base of each half. Beat egg whites with the salt until stiff; beat in sugar gradually to make stiff meringue. Place cantaloupes on ungreased cookie sheet; place 1 scoop vanilla ice cream in each half. Cover with meringue, sealing edges. Sprinkle with almonds. Bake at 500 degrees for 2 to 3 minutes. Serve immediately. Yield: 6 servings.

Mrs. Ronald G. Nicholl, Corr. Sec. OWC
Ketchikan US Coast Guard Base, Alaska

CHARLIE'S CHERRY FAVORITE

3/4 c. sugar
5 tbsp. cornstarch
2 cans sour pie cherries
3/4 c. shortening
1 1/2 c. oatmeal
1 1/2 c. flour
3/4 c. brown sugar
3/4 tsp. soda

Boil first 3 ingredients until thickened. Combine remaining ingredients with pastry blender. Pack half the blended ingredients into 7 1/2 x 12-inch pan; spread with cherry mixture. Spread remaining blended mixture over top. Bake at 350 degrees for 20 minutes. Serve alone or with ice cream. Yield: 8-10 servings.

Mrs. Wendell R. Arndt, Publ. Chm.
Seoul Area American OWC
Yongsan Compound, Seoul, Korea

CHERRIES JUBILEE

2 c. canned black Bing cherries
3/4 c. cherry juice from can
1 c. white corn syrup
1 8-oz. c. brandy
Vanilla ice cream

Heat cherries, juice and syrup in chafing dish until thoroughly warm. Add brandy; stir. Ignite; ladle slowly over individual servings of ice cream. Yield: 4-6 servings.

Mrs. Donald F. Ryder, OWC
FOCCPAC, Hawaii

CRANBERRY CRUNCH

1/2 c. flour
Butter
1 1/4 c. brown sugar
1 c. rolled oats
1 can whole cranberry sauce
1/4 c. chopped pecans
Whipped cream or topping (opt.)

Combine flour, 1 stick butter, brown sugar and oats; mix well. Spread 1/2 of the sugar mixture in greased 8 x 8-inch pan; cover with cranberries. Spread remaining mixture over top; dot with extra butter and pecans. Bake at 350 degrees for 30 minutes or until bubbly. Serve with whipped cream, if desired. Yield: 6-12 servings.

Mrs. Henry A. Renken, Hon. Pres. OWC
Great Lakes NTS, Illinois

CRUNCHY PEACHES 'N' CREAM

1 No. 2 1/2 can peaches, drained
1 c. peach preserves
1 tbsp. brandy or 1 tsp. lemon juice
1/2 c. brown sugar
1/2 c. crumbled cornflakes
1 tsp. cinnamon
1 qt. vanilla ice cream

Place peaches in 9 x 9-inch casserole. Mix 1/2 cup peach juice with peach preserves and brandy; pour over peaches. Mix sugar, cornflakes and cinnamon; sprinkle over peaches. Bake for 15 minutes at 375 degrees. Place hard-frozen ice cream in 6 individual dishes; spoon peach mix over top. Spoon 1/2 teaspoon brandy over finished dessert; serve flaming for really festive look.

Mrs. Damon H. Thomas, Pres. OWC
Ft. Wainwright, Alaska

DUMP DEEP DISH PIE

2/3 stick butter
1/2 c. sugar
1/2 c. flour
1/2 c. milk
1 tsp. baking powder
Pinch of salt
2 c. sweetened fruit

Melt butter in oblong pan. Mix sugar, flour, milk, baking powder and salt in another dish. Pour over melted butter; top with fruit and juice. Bake at 425 degrees until crust is done.

Mrs. Jack Royster, Corr. Sec. OWC
Whiteman AFB, Missouri

FRESH FRUIT MEDLEY

3 bananas, sliced
1 c. pineapple chunks, fresh or canned
2 oranges, sectioned
2 peaches, sliced
1/2 c. strawberries (opt.)
1/2 c. small marshmallows (opt.)
3/4 c. sugar

Combine fruit and marshmallows with sugar; toss lightly. Cover; chill for 1 hour. Serve as appetizer, salad or dessert. Yield: 6 servings.

Mrs. G. P. Bienstadt, OWC
Memphis NAS, Tennessee

FLORIDA AMBROSIA

2 Florida grapefruit, peeled and sectioned
3 Florida oranges, peeled and sectioned
2 Florida tangerines, peeled and sectioned
1/3 to 1/2 c. sugar
1/2 c. shredded coconut

Remove membrane from grapefruit and orange sections. Cut tangerine sections into halves; remove seeds. Turn half the fruit into serving dish; sprinkle with half the sugar and coconut. Repeat procedure. Chill for at least 1 hour before serving. Yield: 8 servings.

Photograph for this recipe on page 267 .

GRAPE CUP

20 lge. marshmallows
1/2 c. grape juice
1 pt. whipping cream, whipped
1 pkg. frozen black cherries, thawed

(Continued on next page)

Melt marshmallows and grape juice in saucepan; cool to jelly consistency. Fold cream into grape mixture. Place in stemmed glasses; spoon on cherries. Chill for at least 2 hours. Yield: 6 servings.

Mrs. David D. Hutchinson, Asst. Chm. Ways and Means OWC
Davis Monthan AFB, Arizona

GARDELLA SPECIAL

1 half gal. vanilla ice cream
1 No. 2 1/2 can fruit cocktail, drained
1 bottle port or Burgundy
8 to 10 maraschino cherries (opt.)

Place 1 or 2 scoops vanilla ice cream in dessert or parfait glass; top with 2 tablespoons fruit cocktail. Pour 2 tablespoons port over fruit. Top with maraschino cherry, if desired. Good to serve after heavy meal.
PERSONAL NOTE: This recipe was passed on from my in-laws; name of dish originated in their restaurant.

Mrs. John K. Gardella, Pres.
Quonset-Davisville NOWC
NAS Quonset Point, Rhode Island

HOT FRUIT CASSEROLE

1/3 c. melted butter or margarine
2 tsp. curry powder
3/4 c. brown sugar
1 No. 2 1/2 can pears, drained and dried
1 No. 2 1/2 can apricots, drained and dried
1 No. 2 1/2 can peaches, drained and dried
12 pineapple chunks
Maraschino cherries

Mix butter, curry powder and brown sugar together. Arrange fruits in 1 1/2-quart casserole; add butter mixture. Looks skimpy but cooks together well; do not cover. Bake for 1 hour at 325 degrees. Yield: 8 servings.

Mrs. Floyd M. Yates, Hon. Pres. Wives' Club
Red Bluff AFS, California

PEACH-CHERRY FLAMBE

1/2 c. peach jam
1 lge. can peach halves, well drained
2 c. dark sweet cherries, well drained

(Continued on next page)

1/2 c. brandy
1 qt. vanilla ice cream

Melt peach jam in chafing dish or electric skillet; add fruit. Heat. Pour brandy into peach halves; light with match. Serve fruit mixture over scoop of vanilla ice cream when flame dies out. Yield: 6-8 servings.

Mrs. Douglas L. Crinklaw, Nav. Com. Sta. OWC
Norfolk, Virginia

HOT FRUIT DISH

10 maraschino cherries
1 15 1/2-oz. can pineapple slices
1 15 1/2-oz. can pear halves
1 15 1/2-oz. can peach halves
3/4 c. brown sugar
4 tsp. curry powder
1/3 c. butter

Drain most of the juice from canned fruit. Place in ungreased casserole. Add sugar, curry powder and butter. Bake for 1 hour at 350 degrees. Serve as accompaniment with meat. Yield: 8 servings.

Mrs. Edwin L. Dennis, Jr., Pres. Cinclant OWC
Atl. Com. Hdgtrs., Norfolk, Virginia

MICHAEL'S ORANGE FLAMBE

1/4 c. cold water
1/3 c. cornstarch
2 c. mandarin orange segments, with juice
1 jigger grand marnier liqueur
1 pt. orange sherbet
4 tsp. grain alcohol or 100 proof rum

Mix water and cornstarch until smooth. Bring orange segments to boil; stir in cornstarch mixture, cooking until thickened. Stir in liqueur; cool. Dip portion of sauce over dipper of sherbet; pour 1 teaspoon grain alcohol over. Ignite; serve flaming. Yield: 4 servings.

Mrs. Andrew P. Rollins, Hon. Pres. OWC
Ft. Leonard Wood, Missouri

PEACH DELIGHT

1/2 c. butter
1 c. flour

(Continued on next page)

1 c. sugar
1 c. milk
4 tsp. baking powder
1/4 tsp. salt
1 tsp. vanilla
5 peeled, sliced and sugared peaches
    or 1 No. 303 can peaches, drained

Preheat oven to 350 degrees. Melt butter in medium-sized glass baking pan. Mix flour, sugar, milk, baking powder, salt and vanilla together by hand. Pour batter into butter; swirl to blend slightly. Drop in peaches. Bake at 350 degrees for 30 minutes. Turn off oven; leave peach delight in oven for 15 minutes. Serve warm with cream, ice cream or whipped cream. Yield: 4 servings.

Mrs. Jey E. Younger, III, Corr. Sec. OWC
Blytheville AFB, Arkansas

PEACH COBBLER

3/4 stick butter
1 c. Bisquick
3/4 c. sugar
1 c. milk
1/4 tsp. cinnamon
1 No. 3 can sliced peaches, drained
4 tbsp. peach syrup

Melt butter in casserole in 350-degree oven. Mix together remaining ingredients. Pour mixture into casserole with butter. Bake for about 30 to 45 minutes or until crust is golden. Yield: 6 servings.

Mrs. Albert F. Disante, Corr. Sec. OWC
Minot AFB, North Dakota

PEACHES IN RED WINE

6 sm. peaches
1 c. sugar
2/3 c. water
Cinnamon
2/3 c. red Burgundy
Whipped cream

Peel peaches; do not remove stones. Place peaches in saucepan with sugar, water and cinnamon to taste. Cover; simmer for about 15 minutes. Add Burgundy; cook, uncovered to consistency of light syrup. Pour over peaches; chill. Serve with whipped cream.

Mrs. L. E. VanBuskirk, Hon. Pres.
Red River Army Depot
Texarkana, Texas

PEACH YUM YUM

3 c. sliced peaches
1 tbsp. sugar
1 tbsp. flour
1/2 c. chopped pecans
1/2 box white cake mix
1/4 lb. butter or oleo, melted

Place peaches in buttered 8 x 8-inch pan; sprinkle with sugar, flour and pecans. Sprinkle white cake mix over all; pour over butter. Do not mix. Bake at 375 degrees for 30 minutes or until crusty, medium brown color appears. Cool. Serve with whipped cream or Cool Whip. Yield: 6 servings.

Mrs. Nelson W. Hardin, Asst. Treas. OWC
Pope AFB, North Carolina

PLUM JUBILEE

1/2 c. currant jelly
1 No. 2 1/2 can plums
1/3 c. plus 1 tsp. brandy
10 vanilla wafers
20 scoops or 1 1/2 qt. vanilla ice cream

Melt jelly in saucepan over low heat; remove seeds from plums. Add plums and juice to jelly and continue heating. Add 1/3 cup brandy when almost boiling. Place a vanilla wafer in each of 10 parfait glasses; moisten each with teaspoon brandy. Place 2 scoops ice cream in each glass. Spoon plum sauce over ice cream. Yield: 10 servings.

Mrs. Norman B. Hopkins, Hon. Pres.
McKee Barracks OWC
Crailsheim, Germany

PINEAPPLE DESSERT

Sliced pineapple
Grated coconut
Sour cream

Place 2 pineapple slices together for each serving. Cover with coconut. Pour sour cream over coconut. Bake at 300 degrees for about 10 minutes. Garnish with cherries or sliced mandarin oranges.

Mrs. H. G. Sparrow, Ed. Newsletter Women's Club
Fort Myer, Virginia

QUICK APPLE BROWN BETTY

2 cans pie-sliced apples
Cinnamon
2 c. brown sugar
1 1/2 c. flour
1/2 c. butter

Place apples in 2-quart glass baking pan. Sprinkle with cinnamon. Mix brown sugar, flour and butter until crumbly. Dot over apples. Bake at 375 degrees for 30 to 40 minutes or until crisp.

Mrs. John Garver, Pres. Woman's Club
West Point, New York

QUICK CAMPING DESSERT

1 can Pillsbury refrigerator biscuits
1 can blueberry, apple, blackberry or
**   cherry pie filling**
Oil
Powdered sugar

Roll each biscuit or pat with hands to flatten; place 1 tablespoon filling on half the biscuit. Fold over; seal. Fry in skillet with about 1/2 inch oil until brown. Roll in powdered sugar. Yield: 6 servings.

Mrs. William Sims, Hon. Pres. OWC
Yuma MCAS, Arizona

QUICK FRUIT COBBLER

1/2 c. margarine
1 c. Bisquick
1 c. sugar
1 c. milk
1 30-oz. can sliced peaches or blackberries

Preheat oven to 350 degrees. Melt margarine in small saucepan; pour into 13 x 9 1/2 x 2-inch loaf pan, covering bottom of pan. Combine Bisquick, sugar and milk in small mixing bowl; beat smooth with mixer or egg beater. Pour evenly over margarine. Pour fruit carefully over Bisquick mixture, spreading evenly; do not stir in. Bake for 1 hour at 350 degrees. Serve warm or chilled, topped with whipped cream, if desired. Yield: 12 servings.

Mrs. Elgin R. Christian, Ways and Means Chm. NMS OWC
Washington, District of Columbia

QUICK FRUIT SALAD DESSERT

1 No. 2 1/2 can fruit cocktail, chilled
2 bananas, diced
1 c. miniature marshmallows
1/2 c. pecans or walnuts
1/2 c. mayonnaise
1/2 c. shredded coconut (opt.)

Drain fruit cocktail well; combine with remaining ingredients. Toss lightly. Yield: 8 servings.

Mrs. Gary Farmer, Treas. OWC
Kingsley Field AFB, Oregon

QUICK MANDARIN DESSERT

1 jar orange marmalade
4 cans mandarin oranges
1 c. sour cream

Melt marmalade in small saucepan. Divide oranges among 8 sherbet glasses; spoon marmalade over. Top with dollop of sour cream. Yield: 8 servings.

Mrs. Phillip Kamish, Corr. Sec.
Bentwaters-Woodbridge OWC
RAF Bentwaters, England

CHOCOLATE-MINT MERINGUE DROPS

2 egg whites, beaten stiff
1/4 tsp. salt
1/2 tsp. cream of tartar
3/4 c. sugar
Green food coloring
1 6-oz. pkg. mint-flavored chocolate chips

Preheat oven to 375 degrees. Beat egg whites stiff. Add salt, cream of tartar and sugar gradually to egg whites. Add few drops coloring to shade desired. Fold in chocolate chips. Drop by teaspoonfuls onto greased cookie sheet. Place in oven; turn oven off at once. Let stand in oven for at least 2 hours; remove from sheet with spatula. Yield: 36 cookies.

Mrs. Wilfred C. Burton, Women's Club
US Mil. Acad., West Point, New York

MOCHA BROWNIE TORTE

1 1 1/2-lb. pkg. fudge brownie mix
1/4 c. water
2 eggs
1/2 c. chopped pecans
1 1/2 c. heavy cream
1/3 c. brown sugar
4 tsp. instant coffee powder
Shaved semisweet chocolate

Preheat oven to 350 degrees. Grease two 9-inch round layer cake pans. Blend brownie mix with water and eggs; stir in pecans. Spread in prepared pans. Bake for 20 minutes. Cool in pans on wire rack for 5 minutes before turning out of pans to cool completely. Beat cream just until it begins to thicken; add sugar and coffee powder, beating until stiff. Fill layers with cream; frost top and sides. Sprinkle with shaved chocolate. Chill for 1 hour or more. Yield: 10-12 servings.

Mrs. Ralph D. Hill, Family Services Chm.
Point Arena AF, California

POUND CAKE TORTE

1 frozen pound cake
2 pkg. German's sweet chocolate
1/4 c. strong coffee
1/2 pt. whipping cream, whipped
1/2 tsp. almond flavoring
Slivered almonds

Slice frozen cake lengthwise to make 6 layers, using electric knife. Melt chocolate with coffee; cool. Fold into whipped cream flavored with almond. Spread between cake layers; frost top and sides. Decorate with almonds. Yield: 8-10 servings.

Mrs. William R. Jarrell, OWC
US Air Force Academy, Colorado

MOCHA VELVET TORTE

1 12-oz. loaf pound cake
1 pkg. instant chocolate pudding mix
1 tbsp. instant coffee powder
1 2-oz. package dessert topping mix
1 1/2 c. milk

Slice cake horizontally into 4 layers. Place pudding mix, instant coffee, dessert topping and milk in mixing bowl; beat till fluffy and of spreading consistency. Spread 3 cake layers with frosting; stack together. Top with fourth layer; frost top and sides. Chill. Yield: 10 servings.

Mrs. Myron W. Crow, American OWC
AFNORTH Kolsas, Norway

RITZ CRACKER PIE

1/2 tsp. baking powder
4 egg whites, beaten stiff
1 c. sugar
1/2 tsp. vanilla
1/2 c. pecans
19 Ritz crackers, coarsely crumbled

Add baking powder to egg whites; mix in sugar, vanilla and pecans. Fold in crackers. Place in well-greased 9-inch pie pan. Bake for 30 minutes in 325-degree oven. Cool; refrigerate. Serve with whipped cream or ice cream. Yield: 6-8 servings.

Mrs. A. C. Agan, OWC
Wife of Commanding General ADC
Ent AFB, Colorado

RITZIE PIE

1 c. sugar
3 egg whites, beaten stiff
1 tsp. baking powder
20 crumbled Ritz crackers
3/4 c. chopped walnuts

Fold a little sugar at a time into egg whites; add baking powder with last tablespoon sugar. Add crackers and nuts; place in pie pan. Bake at 350 degrees for 20 to 25 minutes. Chill; serve with whipped cream or ice cream. Yield: 8-12 servings.

Mrs. Paul H. Reynolds, Pres. OWC
Sharpe Army Depot, California

SODA CRACKER PIE

3 egg whites
1/2 tsp. cream of tartar
1 c. sugar
12 soda crackers, finely crushed
1 c. chopped pecans
1 pkg. Dream Whip, prepared according to
    package instructions

Beat egg whites with cream of tartar until foamy; beat in sugar until stiff. Add remaining ingredients; mix well. Place into well-buttered 10-inch pie tin. Bake for about 20 minutes at 350 degrees. Cool; cover with Dream Whip. Yield: 8 servings.

Mrs. Don Conwell, Sec. OWC
Peshawar Air Station, Pakistan

SODA CRACKER PIE

1/8 tsp. salt
1 tsp. vanilla
1 c. sugar
3 egg whites, beaten stiff
3/4 c. chopped walnuts
3/4 c. crushed crackers, with unsalted tops
1 tsp. baking powder
1/2 pt. whipping cream, whipped and
    sweetened to taste

Beat salt, vanilla and sugar into egg whites thoroughly; fold in walnuts and crackers, reserving a few walnuts. Add baking powder; stir well. Place in ungreased 9-inch pie pan. Bake for 25 minutes at 325 degrees. Cool completely; spread with whipped cream. Sprinkle with reserved nuts. Refrigerate for at least 4 hours before serving. Yield: 8 servings.

Mrs. Walter W. White, Ways and Means Chm. USCG OWC
Long Beach, California

APPLE PIE WITH A DIFFERENCE

1 lge. frozen pie shell
Flour
2 beaten eggs
Dash of salt
2 tbsp. lemon juice
1 tsp. vanilla extract
1 1/2 c. sour cream
1 tsp. cinnamon
2 21-oz. cans apple pie filling
1/4 c. soft butter
1/4 c. chopped walnuts
1/2 c. firmly packed brown sugar

Place pie shell in plate as directed. Add 2 tablespoons flour to eggs; blend. Add salt, lemon juice, vanilla extract, sour cream and 1/2 teaspoon cinnamon; mix well. Fold in pie filling; turn into shell. Bake at 350 degrees for 40 minutes. Mix remaining cinnamon, butter, nuts, brown sugar and 1/3 cup flour. Crumble over pie; continue baking for 15 to 20 minutes or until pie is set and topping is slightly brown. Serve slightly warm with a wedge of cheddar cheese, if desired. Yield: 6-8 servings.

Mrs. W. D. Johnson, Jr., Nursery Chm. C and OWC
McKee Barracks, West Germany

APRICOT CHIFFON PIE

LACY COCONUT CRUST:

1 tsp. butter or margarine
1 3 1/2-oz. can flaked coconut

(Continued on next page)

FILLING:

1 envelope unflavored gelatin
1/3 c. sugar
Dash of salt
1 12-oz. can apricot nectar
1 tsp. lemon juice
1/8 tsp. almond extract
2 egg whites, unbeaten

Butter 9-inch pie plate. Press coconut against sides and bottom of pie plate. Bake at 325 degrees for 10 minutes or until edges are golden. Cool. Thoroughly mix gelatin, sugar and salt. Heat apricot nectar in saucepan just to boiling; add to gelatin mixture, stirring until dissolved. Add lemon juice and almond extract; chill till partially set. Add egg whites; beat till soft peaks form. Pile into cooled coconut crust; chill until firm. Yield: 7 servings.

Mrs. Lawrence M. Lyon, Rec. Sec. OWC
Beale AFB, California

APRICOT PASTRIES

1 pkg. refrigerated crescent rolls
1/2 c. apricot jam
1 c. sour cream
1 beaten egg
1 tbsp. sugar
1/2 tsp. vanilla

Preheat oven to 425 degrees. Unroll crescent rolls; pat into buttered 13 x 9 x 2-inch baking dish. Spread with jam. Bake for 15 minutes; remove from oven. Reduce heat to 325 degrees. Combine remaining ingredients. Pour evenly over rolls; return to oven. Bake for 5 to 6 minutes more. Serve warm. Yield: 12 servings.
PERSONAL NOTE: This is quick for a busy day when you want to give your family something special . Good too for something to serve with the coffee at a meeting.

Mrs. John W. Clifford, Pres. OWC
Fort Sill, Oklahoma

CHERRY-BANANA PIE

2 bananas, sliced
1 baked 9-inch pie crust
1 can cherry pie filling
Whipped cream

Arrange bananas in pie shell. Pour filling over; chill. Serve with whipped cream. Yield: 6 servings.

Mrs. James Meidl, Treas. OWC
Fort Benjamin Harrison, Indiana

BLUEBERRY CREAM PIE

1 pkg. vanilla pudding, regular or instant
1 1/2 c. milk
1/2 c. heavy cream, whipped
1 baked 8-inch pie shell
1 can blueberry pie filling

Make pudding as package directs using 1 1/2 cups milk; refrigerate until cold. Fold in whipped cream; turn into baked pie shell. Refrigerate until firm. Carefully spoon blueberry pie filling over pudding in pie shell. Refrigerate until ready to serve. Yield: 6-8 servings.

Mrs. F. L. Farrell, Program Chm.
Kaneohe MCAS, Oahu, Hawaii

CHESS-MERINGUE PIE

1 stick margarine, melted
1 c. sugar
3 egg yolks
1/2 c. canned milk
1 tsp. vanilla
Unbaked pie shell
3 egg whites, beaten till stiff

Mix ingredients together; pour into pie shell. Bake at 350 degrees for 30 minutes. Top with meringue. Bake for 15 to 20 minutes. Yield: 6 servings.

Mrs. Robert B. Moffitt, Nursery Chm. OWC
Ft. Riley, Kansas

CHOCOLATE CANDY BAR ICEBOX PIE

9 plain Hershey bars
1/2 c. cream or milk
1 10-oz. pkg. marshmallows
2 1/2 c. whipped cream with sugar and
    vanilla added
1 c. pecans

(Continued on next page)

2 8 or 9-inch baked pie shells, pastry or
   meringue
Grated chocolate

Place first 3 ingredients in saucepan. Heat, stirring until melted. Remove from heat; cool to room temperature. Fold in 1 1/2 cups whipped cream and pecans. Pour into cooled pie shells; top with 1 cup whipped cream. Grate chocolate on top; refrigerate. Almond Hershey bars and almonds may be substituted for plain bars. Yield: 16 servings.

Mrs. James C. Snell, OWC
Handorf, Germany

CHOCOLATE CHIP PIE

3 eggs, beaten
1/8 tsp. salt
1 tsp. vanilla
1/2 c. sugar
1 1/4 c. white corn syrup
2/3 c. walnut halves
1 c. semisweet chocolate chips
1 unbaked pie shell
1/2 c. heavy cream, whipped

Preheat oven to 375 degrees. Combine in medium-sized bowl eggs, salt, vanilla, sugar and syrup, beating until just blended. Stir in walnut halves and chocolate pieces. Pour mixture into pie shell. Bake for 45 minutes or until top is evenly puffed up and starts to crack. Top each serving with whipped cream and walnut halves, if desired. Pie freezes well. Yield: 8 servings.

Mrs. Thomas J. Scarfato, Coffee Chm.
Willow Grove NAS, Pennsylvania

CHOCOLATE CHIP PIE

3 1/2 c. miniature marshmallows or 30 lge.
   marshmallows
1/2 c. milk
1 c. heavy cream
1 tbsp. confectioners' sugar
2 1-oz. sq. unsweetened chocolate, shaved
1 graham cracker crust for 8-inch pie

Combine marshmallows and milk in large saucepan or double boiler. Cook over low heat until marshmallows melt; cool thoroughly. Whip cream with confectioners' sugar; fold into marshmallow mixture. Add chocolate; stir in gently. Pour into graham cracker crust. Chill until set. Garnish with chocolate shavings, if desired. Yield: 6 servings.

Mrs. Steven Fisher, Custodian OWC
Fairchild AFB, Washington

CHOCOLATE PIE

1 giant chocolate-almond bar
2 c. whipping cream
1 graham cracker pie crust

Melt chocolate bar in double boiler over low heat; cool. Add to whipped cream; pour into cracker pie crust. Chill for 2 hours or longer. Yield: 6 servings.

Mrs. W. C. Morrill, CGOWC
St. Louis, Missouri

COTTAGE CHEESE PIE

1 sm. carton cottage cheese
3 tbsp. butter, melted
1 c. sugar
1 tsp. lemon rind, grated
1 tsp. lemon juice
2 slightly-beaten eggs
1 1 1/2-oz. box raisins (opt.)
1/2 c. chopped pecans (opt.)
1 9-inch unbaked single pie shell

Mix first 8 ingredients together; pour into pie shell. Bake at 350 degrees for 45 to 50 minutes. Chill for at least 2 hours before serving. Yield: 6 servings.

Mrs. James G. Jaborek, 2nd VP OWC
Itazuke AFB, Japan

CRAZY CRUST CHERRY PIE

1 c. all-purpose flour
2 tbsp. sugar
1 tsp. baking powder
1/2 tsp. salt
3/4 c. water
2/3 c. solid vegetable shortening
1 egg
1 1-lb. 5-oz. can cherry pie filling

Combine in small mixing bowl flour, sugar, baking powder, salt, water, shortening and egg. Blend well at lowest speed of mixer. Spread batter in 9 or 10-inch deep dish pie pan. Carefully spoon filling into center of batter. Do not stir. Bake at 425 degrees for 35 to 40 minutes or until crust is golden brown. Yield: 6 servings.

Mrs. Kent Huggins, Asst. Treas. OWC
Pease AFB, New Hampshire

CRUSTLESS APPLE PIE

1 can apple pie filling
1 c. flour
1 c. sugar
1 tsp. baking powder
1 egg
Butter

Pour apple pie filling in 8 or 9-inch pie plate. Combine flour, sugar and baking powder. Break egg over; mix well. Pour topping over pie filling. Dot with butter. Bake in 350-degree oven for 30 minutes. Serve warm with ice cream, if desired.

Mrs. Harold R. Hensle, NOWC
Naval Hospital, San Diego, California

CUSTARD PIE

2 1/2 c. scalded milk
1/2 c. sugar
1/4 tsp. salt
4 eggs, slightly beaten
1 tsp. vanilla
1 unbaked 9-inch pie shell
Nutmeg

Combine milk, sugar and salt. Stir until sugar is dissolved. Very gradually add milk mixture to eggs; stir until well blended. Stir in vanilla. Pour mixture into unbaked shell in glass pie plate. Generously sprinkle top with nutmeg. Bake at 400 degrees until knife inserted in center comes out clean. Yield: 6-8 servings.

Mrs. John C. Herring, Treas. OWC
F. E. Warren AFB, Wyoming

EASY PEACH PIE

Pastry for 9-inch 1-crust pie
2 tbsp. chopped almonds
1 pkg. vanilla instant pudding
1 c. milk
1 c. chilled whipping cream
1 1-lb. 4-oz. can sliced peaches, drained

Prepare pastry as directed except for stirring in almonds before adding water. Bake pie shell. Blend pudding and milk in small mixing bowl at low speed. Add cream; beat at medium speed for 3 to 5 minutes or until soft peaks form. Fold in peaches, reserving about 1/2 cup for garnish. Pour into pie shell. Arrange peach slices on top of pie. Refrigerate for several hours or until filling is firm. Yield: 8-10 servings.

Mrs. Raymond Gallagher, Hon. Pres. OWC
Custer AFS, Michigan

FUDGE PIE

1 1/2 c. sugar
3 tbsp. cocoa
3 tbsp. flour
3 tbsp. butter or margarine at room
    temperature
3 egg yolks
3/4 c. milk
1 tsp. vanilla
3/4 c. nuts (opt.)
1 9-inch unbaked pie shell

Stir sugar, cocoa, flour and butter together; add egg yolks. Stir; do not beat. Add milk, vanilla and nuts. Mix lightly; pour in pie shell. Cook for 40 minutes in 350-degree oven. May be served warm or cold with vanilla ice cream, if desired. Yield: 6 servings.
PERSONAL NOTE: While living in Franklin, Louisiana in 1960, I obtained Favorite Sugar Recipes from Louisiana Plantations, put out by the extension service. This came to be one of my family's favorites as it is so easy and so good.

Mrs. Charles K. Townsend, Pres. ESSA OWC
Washington Science Center, Washington, D. C.

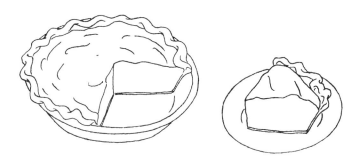

GRASSHOPPER PIE

24 Hydrox or Oreo cookies, rolled till fine
4 tbsp. butter, melted

FILLING:

25 lge. marshmallows
1/2 c. milk
2 tbsp. creme de cacao
2 tbsp. creme de menthe
1/2 pt. cream, whipped

Make crust by combining cookie crumbs and butter, reserving 1 tablespoon crumbs for top. Press crumbs into 8 or 9-inch pie plate. Heat marshmallows and milk in saucepan until marshmallows melt; cool. Add creme de cacao and creme de menthe. Fold whipped cream into above mixture. Pour into prepared crust; sprinkle with reserved crumbs. Chill for at least 8 hours. Keeps for several days. Yield: 6-8 servings.

Mrs. Ephraim P. Holmes, Cinclant OWC
Norfolk, Virginia

GUAVA CHIFFON PIE

1 6-oz. can frozen guava nectar
2 tbsp. water
1 pkg. lemon Jell-O
1 6-oz. can evaporated milk, icy cold
2 tbsp. lemon juice
1 baked pie shell or crumb crust
1 pkg. Dream Whip, whipped

Empty guava nectar into saucepan. Swish out can with water; add to saucepan. Boil guava juice. Add Jell-O; stir to dissolve. Cool till syrupy. Whip milk till stiff; add lemon juice. Fold Jell-O mixture into whipped milk. Pour into baked pie shell or crumb crust; chill till firm. Frost with Dream Whip. Make pie prettier color by adding few drops of red food color to guava mixture. Yield: 6-8 servings.
PERSONAL NOTE: This pie drew raves from all our Mainland visitors and from our Hawaiian friends and neighbors too. Fortunately, frozen guava nectar is available in many metropolitan Mainland areas now.

Mrs. Charles F. Kellenbarger, MOWC Pres.
Yuma MCAS, Arizona

LEMON HEAVEN PIE

3 or 4 eggs
1/2 c. sugar
4 tbsp. lemon juice
Pinch of salt
1 c. whipped cream
Cookies or cracker crumbs

Beat egg yolks and 1 egg white. Add sugar, lemon juice and salt. Cook for 5 minutes in double boiler or until mixture is thick; cool. Beat remaining egg whites until stiff; fold into lemon mixture. Fold in whipped cream carefully. Pour into crumb-lined 8 or 9-inch pan. Chill for at least 1 hour. Yield: 6-8 servings.

Mrs. C. W. Johnson, OWC
Fallon AFS, Nevada

STRAWBERRY PARFAIT PIE

1 sm. pkg. strawberry Jell-O
1 1/4 c. hot water
1 pt. vanilla ice cream
1 12-oz. box sliced strawberries, thawed
    and drained
1 baked pie shell or graham cracker crust

Dissolve Jell-O in hot water in 2-quart saucepan. Add ice cream by spoonfuls, stirring until melted. Chill until thickened but not set for 15 to 25 minutes. Fold in berries. Turn in pie shell. Chill until firm. Yield: 6-8 servings.

Mrs. Lawrence Curtis, Treas. OWC
Seymour Johnson AFB, North Carolina

GREEN TOMATO PIE

5 med.-sized green tomatoes, peeled and
    diced
1 tbsp. vinegar
Dash of salt and pepper
Water
1 c. sugar
1/2 tsp. cinnamon
1 tbsp. flour
1/2 tsp. lemon extract
Butter
Pastry for 2-crust pie

Place tomatoes in bowl; add vinegar, salt, pepper and enough water to cover. Let stand. Squeeze out tomatoes; return to bowl. Add sugar, cinnamon, flour and lemon extract. Dot with butter; mix well. Pour into pie shell; cover with remaining rolled out dough. Bake at 425 degrees till browned. Yield: 6 servings.

Mrs. Joy M. Strayer, Pres. OWC
Incirlik AFB, Turkey

STRAWBERRY 'N' WINE PIE

1/2 c. rose or port wine
3/4 c. water
1 regular pkg. strawberry flavored gelatin
1 10 to 12-oz. pkg. frozen sliced strawberries
2 tsp. lemon juice
2 3-oz. pkg. cream cheese
2 tbsp. milk
1 9-inch baked pie shell
Whipped cream

Heat wine and water in saucepan to almost boiling; remove from stove. Add gelatin; stir until dissolved. Add strawberries and lemon juice to hot gelatin. Break up strawberries to hasten thawing. Chill until mixture begins to thicken. Whip cream cheese and milk together with fork until creamy. Spread over bottom and sides of baked pie shell. Pour in partially thickened gelatin mixture. Refrigerate until firm. Serve individual pieces with whipped cream. Pie will keep for several days in refrigerator. Yield: 6-8 servings.

Mrs. Carl G. Eyler, Hon. Adv. OWC
Laughlin AFB, Texas

APPLE-WALNUT PUDDING

1 c. sugar
1/4 c. butter
1 egg, unbeaten
2 c. shredded apples
1 c. flour
1 tsp. soda
1 tsp. cinnamon

(Continued on next page)

1/2 tsp. nutmeg
1/4 tsp. salt
1/2 c. chopped walnuts

Beat first 3 ingredients until fluffy; stir in apples. Add dry ingredients and walnuts; blend well. Place in greased and floured 9-inch square pan or 6 cup mold. Bake at 350 degrees for 45 minutes. Yield: 8 servings.

Mrs. Thomas E. J. Jacobi, NOWC
Ft. Meade, Maryland

CARAMEL PUDDING

4 to 6 cans sweetened condensed milk

Place cans of milk in kettle large enough so that they may be completely covered with water. Simmer for 3 hours. Be sure cans are kept covered with water. Remove cans from water; cool at room temperature. May be stored on shelf for 6 months or more. Serve with cookies, whipped cream, nuts or all three. Decorate with cherry.

Mrs. Warren E. Porter, Welfare Chm. Women's Club
Walter Reed Army Hospital, Washington, District of Columbia

COLD LEMON SOUFFLE

3 eggs
Juice of 1 1/2 lemons
1 pkg. unflavored gelatin, softened in 2 tbsp.
   cold water dissolved over boiling water
1/2 c. sugar
Pinch of salt
1/4 c. cream, whipped

Beat eggs until creamy; add lemon juice and gelatin. Add sugar, salt and cream. Place mixture in serving dish; keep cool until ready to use. Serve with cream, if desired. Yield: 6 servings.

Mrs. Frank W. Norris, Hon. Pres. Woman's Club
Wife of Commanding General
Norfolk, Virginia

DATE UPSIDE-DOWN CAKE

1 c. dates
2 tbsp. butter
1 c. boiling water
1 egg
1 1/2 c. flour
1/2 c. sugar
1 c. brown sugar
1 tsp. soda
1/2 tsp. baking powder
1/2 tsp. salt
1/2 c. broken walnuts

TOPPING:

1 1/2 c. brown sugar
1 1/2 c. boiling water

Snip dates into 9-inch baking dish; add butter. Pour over boiling water; stir. Add remaining cake ingredients. Beat with fork until blended. Smooth in pan; sprinkle brown sugar over. Pour boiling water over slowly. Bake at 375 degrees for 40 minutes. Yield: 6 servings.

Mrs. Robert Doane, Ed. Roadrunner OWC
Fort Bliss, Texas

EDITH'S BROWN SUGAR PUDDING

1 c. brown sugar
2 c. boiling water
2 tbsp. butter
1 c. sifted flour
1/2 c. sugar
2 tsp. baking powder
1/2 c. raisins
1/2 c. milk or water

Preheat oven to 375 degrees. Combine brown sugar, boiling water and butter in 2-quart casserole. Bake while mixing batter. Sift flour, sugar and baking powder together. Add raisins and milk. Mix thoroughly, but do not beat. Remove casserole from oven. Drop batter into syrup by spoonfuls. Bake for 20 to 25 minutes. Yield: 4 servings.

Mrs. Donald J. Cole, Gorm. Ed. OWC
Fort Richardson, Alaska

PEACH DUMPLINGS

2 tbsp. brown sugar
Sugar
1 tsp. sugar
1/2 c. peach syrup
1 c. orange juice
3 tbsp. milk

(Continued on next page)

1/4 tsp. fine grated lemon peel
1/8 tsp. almond extract
1/2 c. pkg. biscuit mix
1 1-lb. 3-oz. can freestone peach halves

Combine brown sugar and 1 tablespoon sugar; heat peach syrup, sugar mixture and orange juice to a boil. Stir milk, lemon peel and extract into packaged mix in bowl. Drop by tablespoonfuls into syrup to make 4 dumplings. Cover; cook at slow boil for 10 minutes. Sprinkle 1 teaspoon sugar mixed with pinch of cinnamon over each dumpling; cover. Cook for about 5 minutes. Divide peaches evenly among 4 dessert dishes; add syrup from skillet and dumplings. Yield: 4 servings.

Mrs. Charles Carpenter OWC
Ellsworth AFB, South Dakota

SHERRIED LEMON PUDDING

1 3/4 c. cold milk
1/4 c. sherry
1 3 3/4-oz. pkg. instant lemon pudding
1/4 tsp. lemon rind
Pinch of salt

Pour milk and sherry into bowl. Add instant pudding, lemon rind and salt. Beat slowly with rotary beater or at low speed of electric mixer until well blended, for 1 or 2 minutes. Chill. Yield: 4 servings.

Mrs. Michael J. Golojuch OWC
Makah AFS, Washington

WEST POINT CHERRY PUDDING

1 c. flour
1 c. sugar
1 tsp. baking powder
1/2 tsp. salt
1 egg
2 c. drained sour cherries

SAUCE:

1/2 c. butter
1/2 c. heavy cream
1 c. sugar

Mix sifted dry ingredients. Add egg and cherries; mix just enough to blend. Pour into 9 x 9-inch pan. Bake at 350 degrees for 50 minutes. Melt butter in saucepan over low heat; add cream and sugar. Cook until sugar melts. Pour warm sauce over pudding. Yield: 6-8 servings.

Mrs. M. D. Johnson, Gourm. Chm. OWC
West Point, New York

Low-Calorie
Dishes

RECIPE FOR PARTY MEAT PATTIES ON PAGE 363

CABBAGE-PEPPER RELISH

3 c. shredded cabbage
1 chopped green pepper
1/2 c. vinegar
1/4 c. water
1 1/2 tsp. salt
1/2 tsp. celery seeds
1/4 tsp. pepper
1/4 tsp. paprika
1 tsp. artificial sweetener

Combine all ingredients. Marinate for at least 1 hour. No calories. Yield: 4-6 servings.

Mrs. H. F. Szemplinski, OWC
Hancock Field AFB, New York

DIETER'S DIP
(120 calories per cup)

Garlic powder
Salt
Tabasco sauce
Worcestershire sauce
1 7-oz. can minced clams, drained
1 pt. yogurt
Paprika

Stir first 5 ingredients into yogurt until thoroughly blended. Chill for at least 2 hours. Sprinkle with paprika. Serve on bed of crushed ice, surrounded by any or all of following: julienne strips of prepared raw carrots, celery, broccoli, beets, rutabagas, fingers of cucumber strips, cauliflower flowerets and whole cherry tomatoes and radishes. Few drops of food color added to yogurt can be used to complement color scheme. Yield: 8-10 servings.

Mrs. John M. Kiernan, Jr., Rec. Sec.
Mannheim Officers and Civilians Wives Club
Worms, Germany

LOW-CAL CLAM DIP
(13 calories per tablespoon)

1 c. low-calorie cottage cheese
1 7-oz. can minced clams
1 tsp. chopped chives
1/4 tsp. salt
1/8 tsp. thyme

Combine all ingredients; chill. Serve with raw vegetables. Yield: 8-12 servings.

Mrs. Donald Holmes, Past Pres. NOWC
San Francisco Bay Naval Shipyard, California

FAMOUS SENATE RESTAURANT BEAN SOUP

2 lb. small navy pea beans, washed till white
    and drained
4 qt. hot water
1 1/2 lb. smoked ham hocks
1 lge. onion, chopped, braised in butter
Salt and pepper to taste

Combine beans, hot water and ham hocks in large kettle. Place on fire with 4 quarts hot water. Add ham hocks. Boil gently for 3 hours; add onion. Add salt and pepper just before serving because salt causes beans to be tough and hard. Yield: 8 servings.
PERSONAL NOTE: This was published by Heloise Cruse some years ago. I have never seen it since so wanted to share it with you.

Mrs. Howard L. Rust, Parlm. OWC
Upper Heyford, England

LOW-CALORIE DIP

2 tbsp. milk
1/2 tsp. Worcestershire sauce
1 12-oz. carton cottage cheese
1 envelope Good Seasons cheese-garlic salad
    dressing mix

Place all ingredients in blender; mix thoroughly until smooth. Serve with strips of raw vegetables; extra low calorie.

Mrs. H. L. Hinkley, Parlm. OWC
Ft. Ritchie, Maryland

LOW-CAL PARTY DIP

1 c. diet cottage cheese
1 tbsp. lemon juice
1/2 c. chives or green onions
1/2 tsp. vegetable salt
1/2 tsp. rose paprika
Celery slices (opt.)
Summer squash slices (opt.)
Buttermilk

Mix first 6 ingredients for 1 minute in electric blender with enough buttermilk for consistency of mayonnaise. Chill in refrigerator. Use tender sprigs of very young cauliflower, unpeeled thin wedges of cucumbers, small tomatoes, carrots and celery to dip.

Barbara J. Kelley, OWC
Camp Pendleton, California

LOW-CAL VEGETABLE SOUP
(60 calories per serving)

3 c. water
2 beef bouillon cubes

(Continued on next page)

2 chicken bouillon cubes
1 1-lb. 3-oz. can tomatoes
1 med. onion, chopped
1/2 c. carrots, thinly sliced
2 stalks celery, cut in 1/2-inch slices
3 peppercorns
1/2 tsp. dried sage
1 tsp. salt
1/4 c. grated Parmesan cheese

Combine all ingredients except cheese in 2-quart saucepan; cover. Simmer for 1 hour. Serve sprinkled with Parmesan cheese. Yield: 5 servings.

Mrs. Morris S. Shimanoff, MOWC
Camp Pendleton, California

PICKLED CABBAGE

1/2 head cabbage, grated
1 green pepper, grated
1 carrot, grated
2 green onions, grated
Salt and pepper to taste

DRESSING:

4 tbsp. vinegar
Artificial sweetener to equal 1 1/2 tbsp.
    sugar
3/4 c. water

Mix all vegetables, adding salt and pepper as desired. Mix Dressing; combine with vegetables. Chill before serving. Yield: 4-6 servings.

Mrs. William J. Mulligan, OWC
China Lake NWC, California

THIRTY-CALORIES-PER-CUP SOUP

6 beef bouillon cubes
3 carrots, sliced
1 onion, sliced
1 sm. head cabbage, chopped
6 c. water
3 celery stalks, diced

Combine all ingredients in large kettle. Simmer until vegetables are tender.

Mrs. Albert R. Elmore, OWC
Othello OWC
Othello AFS, Washington

APPLESAUCE-PUMPKIN PIE

1 c. canned pumpkin
1 c. unsweetened applesauce

(Continued on next page)

4 tsp. Sucaryl
1/2 tsp. salt
1 1/2 tsp. cinnamon
1 1/2 tsp. nutmeg
1/2 tsp. allspice
1/2 tsp. cloves
1/4 tsp. ginger
4 eggs, beaten
1 c. milk
1 9-inch unbaked pie shell

Combine pumpkin, applesauce, Sucaryl, salt and spices; blend well. Add eggs and milk, mixing well. Pour into unbaked pie shell. Bake in 425-degree oven for 45 minutes or until knife inserted near center comes out clean. Yield: 6 servings.

Mrs. James R. Witt OWC
Kingsley AFB, Oregon

APPLE SNOW

1/2 envelope Knox gelatin
1 tsp. Sucaryl
1/4 tsp. salt
3/8 c. water
1/4 tsp. grated lemon rind
1/2 tbsp. lemon juice
8 oz. applesauce
1 egg white, beaten stiff

Combine and dissolve first 4 ingredients in top of double boiler. Add remaining ingredients; mix thoroughly. Chill before serving. Yield: 4 servings.

Mrs. Thomas L. Waters, Hosp. Chm. OWC
Redstone Arsenal, Alabama

BERRY-ICE CREAM FLOAT

1 envelope unflavored gelatin
1/4 c. cold water
2 c. berries, mashed
1 tsp. liquid non-sugar sweetener
1 tbsp. lemon juice
1/8 tsp. salt
1 drop red food coloring
1/3 c. dry powdered milk
1/4 c. ice water

Soften gelatin in cold water in saucepan. Dissolve by boiling; stir until completely dissolved. Combine berries, sweetener, lemon juice, salt and coloring; add to softened gelatin. Chill until mixture begins to thicken. Combine dry milk and ice water; beat at high speed of electric or hand mixer until stiff. Fold into gelatin; spoon into cups. One cup equals 1 fruit and 1/4 cup whole milk on restricted diet. Yield: 6 servings.
PERSONAL NOTE: I am a member of the TOPS Club (take off pounds sensibly) and this recipe evolved during our discussion on low-calorie dishes.

Mrs. C. W. Macks, OWC
Randolph AFB, Texas

DIETER'S CHEESECAKE

2 8-oz. pkg. low calorie cream cheese, softened
3/4 c. low calorie sugar
4 eggs, separated
1/2 pt. sour cream
Margarine
Graham cracker crumbs

Blend cheese, sugar and egg yolks thoroughly. Beat egg whites until stiff. Add sour cream to cream cheese mixture. Fold in egg whites. Grease pan with margarine. Sprinkle in graham cracker crumbs. Pour filling into crust. Bake for 35 minutes in 350-degree oven. Cool.

Mrs. George C. Van Natta, VP CGOWC
Galveston, Texas

DIETER'S GELATIN

1 bottle diet soda, favorite flavor
1 pkg. unflavored gelatin
Fresh fruit or raw vegetables

Reserve 1/4 cup of the soda; place remaining soda in saucepan. Bring to a boil. Dissolve gelatin in reserved soda; add boiled soda. Pour into dishes to cool. Add fresh fruit; chill.

Mrs. Claude W. Roesner, Soc. Chm. Joint OWC
El Centro, California

DIET WATCHER'S MALTED

1/2 c. diet soda, any flavor
1 c. skim milk
6 thin ice cubes

Place all ingredients in blender; mix well. Yield: 1 serving.

Mrs. Ronald D. Ross, Wife of Commander OWC
Watertown AFS, New York

HOMEMADE PEACH ICE CREAM

12 fresh peaches, thinly sliced
2 c. low calorie Sugar Twin
2 eggs
1 can evaporated milk
1 tbsp. vanilla extract
1/2 gal. skim milk

Combine peaches and 1 cup low calorie sugar. Set aside for 15 minutes. Beat eggs with remaining sugar; add evaporated milk and vanilla extract. Mash peaches with hand beater or low speed of portable. Add these ingredients, combined, to freezer container; fill with skim milk. Follow directions for electric freezer or hand crank. Yield: 1 gallon.

Mrs. Roger B. Boerner, Pres.
Ft. Fisher AFS, North Carolina

FROZEN CHOCOLATE MOUSSE
(110 calories per serving)

> 1 tsp. unflavored gelatin
> 2 tbsp. water
> 1 1-oz. sq. unsweetened chocolate
> 1/4 c. hot water
> 1/4 tsp. salt
> 1 tbsp. liquid sweetener
> 1 tsp. vanilla
> 2/3 c. ice water
> 1/8 tsp. cream of tartar
> 2/3 c. nonfat dry milk

Soften gelatin in 2 tablespoons water. Melt chocolate in top of double boiler over gently boiling water; add hot water. Stir until smooth; remove from heat. Add softened gelatin; stir until dissolved. Add salt, liquid sweetener and vanilla; chill until slightly thickened. Combine ice water and cream of tartar in small bowl; add dry milk. Beat for 5 minutes on high speed forming stiff peaks. Gently fold in chocolate mixture; pour into 1-quart mold. Freeze for 6 hours. Yield: 4 servings.

Mrs. Robert W. McCortney, Pres. OWC
Fort Holabird, Maryland

FRUIT CREME DE MENTHE
(40 calories per serving)

> 1 can diet fruit cocktail
> 1/2 c. any fresh fruit, cut up
> 1 tbsp. creme de menthe
> 1/2 tsp. liquid artificial sweetener

Combine all ingredients. Freeze for 40 minutes, stirring occasionally.

Mrs. Daniel Robinson OWC
Fort Fisher AFS, North Carolina

FRUIT DELIGHT PIE
(717 calories per pie)

> Water
> 1 1-lb. can low calorie fruit cocktail, drained and
>   juice reserved
> 1 4-serving envelope low calorie lemon gelatin
> 12 ladyfingers, split and cut in half
> 1 envelope low calorie whipped topping mix
> 1/2 tsp. nutmeg

Add enough water to fruit cocktail juice to make 2 cups liquid; bring to boil. Dissolve gelatin; chill until very thick. Line 9-inch pie pan with ladyfingers. Prepare whipped topping mix as directed on package; add nutmeg before whipping. Beat thickened gelatin with rotary beater or electric mixer until fluffy and thick; fold in 1 cup whipped topping and fruit cocktail. Spoon into pie pan; chill for at least 2 hours or until set. Garnish with remaining whipped topping. Yield: 6-8 servings.

Mrs. Edison D. Guthrey, W and M Chm.
Kelly AFB, Texas

IRISH COFFEE SODA

1 scoop dietetic coffee ice cream
1 low-calorie coffee soda
1 tbsp. Irish whisky (opt.)
2 tbsp. whipped cream or Cool Whip
Dash of nutmeg

Stir ice cream into glass of coffee soda; add Irish whiskey. Top with a dollop of whipped cream; sprinkle with nutmeg. Yield: 1 serving.

Mrs. Warren C. Mitchell, Luncheon Chm. CGOWC
Governors Island, New York

LIME SNOW PIE
(163 calories per serving)

1 envelope unflavored gelatin
1/4 c. cold water
3 eggs, separated
1/2 c. lime juice
1/2 c. sugar
1/2 tsp. salt
1 tsp. grated lime rind
Green food coloring to shade desired
1/2 c. undiluted evaporated milk
1/2 c. Vanilla Slim Topping

Soften gelatin in cold water. Beat egg yolks in top of double boiler; stir in lime juice, 1/4 cup sugar and salt. Cook over boiling water, stirring till thickened. Remove from heat; stir in gelatin to dissolve. Add lime rind and food coloring; refrigerate until cold but still syrupy. Freeze milk in ice tray until soft crystals form 1-inch from the edge. Beat egg whites to stiff peaks; beat in remaining sugar gradually to straight, stiff peaks. Fold in lime mixture quickly and thoroughly. Turn icy milk into cold bowl; beat to soft peaks with electric mixer. Fold into lime mixture quickly; turn into pie crust. Refrigerate. Top with Vanilla Slim Topping; refrigerate until serving time.

VANILLA SLIM TOPPING:

1/4 tsp. unflavored gelatin
3/4 tsp. cold water
1 tsp. sugar
Pinch of salt
1 tbsp. nonfat dry milk
1/4 tsp. vanilla extract
1/2 c. Whipped Topping

Soften gelatin in cold water; dissolve over hot water. Remove from heat. Add sugar, salt, dry milk and vanilla extract; fold in Whipped Topping. Top pie with 1/2 cup. Tint half the pie topping green, leaving remaining portion white. Swirl both portions over pie.

(Continued on next page)

WHIPPED TOPPING:

2 tbsp. cold water
2 tbsp. nonfat dry milk
3/4 tsp. sugar
3/4 tsp. lemon juice
1/8 tsp. vanilla

Place cold water in bowl; sprinkle on dry milk. Beat until thick. Add sugar, lemon juice and vanilla extract gradually, continuing to beat till stiff enough to hold soft peaks. Yield: 8 servings.

Mrs. James F. Rosborough, Jr., Pres. OWC
Oakland Naval Hospital, California

LEMON FROST
(100 calories per serving)

1 egg, separated
1/3 c. water
1/3 c. nonfat dry milk
1/3 c. sugar
1 tsp. grated lemon peel
3 tbsp. lemon juice
Dash of salt

Combine egg white, water and dry milk; beat to very stiff peaks. Blend next 4 ingredients and slightly beaten egg yolks; beat into egg white mixture gradually. Spoon lemon mixture into refrigerator tray; freeze. Cut in 6 squares; garnish with mint leaves, if desired. Yield: 6 servings.

Mrs. Jack O. Raun, Soc. Chm.
616 AC & W Sqdn. Wasserkuppe AFS, Germany

LIME BARS
(100 calories per serving)

1 egg white
1/3 c. water
1/3 c. nonfat dry milk
1/3 c. sugar
Grated lime peel
1 tbsp. lime juice
Dash of salt in slightly-beaten egg yolk
3 tbsp. vanilla wafer crumbs

Combine first 3 ingredients; beat until stiff peaks form. Blend sugar, peel, juice, salt and egg yolk. Add slowly to egg white mixture. Sprinkle 2 tablespoons vanilla wafer crumbs into refrigerator tray. Spoon in lime mixture. Dust with remaining crumbs; freeze. Garnish with mint sprig.

Mrs. Harold H. Freeland, Adv. O and CWC
U S Navy Com. Sta. Harold E. Holt, Australia

LO CAL BREAD PUDDING
(132 calories per serving)

5 slices old bread
1/3 c. raisins
Warm water
2 c. skim milk
1 tbsp. liquid sweetener
1/4 tsp. vanilla
2 eggs, beaten

Cut bread into cubes; place in buttered 1-quart casserole. Soak raisins in warm water till plump; drain. Sprinkle over bread cubes. Scald milk; add sweetener and vanilla. Stir slowly into eggs. Pour mixture over bread and raisins. Bake in 350-degree oven for 55 minutes or until brown and silver knife comes out clean. Serve warm or cold. Yield: 6 servings.

Mrs. Charles V. Heath, 1st. VP OWC
USA Hosp., Ft. Stewart, Georgia

LOW-CAL ORANGE MOSS

2 pkg. or 2 tbsp. gelatin
1/2 c. cold water
1/2 c. hot water
2 tbsp. Sucaryl sweetener
4 tbsp. lemon juice
1 c. fresh or frozen orange juice
2 tbsp. grated orange peel
3 egg whites, stiffly beaten
Fresh orange sections, soaked in rum and sugar
Fresh strawberries
Mint leaves
Cool Whip
Blanched almonds

Soak gelatin in cold water; dissolve in hot water. Add sweetener, fruit juices and grated orange peel. Chill until partially congealed. Fold in egg whites. Turn into oiled 1 1/2-quart ring mold; chill. Turn out on tray; surround with orange sections, fresh strawberries and mint leaves. Fill center with Cool Whip; top with blanched, toasted almonds. Yield: 6 servings.

Mrs. James C. Sherrill, Hon. Pres. OWC
Travis AFB, California

LOW-CALORIE CHOCOLATE CAKE AND FROSTING
(71 calories per serving)

3/4 c. sifted flour
1 tsp. baking powder
1/4 tsp. soda
1/4 tsp. salt
3 tbsp. cocoa
1/4 c. cold coffee
1 egg, beaten
1 tbsp. artificial liquid sweetener
1/4 c. water
1 tbsp. salad oil
1 tsp. vanilla

(Continued on next page)

FROSTING:

1/2 tsp. unflavored gelatin, soaked in 2 tbsp.
    water
3 tbsp. non-fat dry milk
1 1/2 tsp. lemon juice
1/2 tsp. liquid artificial sweetener
1 tsp. vanilla

Sift flour, baking powder, soda and salt together. Blend cocoa and coffee. Combine egg, liquid sweetener, water, salad oil and vanilla; stir until smooth. Stir in cocoa and coffee mixture. Add dry ingredients. Line 1 8-inch round layer cake pan with paper; grease with 1/8 teaspoon butter. Pour batter into pan; cover pan with foil. Place in shallow pan of water. Bake in 350-degree oven for 25 minutes. Remove from pan onto cake rack; cool. Cut layer into half crosswise to make 2 layer cake. Dissolve gelatin over hot water. Combine all remaining ingredients in small mixer bowl; beat on high speed for about 15 minutes. Add gelatin very gradually, continuing to beat until Frosting will stand in peaks. Fill and frost cake. Yield: 8 servings.

Mrs. R. D. Baker, Publ. Dir. OWC
Camp Lejeune, North Carolina

LOW-CAL STRAWBERRY CHARLOTTE

1 envelope unflavored gelatin
1/4 c. water
4 egg yolks
1 1/2 qt. fresh or whole frozen strawberries
1 1/3 c. ice water
1 1/3 c. dry skim milk
1 tbsp. lemon juice
Artificial sweetener to taste
16 ladyfingers

Chill beaters and bowl. Soften gelatin in 1/4 cup water; add egg yolks. Cook over boiling water until egg yolks thicken; chill in refrigerator. Puree strawberries in blender. Add ice water to dry skim milk gradually; stir in juice and artificial sweetener. Beat until as stiff as whipped cream; fold in strawberry puree and egg yolk mixture. Line sides and bottom of 2-quart souffle dish with ladyfingers; pour in strawberry mixture. Top with ladyfingers; cover with waxed paper. Refrigerate for at least 6 hours or overnight. Yield: 12 servings.

Mrs. J. A. Brown, Hon. Chm.
Norfolk NSY, Portsmouth, Virginia

LOW-CALORIE PANCAKES

1/2 lb. cottage cheese, sieved or mashed fine
3 tbsp. flour
1 tsp. salt
3 eggs
1 tbsp. sugar
Low calorie syrup or jam or powdered sugar

Combine first 5 ingredients; beat well. Drop amount the size of silver dollar onto hot Teflon griddle; brown. Turn with care; brown other side. Serve immediately with very little syrup or jam or sprinkled with powdered sugar. Yield: 4 servings.

Mrs. J. Walter Poorman, OWC
Moron AB, Spain

MALIBU ORANGE SOUFFLE
(120 calories per serving)

1 envelope unflavored gelatin
1/2 c. sugar, divided
1 c. water
1 6-oz. can frozen juice concentrate
1/2 c. instant non-fat dry milk crystals
2 tbsp. lemon juice

Mix together gelatin and 1/4 cup of the sugar in saucepan; stir in water. Cook over low heat, stirring occasionally, until mixture is consistency of unbeaten egg white. Stir in frozen juice concentrate; chill. Prepare milk according to package directions; beat until soft peaks form. Add lemon juice; continue beating until firm peaks form. Add remaining sugar gradually; fold into gelatin mixture. Turn into serving bowl; chill until firm. Garnish with whipped topping and cantaloupe, white grapes, blueberries or other fresh fruit, if desired. Yield: 8 servings.

Joan Rogers, Wlfr. Chm. OWC
Little Rock AFB, Arkansas

ORANGE-GLAZED PEARS
(45 calories per serving)

2 1-lb. cans diet pear halves
1 c. orange juice
2 tbsp. low calorie apricot preserves
6 to 12 mint sprigs

Turn pear halves into sieve; drain, discarding liquid. Combine orange juice and apricot preserves in heavy medium-sized skillet; heat to boiling, stirring constantly. Reduce heat. Place pear halves cut-side down in skillet; simmer for 15 minutes or until glazed, basting often. Stand pears, 2 halves together as whole pear, in shallow serving dish; spoon glaze over. Top with mint; chill for 1 hour. Serve 1/2 pear per person.

Mrs. Gilbert F. Baker, Ladies Club
Letterkenny AD, Pennsylvania

PLUM WHIP

1 envelope unflavored gelatin
1/4 c. cold water
1 1-lb. can dietetic red plums
6 to 8 drops red food coloring
1 tbsp. lemon juice
2 egg whites
Dash of salt
1 1/4-oz. envelope low calorie dessert
    topping mix, prepared

Soften gelatin in cold water. Sieve plums and juice into saucepan; heat till boiling. Add softened gelatin, food coloring and lemon juice, stirring till dissolved. Cook till partially thickened. Beat egg whites and salt till soft peaks form; add plum mixture gradually, beating till fluffy. Fold half the topping into plum mixture; use remaining topping as garnish. Yield: 10 servings.

Mrs. James W. Davis, Sec. OWC
George AFB, California

LOW-CALORIE APRICOT CLOUD PIE

16 sm. graham crackers, crushed
Non-caloric sweetener
3 tbsp. melted butter
1 tbsp. plain gelatin
Cold water
1/4 tsp. salt
2 tbsp. lemon juice
1 12-oz. can non-caloric apricot juice
1/2 c. evaporated milk, chilled

Combine graham crackers, 3/4 teaspoon non-caloric sweetener and melted butter. Press into 9-inch pie plate; chill until firm. Soften gelatin in cold water according to package directions. Add 1 tablespoon non-caloric sweetener, salt and lemon juice; dissolve in heated apricot juice. Chill until mixture begins to thicken. Beat evaporated milk until stiff. Fold into gelatin mixture; pour into crust. Chill until firm. Yield: 6 servings.

Mrs. David B. Smith, Hon. VP
Templehof OWC
Berlin, Germany

ORANGE SHERBET

4 tbsp. concentrated frozen orange juice
4 oz. skimmed milk powder
3 drops liquid non-sugar sweetener

Combine all ingredients in blender; mix thoroughly. Pour into 2 sherbet glasses; place in freezer for 1 hour or until slightly frozen. Yield: 2 servings.

Mrs. Robert Lawrence, Pres. Joint OWC
El Centro NAF, California

QUICK TORTONI

1 c. non-fat dry milk
1 c. ice water
6 tbsp. sugar
1 tsp. almond extract
1/2 c. finely chopped blanched almonds

Stir milk into ice water; beat with electric mixer at high speed until stiff. Beat in sugar and almond extract; fold in almonds. Spoon mixture into fluted paper baking cups; set into muffin pans. Freeze for 3 to 4 hours or until firm. Yield: 6 servings.

Mrs. A. F. Cornell, Pres. O and CWC
US Nav. Com. Sta. Harold E. Holt, Exmouth, Western Australia

POOR MAN'S CHARLOTTE RUSSE

1 pkg. vanilla Whip 'n' Chill
1/2 c. cold skim milk
1/4 c. cold water
1/4 c. rum or sherry

(Continued on next page)

Blend Whip 'n' Chill thoroughly at low speed of electric mixer with cold milk. Whip at high speed for about 1 minute. Blend in cold water and 1/4 cup rum at low speed. Whip at high speed for about 2 minutes. Refrigerate until cold for about 1 hour. Yield: 4 servings.

Mrs. Joseph W. Weaver, Pres. OW League
NAS, Pensacola, Florida

PINEAPPLE FLUFF
(53 calories per serving)

1 envelope lemon D-Zerta
1 1/4 c. boiling water
Non-calorie sweetener
Low calorie whipped topping, prepared
1 14-oz. can low calorie pineapple tidbits,
    drained and juice reserved

Dissolve D-Zerta in boiling water. Add enough water to reserved juice to make 3/4 cup liquid. Stir into gelatin with non-caloric sweetener to equal 2 teaspoons sugar; chill until sightly thickened. Blend in whipped topping and pineapple; chill until firm. Yield: 8 servings.

Mrs. John D. Williston, Treas. OWC
Lakehurst Naval Air Station, New Jersey

RASPBERRY BAVARIAN
(63 calories per serving)

1 3-oz. raspberry flavored D-Zerta
1 c. hot water
3/4 c. cold water
3 tbsp. lemon juice
3/4 c. red raspberries, thawed
3 tbsp. non-fat dry milk
3 tbsp. ice-cold water

Dissolve gelatin in hot water; add 3/4 cup water and lemon juice. Refrigerate until mixture begins to thicken. Drain raspberries, reserving juice. Beat non-fat dry milk solids with ice-cold water until consistency of whipped cream. Beat gelatin until frothy. Fold whipped milk into gelatin; add raspberries carefully. Spoon into 6 sherbet glasses; chill. One tablespoon raspberry juice may be spooned over each serving, if desired.

Mrs. Neil Shoop, Pres. OWC
Finley AFS, North Dakota

SHERRY GLACE

1/2 gal. vanilla ice milk
1/4 c. sherry
12 macaroons, broken into small pieces

Soften ice milk at room temperature. Stir in sherry and macaroons which have been broken into small pieces; refreeze. For a chewy-type macaroon, use nuts as well as coconut. Yield: 10 servings.

Mrs. Frank E. Rouse, Hon. Pres. OWC
Kelly Air Force Base, Texas

REAL STRAWBERRY PIE
(173 calories per serving)

    1 1/4 c. crushed graham cracker crumbs
    1/4 c. diet margarine, softened
    1 tsp. Sweet-10
    1 envelope strawberry D-Zerta
    1 1/4 c. boiling water
    1 pt. dietetic vanilla ice cream
    1 c. drained, artificially sweetened, sliced
        fresh strawberries
    5 whole strawberries

Combine crumbs, margarine and Sweet-10; press firmly against sides and bottom of 9-inch pie pan. Bake at 375 degrees for 8 minutes; cool. Dissolve D-Zerta in boiling water; stir in ice cream till melted. Chill till quite thick, for about 10 minutes. Fold in strawberries; pour into crumb crust. Chill; garnish with whole strawberries. Yield: 6 servings.

Mrs. James D. Edwards, Pres. OWC
Laredo AFB, Texas

RICE FLUFF

    2 c. precooked rice, cooked and drained
    1 lge. can low calorie fruit cocktail, drained
    1 pkg. Dream Whip, prepared according to directions
        low calorie sweetener
    Sugar or low calorie sweetener to taste

Combine all ingredients; chill in refrigerator for 15 minutes before serving. One package fresh, frozen fruits may be substituted for fruit cocktail. Yield: 6 servings.
PERSONAL NOTE: This originated as Mother's recipe made with "farm fresh" cream. I have modified same for sake of maintaining that "girlish" figure.

Mrs. C. W. Thompson, III, OWC
Birkenfeld, Germany

SLIM SPANISH CREAM

    1 1/2 c. powdered skim milk
    3 1/2 c. water
    1 pkg. gelatin, soaked in 1/2 c. water
    3 eggs, separated
    1 whole egg
    1/4 tsp. salt
    2 tbsp. Sucaryl
    3 tbsp. sugar

Scald powdered milk and water. Add gelatin. Beat egg yolks and whole egg slightly. Pour hot milk into beaten yolks while stirring. Add salt and Sucaryl; return to heat. Continue stirring over low heat with metal spoon until custard thickens and coats spoon; remove immediately. Continue stirring; cool till just warm. Beat egg whites and sugar; fold into custard. Refrigerate in sherbet glasses or serving dish. Yield: 8 servings.

Mrs. Noel Gayler, Adv. OWC
Offutt AFB, Nebraska

SPANISH CREAM

1 envelope unflavored gelatin
6 tbsp. sugar or substitute
1/2 tsp. salt
2 eggs, separated
2 c. non-fat milk
1 tsp. vanilla

Mix gelatin, 2 tablespoons sugar and salt in saucepan. Beat egg yolks and 1 cup milk. Add to gelatin mixture over low heat; stir constantly. Remove from heat when slightly thickened; add 1 cup milk and vanilla. Chill until mixture is thickened. Beat egg whites till stiff; add remaining sugar while beating. Fold in gelatin; pour into 4-cup mold or individual molds. Chill. Yield: 8 servings.

Mrs. G. L. Tarleton, Hon. Pres.
Argentia 'O' Wives
Newfoundland, Canada

STRAWBERRY CHIFFON PIE
(252 calories per pie)

1 pkg. low calorie strawberry gelatin
1 envelope gelatin, softened in 1/4 c. cold water
1 envelope low calorie whipped topping
8 graham crackers, crushed
1/2 box fresh strawberries, sliced

Make strawberry gelatin according to directions on package. Add soaked gelatin to hot mixture; stir until dissolved. Cool mixture with ice cubes. Combine whipped topping made according to directions. Add enough whipped topping to hold cracker crumbs together. Press into pie pan. Reserve enough topping to garnish pie top. Combine remaining topping with gelatin mixture and strawberries. Pour into pie shell; garnish with topping and several sliced strawberries.

Mrs. Paul T. Widener, Courtesy Chm., OWC
Williams AFB, Arizona

STRAWBERRY FLUFF

1 pkg. strawberry gelatin
1 c. hot water
1 c. cold water
1 c. strawberry yogurt
1/2 c. sour cream

(Continued on next page)

Dissolve gelatin in hot water. Add cold water; chill until slightly thickened. Reserve 1/2 cup mixture for garnish. Place remaining gelatin in bowl over ice and water; whip with beater until fluffy and thick like whipped cream. Add yogurt; mix lightly. Spoon half way up into parfait glasses; add layer of reserved gelatin. Finish with yogurt mixture. Top with dab of sour cream. Yield: 6 servings.

Mrs. William J. Perry, Treas. OWC
Defense Electronics Supply Center, Dayton, Ohio

STRAWBERRY MOUSSE
(68 calories per serving)

1 3-oz. pkg. strawberry gelatin
1 c. boiling water
1 c. cold water
Liquid artificial sweetener
1/4 c. instant non-fat dry milk
1/4 c. ice water
1 tbsp. lemon juice

Dissolve gelatin in boiling water; add cold water and 1 tablespoon artificial sweetener. Chill until slightly thickened. Beat gelatin over ice until very light and fluffy. Whip dry milk with ice water until soft peaks form, 3 to 4 minutes. Add lemon juice and 1 1/2 teaspoons liquid sweetener; beat until stiff for 3 to 4 minutes. Fold in whipped milk mixture; pour into 1 1/2-quart mold or individual serving dishes. Chill until firm. Unmold; garnish with fresh strawberries. Yield: 6 servings.

Mrs. Ronald R. Kenyon, Publ. Chm. OWC
Fairchild AFB, Washington

LOW-FAT BUTTERMILK PANCAKES

1 egg
1 tsp. soda
1 c. buttermilk
3/4 c. flour
1/4 tsp. salt

Beat egg; stir soda into buttermilk. Add to egg. Stir in flour and salt. Brown on lightly greased griddle or Teflon griddle or electric frypan. For variety add 1 large ripe banana, thinly sliced or 1 cup frozen or fresh blueberries or 1 tart juicy apple, thinly sliced. Yield: 7-8 pancakes.

Mrs. James F. Agnew, Chaplains' Wives Club
Portsmouth, Virginia

LOW-SODIUM MEAT MARINADE

1/2 c. white vinegar
1/2 c. salad oil
1/2 c. lemon juice
1/2 tsp. freshly-ground pepper
1 clove of garlic, minced, if desired
1 sm. to med. onion, sliced thin

(Continued on next page)

Mix ingredients; store in tightly covered glass container until needed. Place meat such as chuck roast in glass or crockery baking dish. Spread marinade over top. Cover tightly with lid or plastic wrap. Let stand for several hours or overnight, depending on meat thickness. Turn meat; spread again with same marinade, now mixed with meat juices. Let stand until ready to cook. Remove meat; pat dry. Meat can now be oven or pan broiled, or oven-roasted, depending on type of meat. Remove as much fat as possible from pan of drippings when meat has been cooked; add used marinade to pan. Simmer to make delicious gravy.

Mrs. John F. Wilbert, SSC Rep. OWC
U.S.N.T.C.
Bainbridge, Maryland

BAKED ENDIVE

4 fine endive
4 thin slices boiled ham
4 hard-boiled eggs, halved
1/2 c. melted low-calorie oleo
1/2 tsp. ground nutmeg

Boil fresh endive in salted water in saucepan for 10 to 12 minutes or until tender. Drain thoroughly. Wrap each endive in slice of ham; place in buttered baking dish. Surround with eggs. Pour oleo over endive; sprinkle with nutmeg. Bake for 10 minutes at 400 degrees. Endive may be canned, or if not available, celery hearts may be substituted. Yield: 4 servings.
PERSONAL NOTE: I am usually busy and of course watching my pounds so this a little out of the ordinary recipe comes in handy for guests too. It may easily be multiplied.

Mrs. Richard D. Small, Pres. OWC
Kelly AFB, Texas

BEEF AND GREEN BEANS
(230 calories per serving)

1/2 lb. lean, tender beef, cut in strips
2 tbsp. Wesson oil
1 med. onion, chopped
1 c. cut green beans, raw or frozen
1 med. green pepper, sliced
1 c. sliced celery
4 tsp. cornstarch
1 tbsp. soy sauce
3/4 c. mushroom liquid and water
Salt and pepper to taste
1 4-oz. can mushrooms
Pimentos

Brown meat in hot oil in large heavy skillet; add next 4 ingredients. Cook for 3 to 5 minutes. Combine cornstarch, soy sauce, liquid and seasonings; add to skillet, stirring to mix thoroughly. Add mushrooms; stir, cooking until liquid is clear and shiny. Garnish with pimentos. Yield: 4 servings.
PERSONAL NOTE: This is an Oriental creation with ingredients readily available at the grocer's.

Mrs. W. K. Hauth, Jr., Chm. Chaplains WC
USN, Norfolk, Virginia

BEEF STROGANOFF

1 tsp. salt
1/8 tsp. pepper
1 1/2 lb. beef, cut in strips
1/4 c. flour
2 tbsp. butter
1 c. sliced onions
1 clove of garlic, minced
1/2 c. water
1 tsp. Worcestershire sauce
3 tbsp. catsup
1 4-oz. can mushrooms
3/4 c. buttermilk

Salt and pepper beef strips; toss in flour. Brown in butter in skillet; add onions and garlic. Cook for 3 to 4 minutes; add water, Worcestershire sauce, catsup and mushrooms. Simmer until beef is tender for 1 hour. Add buttermilk; heat through. Let simmer without lid if thicker sauce is desired. Serve over rice, if desired. Yield: 3-4 servings.

Mrs. Richard S. Ribinski, OWC
Barksdale AFB, Louisiana

BEEF-VEGETABLE LOAF
(160 calories per serving)

1/2 c. finely-chopped celery
1/4 c. finely-chopped onion
1/4 c. finely-chopped mushrooms
1/4 c. finely-chopped green beans
1/4 c. grated carrot
1 lb. lean ground beef
1/2 c. drained, canned tomatoes, chopped
1 tsp. Worcestershire sauce
2 eggs, beaten
1 tsp. salt
1/4 tsp. dry mustard
1/8 tsp. pepper
1/8 tsp. oregano

Mix all ingredients for meat loaf; pack mixture lightly in 9 1/2 x 5 1/4 x 2 3/4-inch loaf pan. Bake at 350 degrees for 1 hour and 15 minutes. Loosen meat gently from sides of pan. Pour off excess juices. Invert onto platter; remove pan. Yield: 6 servings.

Mrs. Walter Crowther, Publ. Chm. OWC
Suffolk County AFB, New York

GROUND BEEF CASSEROLE
(200 calories per serving)

1 lb. ground round steak, lean
5 tomatoes, quartered
1/2 lb. string beans, cut up
1 lge. green pepper
6 stalks celery, chopped
1/4 lb. mushrooms
1 med. head cabbage, chopped
Dash of pepper
1/4 tsp. garlic powder

(Continued on next page)

361

Brown meat in frying pan, previously sprayed with Pam. Add remaining ingredients. Cook until tender. Season with salt substitute, if desired. Yield: 4 servings.

Mrs. John P. Kelley, NOWC
Camp Pendleton, California

BEEF AND VEGETABLES

3 tbsp. vegetable oil
1 lb. top beef round steak, fat trimmed, cut
    in 1/4-inch strips
2 tbsp. flour
1 tsp. salt
Dash of Accent
1 c. sliced celery
1/2 green pepper, sliced
1 med. onion, sliced
1 8-oz. can sliced mushrooms
1 pkg. frozen French-style string beans
3 tbsp. soy sauce

Heat oil in electric frying pan to 375 degrees. Toss meat, flour, salt and Accent in paper bag until meat is coated. Brown quickly in oil. Add celery, pepper, onion and mushrooms. Toss together with meat. Place frozen beans on top; pour soy sauce through beans. Cover; reduce heat to 325 degrees. Cook for 15 minutes or only until beans are done. Yield: 4 servings.

Mrs. Irvin E. Eagerton, OWC
Naval Air Station, Cecil Field, Florida

GERMAN MEATBALLS
(150 calories per serving)

2 med. potatoes, cut into shreds
1/2 med. onion, finely cut
1 tsp. powdered lemon peel
4 sprigs parsley, chopped
1 egg, beaten
1 lb. lean ground beef
1/2 tsp. salt
1/4 tsp. pepper
1/2 tsp. caraway seed
2 tbsp. flour
2 tbsp. low-calorie margarine
2 beef bouillon cubes
2 c. boiling water

Combine potatoes, onion, lemon peel and parsley with beaten egg; set aside. Mix ground beef with seasonings and caraway seed. Combine both mixtures, being certain to mix thoroughly. Form into sixteen 1/2-inch balls; dip balls in flour. Brown in margarine in skillet. Dissolve bouillon cubes in boiling water; add to meatballs. Cover. Simmer for 30 minutes. Yield: 8 servings.
PERSONAL NOTE: While pregnant with my second child, I was overweight conscious and starving. I began trying all kinds of low-calorie recipes and with a bit of improvision the above was a favorite.

Mrs. Albert F. Lockwood, NOWC
US Naval Station, Bermuda

HUNGARIAN BEEF
(345 calories per serving, without noodles)

2 lb. beef round, cut into 1 1/2-inch pieces
2 tbsp. flour
2 tsp. paprika
Dash of nutmeg
1 tsp. salt
2 tbsp. oil
1 c. beef bouillon
1/4 c. sour cream
Broad cooked noodles
2 tbsp. parsley

Dredge beef with mixture of flour, 1 teaspoon paprika, nutmeg and salt. Brown meat on all sides in oil in skillet. Add bouillon; cover. Simmer for 2 hours or until tender. Add remaining paprika and sour cream; blend until sauce is smooth. Serve with noodles; sprinkle with parsley. Yield: 6 servings.

Mrs. Paul R. Schmidt, 2nd VP OWC
Williams AFB, Arizona

OVEN STEW
(320 calories per serving)

1 1/2 lb. lean chuck, cubed
4 carrots, scraped and sliced in 1-inch pieces
1/3 c. chili sauce
2 sm. onions, peeled and sliced
1/2 lb. mushrooms, cleaned and sliced
1/2 tsp. dill
2 stalks celery, sliced
1/2 c. water
1/2 c. tomato puree
Salt and pepper to taste

Preheat oven to 325 degrees. Stir all ingredients in 2-quart casserole. Bake, covered, for 3 hours. Stir once during cooking. Yield: 6 servings.
PERSONAL NOTE: I received this from a neighbor in California. Because of diets periodically going on in this house, this has been a time saver and is enjoyed.

Mrs. W. N. Alexander, 1st. VP C and OWC
Vogelweh Army Post, Germany

PARTY MEAT PATTIES

1 1/2 lb. ground beef
1 1 5/8-oz. can onion dry soup mix
1 c. water
1/4 c. catsup

Mix ground beef with 2 tablespoons of the onion dry soup mix; shape into 6 patties. Brown patties; pour off excess drippings. Stir in water, soup mix and catsup. Cover; cook over low heat for 15 minutes, stirring occasionally. Uncover; cook until done. Yield: 6 servings.

Photograph for this recipe on page 343.

VEAL CHOPS AMAL FI
(370 calories per serving)

4 veal chops, 1/2-inch thick
2 tbsp. flour
2 tbsp. Wesson oil
1 8-oz. can tomato sauce
1/2 c. water
1 clove of garlic, minced
1/2 tsp. oregano
Salt and pepper to taste
1/2 c. ripe olives, sliced

Dust chops with flour. Heat oil in skillet. Saute chops until browned on both sides. Add tomato sauce, water, garlic and oregano. Simmer for 25 minutes; salt and pepper to taste. Garnish with olives. Yield: 4 servings.
PERSONAL NOTE: I am a member of a TOPS Club; we are always looking for low caloried anything.

Mrs. Walter McDuffy, Wel. Chm. OWC
Minot AFB, North Dakota

YOGURT-BEEF STROGANOFF

2 lb. beef stew meat, cut in cubes
6 tbsp. flour
1 1/2 tsp. salt
1/4 tsp. pepper
4 tbsp. shortening
1 c. chopped onion
1 10 1/2-oz. can beef bouillon
1 tsp. brown sugar
1/4 lb. fresh mushrooms, washed and trimmed
1 c. yogurt
Paprika

Dust meat with flour seasoned with salt and pepper. Brown quickly in hot shortening in skillet. Add onion. Saute until wilted. Combine bouillon and sugar; add to meat. Cover. Simmer for 1 hour and 30 minutes or until meat is tender. Add water if necessary as meat cooks. Add mushrooms; carefully fold in yogurt. Heat slowly, just until hot. Serve immediately over hot buttered noodles or steamed rice, if desired. Sprinkle with paprika. Yield: 6 servings.
PERSONAL NOTE: Every time you use yogurt in place of a cup of sour cream, you eliminate almost 300 calories, and the taste is the same.

Mrs. W. G. Gregg, Sec. CGOWC
Naples, Italy

MILK SHAKE

1 bottle cream soda
3 tbsp. powdered milk
Crushed ice

Place ingredients in blender; whizz till blended. Yield: 1 serving.

Annah V. Estes, Hon. Pres.
Scott AFB, Illinois

CHICKEN HAWAIIAN

3 1 1/2-lb. broiler-fryers, split
1 sm. onion, chopped
1/4 c. soy sauce
1 1/2 c. water

Arrange split chickens, skin side down, in large shallow baking pan. Mix onion, soy sauce and water together in small bowl; pour over chicken. Bake in 350-degree oven for 45 minutes. Turn chicken; baste several times with soy mixture in pan. Bake for 45 minutes longer, or until richly browned and tender. Yield: 6 servings.

Mrs. Bruce B. Knutson, Adv. OWC
Bolling AFB, Washington, D. C.

CHICKEN POT PIE
(335 calories per serving)

Water
1/2 c. instant non-fat dry milk solids
Flour
Salt
1/4 tsp. tarragon
1/4 tsp. parsley
Pepper to taste
3 c. cooked, boned chicken cubes
1 8-oz. can cooked white onions
1/2 c. cooked carrot slices
1/2 c. cooked lima beans
1/2 c. cooked peas
2 tbsp. margarine

Combine 1 1/2 cups water, milk solids, 3 tablespoons flour, 1 teaspoon salt, tarragon, parsley and black pepper to taste. Beat until smooth. Cook over medium heat, stirring constantly, until mixture comes to a boil. Fold in chicken, onions, carrots, beans and peas. Pour into 1 1/2-quart casserole. Combine 1/2 cup flour and 1/8 teaspoon salt. Cut in margarine with pastry blender or two knives. Add 2 tablespoons water; blend with fork. Roll out to cover casserole. Place over casserole; pinch edges firmly to edge of casserole. Prick top with fork. Bake at 400 degrees for 20 minutes. Yield: 6 servings.

Mrs. Robert W. Cummings, Sec.-Treas. NAF Wives
Naval Weapon Center
China Lake, California

GINGER BROILERS
(165 calories per serving)

3 tsp. salt
3/4 tsp. pepper
1 1/2 tsp. powdered ginger
1/2 tsp. garlic powder
3 1 1/2-lb. chicken broilers, split
2 tbsp. butter or oleo
2 tbsp. water

Mix salt, pepper, ginger and garlic powder together; rub into broilers. Melt butter in large baking pan; arrange broilers skin side down. Bake in 400-degree oven for 25 minutes. Reduce heat to 350 degrees. Add water; turn broilers over. Bake for additional 20 minutes. Yield: 6 servings.

Mrs. William B. Kerner, OWC
Naples NAF, Italy

LOW-CAL CHICKEN

Garlic salt or powder
Paprika
1/2 tsp. oregano
1 disjointed chicken or chicken pieces for 4
1/2 c. water
1/3 c. lemon juice
1/2 tsp. grated lemon peel

Sprinkle garlic salt, paprika and oregano on chicken. Place in ungreased Pyrex baking dish in layer. Pour in water. Pour lemon juice over chicken. Sprinkle grated lemon peel on top. Bake at 325 degrees for 1 hour. Yield: 4 servings.

Mrs. Harry W. Konkel, OWC
Norfolk Cinclant Flt., Virginia

ROAST DUCK WITH TANGERINES

3 lge. tangerines
1 3 1/2-lb. duck, quartered
2 c. chicken broth
Water or orange juice
1 tbsp. cornstarch
1 tbsp. lemon juice
12 drops artificial sweetener

Grate 1 tangerine peel; set aside. Place duck in roasting pan; add chicken broth. Bake at 325 degrees for 2 hours, or until tender. Remove duck. Pour off all but 3 tablespoons pan drippings. Squeeze tangerines; measure juice. Add water or orange juice to make 1 cup; pour in pan. Blend cornstarch and lemon juice; stir into liquid in pan. Cook; stir until thickened and clear. Remove from heat; stir in artificial sweetener and grated peel. Pour over duck. Yield: 4 servings.

Mrs. William W. Momyer, Hon. Pres. OWC
Langley AFB, Virginia

CANTONESE SALAD
(1 c. contains 30 calories)

SALAD:

2 sm. tomatoes, cut in pieces
1 c. sliced celery
1 c. radishes
1 green pepper, cut in strips
1 can drained bean sprouts

DRESSING:

2 tbsp. salad oil
2 tbsp. soy sauce
1 tbsp. vinegar
1 tbsp. grated onion
Salt and pepper to taste

Mix Salad ingredients together; chill. Combine Dressing ingredients; chill. Shake well before pouring over Salad. Yield: 4-6 servings.

Mrs. Philip T. Boucher, OWC
Williams AFB, Arizona

CRANBERRY CHIFFON SALAD
(50 calories per serving)

1 envelope unflavored gelatin
1/4 c. cold water
2 c. whole cranberries
1 1/2 c. water
1 1/2 tbsp. no-cal sweetener
1/2 c. unsweetened applesauce
1/2 c. finely-chopped celery
1/4 c. nonfat dry milk
1/4 c. ice water

Soften gelatin in cold water. Combine cranberries in water; cook until skins pop and berries are soft. Force through food mill. Add softened gelatin; stir until dissolved. Add no-cal sweetener and applesauce. Chill until mixture begins to thicken; add celery. Combine dry milk and ice water in small bowl; beat on high speed until consistency of heavy cream. Fold into cranberry mixture carefully. Spoon into lightly-oiled 1-quart mold. Chill until set. Yield: 6 servings.

Mrs. P. Dow Berggren, NOWC
US Nav. Comm. Sta. Adak, Alaska

CUCUMBER-CABBAGE MOLD

2 envelopes unflavored gelatin
2 c. boiling water
2 envelopes Lemon Pillsbury Funny Face
1 3/4 c. cold water
2 tbsp. vinegar
1 tbsp. white horseradish
1/2 tsp. salt
1 lge. cucumber
1 c. cabbage, shredded

(Continued on next page)

Dissolve gelatin in boiling water. Add Lemon Funny Face, cold water, vinegar, horseradish and salt. Chill until partially set. Pour 1/2 cup gelatin mixture into 5 cup ring mold. Cut 10 to 15 paper-thin slices cucumber; arrange in ring mold over gelatin. Pour thin layer of gelatin over top; chill to set. Add cabbage and thin layer of gelatin. Chill until almost set. Dice remaining cucumber to make 1 cup; add, covering with any remaining gelatin. Chill until firm. Yield: 8 servings.

Mrs. Robert L. Crouch, Treas. OWC
Camp Smith Honolulu, Hawaii

GOLDEN SALAD
(38 calores per serving)

1 8-oz. can low calorie pineapple tidbits
1 envelope unflavored gelatin
Non-caloric sweetener to equal 1/4 c. sugar
1/4 tsp. salt
1/4 c. orange juice
1/4 c. vinegar
1/2 c. chopped orange sections
1/2 c. coarsely grated carrots

Drain liquid from pineapple into saucepan; sprinkle gelatin over liquid. Stir over low heat until gelatin is dissolved, 2 to 3 minutes. Add sweetener and salt; remove from heat. Stir in orange juice and vinegar; chill to consistency of unbeaten egg white. Fold in pineapple tidbits, orange sections and carrots; turn into 3-cup mold or individual molds. Chill until firm. Unmold on serving platter; garnish with greens. Serve with low-calorie salad dressing. Yield: 6 servings.

Mrs. Walter F. Bodner, Pres. OWC
Port Angeles AS, Washington

LOW-CALORIE TOMATO SALAD

1 3/4 c. tomato juice
1/4 c. finely chopped celery
3 tbsp. sugar
1 tbsp. chopped onion
1/2 tsp. paprika
1 tbsp. salt
2 whole cloves
1 bay leaf
2 tbsp. lemon juice
1/2 c. chopped green peppers
1 pkg. unflavored gelatin
1/4 c. water

Combine all ingredients except gelatin and water in saucepan; simmer for 10 minutes. Remove bay leaf and cloves. Soak gelatin in water. Add to tomato mixture; cool. Place in refrigerator. May be set in molds. Serve on lettuce plain or with dab of mayonnaise, if desired. Keeps for several days, if covered in refrigerator. Yield: 6-8 servings.

Mrs. Bill E. Myers, OWC
RAF Alconbury, England

LOW-CALORIE SPINACH SALAD

1 1-lb. bag fresh spinach, cleaned and stemmed
1/2 c. Kraft's low-calorie Italian dressing
8 tsp. dried chives
4 hard-boiled egg yolks, diced or sieved
4 slices crisp bacon, crumbled or 8 tsp.
    Bac-Os

Place spinach in bowl; cover with damp paper towel. Refrigerate for 1 hour; drain. Toss spinach with dressing and chives; arrange on salad plates. Sprinkle with egg yolks and bacon. Yield: 8 servings.

Mrs. Dwight O. Monteith, Hon. Pres. OWC
Lowry AFB, Colorado

NO-CALORIE COLESLAW

2 c. finely shredded cabbage
1/2 c. skim milk
1 tbsp. wine vinegar
1/4 tsp. salt
Small amount of granular or liquid sugar substitute,
    to taste

Place shredded cabbage in a small bowl. Combine milk, vinegar and seasonings. Pour over cabbage; mix.
PERSONAL NOTE: The Weight Watchers, Inc. allow no oils in diet recipes. Milk curdles slightly from the vinegar and thickens enough to give suggestion of body to the dressing. Tastes so good that even non-dieters like it.

Mrs. Clifford M. Esler, Jr., NOWC
Mare Island Naval Shipyard
Vallejo, California

SUNSHINE SALAD

2 pkg. low-calorie lemon gelatin
1 tsp. salt
2 c. hot water
2 tbsp. vinegar
2 tbsp. diced pimento
1 1/2 tbsp. diced celery
1 hard-cooked egg, cut in pieces
2/3 c. cut and cooked asparagus spears

Dissolve gelatin and salt in hot water; add vinegar. Chill until slightly thickened. Add pimento, celery, egg and asparagus. Pour into molds. Chill until firm. Yield: 6-8 servings.

Mrs. Jack G. Merrell, Hon. Pres. OWC
Wright Patterson AFB, Ohio

DIETER'S DELIGHT SALAD DRESSING

1 c. white vinegar
1/2 c. salad oil
3 tbsp. brown sugar

(Continued on next page)

Juice of 1 lemon
1/2 tsp. paprika
1 grated onion
1/2 c. catsup

Mix all ingredients together in jar; shake well. Store in refrigerator. Good on green salads.

Mrs. B. L. Morris, OWC
RAF Alconbury
Hunts, England

WEIGHT-WATCHERS COLESLAW
(21 calories per serving)

3 c. finely shredded red or white cabbage
1/2 c. chopped green pepper
1/2 c. thinly sliced carrots
1/2 c. grated cucumbers
1/2 c. finely snipped parsley
Vinegar
Salt and pepper to taste

Mix vegetables and parsley. Add enough vinegar to coat vegetables. Season with salt and pepper. Yield: 6 servings.

Mrs. Richard A. Nelson, OWC
USNAD, McAlester, Oklahoma

ZERO SALAD DRESSING

1/2 c. tomato juice
2 tbsp. lemon juice or vinegar
1 tbsp. onion, finely chopped
Salt and pepper to taste
Chopped parsley or green pepper
Horseradish or mustard

Combine ingredients in jar with a tightly fitted top. Shake well before using.

Mrs. Donald P. Kirkpatrick, Culture Chm. OWC
Davis-Monthan AFB, Arizona

CRAB MEAT A LA DEWEY
(248 calories per serving)

1 c. mushrooms, finely chopped
1/2 green pepper, finely chopped
1 1/2 tbsp. flour
1/3 c. nonfat dry milk
1/2 c. water
1/4 tsp. salt
1/8 tsp. pepper
1 egg yolk
1 lb. picked lump crab meat or 2 7 1/2-oz. cans crab
    meat
1 tbsp. grated Parmesan cheese
1 tbsp. dry bread crumbs

(Continued on next page)

Melt butter in top of double boiler; saute mushrooms and green pepper. Blend in flour. Add dry milk, water and seasonings. Cook until mixture thickens. Add small amount hot mixture to egg and crab meat; blend in remaining egg yolk. Turn into 4 individual casseroles or shells. Sprinkle with mixture of Parmesan cheese and crumbs. Bake at 350 degrees for 30 minutes. Yield: 4 servings.

Mrs. Gary S. Morgan, CG OWC
Traverse City CGAS, Michigan

CRAB MEAT DIVAN
(185 calories per serving)

1 6 1/2-oz. can King crab meat, drained
1 10-oz. pkg. frozen broccoli
1/3 c. mayonnaise
1 1/2 tsp. lemon juice
1/2 tsp. prepared mustard
1 tsp. grated onion
1/4 c. grated process cheese

Preheat oven to 350 degrees. Remove membrane from crab meat; break into large pieces. Cook broccoli according to package directions; drain well. Arrange on ovenproof platter; cover with crab meat. Mix mayonnaise, lemon juice and onion; spoon over crab. Top with cheese. Bake 20 minutes. May be served with melba toast. Yield: 4 servings.

Mrs. Paul G. Jones, Ways and Means Chm. OWC
Beale AFB, California

FISH PIQUANT
(300 calories per serving)

4 onions, sliced
2 lb. fish fillets cod, sole, haddock or
    perch
1/2 c. mayonnaise
2 tsp. Worcestershire sauce
2 tbsp. lemon juice
1/4 c. grated Parmesan cheese
2 tbsp. chopped parsley

Cover onions with water; cook until tender but crisp. Drain; spread onions into shallow well-greased baking dish. Cut fish into individual serving pieces. Place fish pieces over onions. Combine remaining ingredients; blend well. Spread mixture on fish pieces. Bake in 350-degree oven for 30 to 40 minutes or until fish flakes. Yield: 6 servings.

Mrs. Sol Loeser, OWC
Othellow AFS, Washington

ITALIAN-STYLE SHRIMP SIZZLE
(90 calories per serving)

3/4 lb. cleaned and deveined shrimp
1/4 c. low-calorie Italian dressing
2 tsp. lemon juice
1/2 tsp. salt
1/4 tsp. seasoned pepper

(Continued on next page)

Arrange shrimp close together in circle in 9-inch ovenproof glass pie plate. Mix Italian dressing and lemon juice together. Pour over shrimp. Sprinkle with salt and pepper. Broil for about 5 to 7 minutes until shrimp turn pink and are flecked golden brown. Serve each portion with fluffy, steamed rice tossed with 2 tablespoons minced chives; spoon sauce over all. Yield: 4 servings.

Mrs. Robert E. Foster, Pres. OWC
RAF Wethersfield Base, England

SLIM 'N' SPEEDY SHRIMP CREOLE
(345 calories per serving)

2 tbsp. oil
1 med. onion, chopped
1 clove of garlic, minced
1 sm. green pepper, chopped
1/2 c. chopped celery
1 8-oz. can tomato sauce
3/4 c. water
1 lb. cleaned raw shrimp
2 c. hot cooked rice

Heat oil in heavy frying pan or electric skillet; cook onion, garlic, green pepper and celery slowly for about 5 minutes. Stir in tomato sauce and water; simmer for about 10 minutes. Add shrimp; bring to a boil. Cook for 5 minutes. Serve over hot rice. Yield: 4 servings.

Mrs. Thomas J. Hollarn, Nursery Chm. OWC
Mountain Home AFB, Idaho

CALORIE-COUNTER'S VEGETABLE SALAD

1 1-lb. can whole vertical pack Blue Lake
    green beans
1 c. thinly sliced fresh cauliflower
1 c. fresh orange sections
2 tbsp. sliced radishes
1/4 tsp. seasoned salt
Dash of seasoned pepper

LOW-CALORIE SALAD DRESSING:

2 tbsp. instant minced onion
2 tbsp. sugar
2 tsp. cornstarch
1/2 tsp. salt
1/2 tsp. paprika
1 c. water
1/3 c. vinegar
1/2 tsp. Worcestershire sauce
Dash of Tabasco
1 tbsp. salad oil

Drain beans; arrange in bundles, spoke-fashion, on serving plate. Place cauli-flower and orange sections in between beans with cauliflower nearest rim. Center with sliced radishes and a radish rose, if desired. Sprinkle with seasoned salt and pepper over all. Chill. Serve with Low-Calorie Salad Dressing. Combine first 5 Dressing ingredients in saucepan. Stir in water, vinegar, Worcestershire and Tabasco. Cook and stir until mixture comes to boil and is thickened. Remove from heat; stir in oil. Chill. Yield: 6 servings.

Photograph for this recipe on page 383 .

CHINESE-STYLE CABBAGE
(120 calories per serving)

1 lge. onion, chopped
1 1/2 tbsp. margarine
6 c. shredded cabbage
Salt and pepper to taste
3/4 lb. liver, cubed
1/2 c. water
1 tbsp. soy sauce

Cook onion in 1/2 tablespoon margarine until soft and yellow; add cabbage. Season with salt and pepper; cover. Steam until tender, 10 to 15 minutes. Dry liver; season. Brown in remaining margarine; add water. Simmer for 5 minutes; add soy sauce and cabbage. Toss lightly. Yield: 6 servings.

Mrs. Louis Emory, 1st VP OWC
Nurnberg, Germany

GREEN PEPPER SAUTE
(50 calories per serving)

1 c. sliced onion
1 tbsp. salad oil
3 green peppers, sliced in 1/4-inch rings
1/2 lb. fresh mushrooms, sliced or 2 3-oz.
  cans sliced, drained
1 tsp. salt
1/8 tsp. crushed dried red pepper
1/8 tsp. dried oregano leaves

Saute onion in hot oil in skillet, stirring, until golden for about 5 minutes. Add remaining ingredients; cover. Cook over medium heat for 5 minutes, stirring occasionally. Yield: 6 servings.

Mrs. Robert W. Harris, Anglo-American Chm. OWC
Alconbury RAF Base, England

SPANISH GREEN BEANS
(30 calories per serving)

1 10-oz. pkg. frozen cut green beans
1 slice bacon, cut up
1/2 green pepper, seeded, cut up
1/4 sm. onion
2 med. tomatoes, cut up or 1 c. canned
  tomatoes
Salt and pepper

Cook beans according to package directions; drain. Cook bacon in small frypan until crisp. Place green pepper and onion in blender container; cover. Run on high speed until chopped. Empty into frypan with bacon; saute until tender. Puree tomatoes in blender; add to pepper and onion. Simmer for 5 minutes. Pour over cooked green beans; heat. Yield: 4 servings.

Mrs. Orville L. Gilchrist, OWC
COMFAIRWINGSLANT, Norfolk, Virginia

LOW-CALORIE RED CABBAGE

1 sm. head red cabbage
1/2 c. white vinegar
1/2 c. water
1 tsp. sugar or substitute
1 tsp. salt

Cut cabbage as for slaw. Combine with other ingredients in large pot. Simmer till tender for about 20 minutes. Add more water, if necessary. Yield: 6-8 servings.

Mrs. Julius F. Sanks, Wlfr. Chm. OWC
Vandenberg AFB, California

MINT-GLAZED CARROTS
(77 calories per serving)

2 1/2 c. tiny whole carrots
2 tbsp. mint jelly
1 tbsp. butter
Parsley

Cook carrots in saucepan until tender; drain. Add jelly and butter. Heat slowly until jelly and butter are melted and carrots are glazed, turning carrots frequently. Garnish with snipped parsley. Yield: 4 servings.

Mrs. Elwood A. Lloyd, Chm. OWC
Fort Detrick, Frederick, Maryland

SPINACH AND YOGURT

2 pkg. frozen chopped spinach, thawed and drained
Salt to taste
1 carton yogurt
1 c. herbed bread crumbs

Place spinach in casserole; sprinkle with salt. Mix with yogurt; top with bread crumbs. Bake at 350 degrees for 20 minutes.

Mrs. John H. Garrett, Command Rep. GLOW
Great Lakes NS, Illinois

SQUASH CREOLE
(44 calories per serving)

2 lb. sm. yellow squash or zucchini
1 tbsp. butter or margarine
1/2 c. chopped green onion
1 tsp. salt
Dash of pepper
1 1-lb. can stewed tomatoes

Cut squash crosswise on diagonal into 1/2-inch thick slice. Saute onion in hot butter in large skillet for about 3 minutes or until tender. Add sliced squash; salt and pepper. Toss together lightly; cover. Cook over low heat for about 15 minutes or until squash is tender. Add tomatoes; toss to combine. Cover; cook for about 1 minute or until mixture is heated throughout. Yield: 8 servings.

Mrs. George R. Doerr, Hon. Adv. OWC
Cannon AFB, New Mexico

INDEX

RECIPE FOR SOUTH AFRICAN STAR CASSEROLE ON PAGE 143

RECIPES ON PARADE

ORDER FORM 70102
RECIPES ON PARADE

These order blanks are not for use by clubs

Fill in number desired below:	1-02

SPECIALTY SERIES

_____ **Foreign Foods - 1970**
_____ Quick & Easy Dishes - 1969
_____ *Holiday Favorites - (1972)
_____ *Cooking for Two or a Crowd - (1973)
* These are future editions

BASIC FIVE FAVORITES

_____ Meats
_____ Desserts
_____ Salads
_____ Casseroles
_____ Vegetables

☐ $3.95 per book, includes mailing charge - enclosed (check or money order)

☐ Bill me at $4.50 per book (extra added for billing)

☐ $3.50 per book if 3 or more ordered, payment enclosed

Mail to:

_____
Name

_____
Address

_____
City   State   Zip

FAVORITE RECIPES PRESS
Box 3396, Montgomery, Alabama 36109

ORDER FORM 70102
RECIPES ON PARADE

These order blanks are not for use by clubs

Fill in number desired below:	1-02

SPECIALTY SERIES

_____ **Foreign Foods - 1970**
_____ Quick & Easy Dishes - 1969
_____ *Holiday Favorites - (1972)
_____ *Cooking for Two or a Crowd - (1973)
*These are future editions

BASIC FIVE FAVORITES

_____ Meats
_____ Desserts
_____ Salads
_____ Casseroles
_____ Vegetables

☐ $3.95 per book, includes mailing charge - enclosed (check or money order)

☐ Bill me at $4.50 per book (extra added for billing)

☐ $3.50 per book if 3 or more ordered, payment enclosed

Mail to:

_____
Name

_____
Address

_____
City   State   Zip

FAVORITE RECIPES PRESS
Box 3396, Montgomery, Alabama 36109

Gift Order 70102
RECIPES ON PARADE
These order blanks are not for use by clubs.

Please fill in number desired (1-02): ( )**Foreign Foods** ( )Meats ( )Desserts ( )Salads ( )Casseroles ( )Vegetables ( )Quick & Easy Dishes

☐ $3.95 each enclosed   ☐ Bill me at $4.50 each   ☐ $3.50 each enclosed (for 3 or more)

TO: _____
Name of Person to Receive Book

_____
Address

_____
City   State   Zip

_____
My Name

_____
Address

_____
City   State   Zip

FAVORITE RECIPES PRESS   P.O. BOX 3396   MONTGOMERY, ALABAMA 36109

OVER

RECIPE FOR CALORIE-COUNTER'S VEGETABLE SALAD ON PAGE 372

OVER

RECIPES ON PARADE

ORDER FORM

70102

RECIPES ON PARADE

These order blanks are not for use by clubs

Fill in number desired below:	1-02

SPECIALTY SERIES

_____ **Foreign Foods - 1970**
_____ Quick & Easy Dishes - 1969
_____ *Holiday Favorites - (1972)
_____ *Cooking for Two or a Crowd - (1973)
     * These are future editions

BASIC FIVE FAVORITES

_____ Meats
_____ Desserts
_____ Salads
_____ Casseroles
_____ Vegetables

☐ $3.95 per book, includes mailing charge - enclosed (check or money order)

☐ Bill me at $4.50 per book (extra added for billing)

☐ $3.50 per book if 3 or more ordered, payment enclosed

Mail to:

_____
Name

_____
Address

_____
City   State   Zip

FAVORITE RECIPES PRESS
Box 3396, Montgomery, Alabama 36109

ORDER FORM

70102

RECIPES ON PARADE

These order blanks are not for use by clubs

Fill in number desired below:	1-02

SPECIALTY SERIES

_____ **Foreign Foods - 1970**
_____ Quick & Easy Dishes - 1969
_____ *Holiday Favorites - (1972)
_____ *Cooking for Two or a Crowd - (1973)
     *These are future editions

BASIC FIVE FAVORITES

_____ Meats
_____ Desserts
_____ Salads
_____ Casseroles
_____ Vegetables

☐ $3.95 per book, includes mailing charge - enclosed (check or money order)

☐ Bill me at $4.50 per book (extra added for billing)

☐ $3.50 per book if 3 or more ordered, payment enclosed

Mail to:

_____
Name

_____
Address

_____
City   State   Zip

FAVORITE RECIPES PRESS
Box 3396, Montgomery, Alabama 36109

Gift Order

70102

RECIPES ON PARADE

These order blanks are not for use by clubs.

Please fill in number desired (1-02): (   )**Foreign Foods**   (   )Meats   (   )Desserts
(   )Salads   (   )Casseroles   (   )Vegetables   (   )Quick & Easy Dishes

☐ $3.95 each enclosed   ☐ Bill me at $4.50 each   ☐ $3.50 each enclosed (for 3 or more)

TO: _____
Name of Person to Receive Book

_____
Address

_____
City   State   Zip

_____
My Name

_____
Address

_____
City   State   Zip

FAVORITE RECIPES PRESS   P.O. BOX 3396   MONTGOMERY, ALABAMA 36109